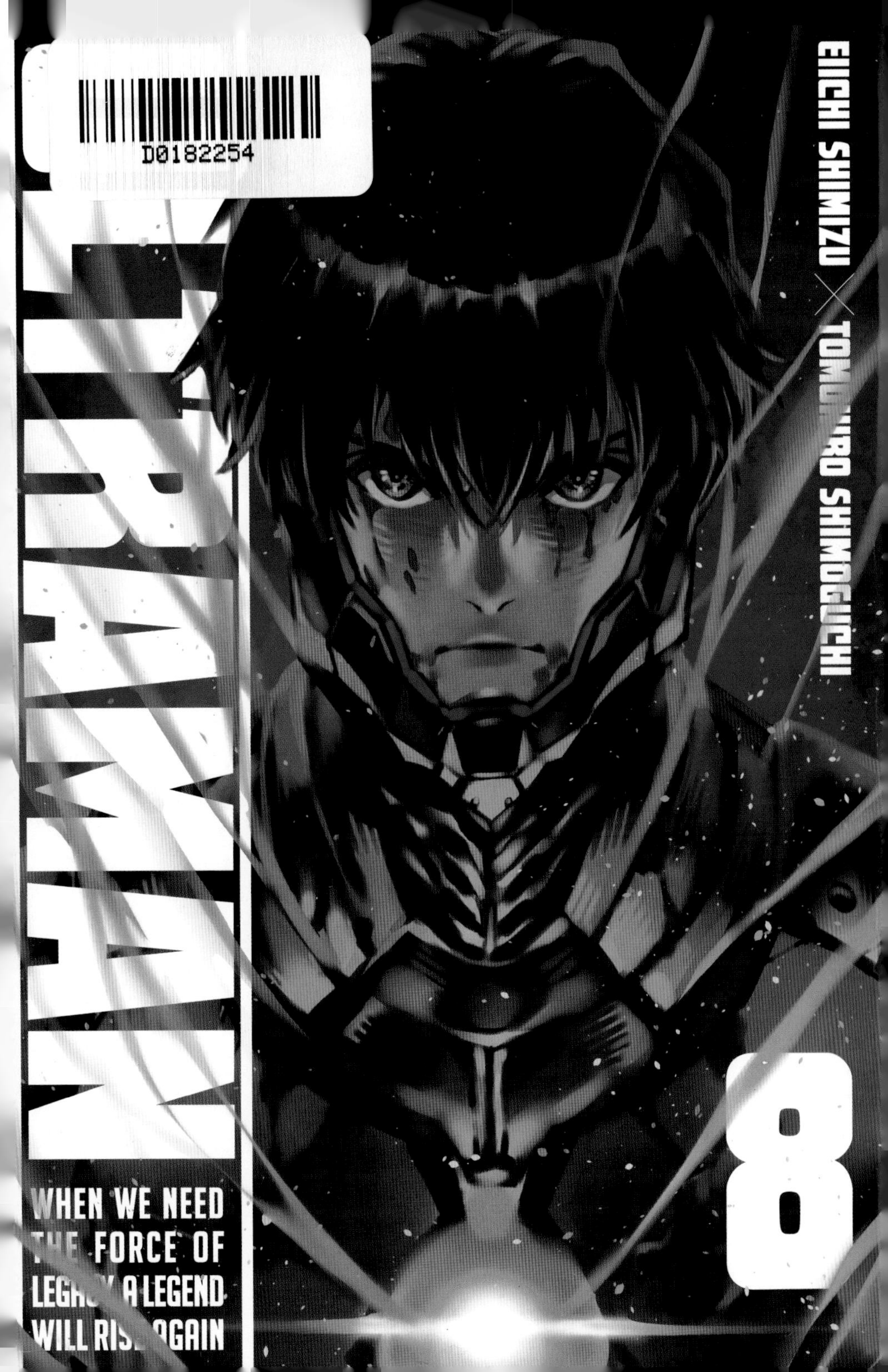
ULTRAMAN
EIICHI SHIMIZU × TOMOHIRO SHIMOGUCHI
8
WHEN WE NEED
THE FORCE OF
LEGACY A LEGEND
WILL RISE AGAIN

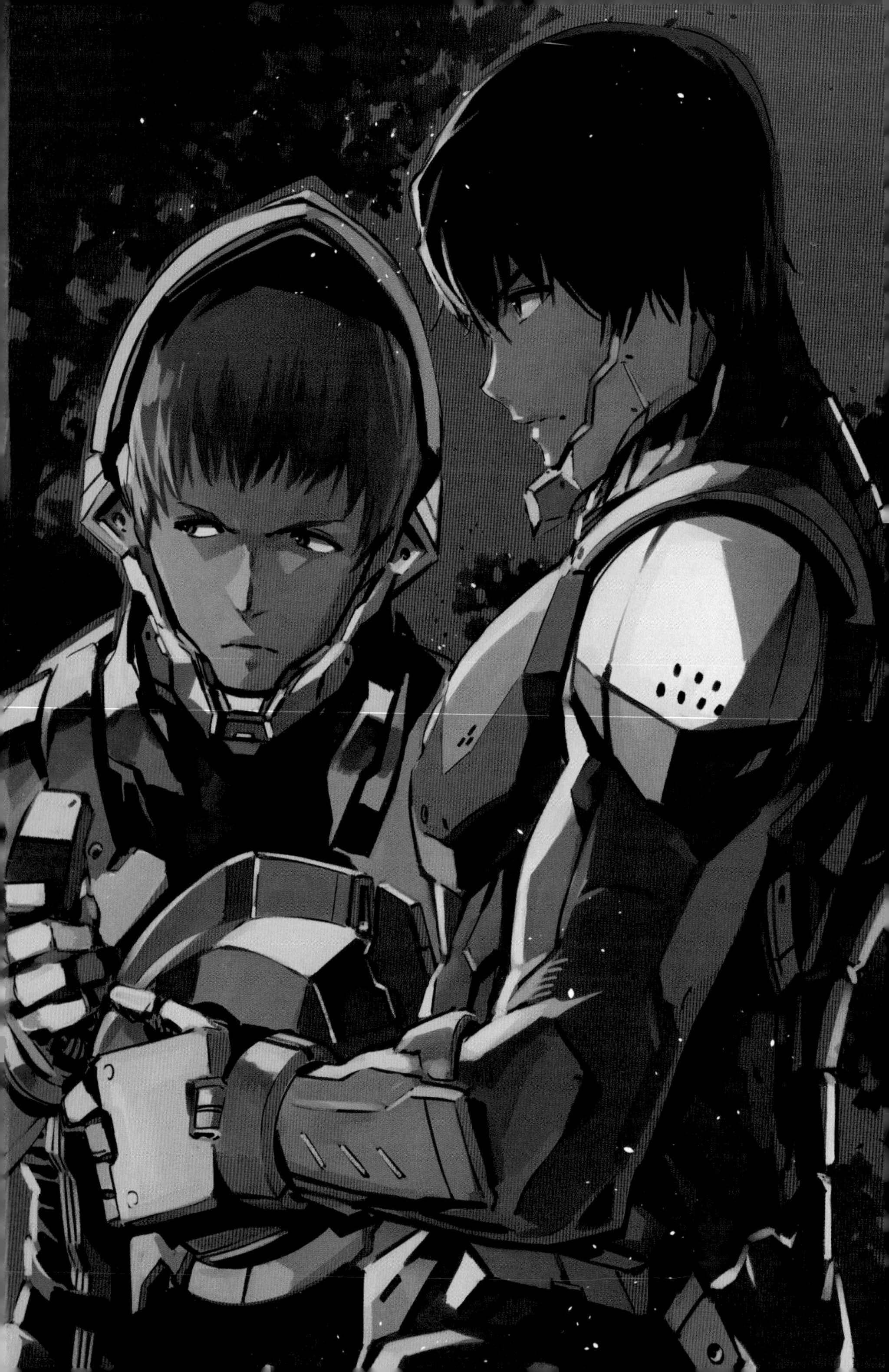

THIS IS THE BEGINNING OF A NEW AGE.

CONTENTS

CHAPTER 48   GALE   005
CHAPTER 49   CONVICTION   025
CHAPTER 50   BIRTH   057
CHAPTER 51   INTRIGUE JUNCTION   089
CHAPTER 52   A NEW GIFT   117
CHAPTER 53   FROM THE EAST, THE LIGHT OF DAWN   145

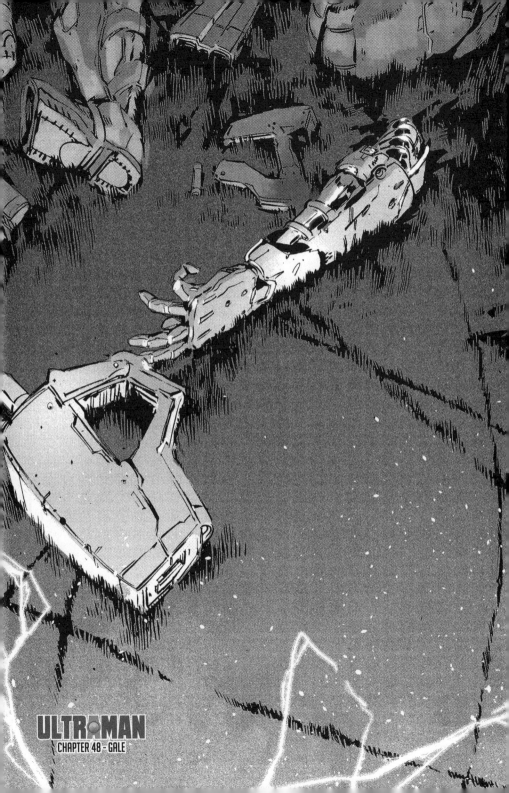

ULTRAMAN
CHAPTER 48 - GALE

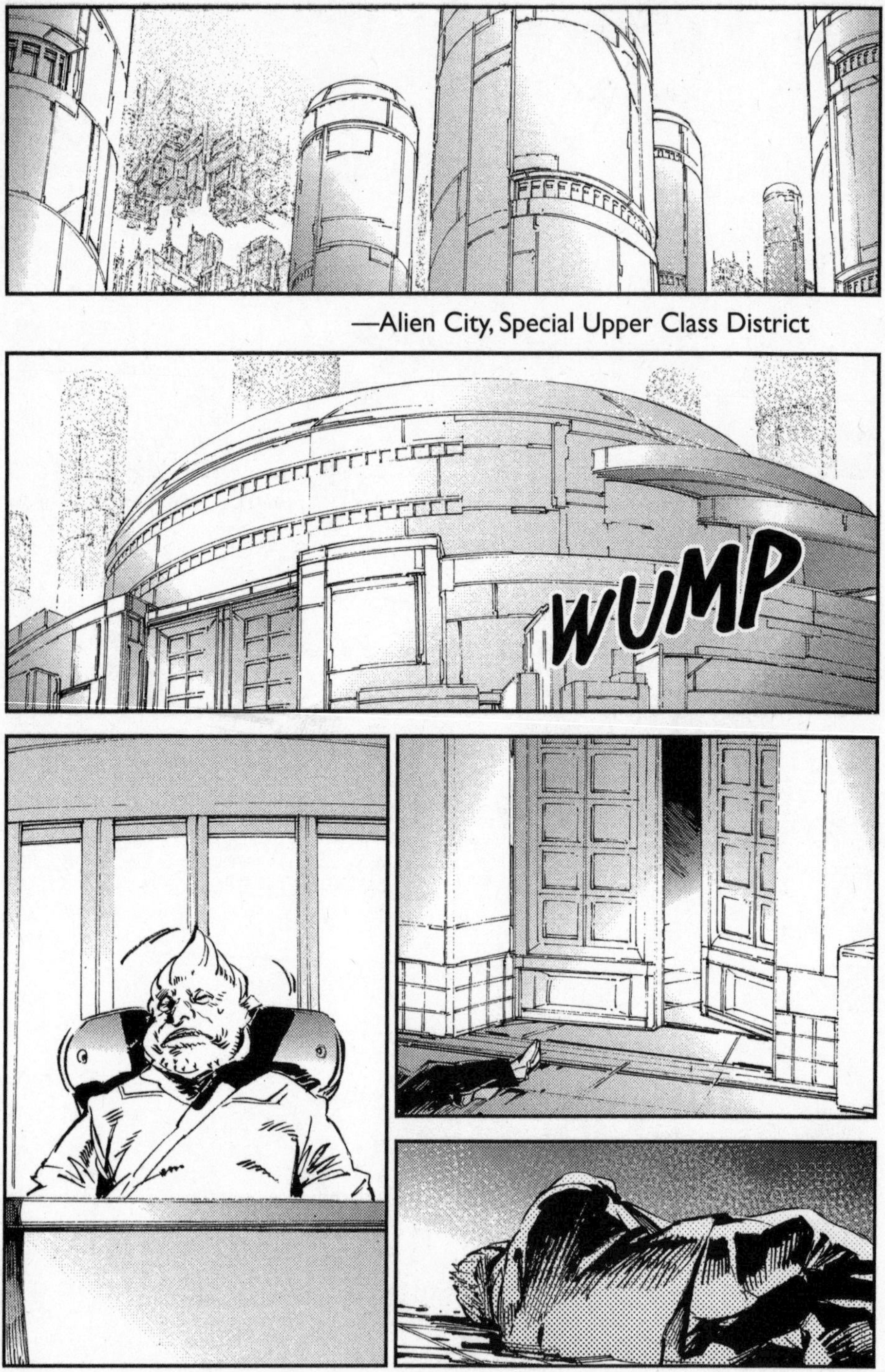
—Alien City, Special Upper Class District
WUMP

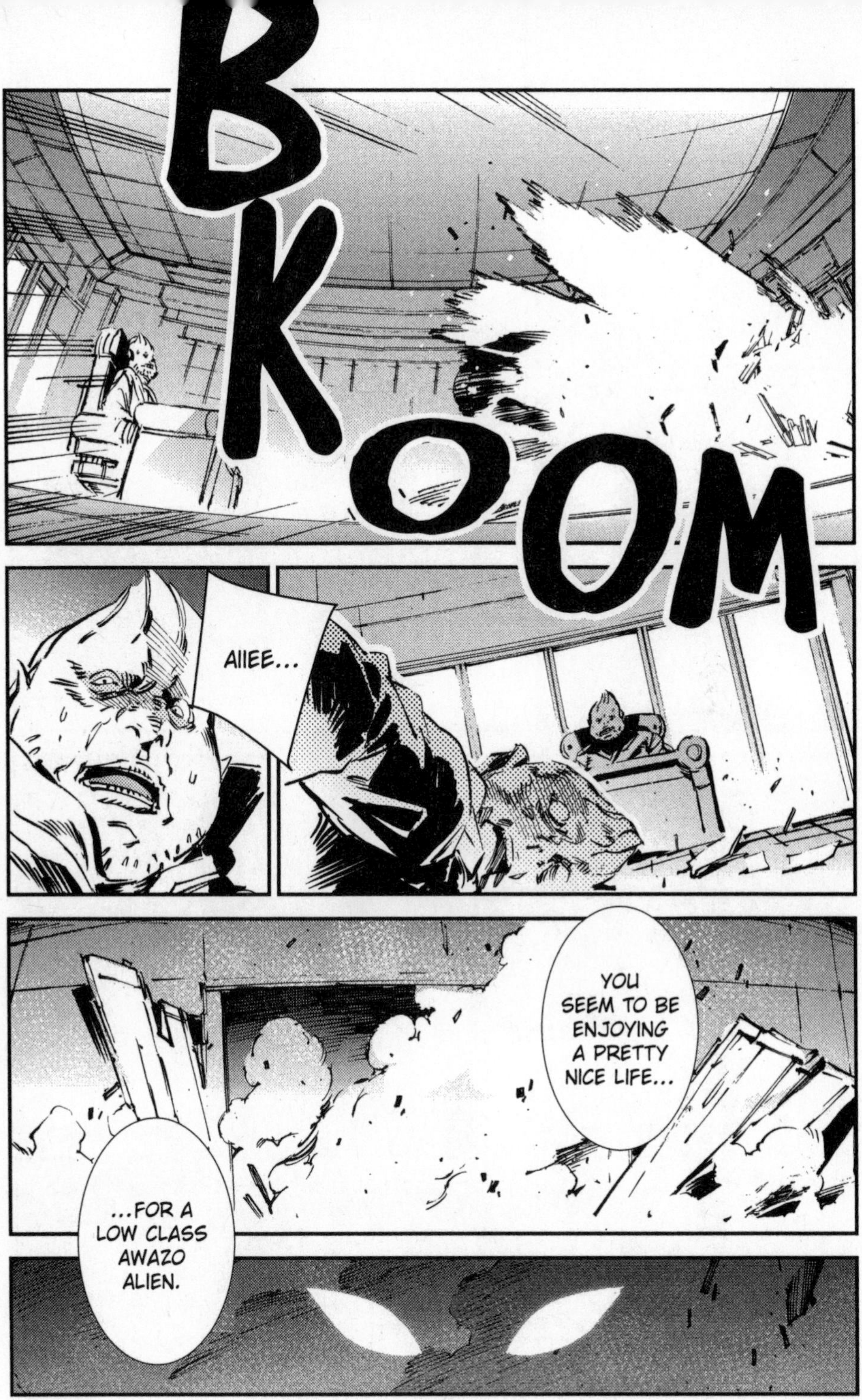
BKOOM
AIIEE...
YOU SEEM TO BE ENJOYING A PRETTY NICE LIFE...
...FOR A LOW CLASS AWAZO ALIEN.

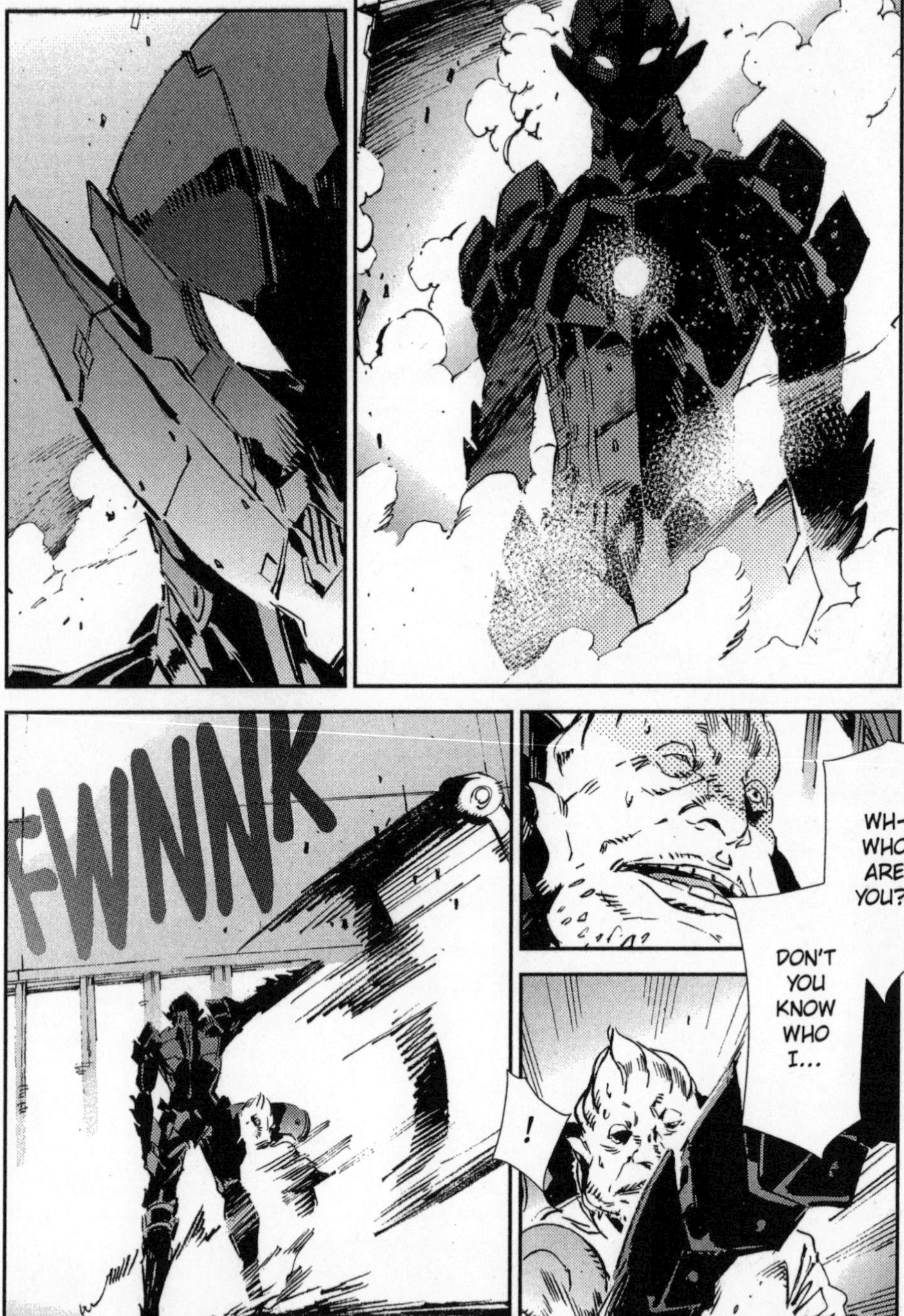
WH- WHO ARE YOU?!
DON'T YOU KNOW WHO I...
!
FWNNK

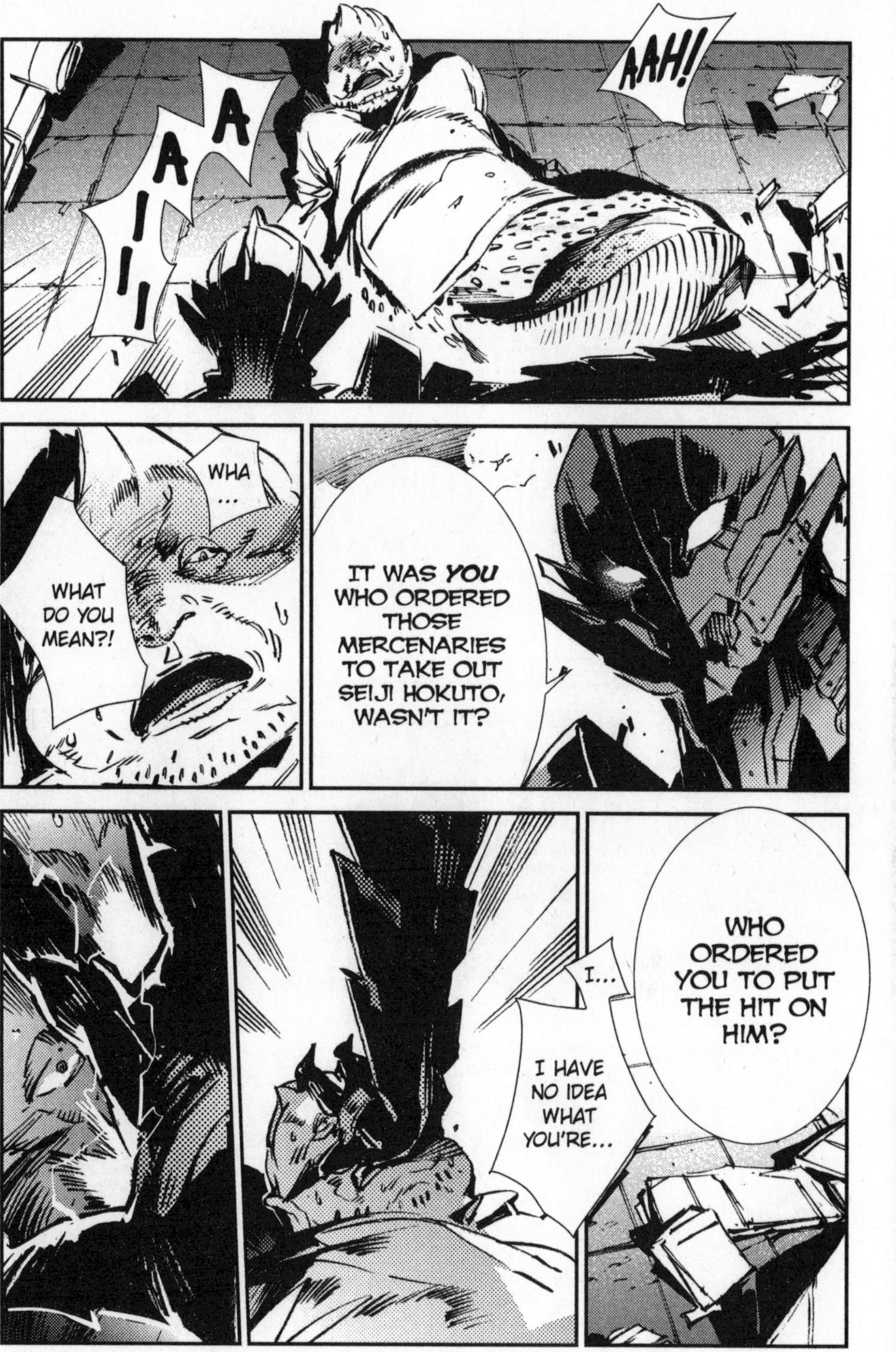
AAH!
AAIII
IT WAS *YOU* WHO ORDERED THOSE MERCENARIES TO TAKE OUT SEIJI HOKUTO, WASN'T IT?
WHA...
WHAT DO YOU MEAN?!
WHO ORDERED YOU TO PUT THE HIT ON HIM?
I...
I HAVE NO IDEA WHAT YOU'RE...

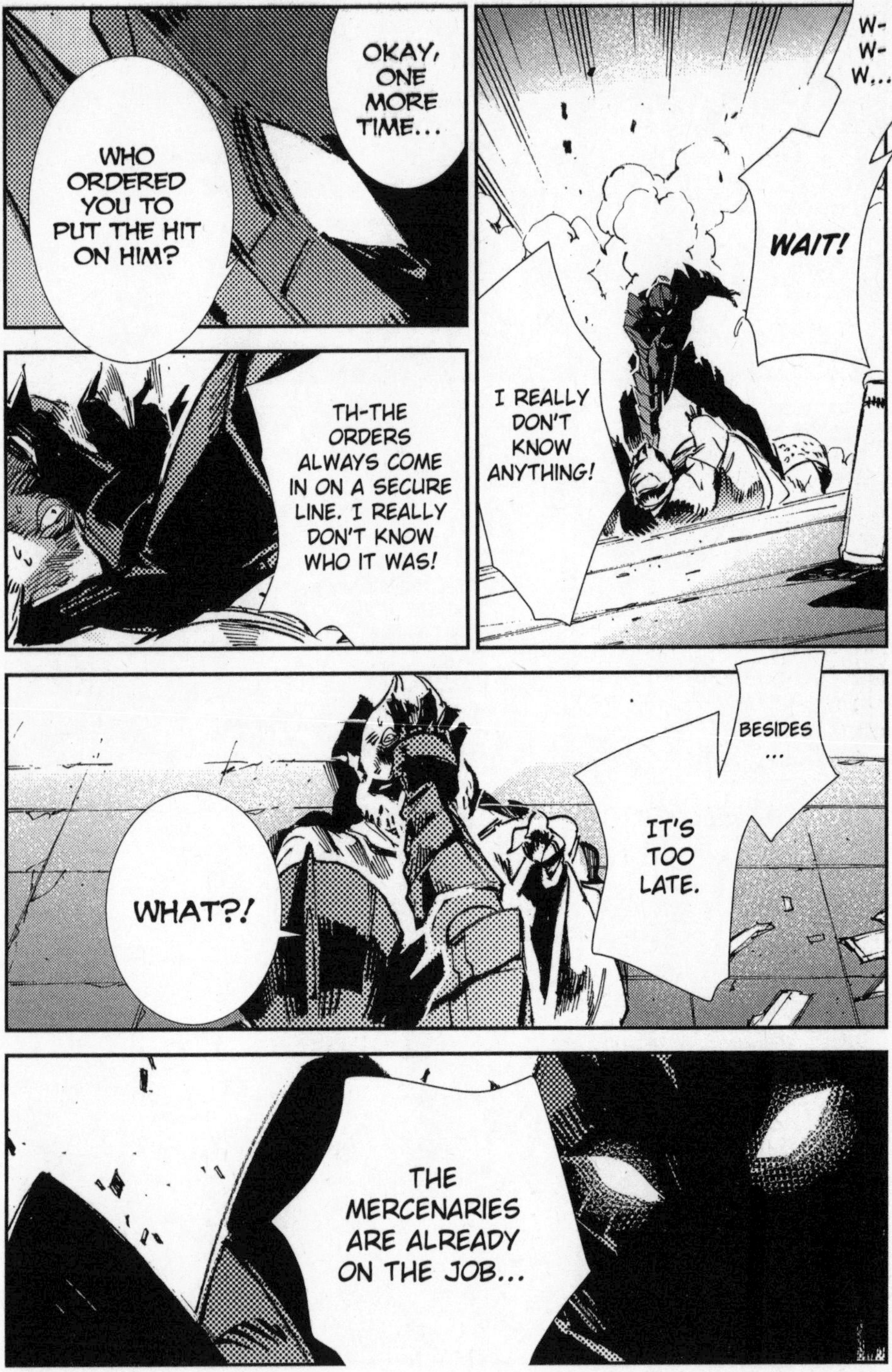
W-W-W...
WAIT!
I REALLY DON'T KNOW ANYTHING!
OKAY, ONE MORE TIME...
WHO ORDERED YOU TO PUT THE HIT ON HIM?
TH-THE ORDERS ALWAYS COME IN ON A SECURE LINE. I REALLY DON'T KNOW WHO IT WAS!
BESIDES...
IT'S TOO LATE.
WHAT?!
THE MERCENARIES ARE ALREADY ON THE JOB...

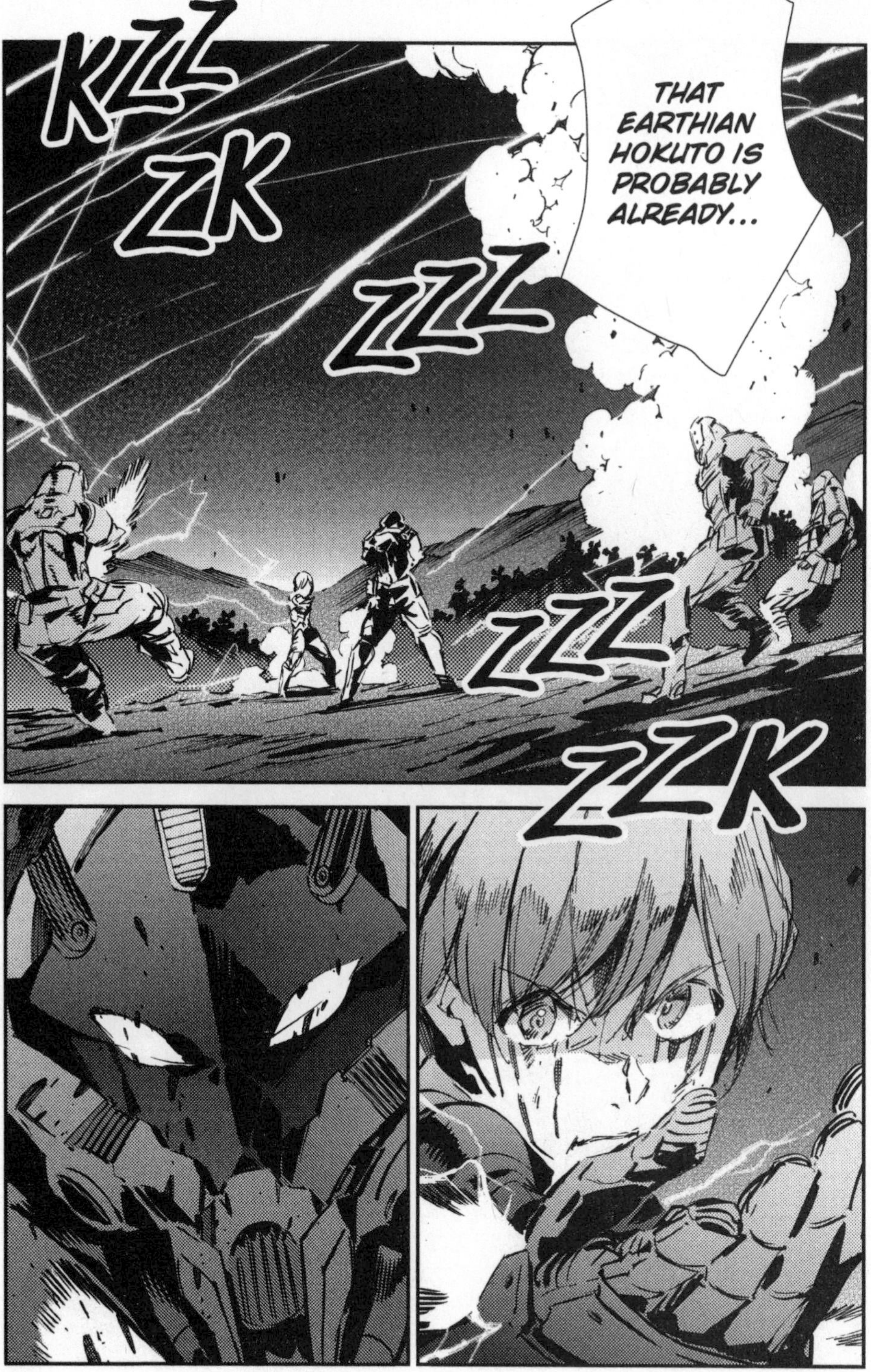
THAT EARTHIAN HOKUTO IS PROBABLY ALREADY...
KZZZ
ZK
ZZZ
ZZZ
ZZZK

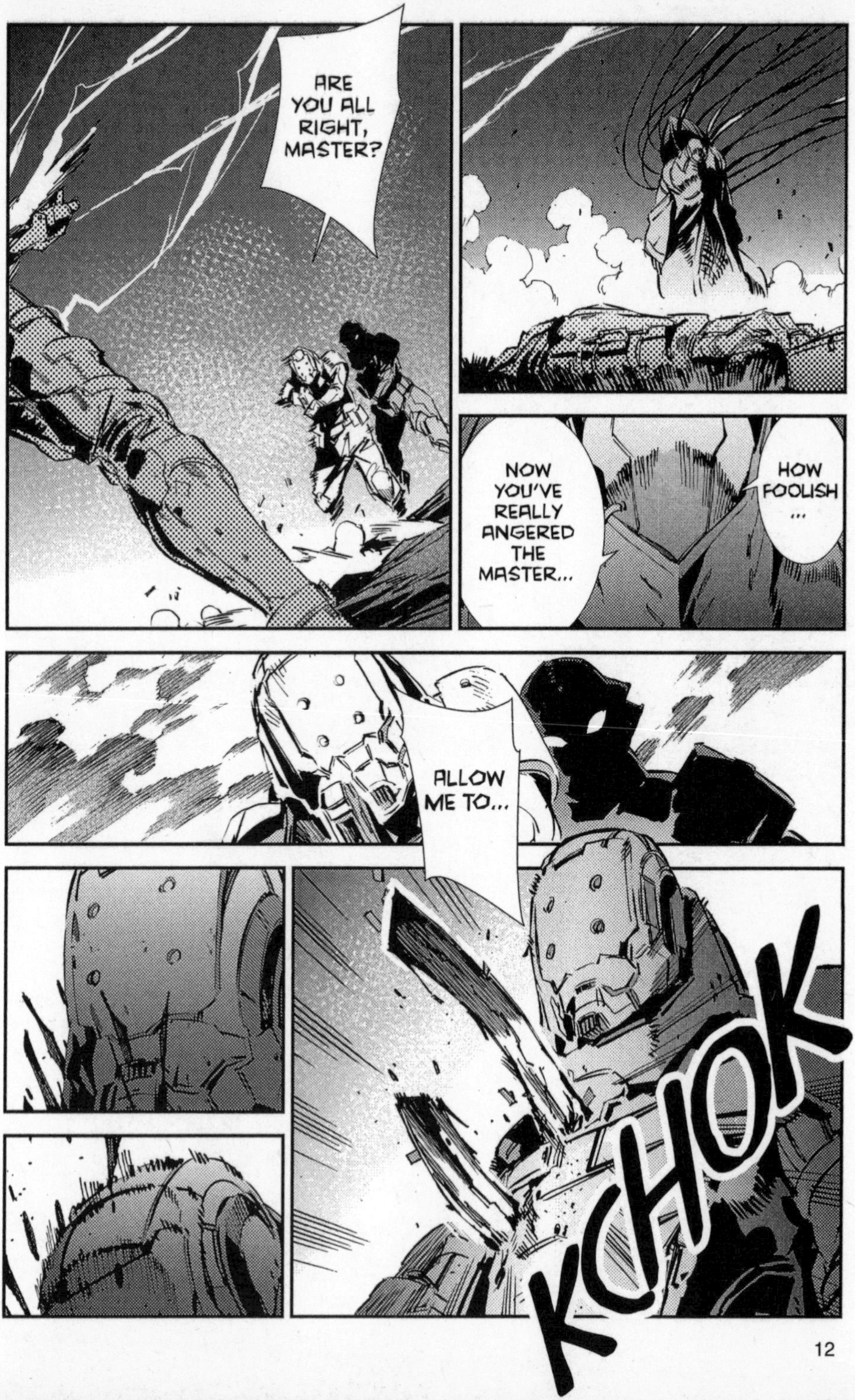
HOW FOOLISH...
NOW YOU'VE REALLY ANGERED THE MASTER...
ARE YOU ALL RIGHT, MASTER?
ALLOW ME TO...
KCHOK

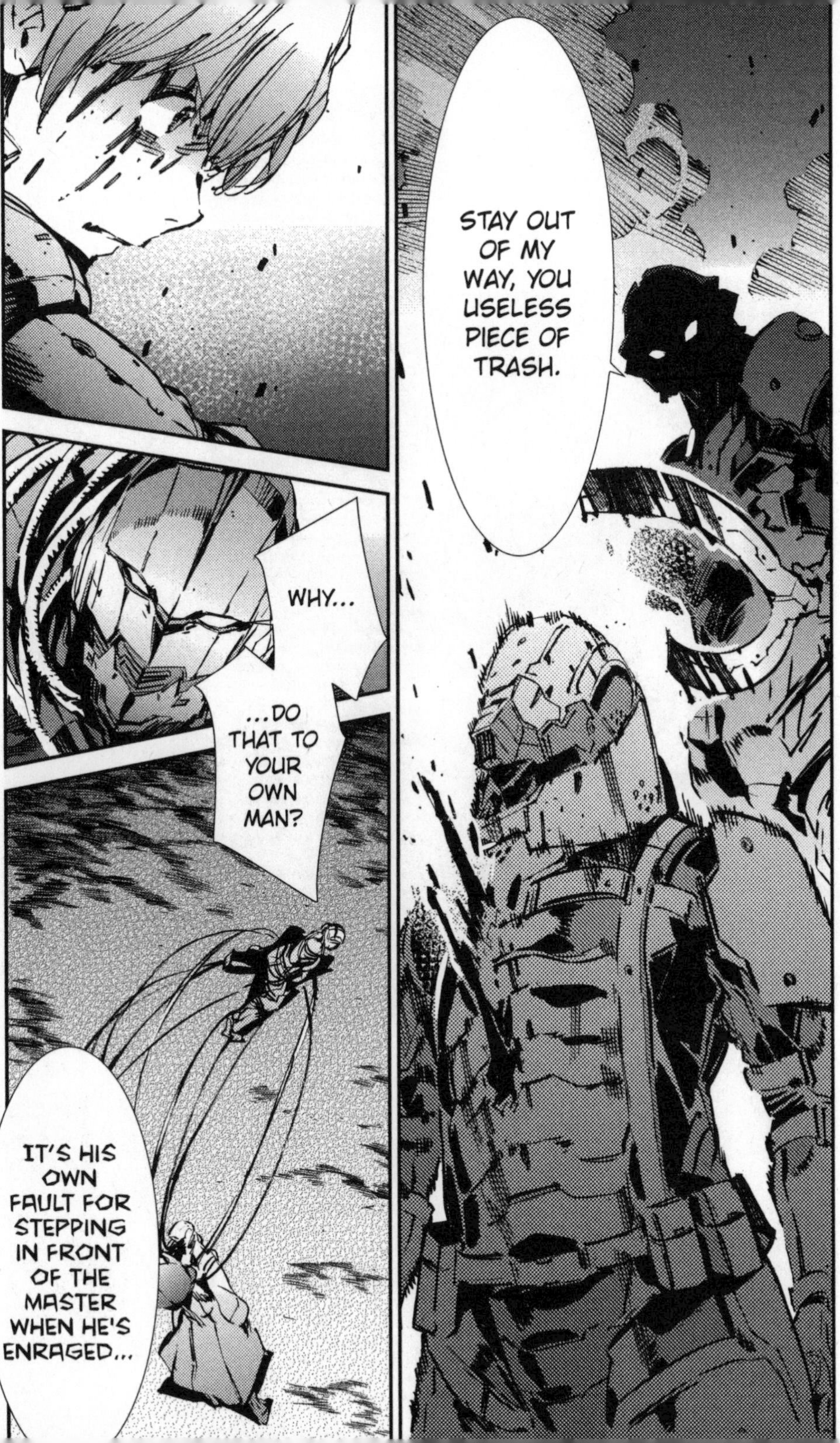
STAY OUT OF MY WAY, YOU USELESS PIECE OF TRASH.
WHY...
...DO THAT TO YOUR OWN MAN?
IT'S HIS OWN FAULT FOR STEPPING IN FRONT OF THE MASTER WHEN HE'S ENRAGED...

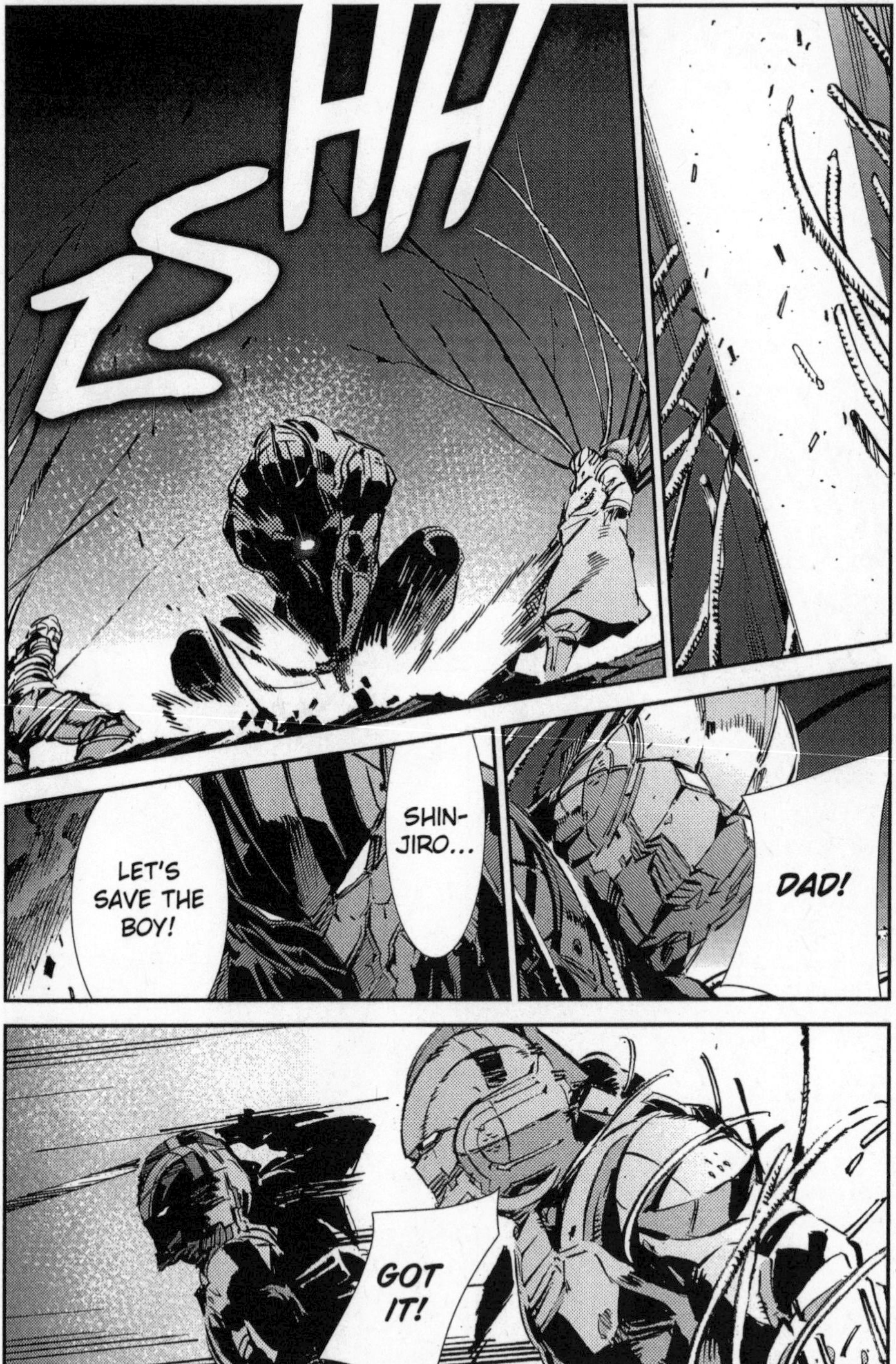
ZSHH
DAD!
SHIN-JIRO...
LET'S SAVE THE BOY!
GOT IT!

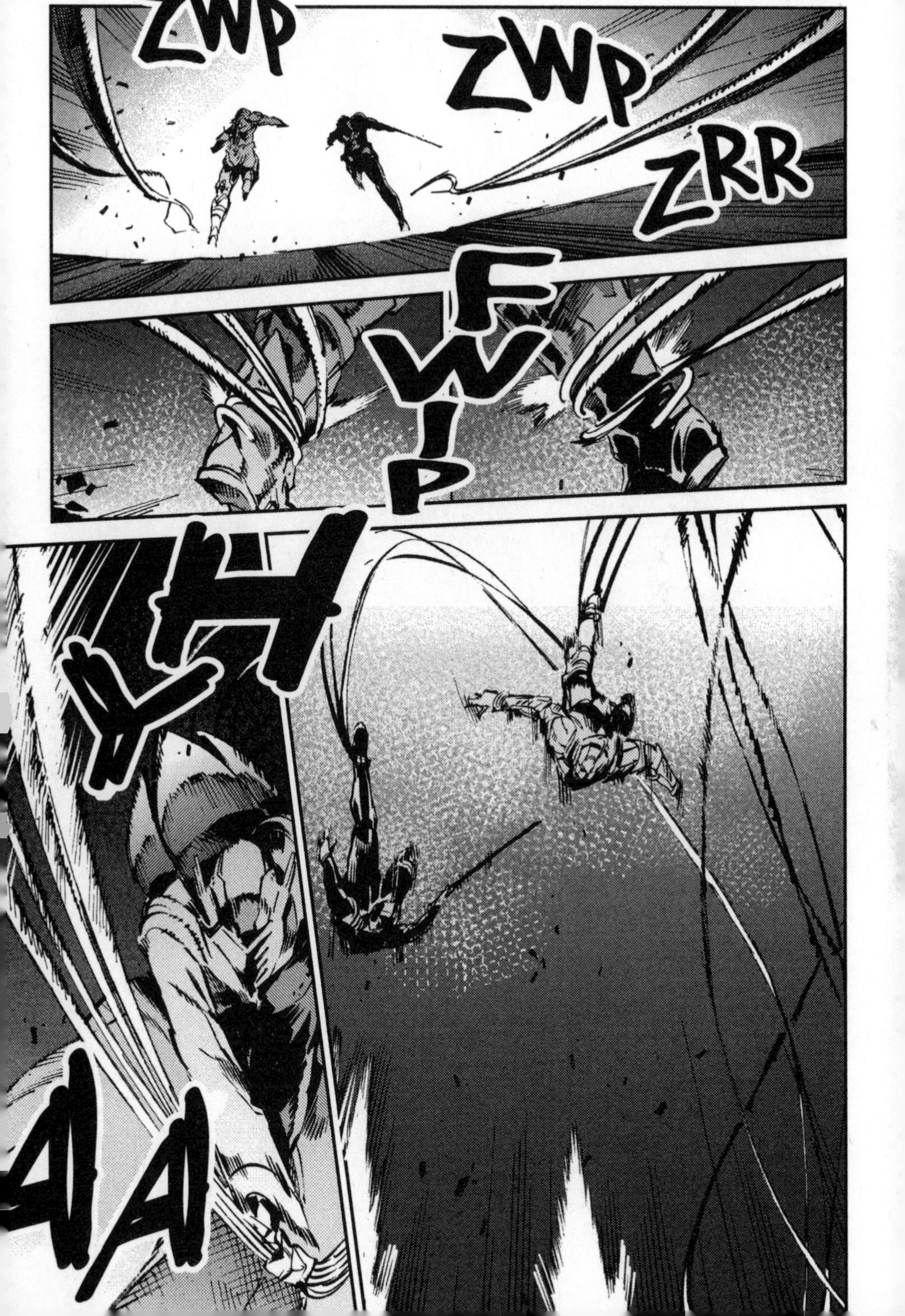
ZWP
ZRR
ZWP
FWIP

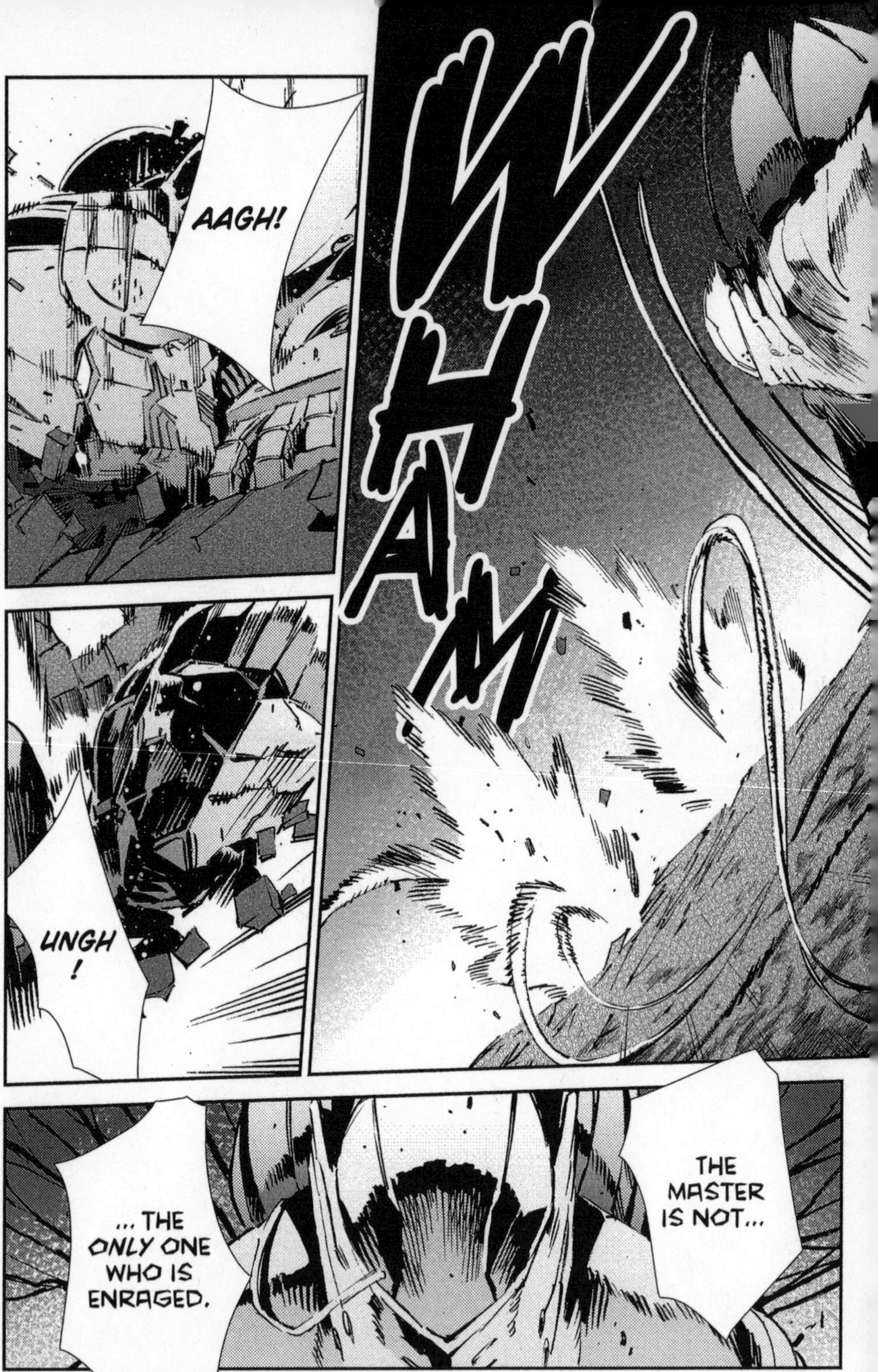
WHAM
AAGH!
UNGH!
THE MASTER IS NOT...
...THE ONLY ONE WHO IS ENRAGED.

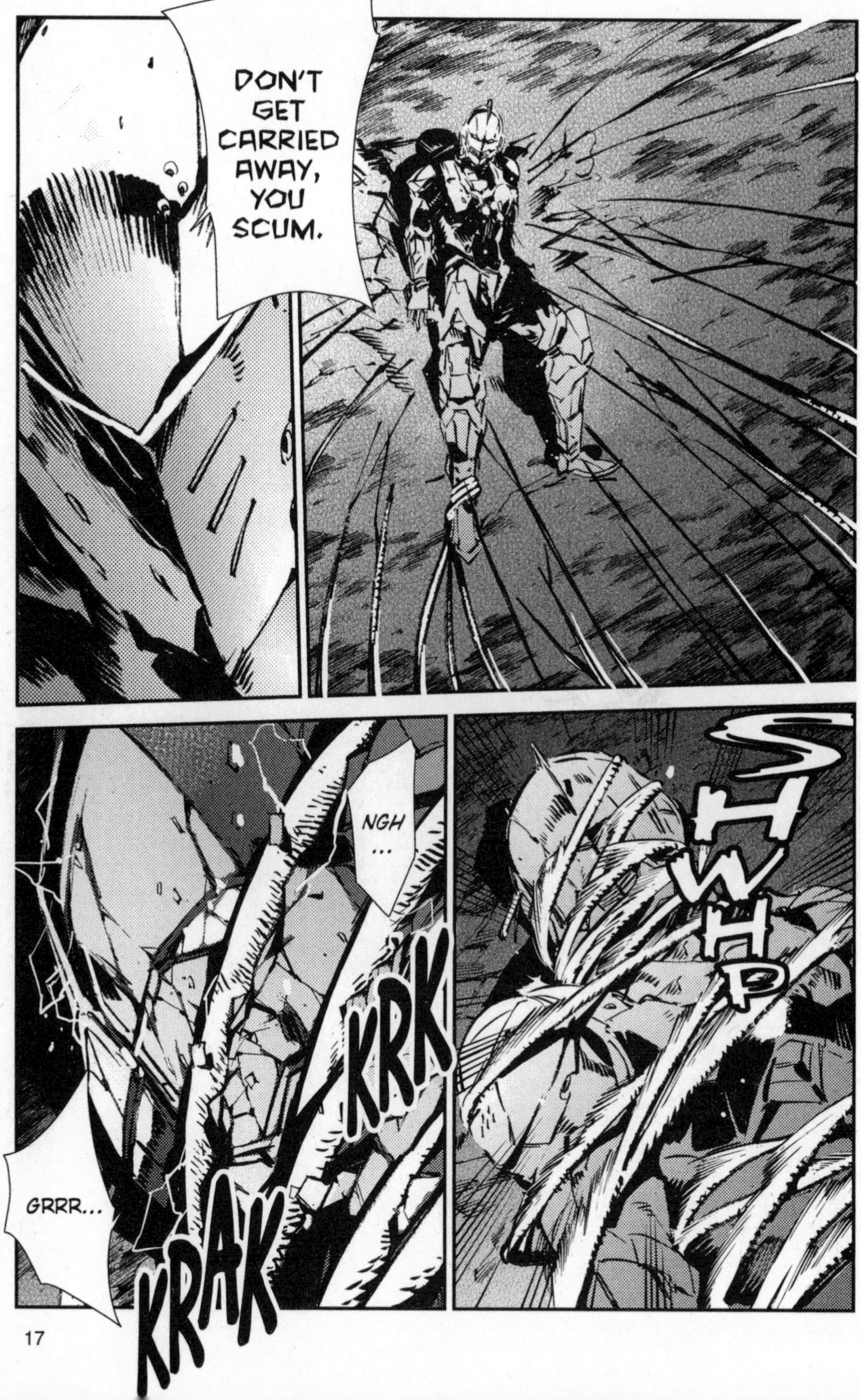

DON'T GET CARRIED AWAY, YOU SCUM.
SHWHP
NGH ...
KRK
GRRR...
KRAK

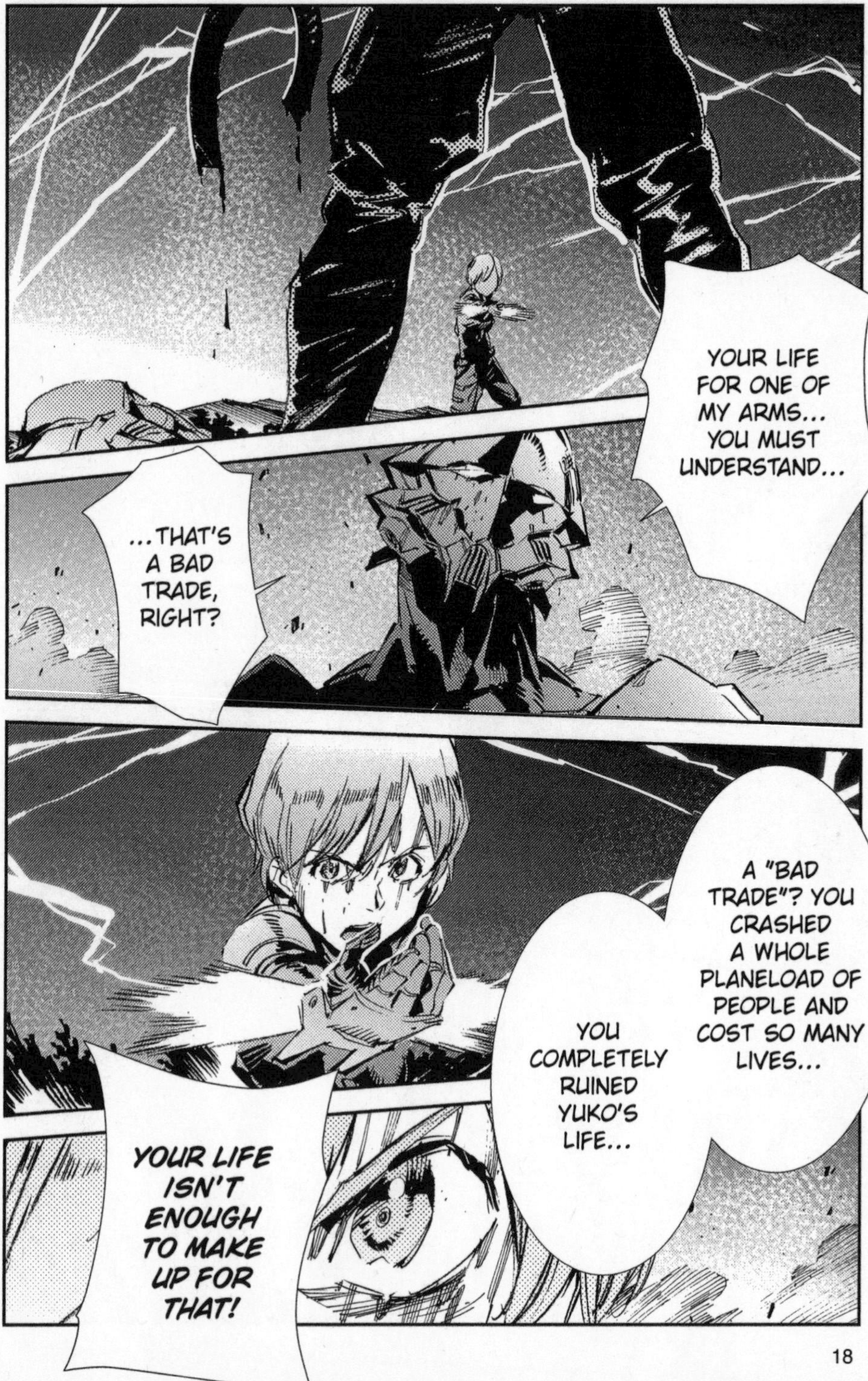
YOUR LIFE FOR ONE OF MY ARMS... YOU MUST UNDERSTAND...
...THAT'S A BAD TRADE, RIGHT?
A "BAD TRADE"? YOU CRASHED A WHOLE PLANELOAD OF PEOPLE AND COST SO MANY LIVES...
YOU COMPLETELY RUINED YUKO'S LIFE...
YOUR LIFE ISN'T ENOUGH TO MAKE UP FOR THAT!

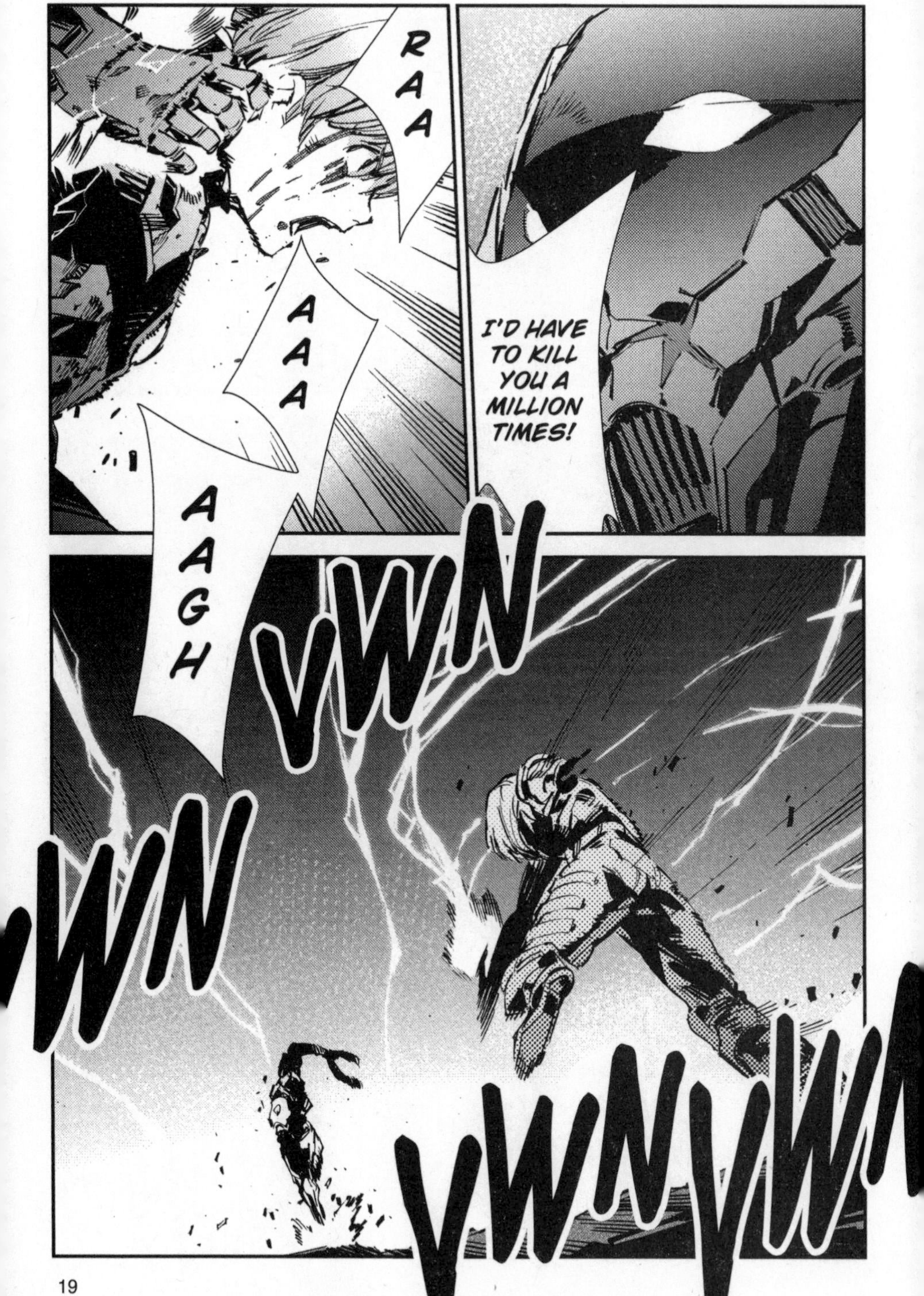
I'D HAVE TO KILL YOU A MILLION TIMES!
RAAAAAAAAGH
VWN
VWN
VWNVWN

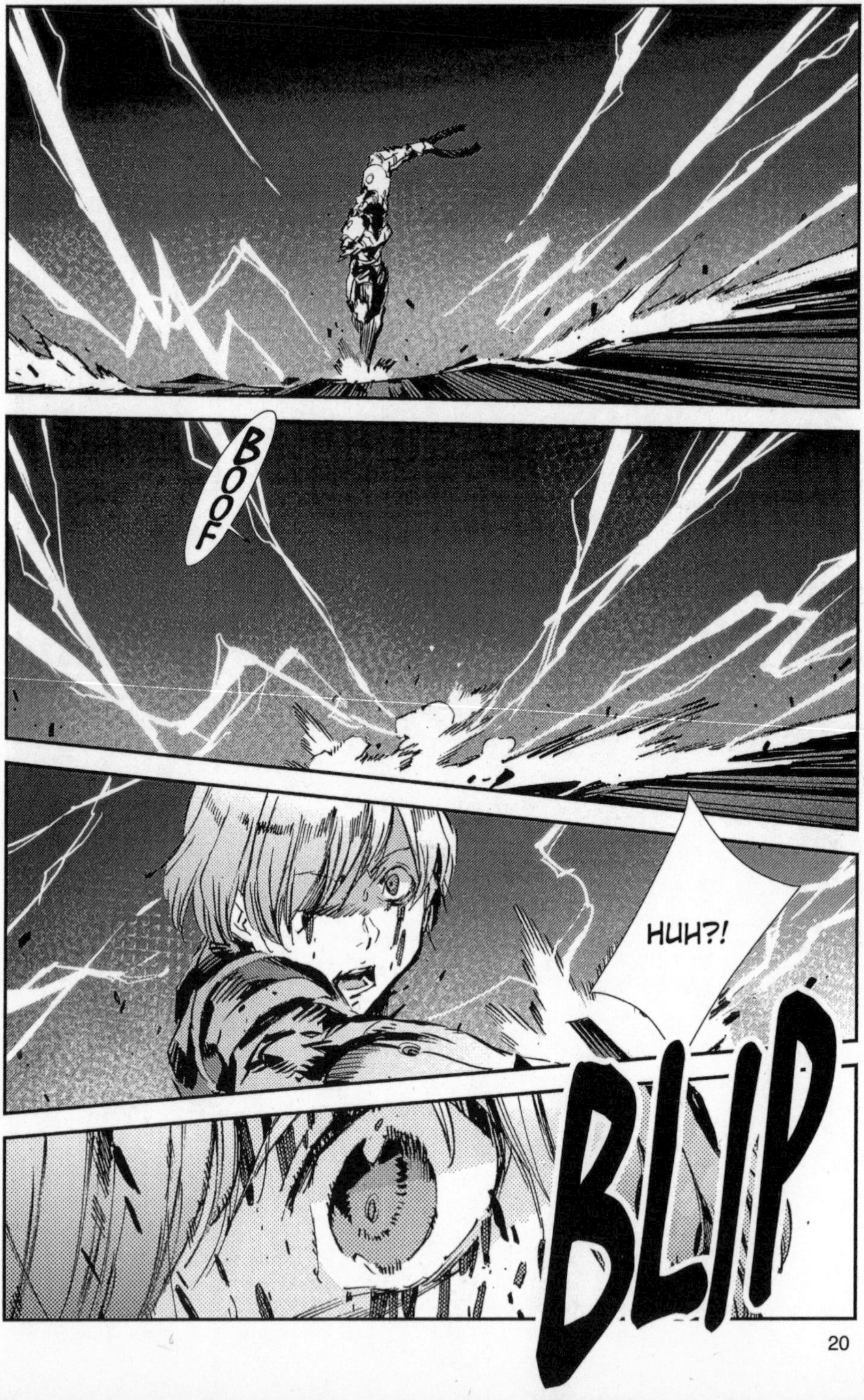
BOOOF
HUH?!
BLIP

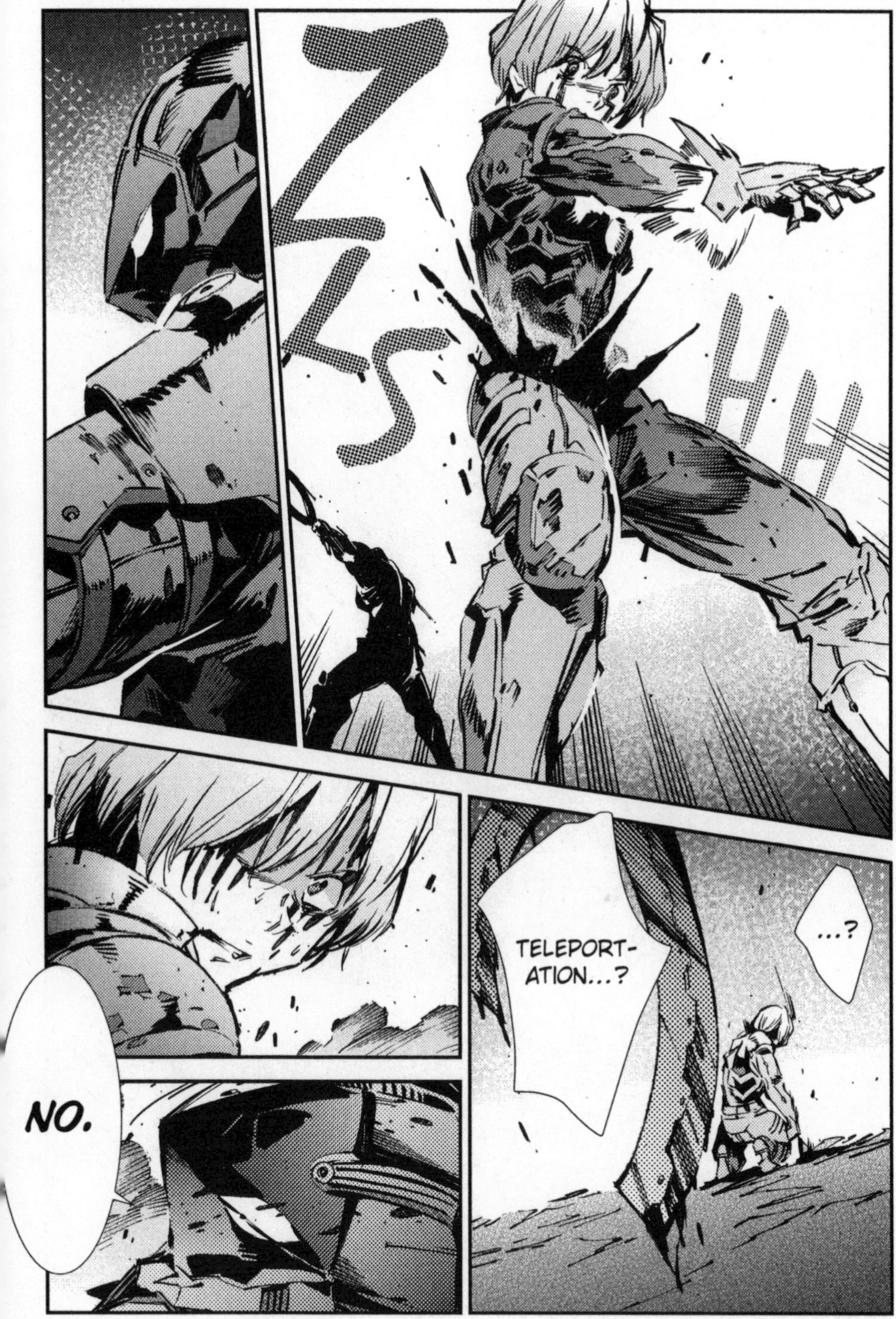
...?
TELEPORT-
ATION...?
NO.

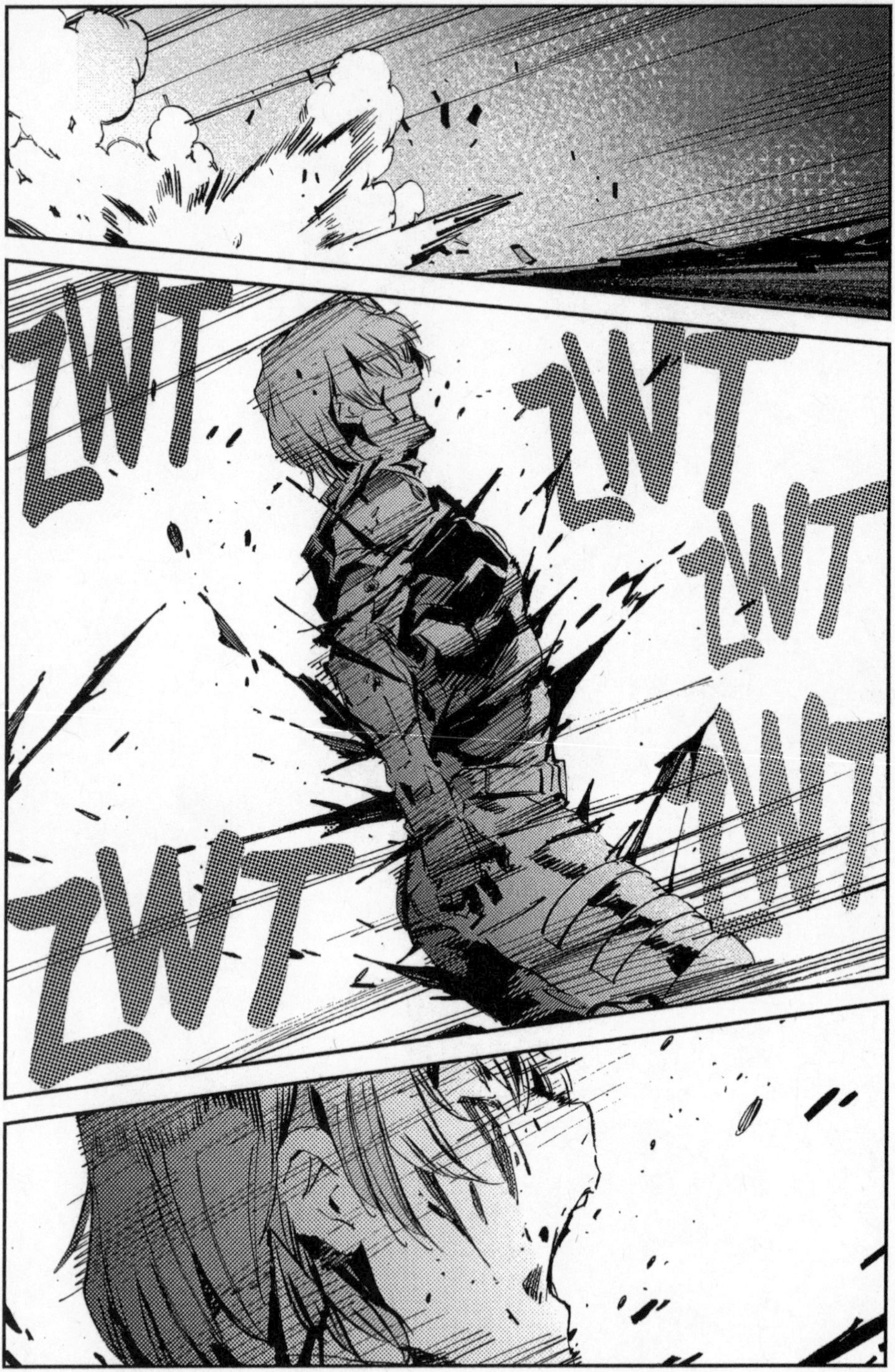
ZWT
ZWT
ZWT
ZWT
ZWT

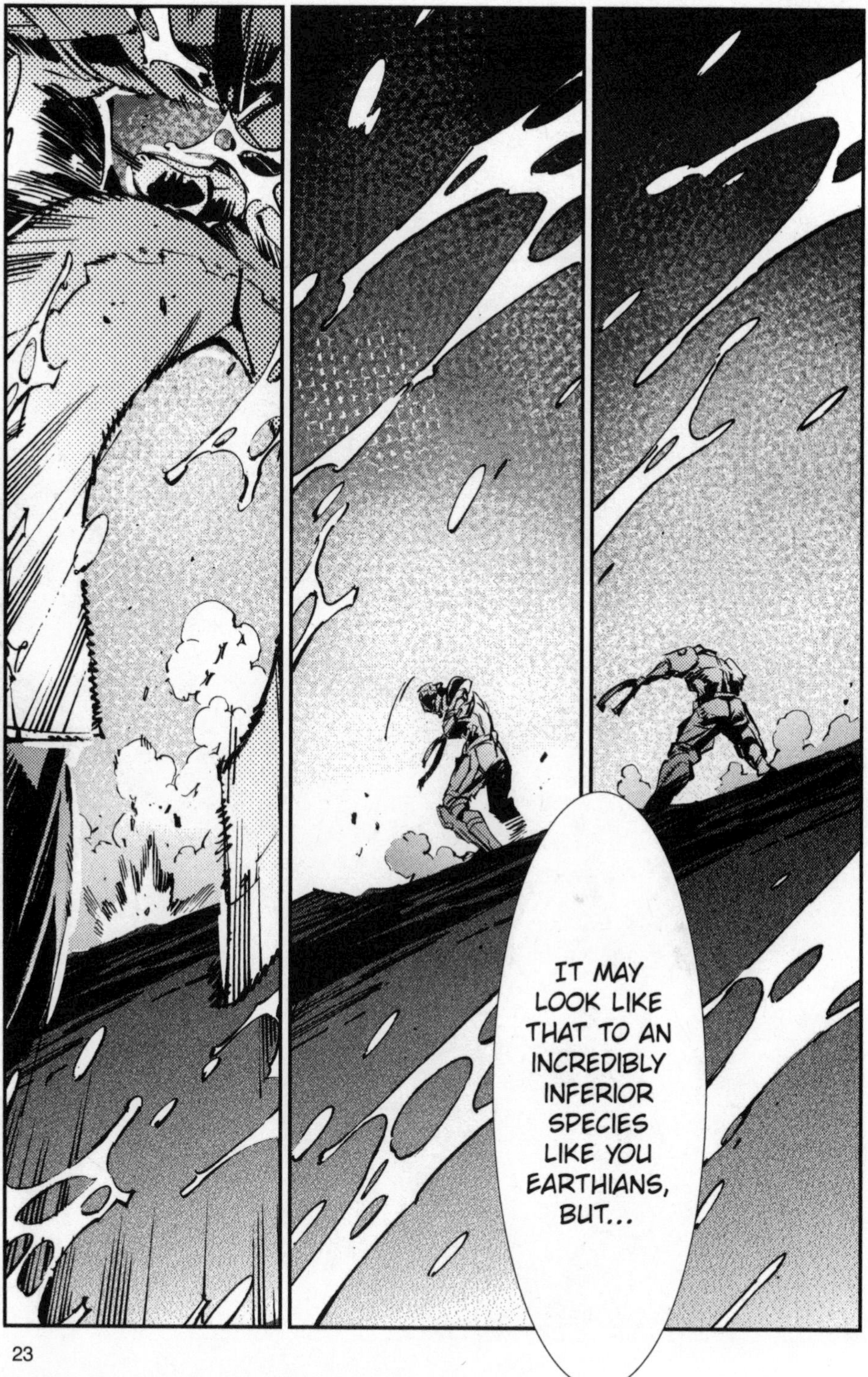
IT MAY LOOK LIKE THAT TO AN INCREDIBLY INFERIOR SPECIES LIKE YOU EARTHIANS, BUT...

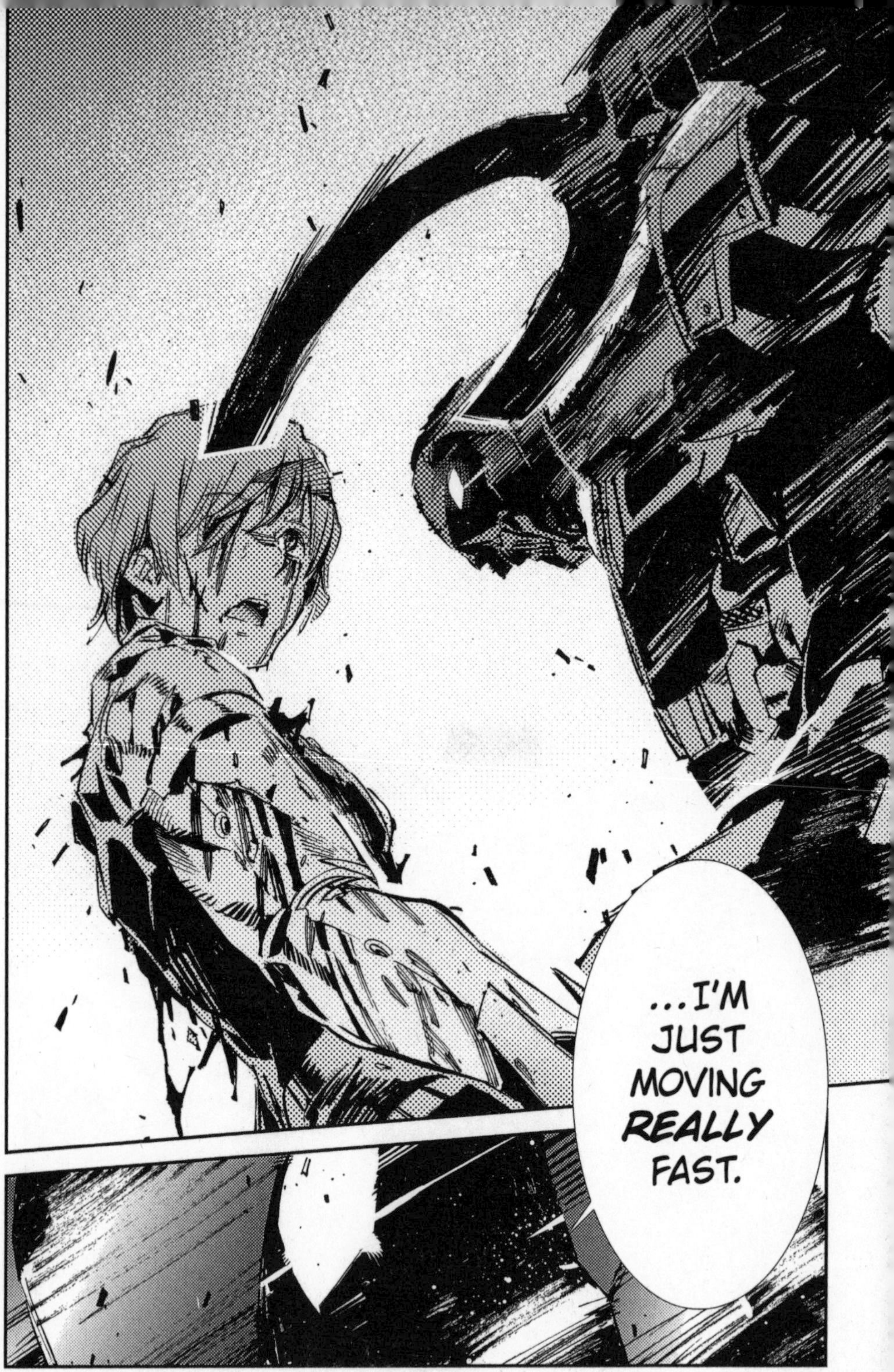
...I'M JUST MOVING REALLY FAST.

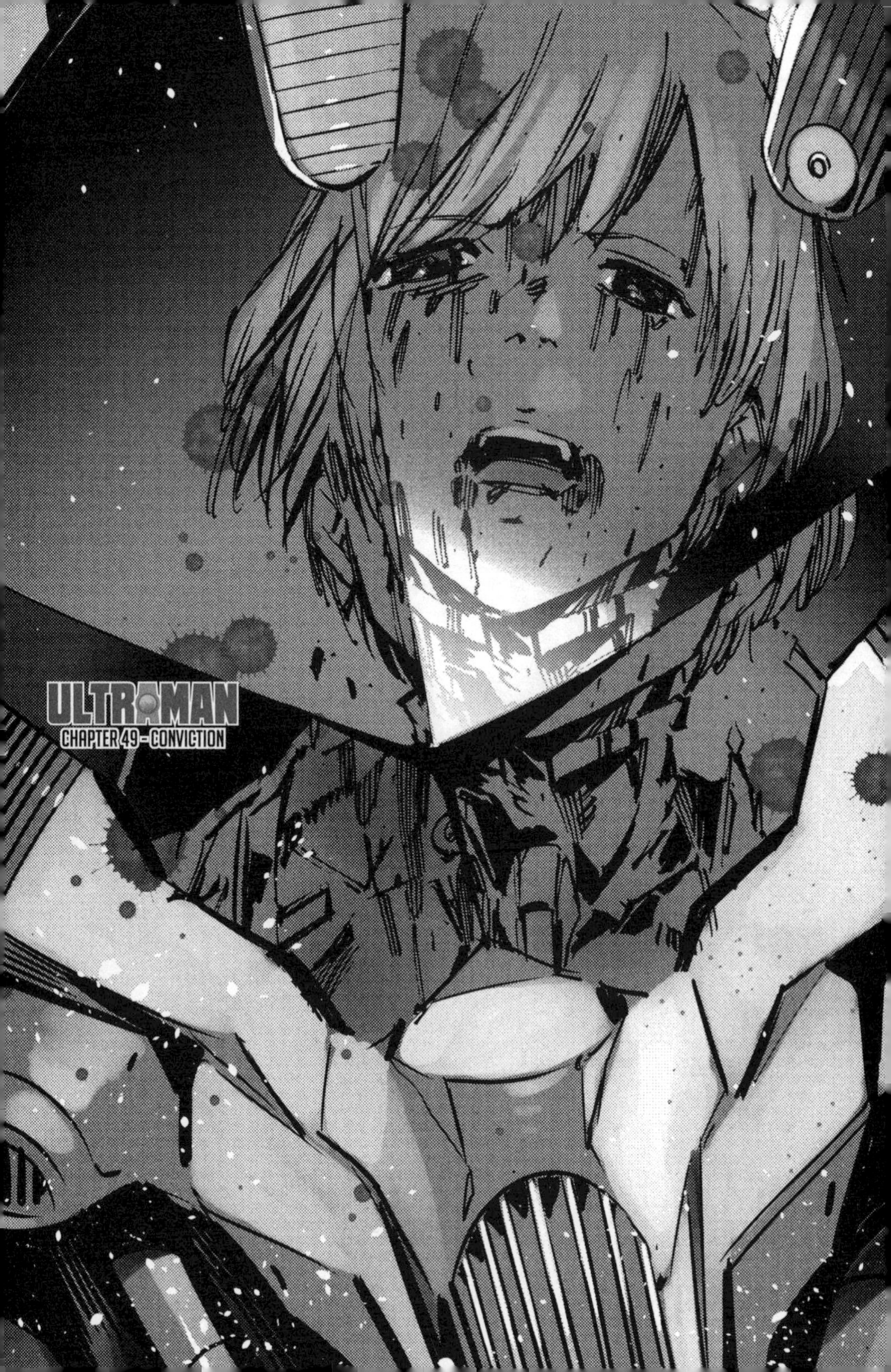
ULTRAMAN
CHAPTER 49 - CONVICTION

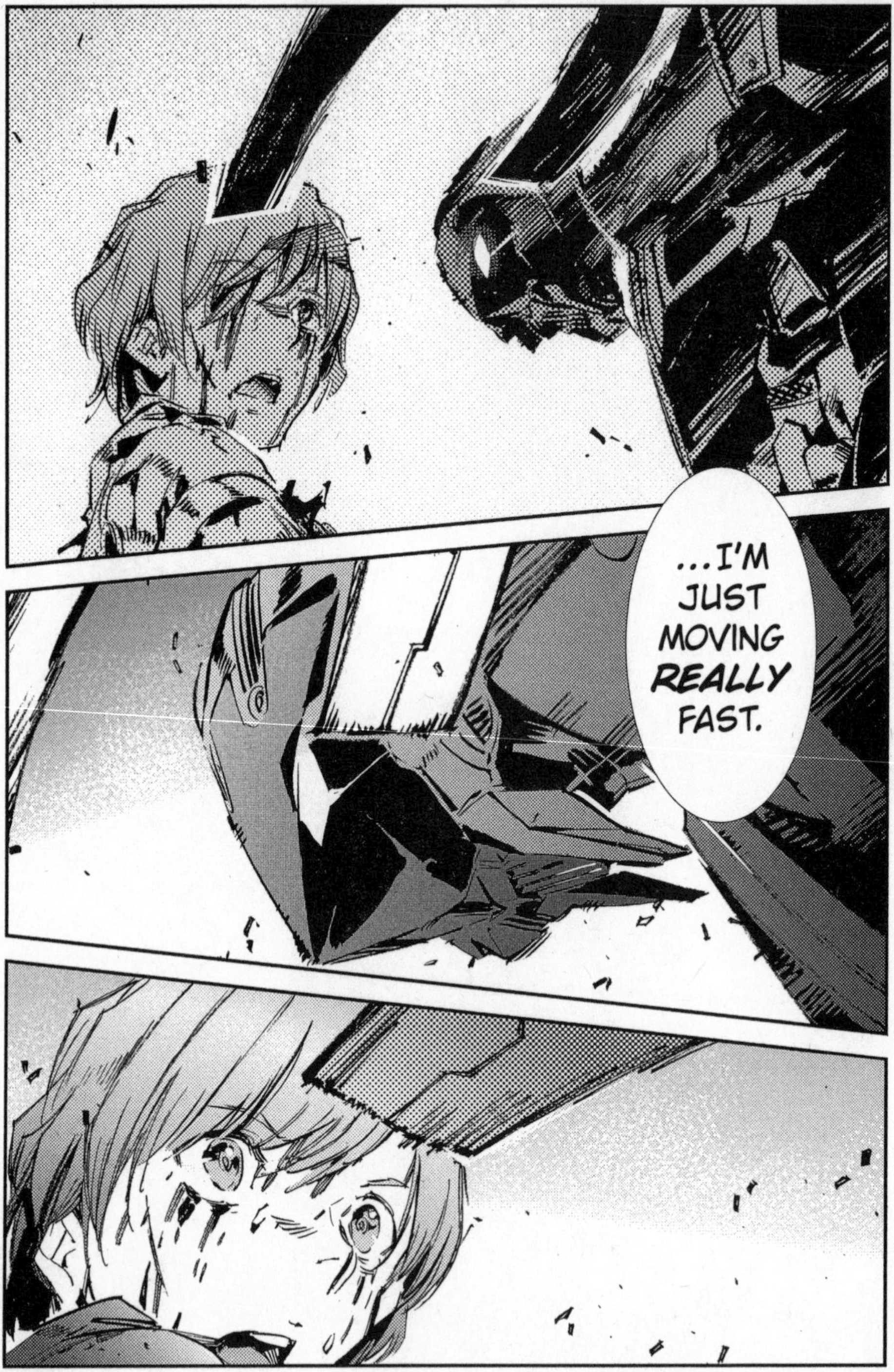
...I'M JUST MOVING REALLY FAST.

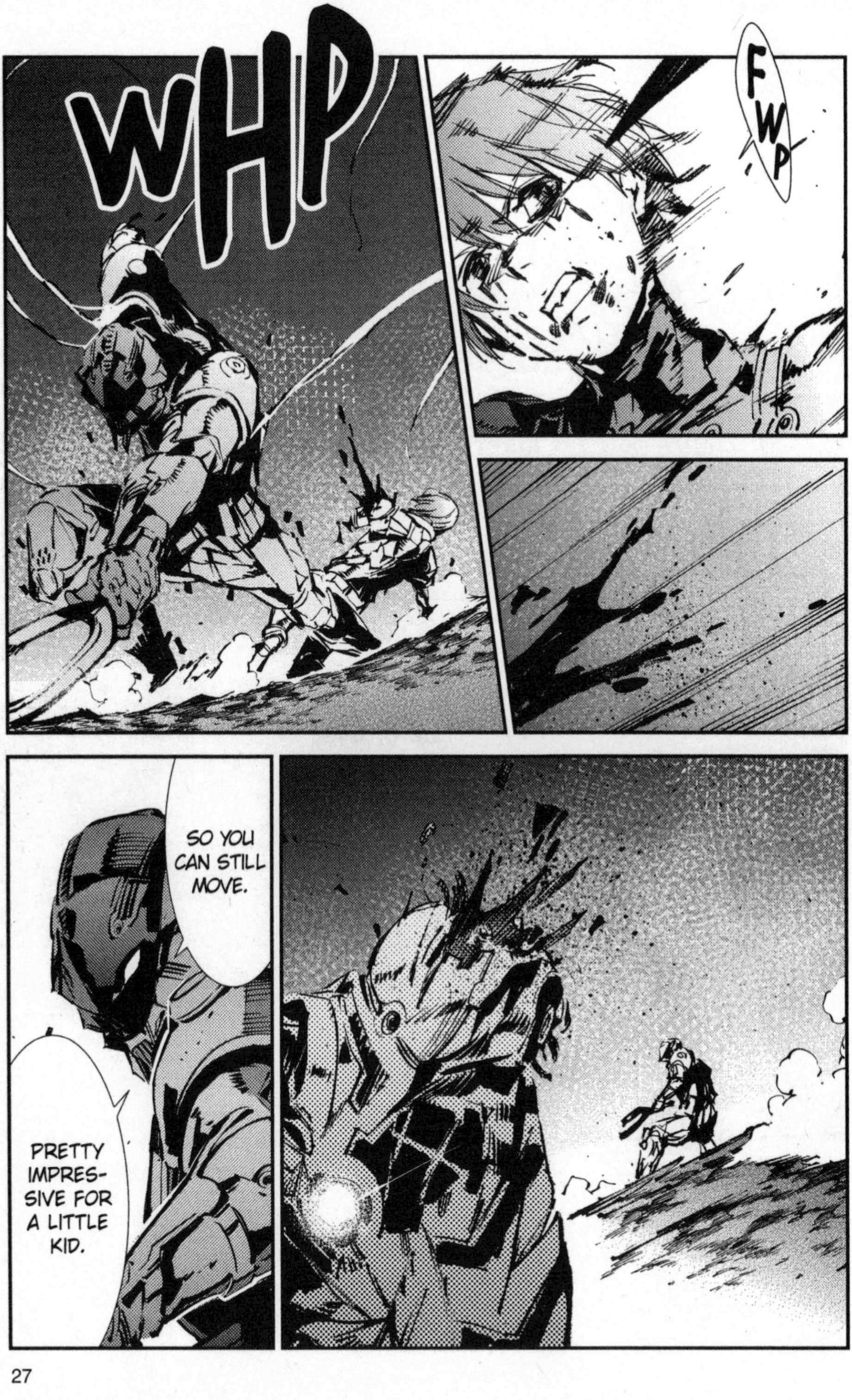
FWP
WHP
SO YOU CAN STILL MOVE.
PRETTY IMPRESSIVE FOR A LITTLE KID.

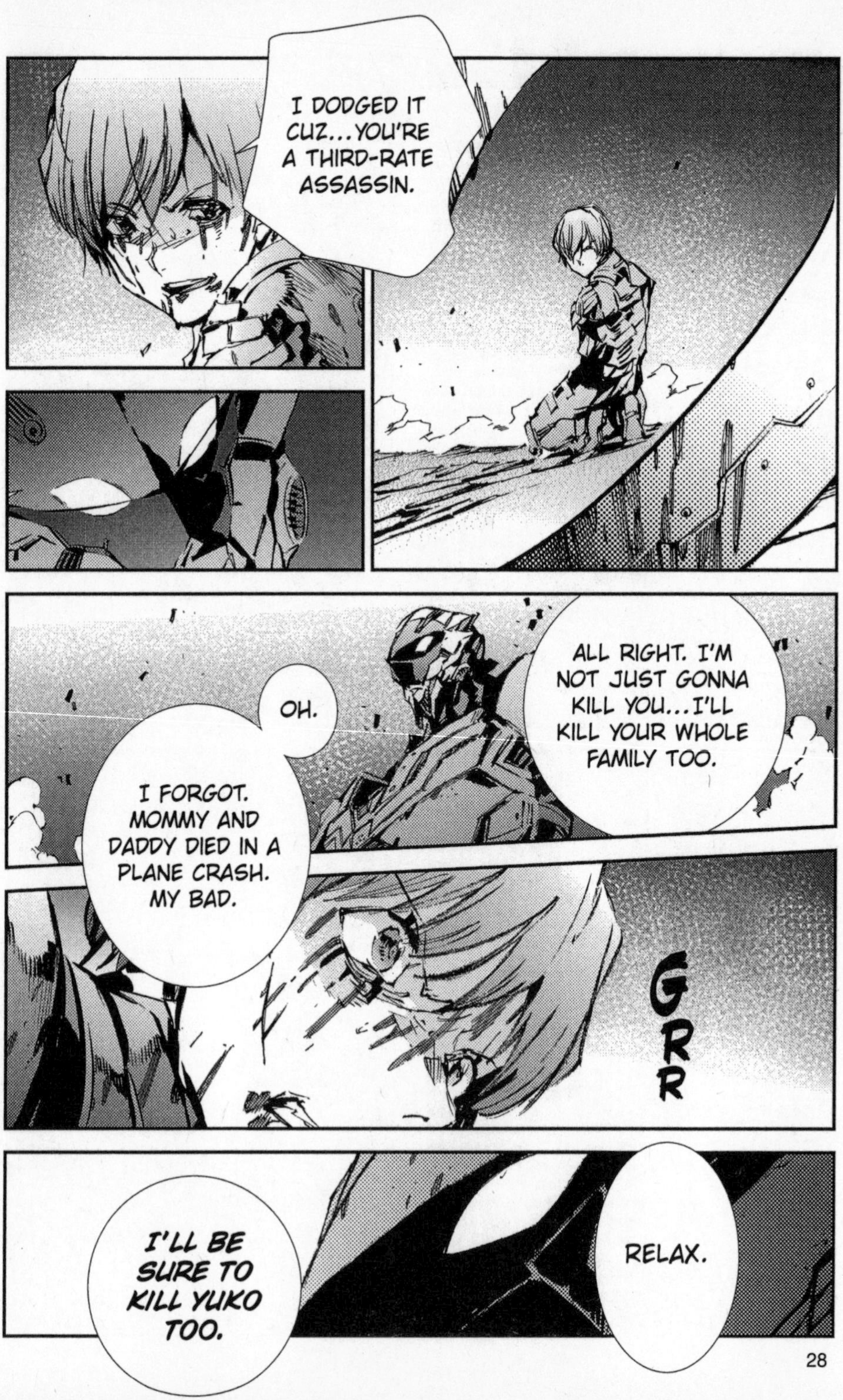
I DODGED IT CUZ...YOU'RE A THIRD-RATE ASSASSIN.
ALL RIGHT. I'M NOT JUST GONNA KILL YOU...I'LL KILL YOUR WHOLE FAMILY TOO.
OH.
I FORGOT. MOMMY AND DADDY DIED IN A PLANE CRASH. MY BAD.
GRR
RELAX.
I'LL BE SURE TO KILL YUKO TOO.

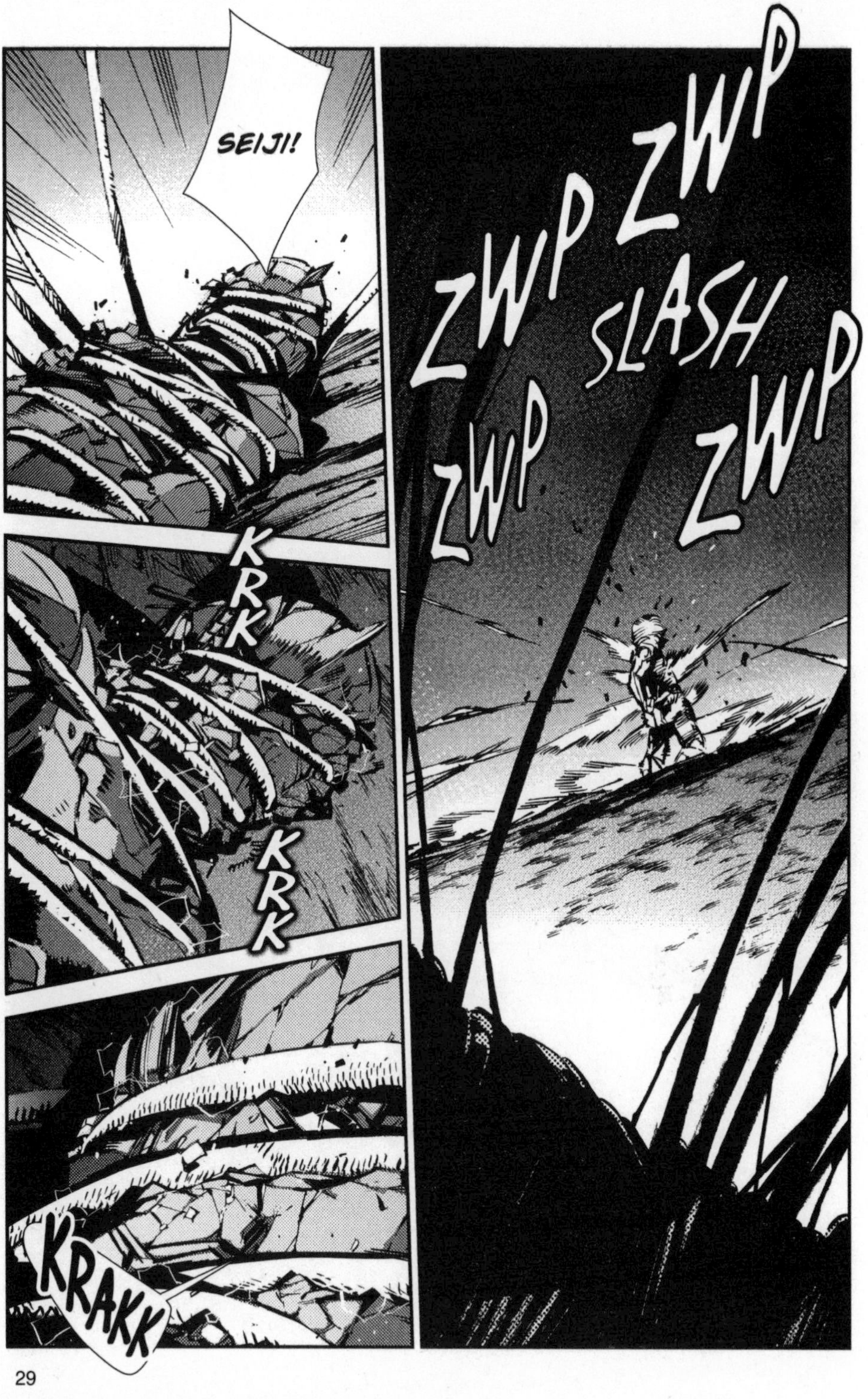
ZWP
ZWP
ZWP
SLASH
ZWP
ZWP
ZWP
SEIJI!
KRK
KRK
KRK
KRK
KRAKK

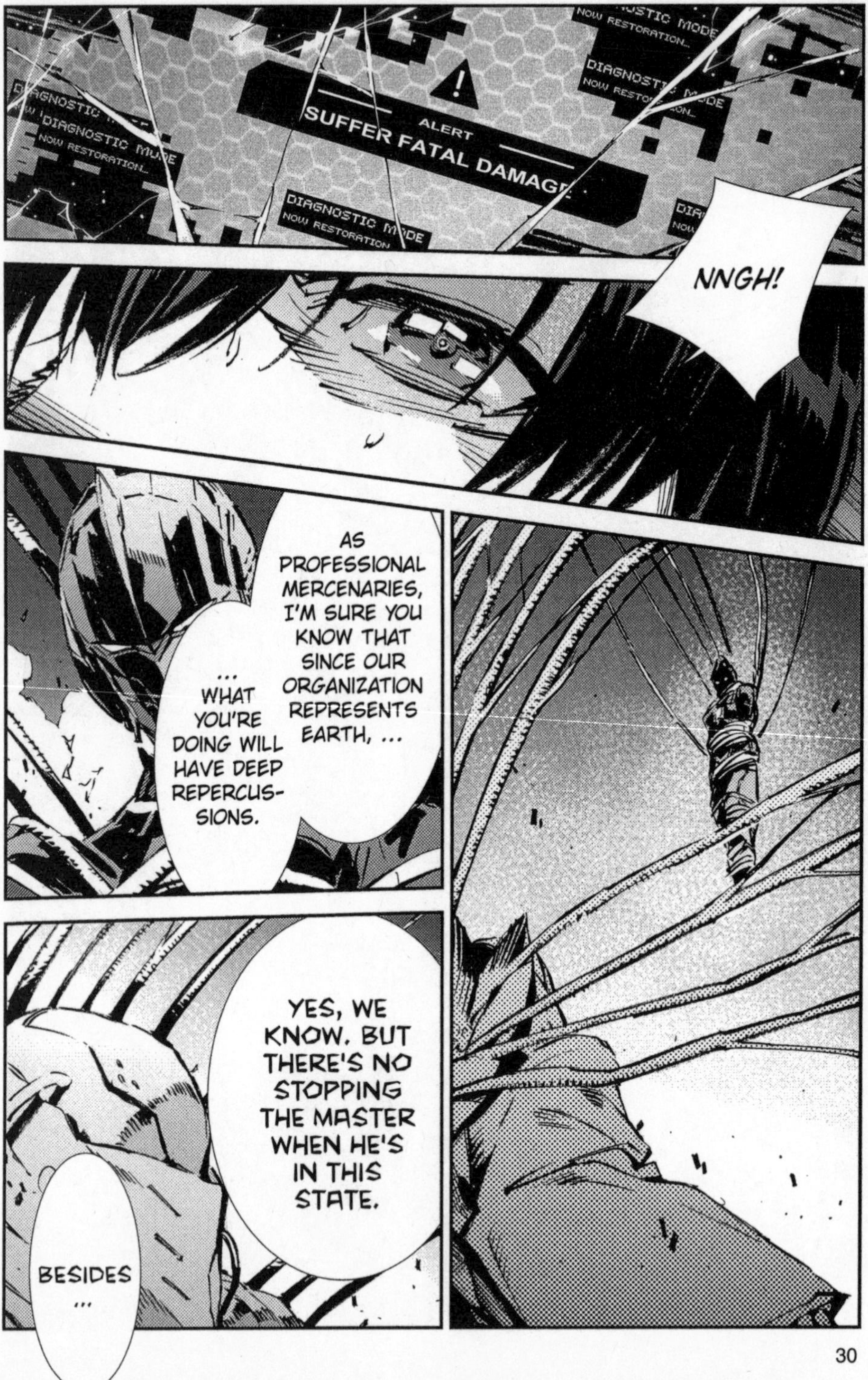
ALERT
SUFFER FATAL DAMAGE
DIAGNOSTIC MODE
NOW RESTORATION...
DIAGNOSTIC MODE
NOW RESTORATION
NNGH!
AS PROFESSIONAL MERCENARIES, I'M SURE YOU KNOW THAT SINCE OUR ORGANIZATION REPRESENTS EARTH, ...
... WHAT YOU'RE DOING WILL HAVE DEEP REPERCUSSIONS.
YES, WE KNOW. BUT THERE'S NO STOPPING THE MASTER WHEN HE'S IN THIS STATE.
BESIDES ...

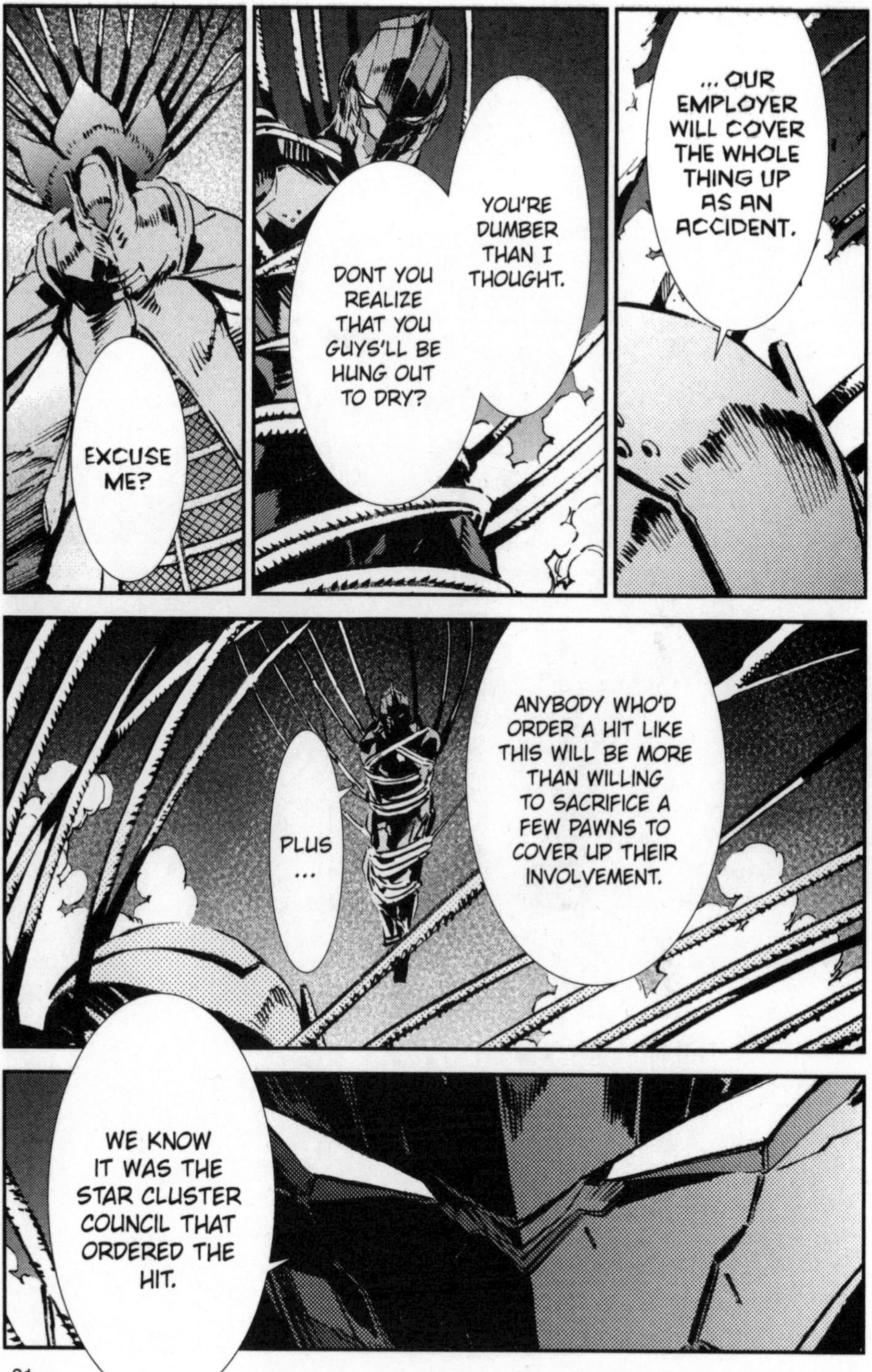
...OUR EMPLOYER WILL COVER THE WHOLE THING UP AS AN ACCIDENT.
YOU'RE DUMBER THAN I THOUGHT.
DONT YOU REALIZE THAT YOU GUYS'LL BE HUNG OUT TO DRY?
EXCUSE ME?
ANYBODY WHO'D ORDER A HIT LIKE THIS WILL BE MORE THAN WILLING TO SACRIFICE A FEW PAWNS TO COVER UP THEIR INVOLVEMENT.
PLUS...
WE KNOW IT WAS THE STAR CLUSTER COUNCIL THAT ORDERED THE HIT.

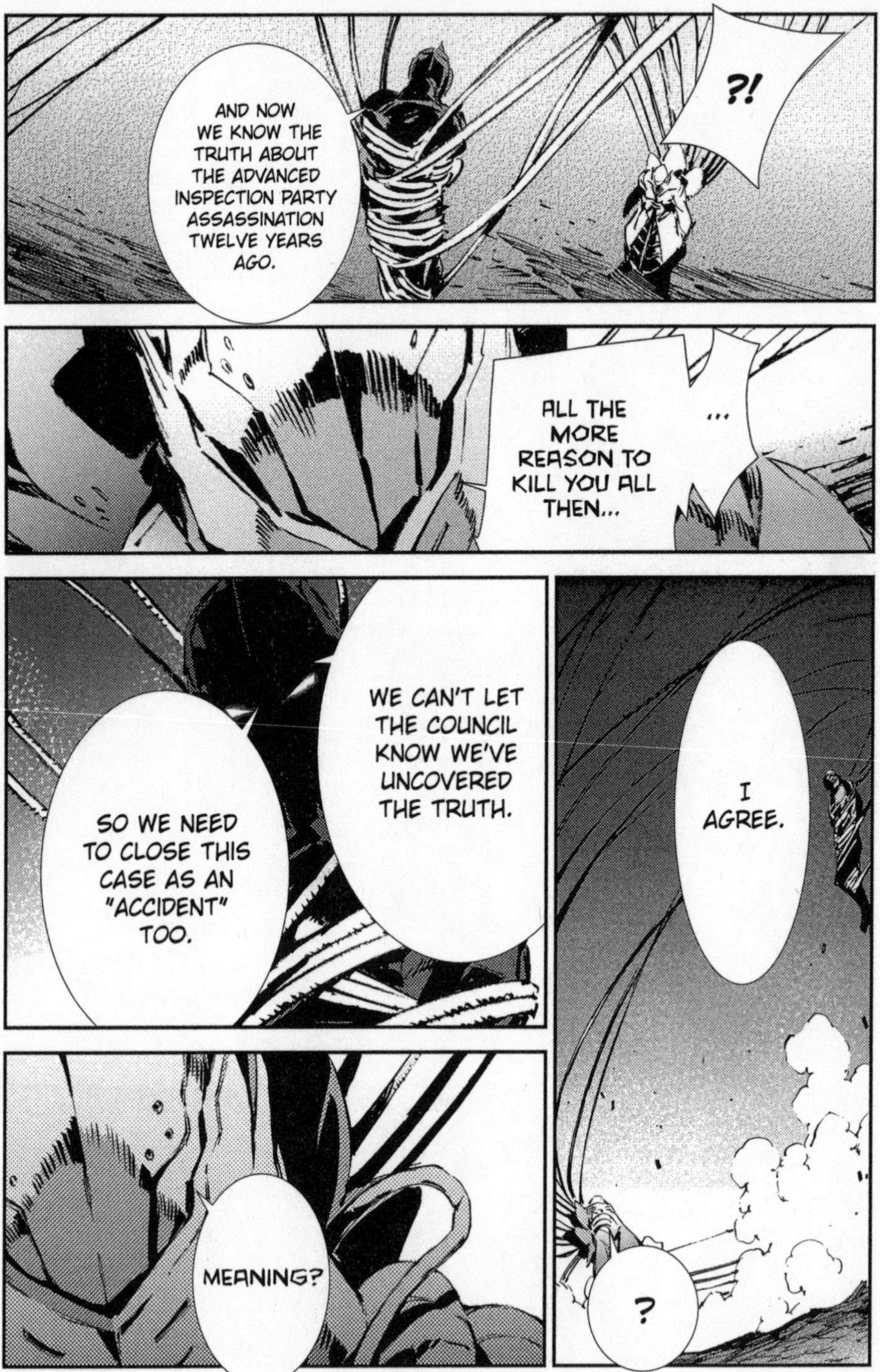
?!
AND NOW WE KNOW THE TRUTH ABOUT THE ADVANCED INSPECTION PARTY ASSASSINATION TWELVE YEARS AGO.
...
ALL THE MORE REASON TO KILL YOU ALL THEN...
I AGREE.
?
WE CAN'T LET THE COUNCIL KNOW WE'VE UNCOVERED THE TRUTH.
SO WE NEED TO CLOSE THIS CASE AS AN "ACCIDENT" TOO.
MEANING?

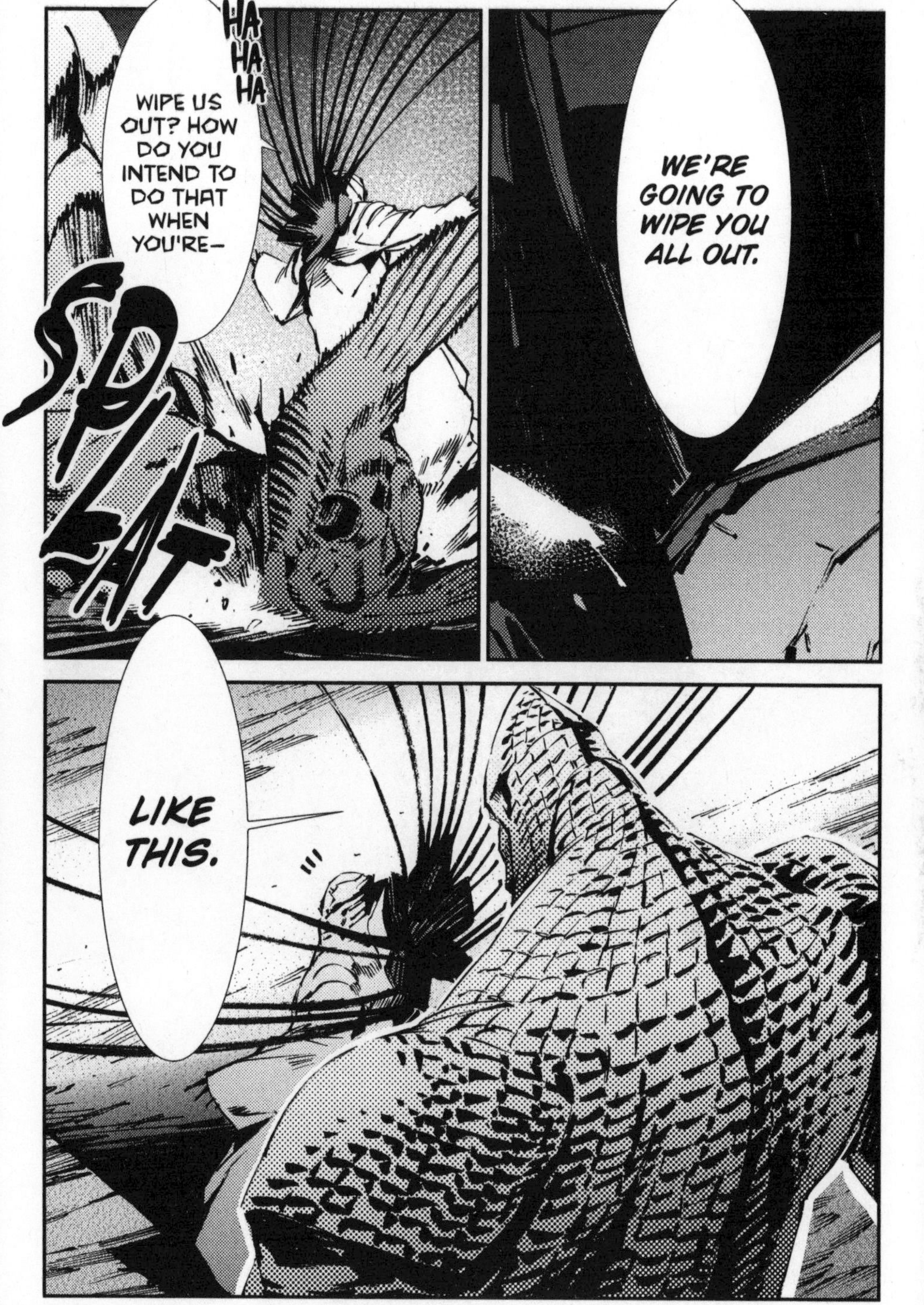
WE'RE GOING TO WIPE YOU ALL OUT.
HA HA HA
WIPE US OUT? HOW DO YOU INTEND TO DO THAT WHEN YOU'RE–
SPLAT
LIKE THIS.
!!

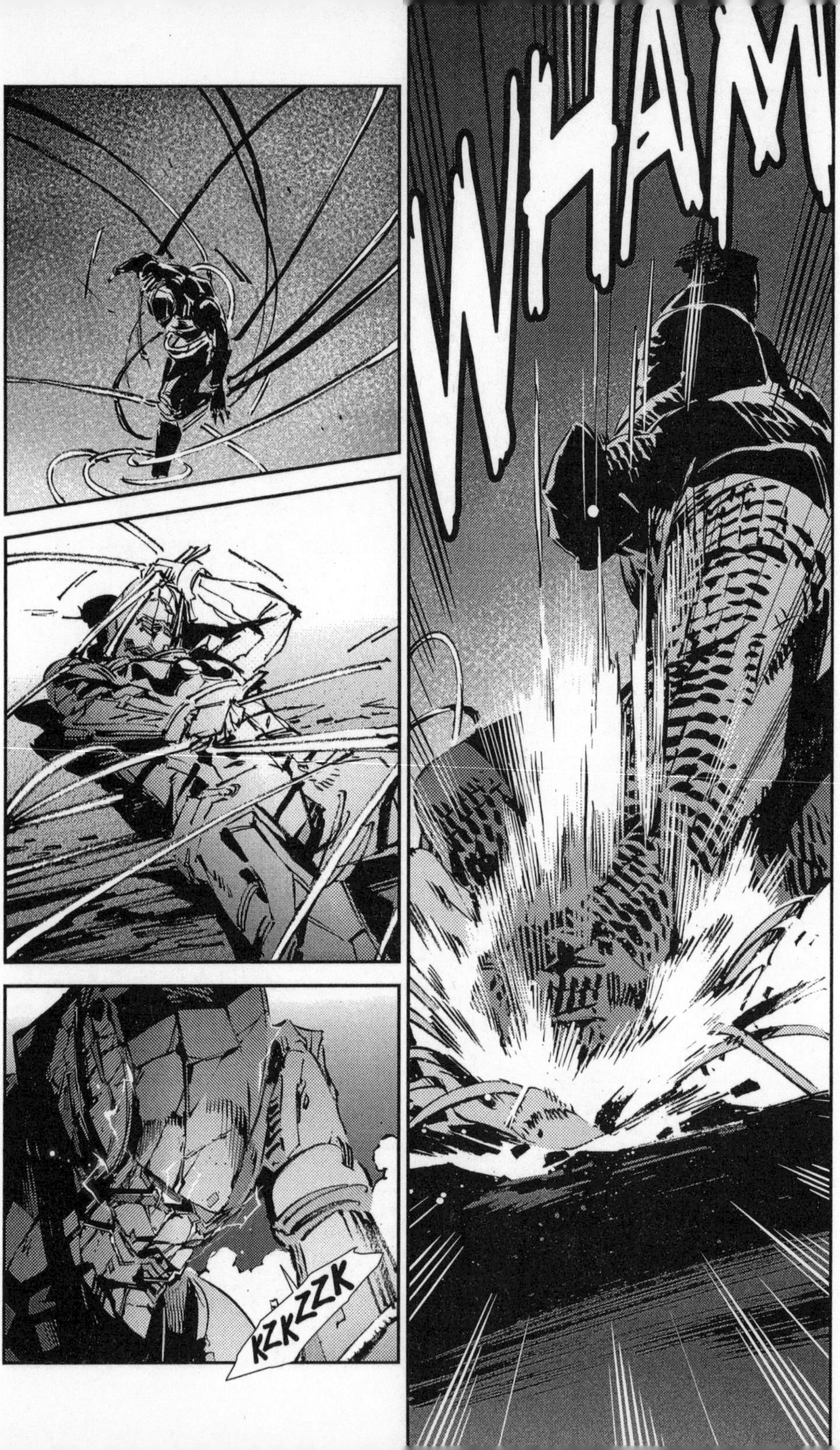
WHAM
KZKZZK

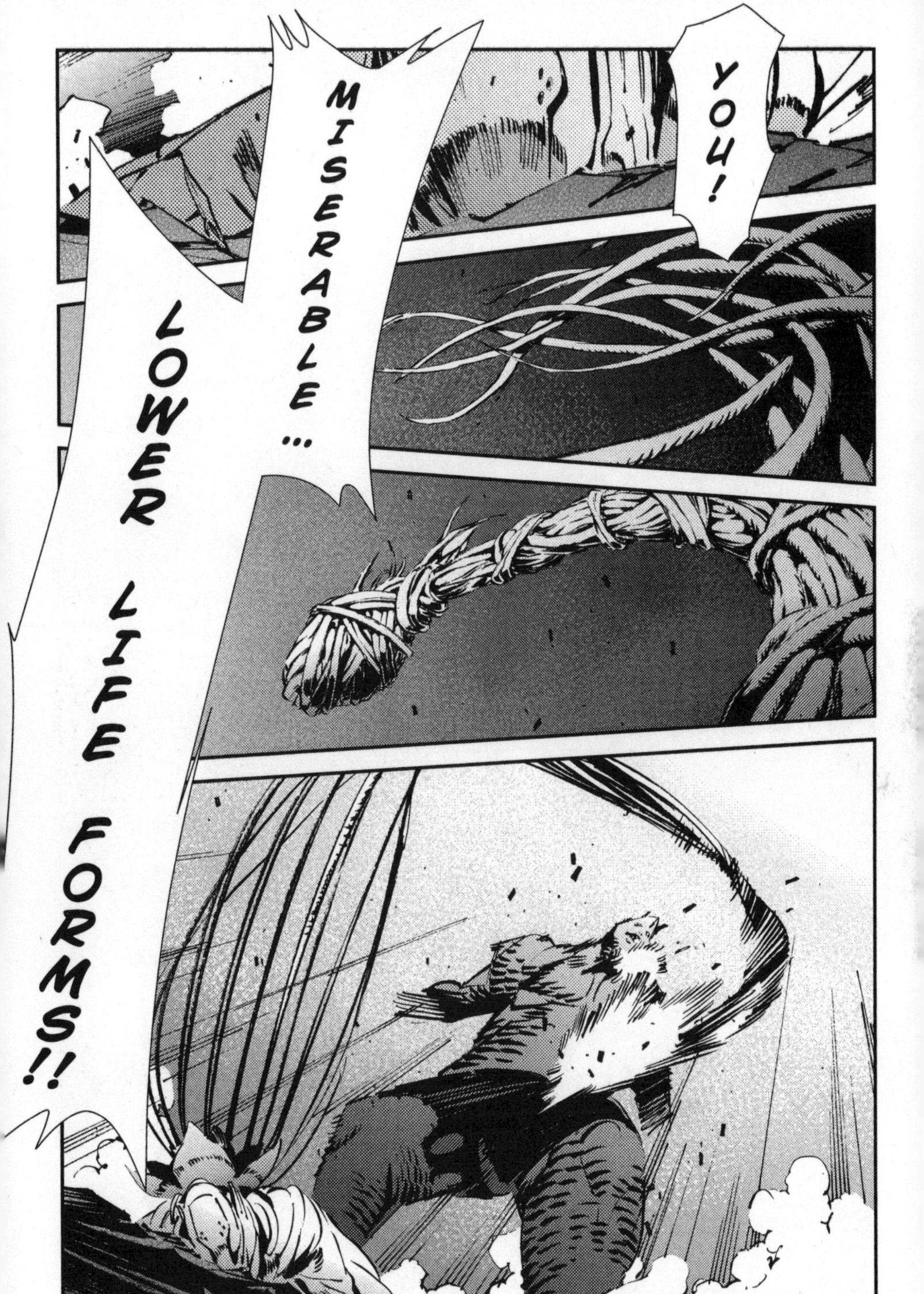
YOU!
MISERABLE...
LOWER LIFE FORMS!!

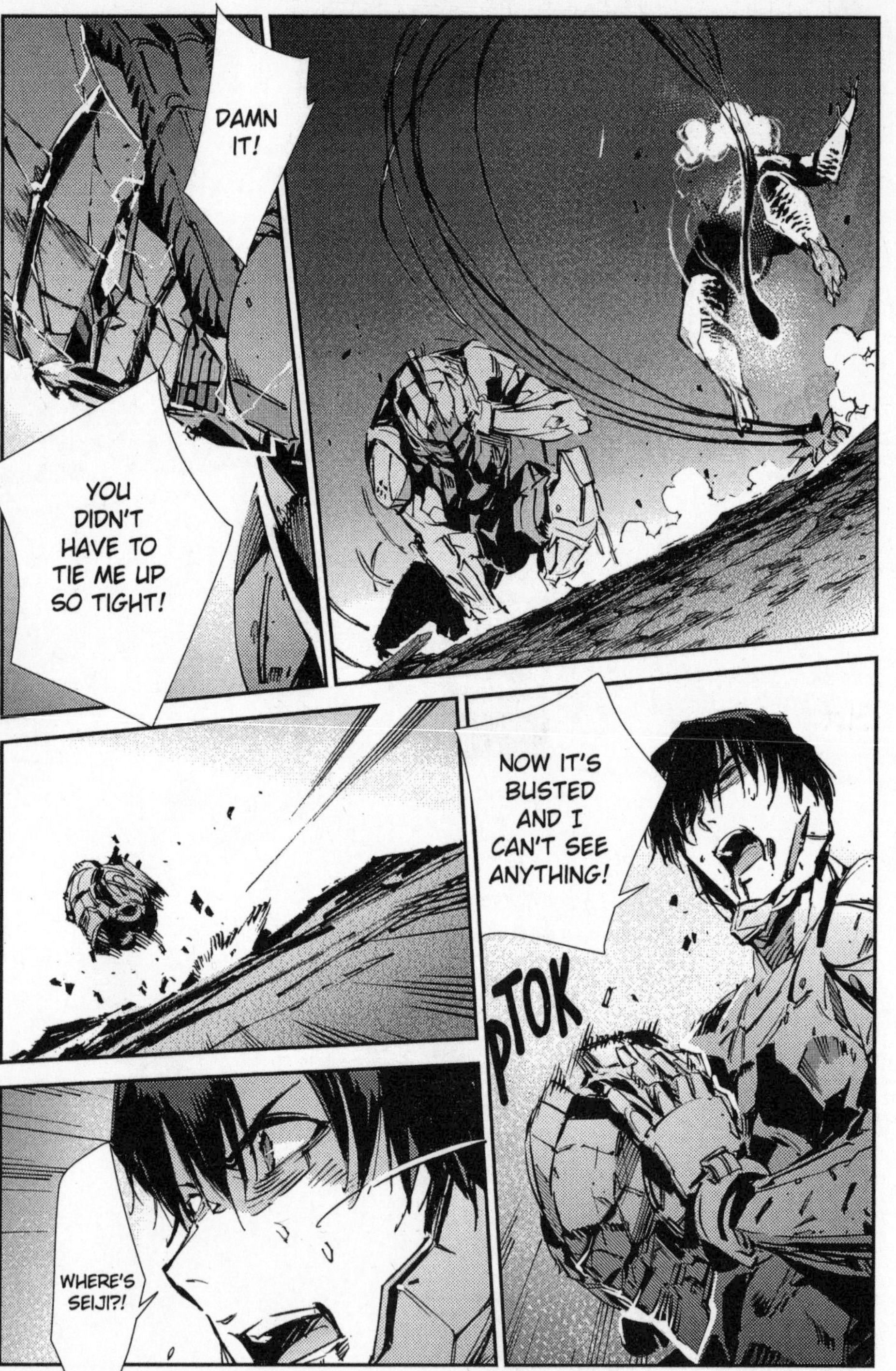
DAMN IT!
YOU DIDN'T HAVE TO TIE ME UP SO TIGHT!
NOW IT'S BUSTED AND I CAN'T SEE ANYTHING!
PTOK
WHERE'S SEIJI?!

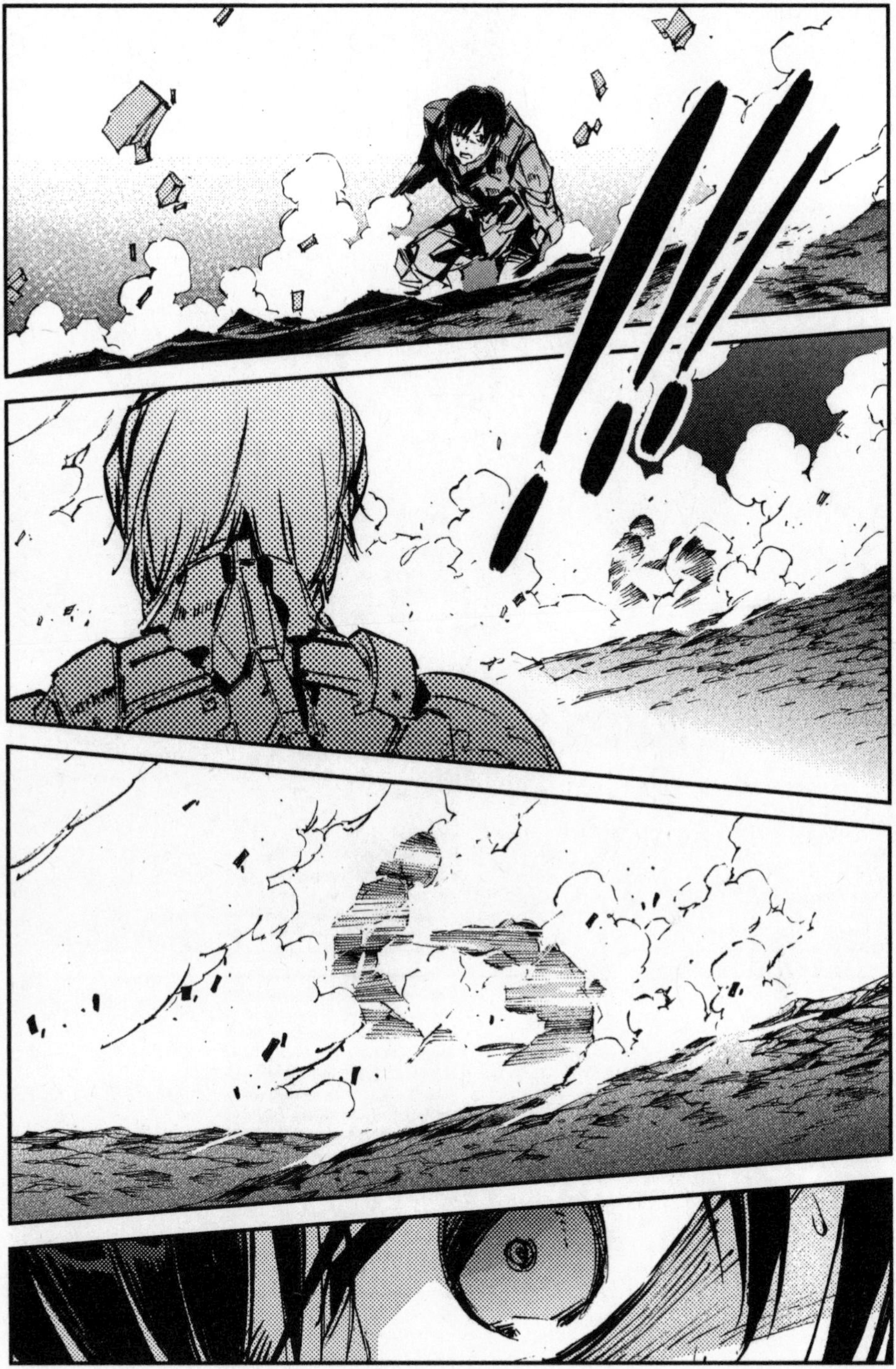

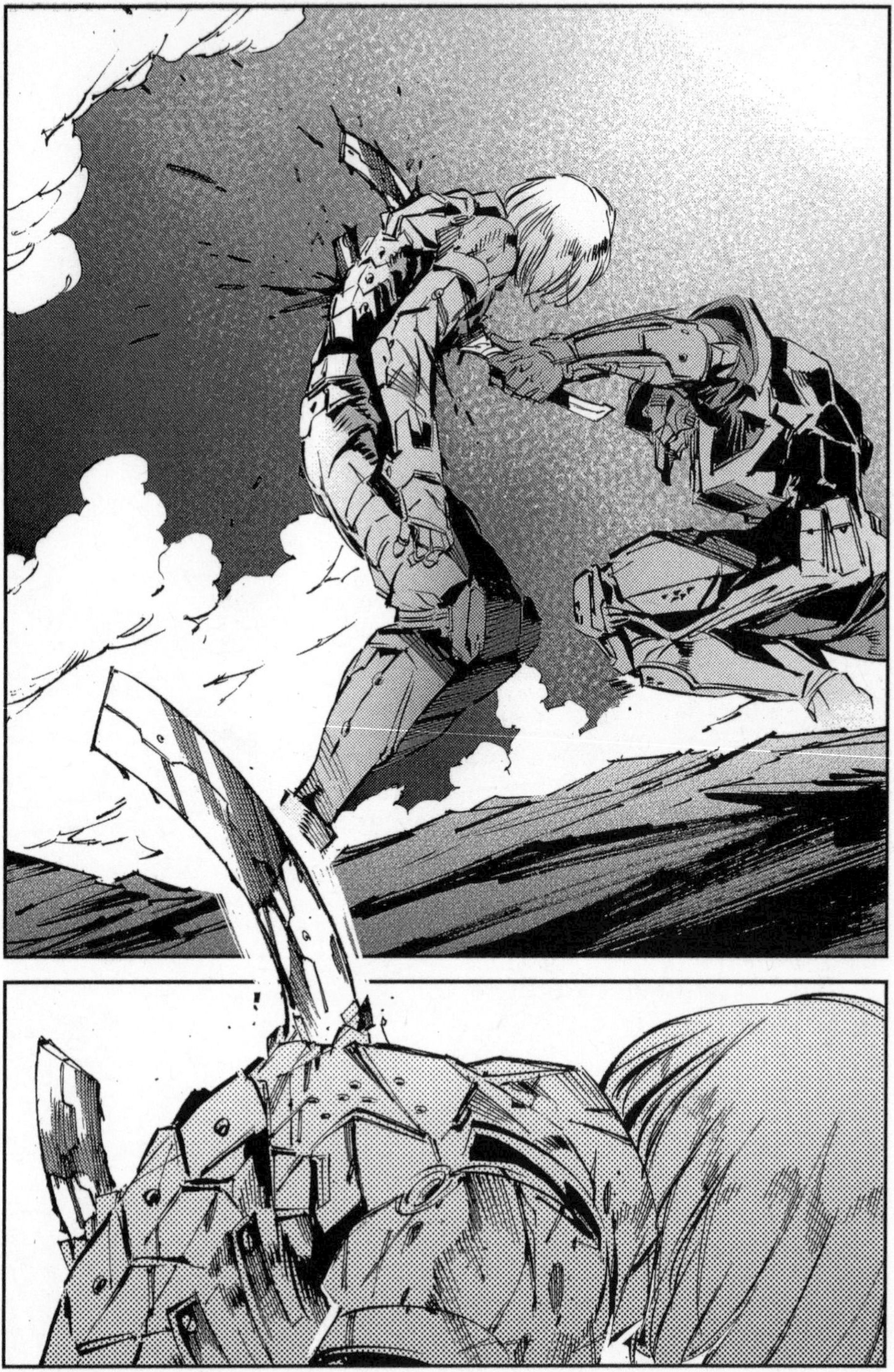

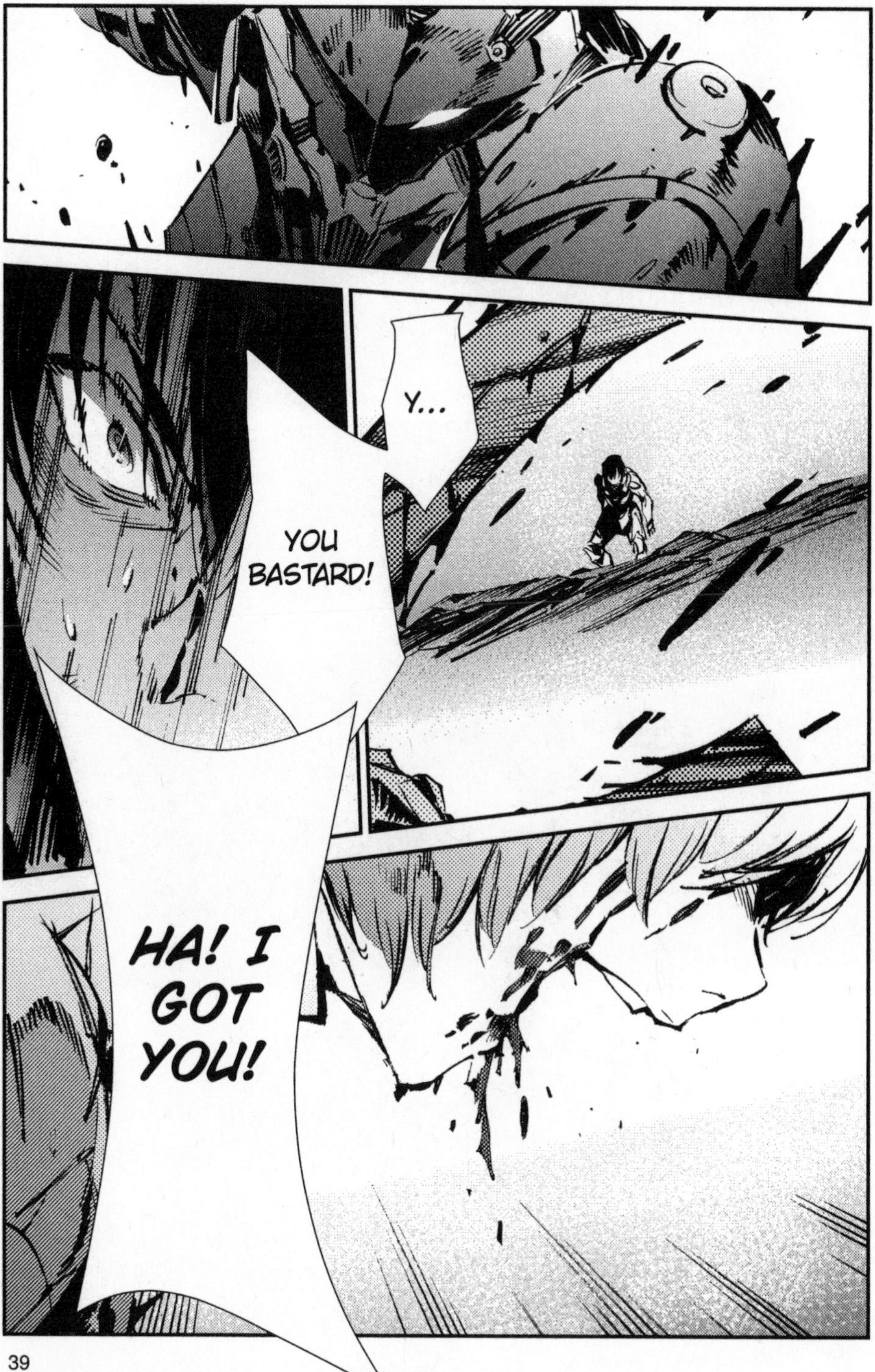
Y...
YOU BASTARD!
HA! I GOT YOU!

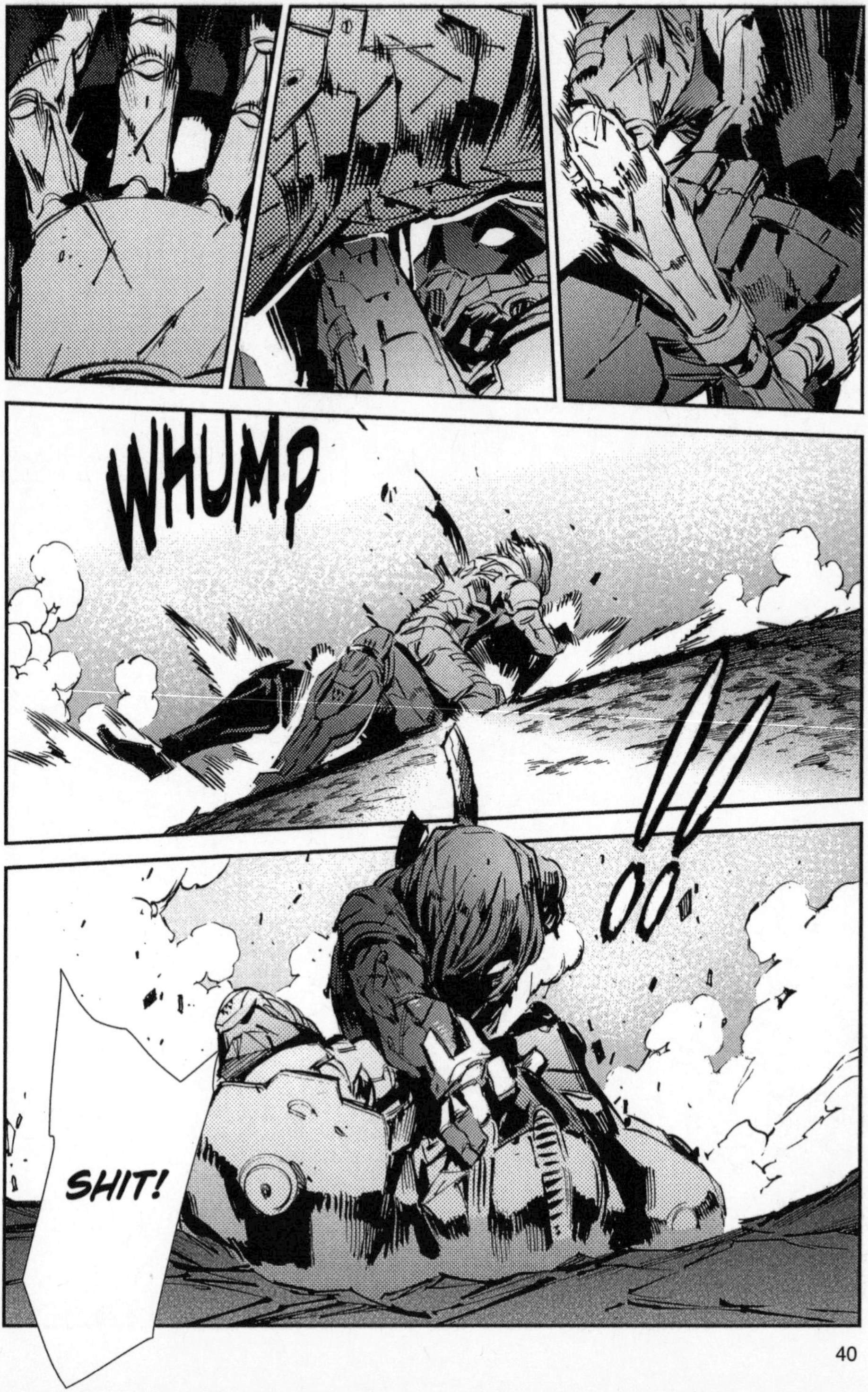
WHUMP
!!
SHIT!

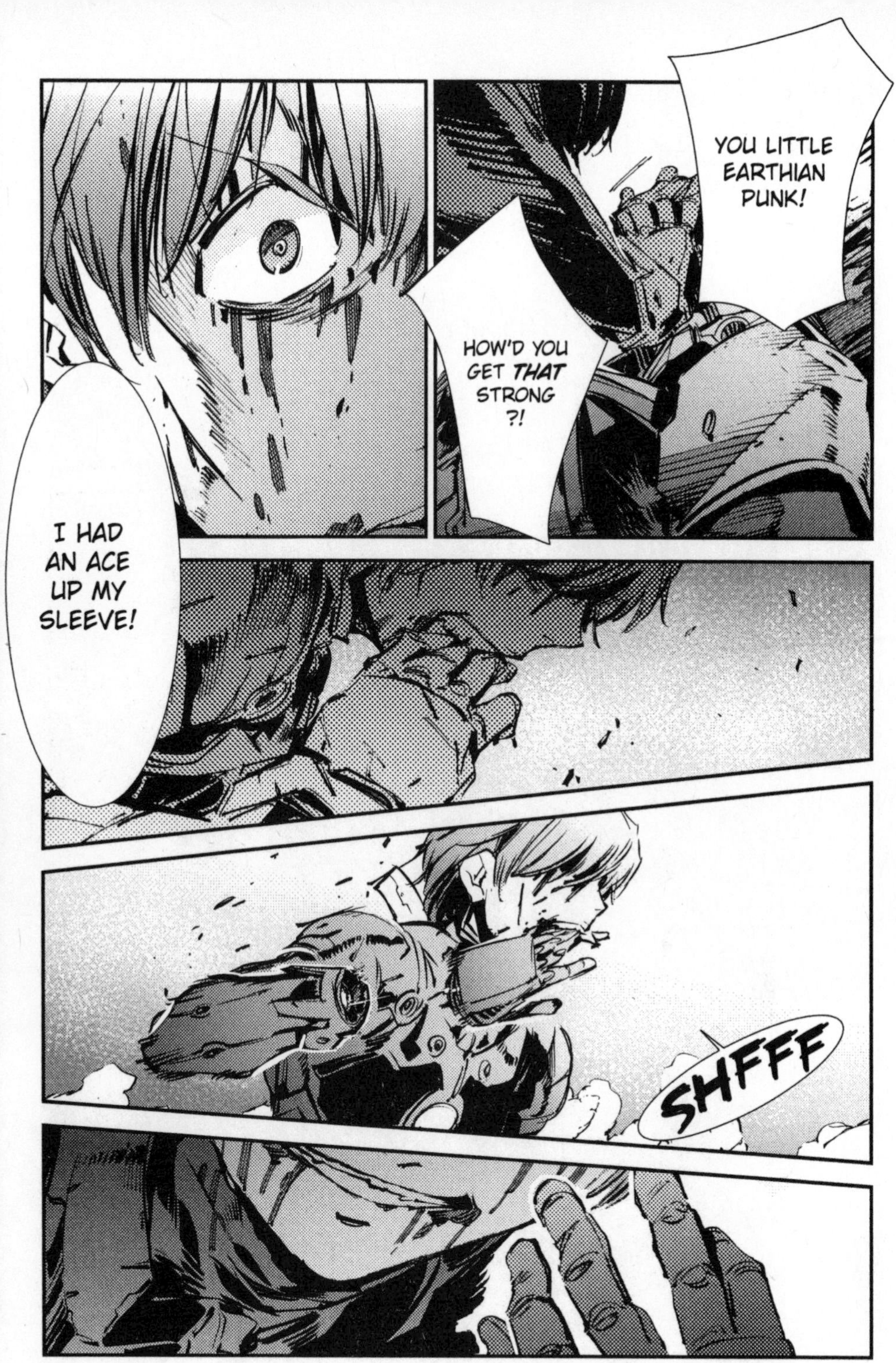
YOU LITTLE EARTHIAN PUNK!
HOW'D YOU GET ***THAT*** STRONG ?!
I HAD AN ACE UP MY SLEEVE!
SHFFF

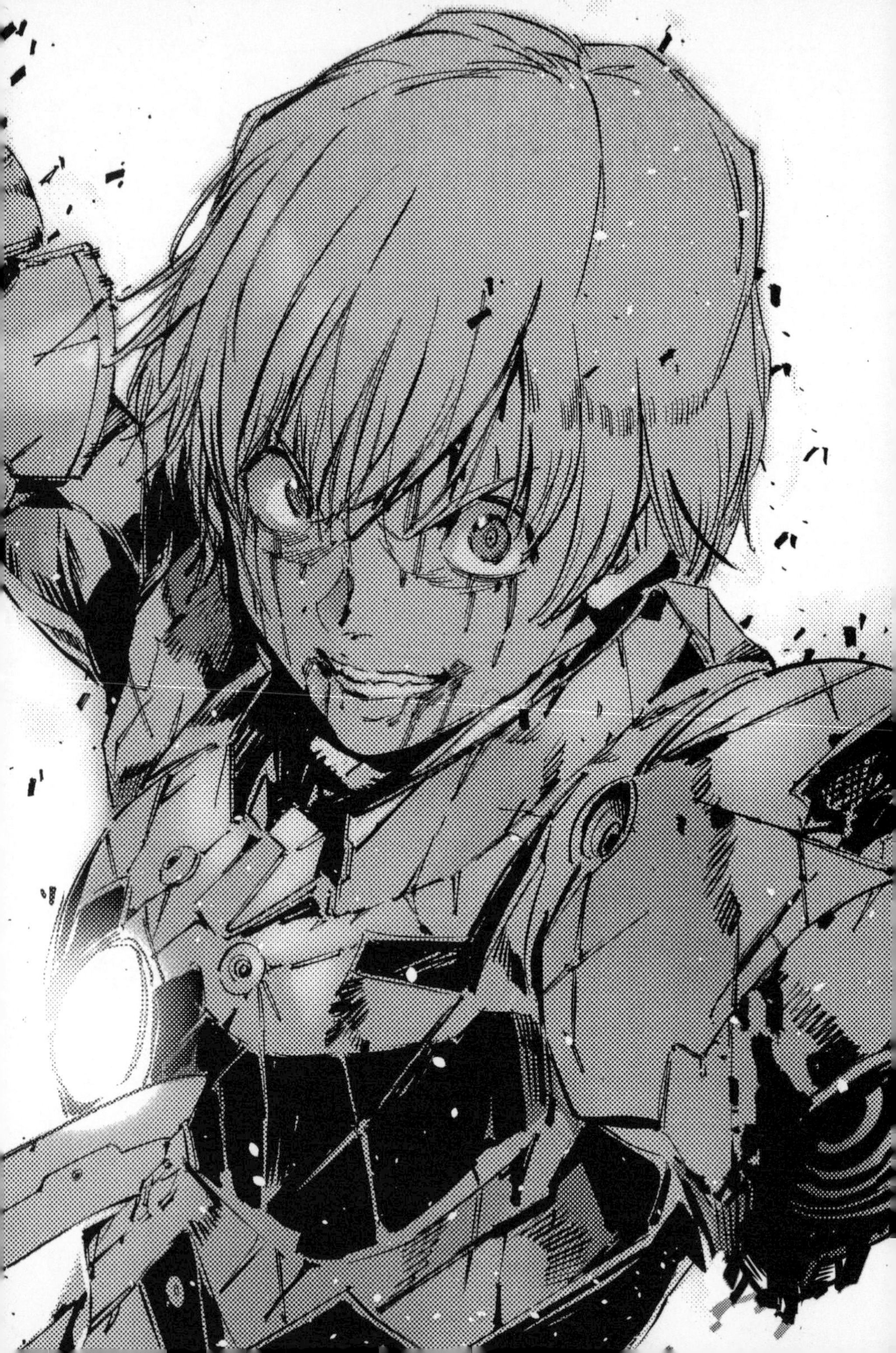

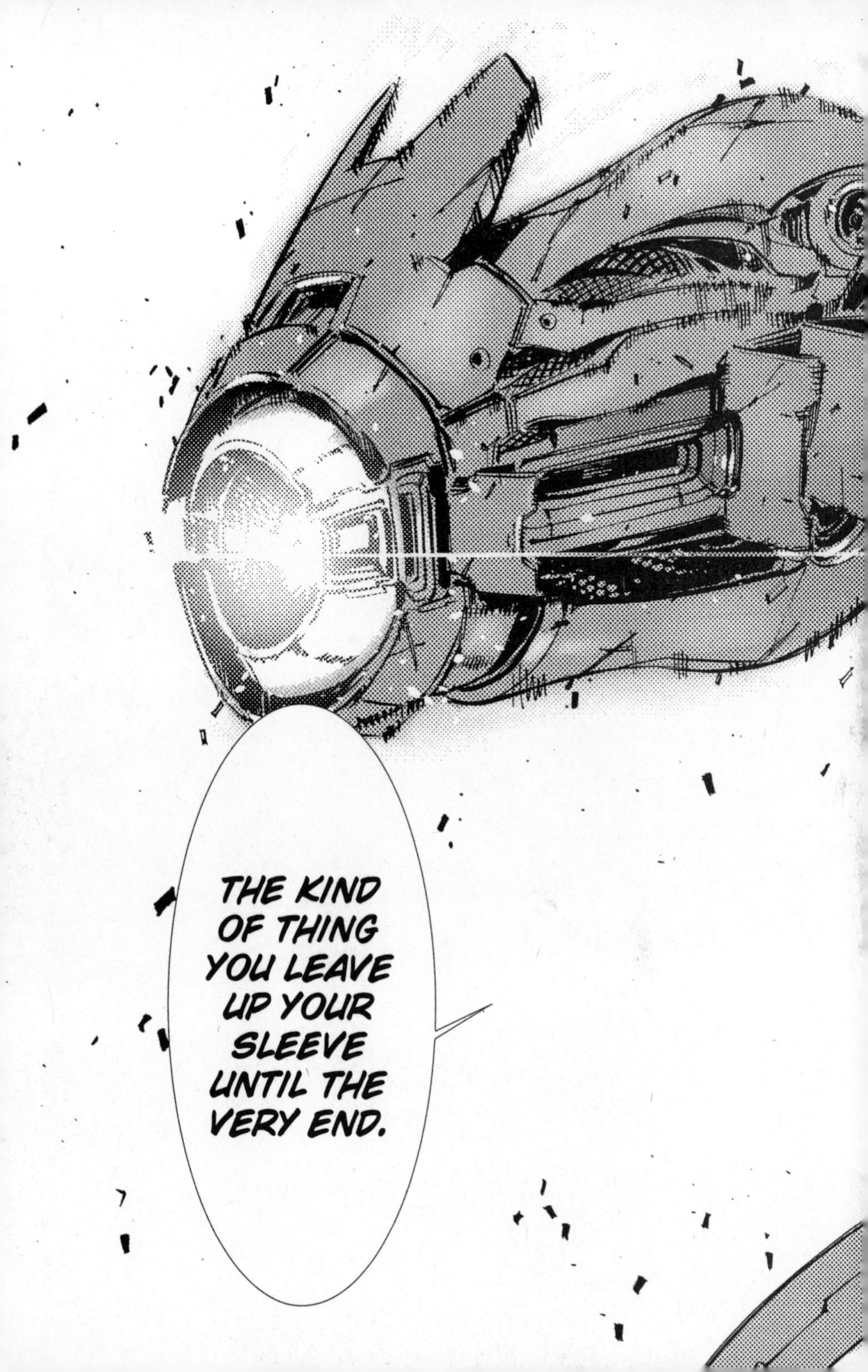
THE KIND OF THING YOU LEAVE UP YOUR SLEEVE UNTIL THE VERY END.

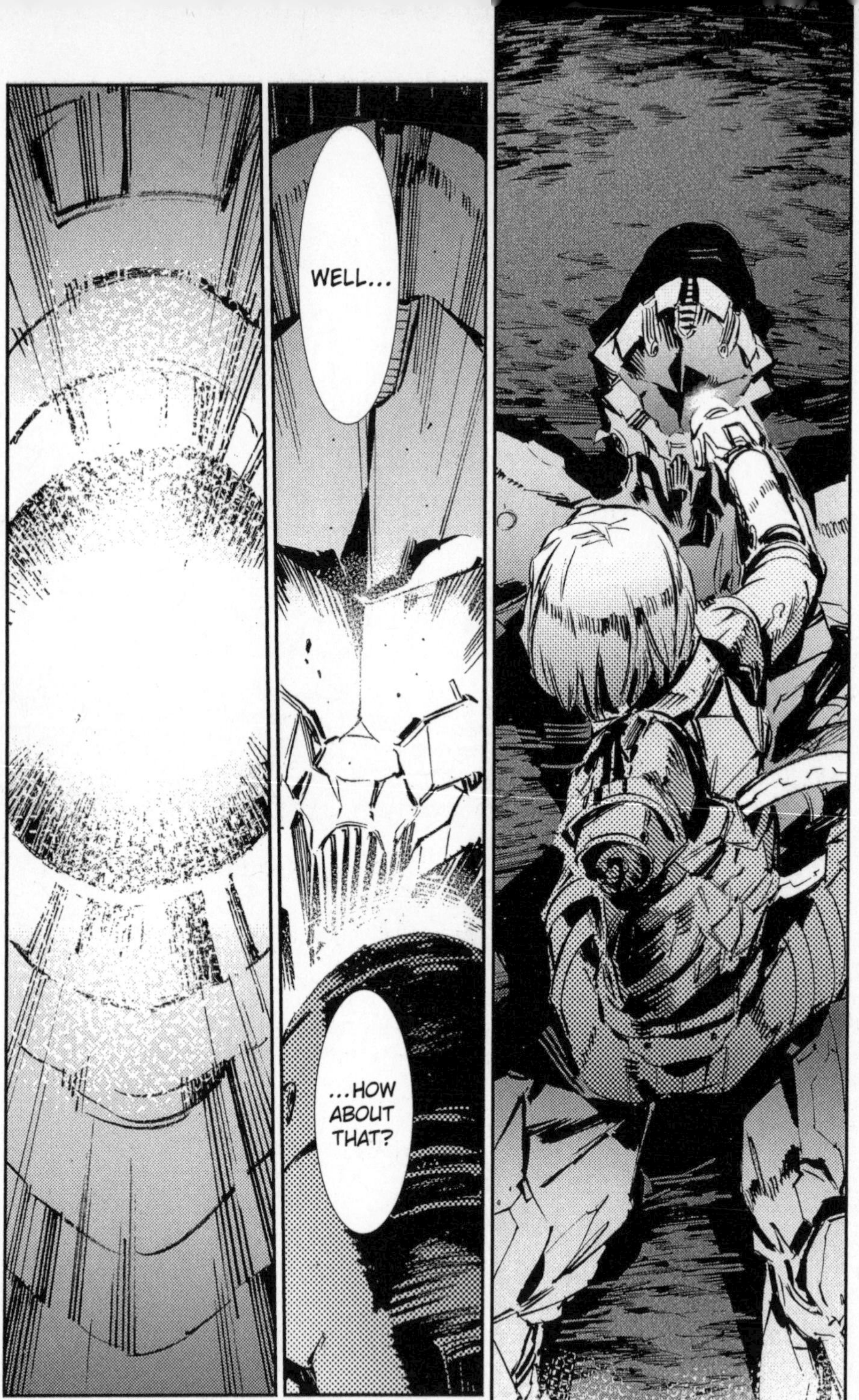
WELL...
...HOW ABOUT THAT?

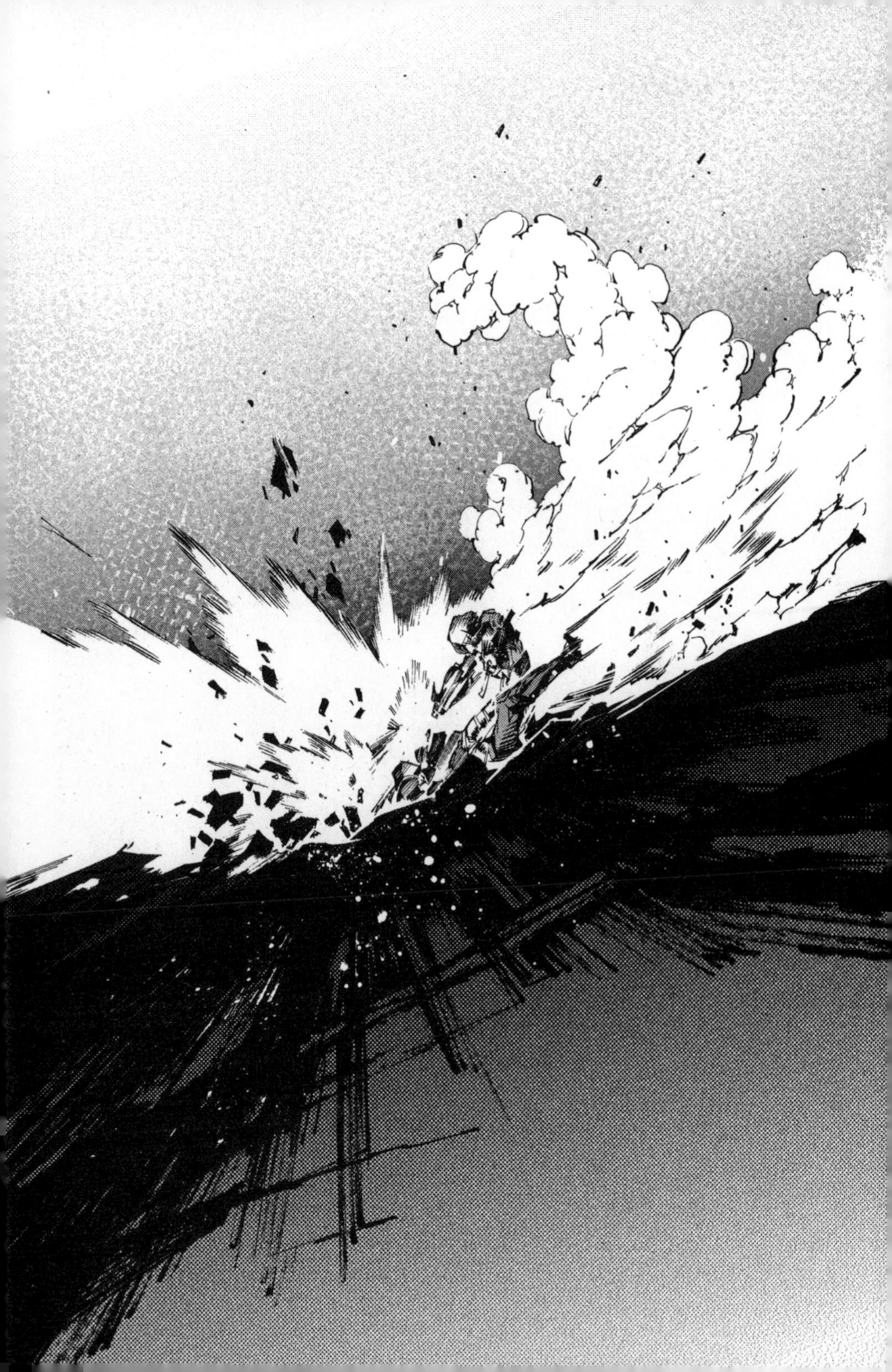

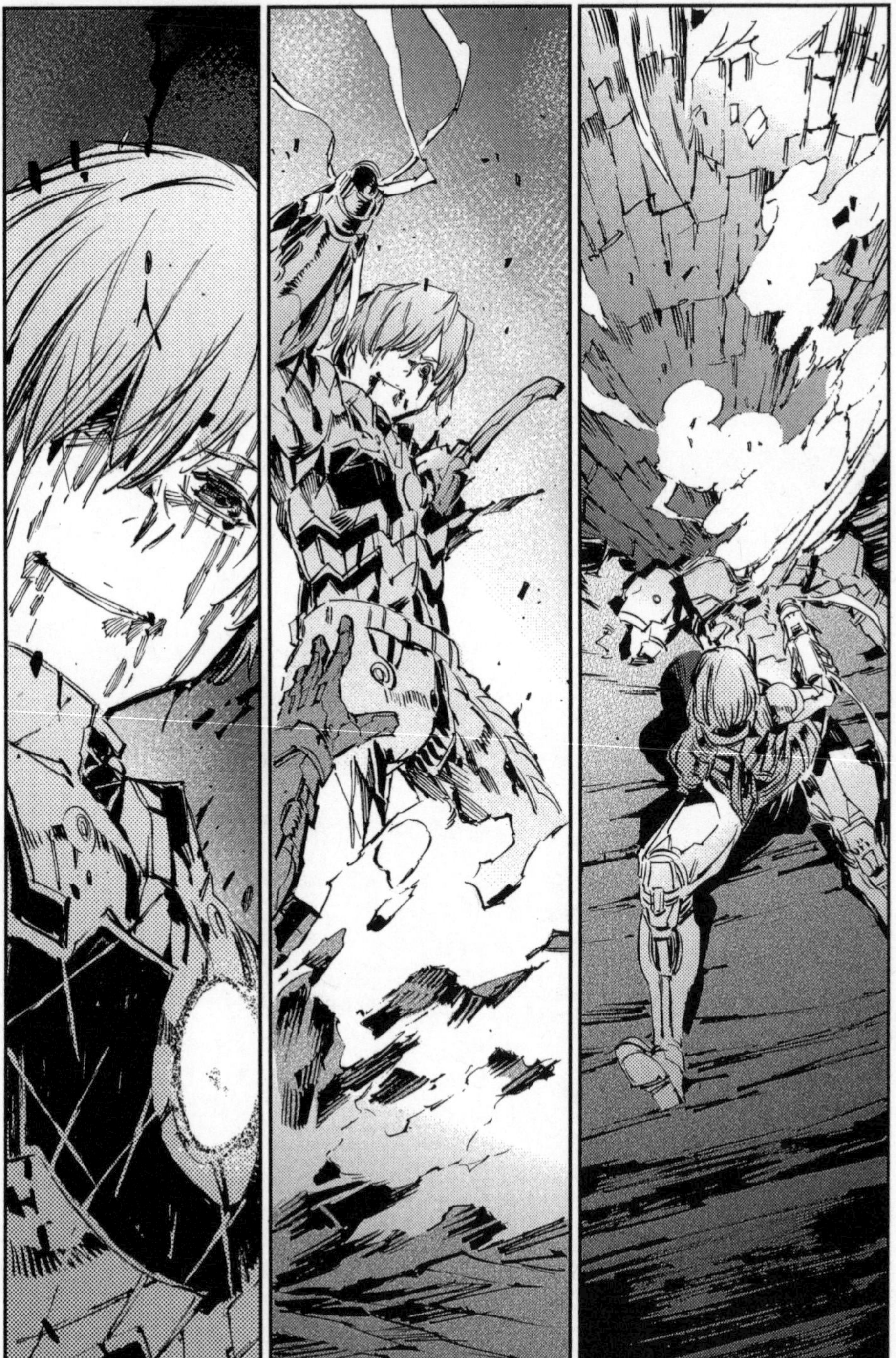

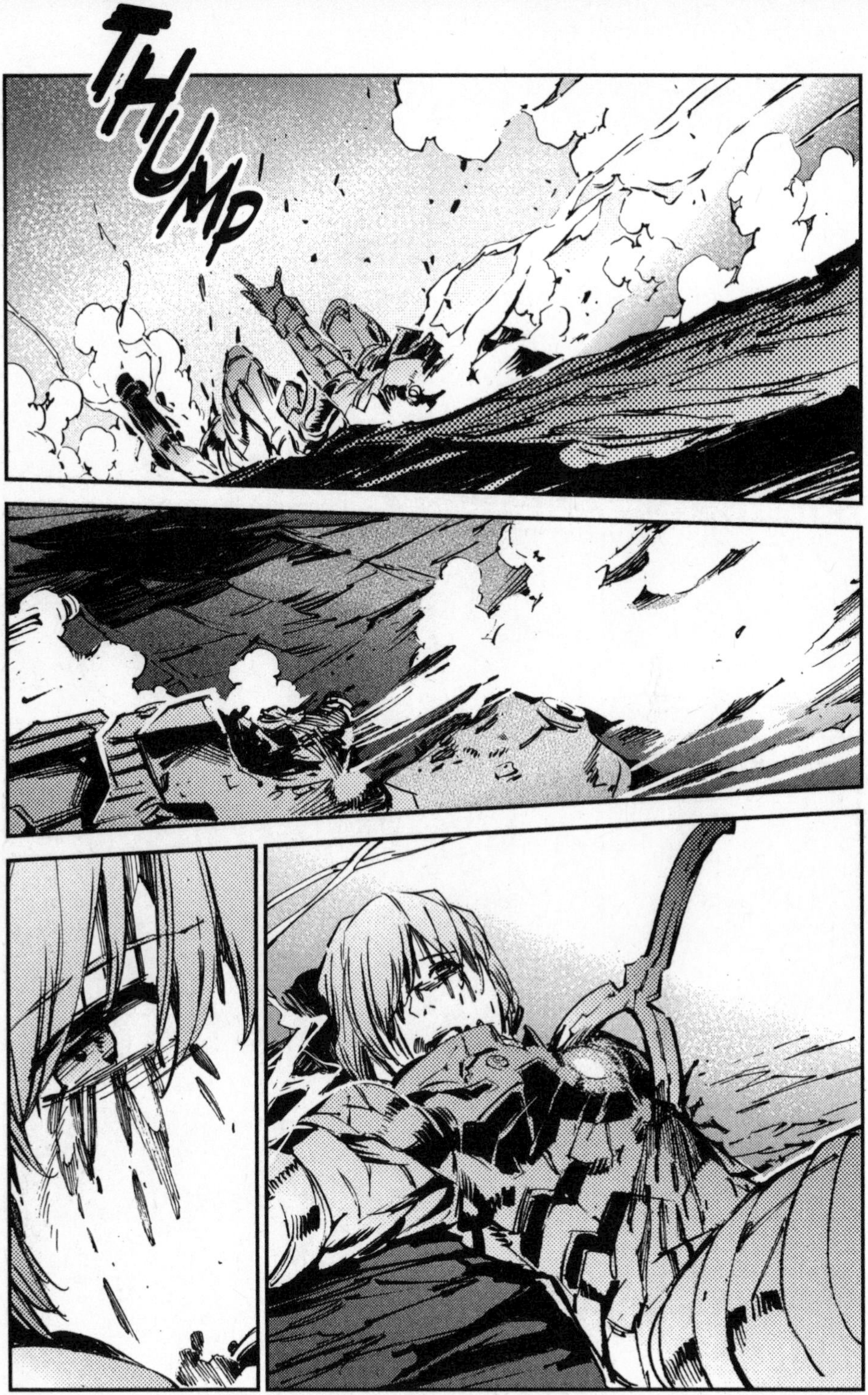
THUMP

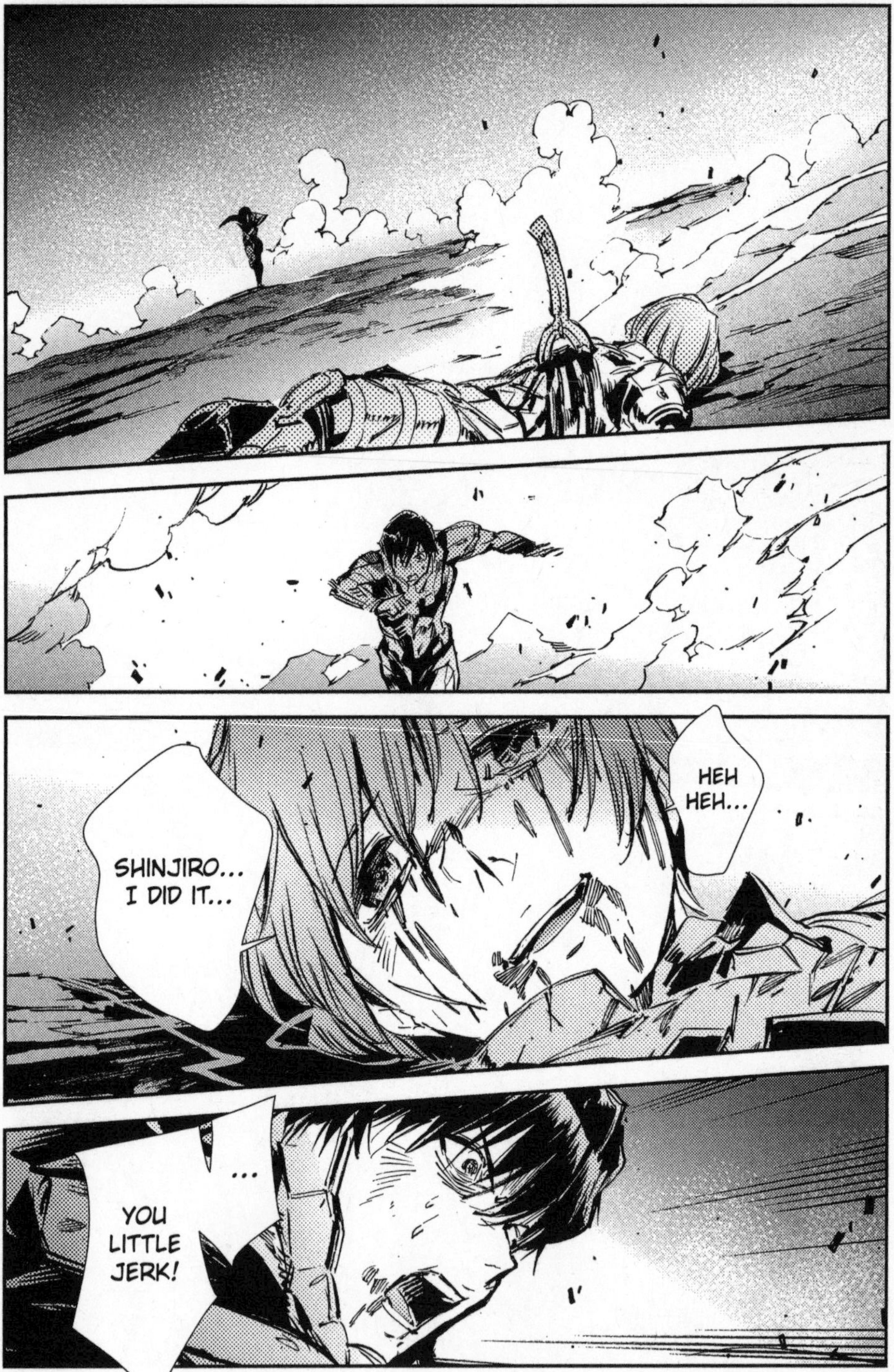
HEH HEH...
SHINJIRO... I DID IT...
...
YOU LITTLE JERK!

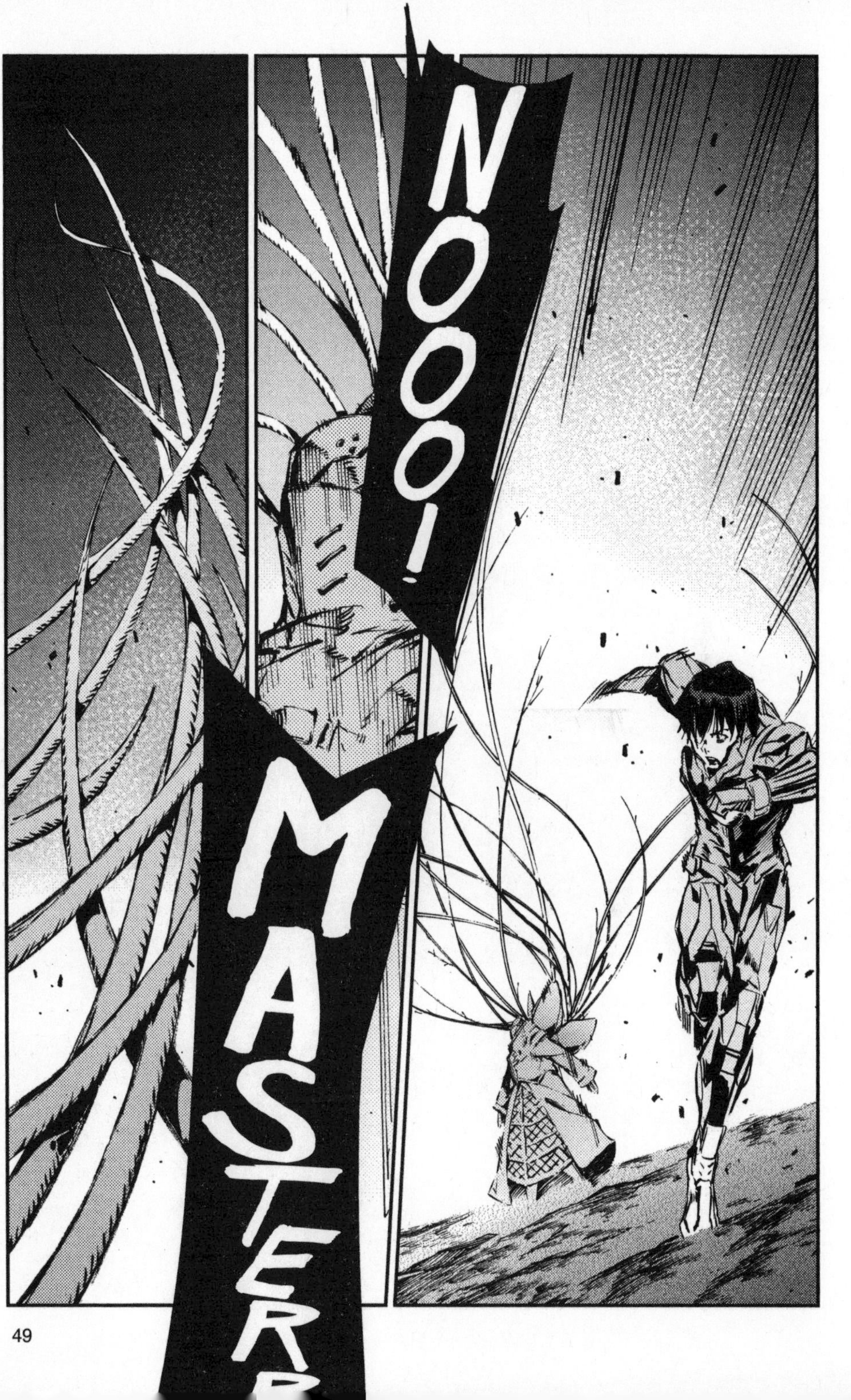
NOOO!
MASTE

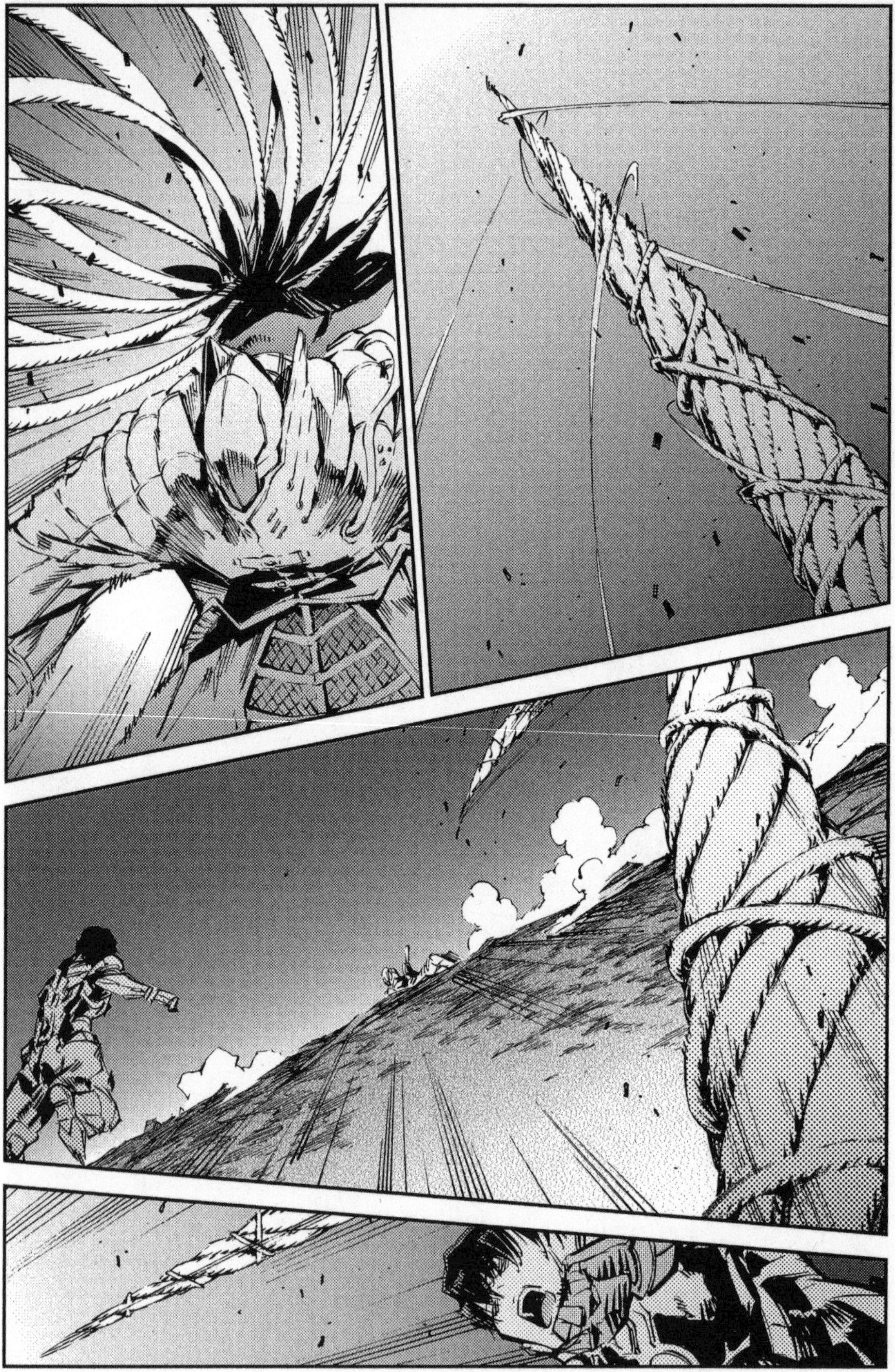

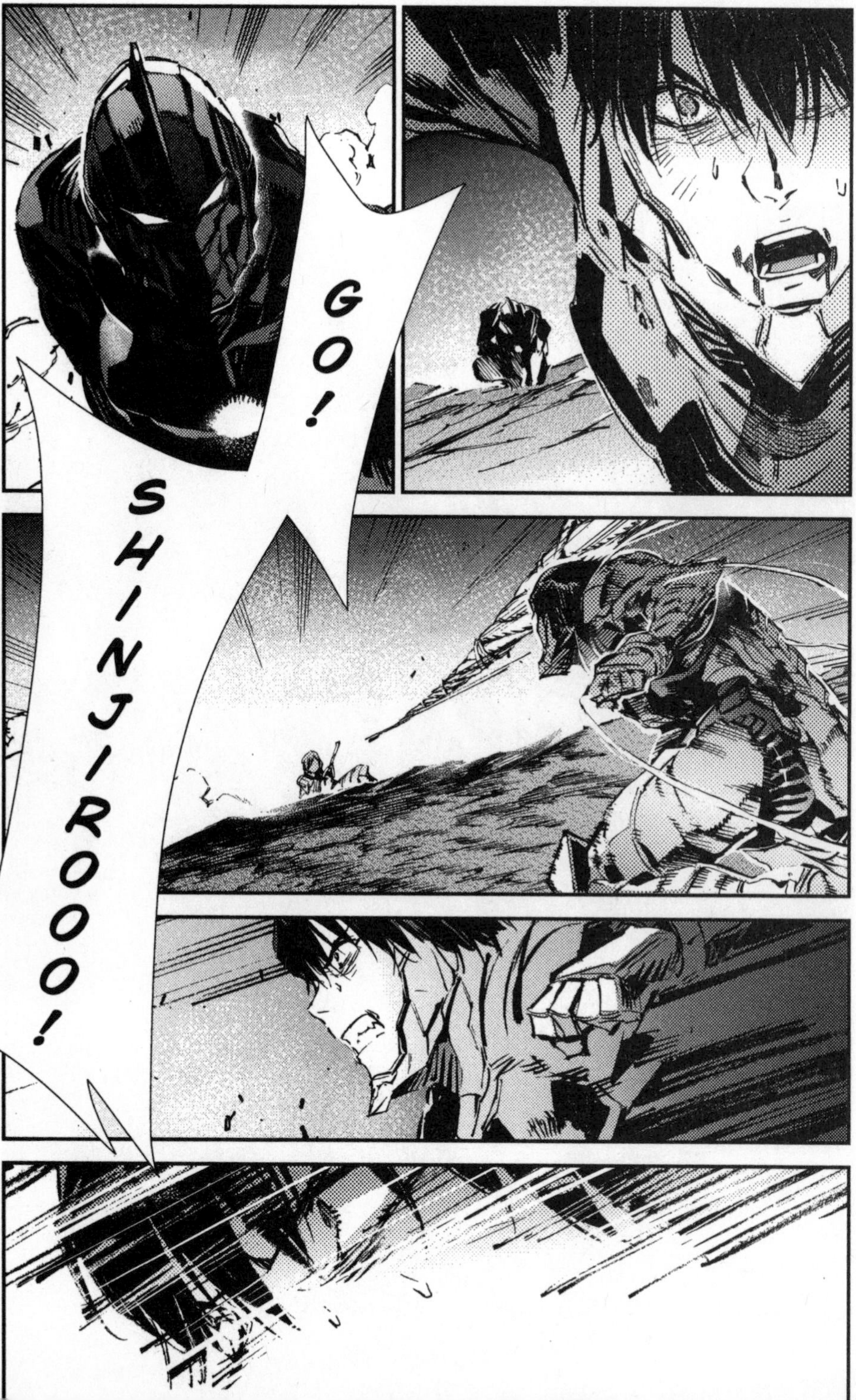
GO! SHINJIROOOO!

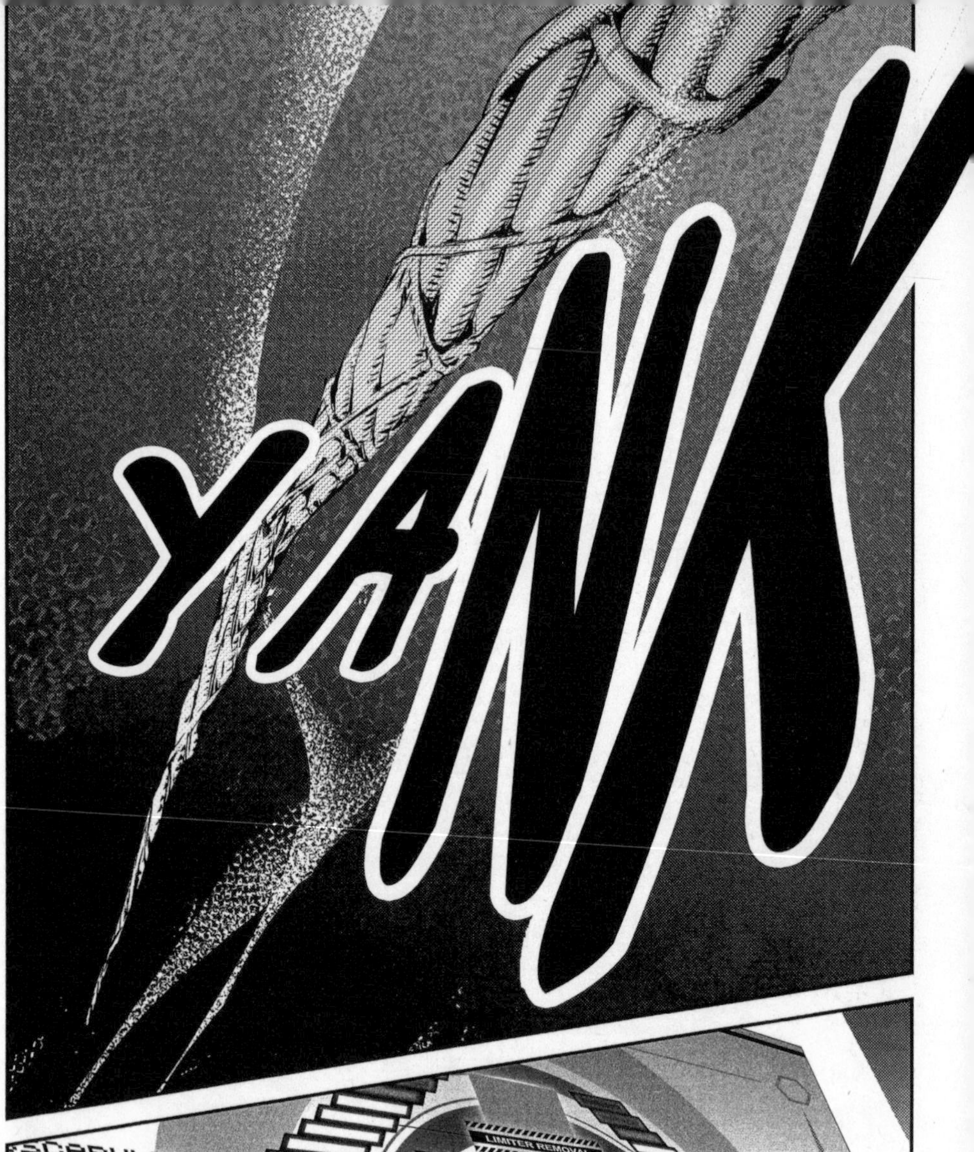
YANK
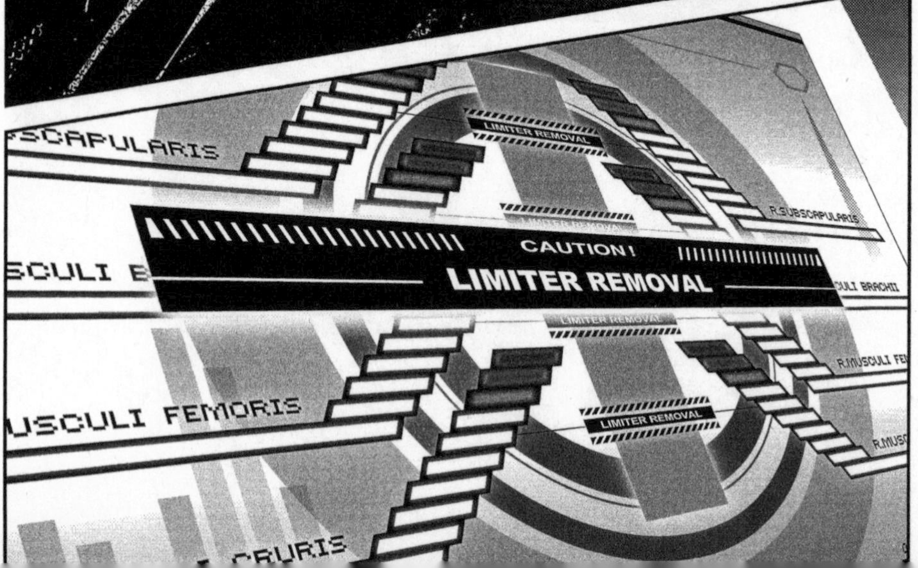
SCAPULARIS
LIMITER REMOVAL
R.SUBSCAPULARIS
LIMITER REMOVAL
CAUTION!
SCULI B
LIMITER REMOVAL
CULI BRACHII
LIMITER REMOVAL
R.MUSCULI FEM
USCULI FEMORIS
LIMITER REMOVAL
R.MUSC
CRURIS

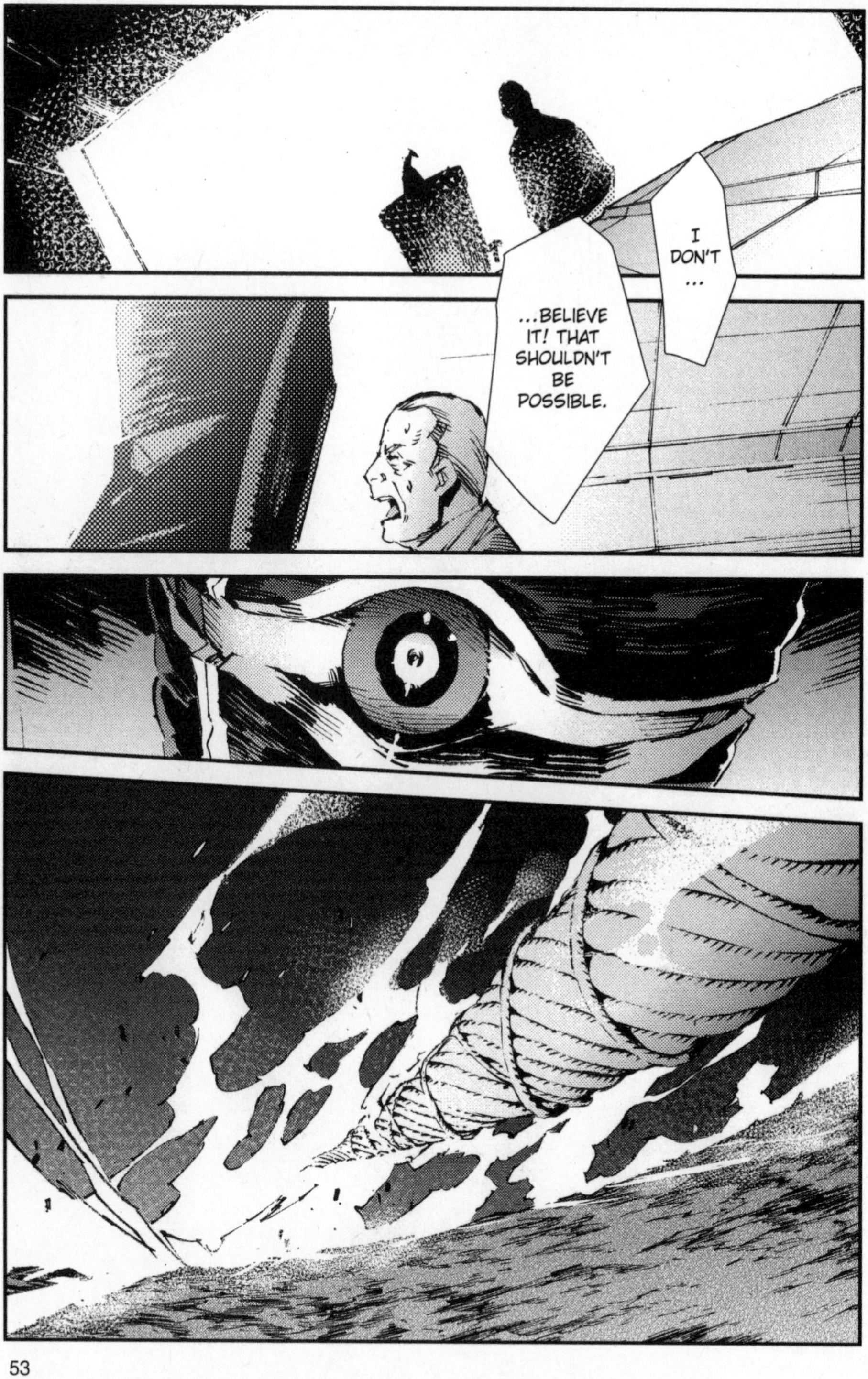
I DON'T ...
...BELIEVE IT! THAT SHOULDN'T BE POSSIBLE.

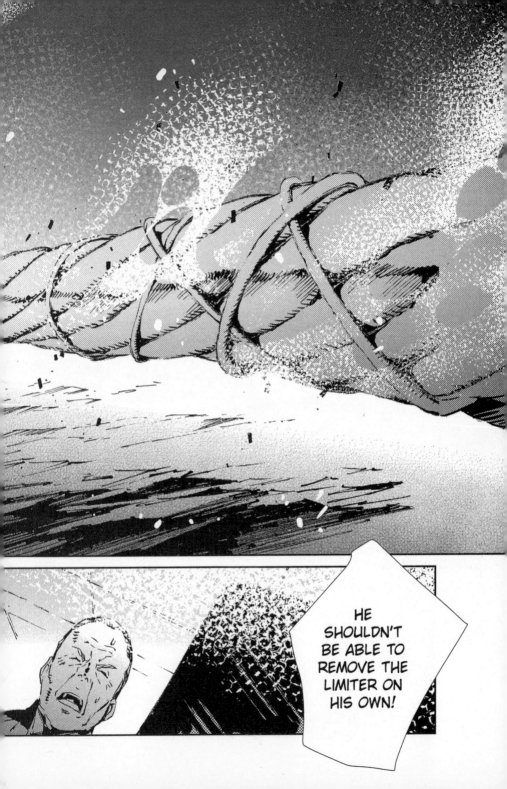

HE SHOULDN'T BE ABLE TO REMOVE THE LIMITER ON HIS OWN!

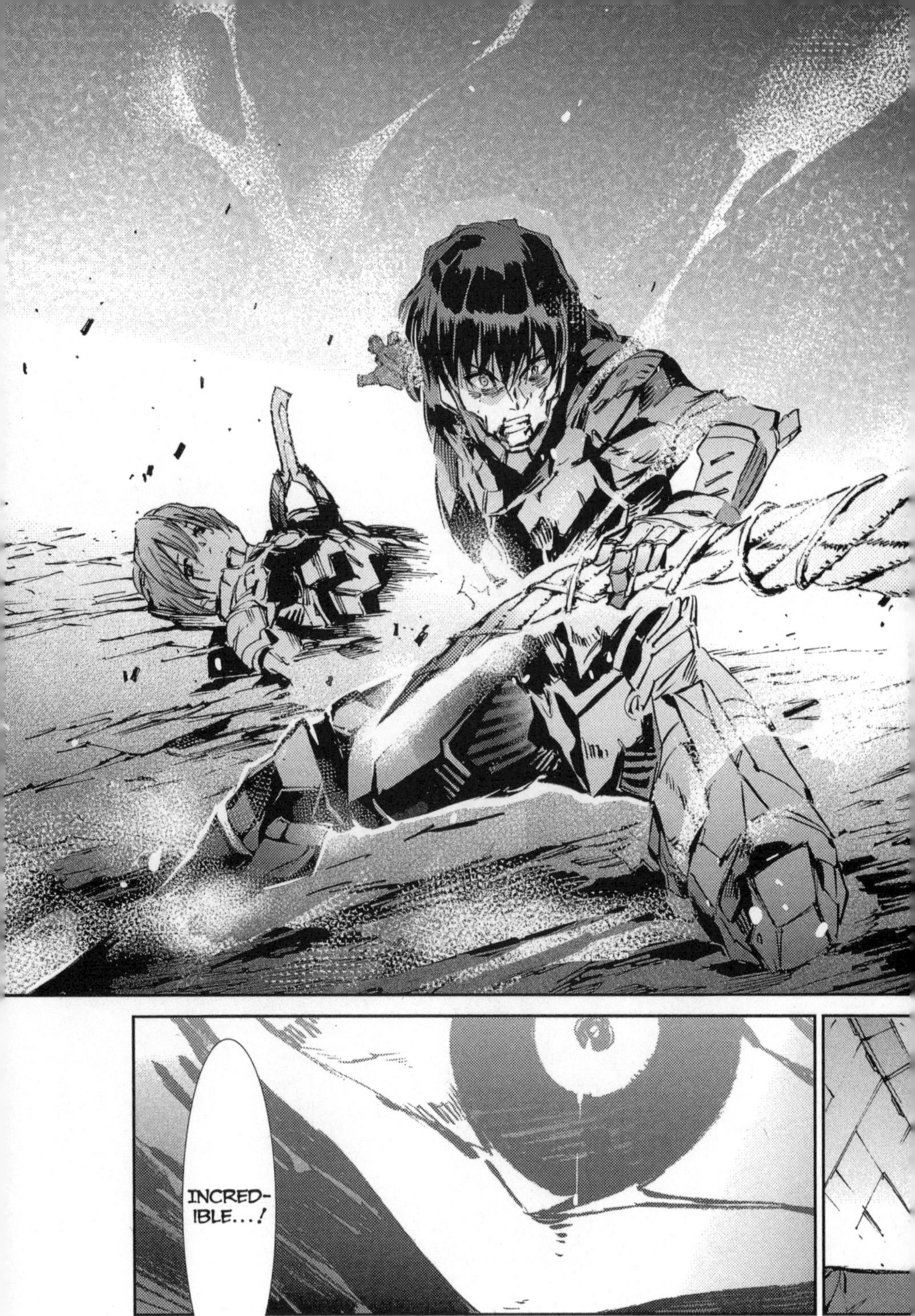
INCRED-IBLE...!

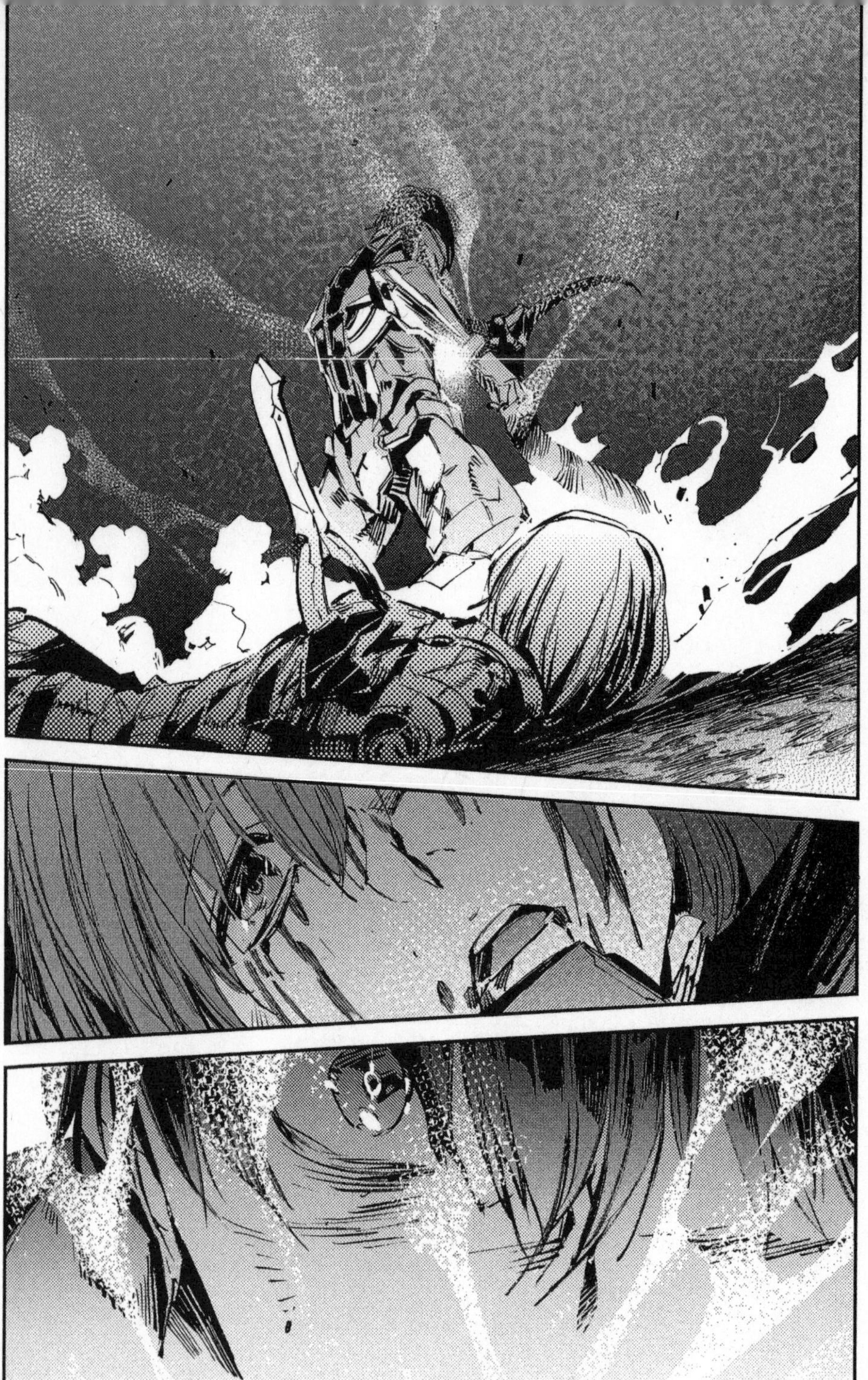

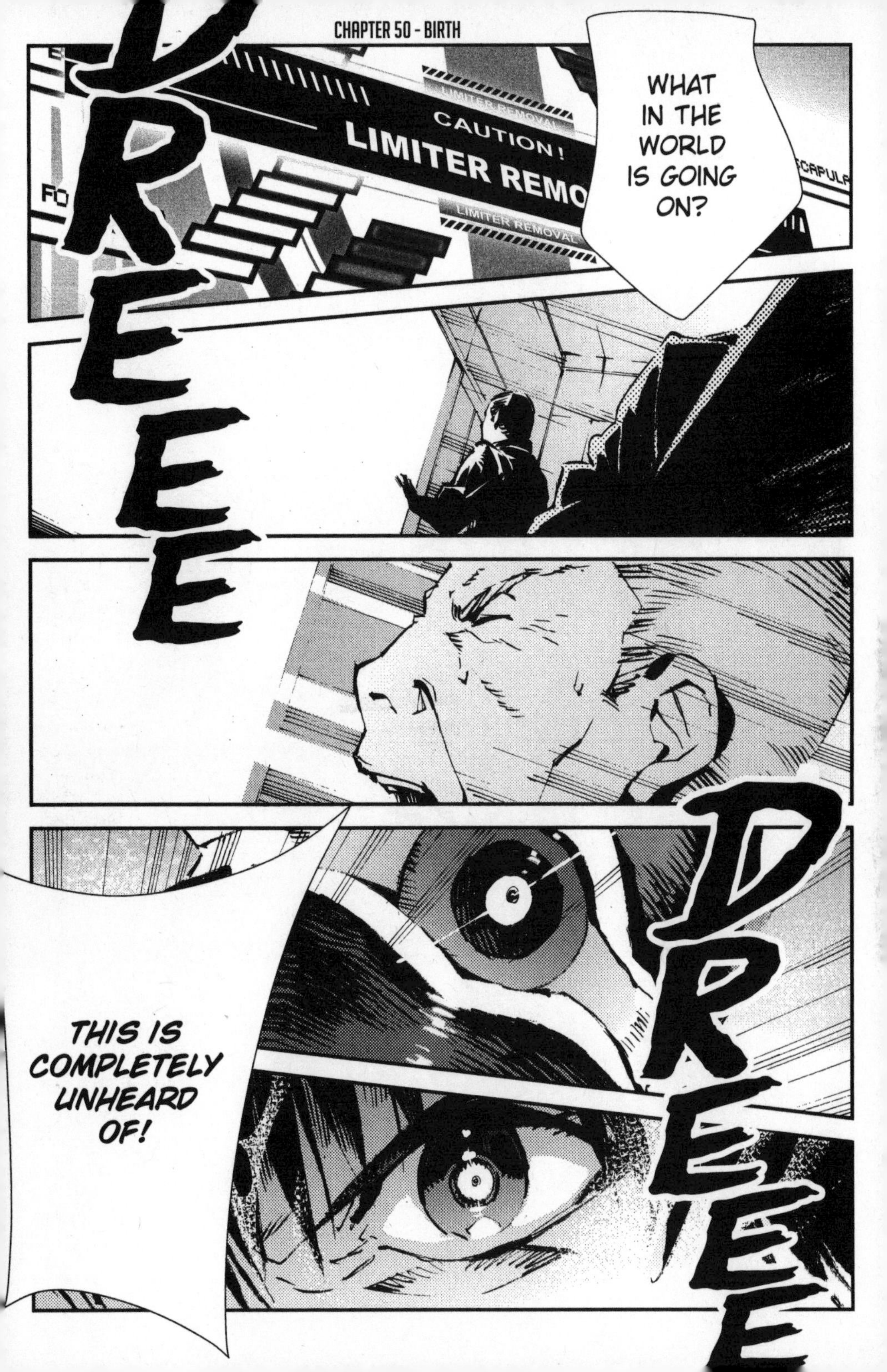
WHAT IN THE WORLD IS GOING ON?
LIMITER REMOVAL
CAUTION!
LIMITER REMOVAL
KREEE
DREEE
THIS IS COMPLETELY UNHEARD OF!

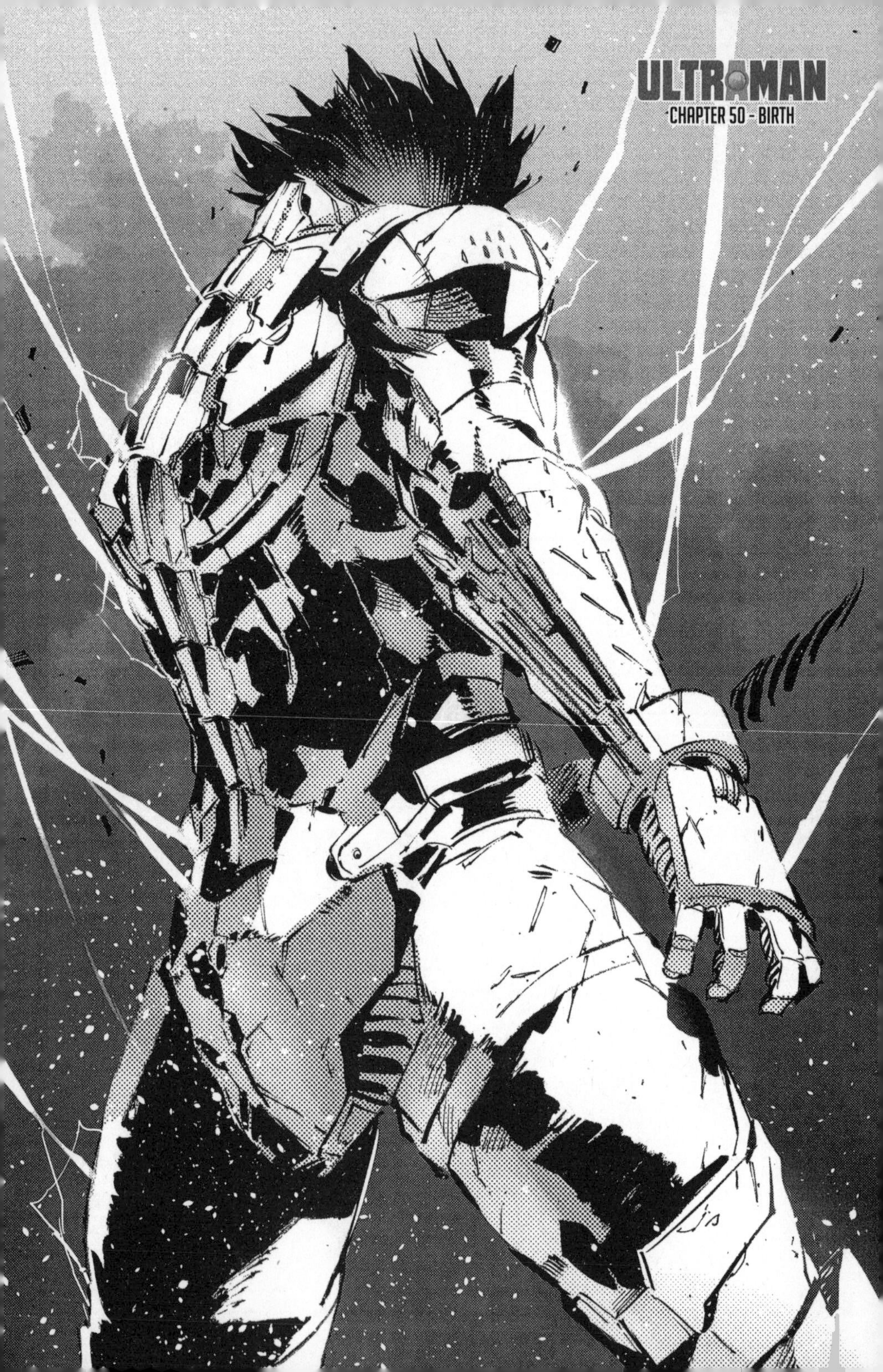
ULTRAMAN
CHAPTER 50 - BIRTH

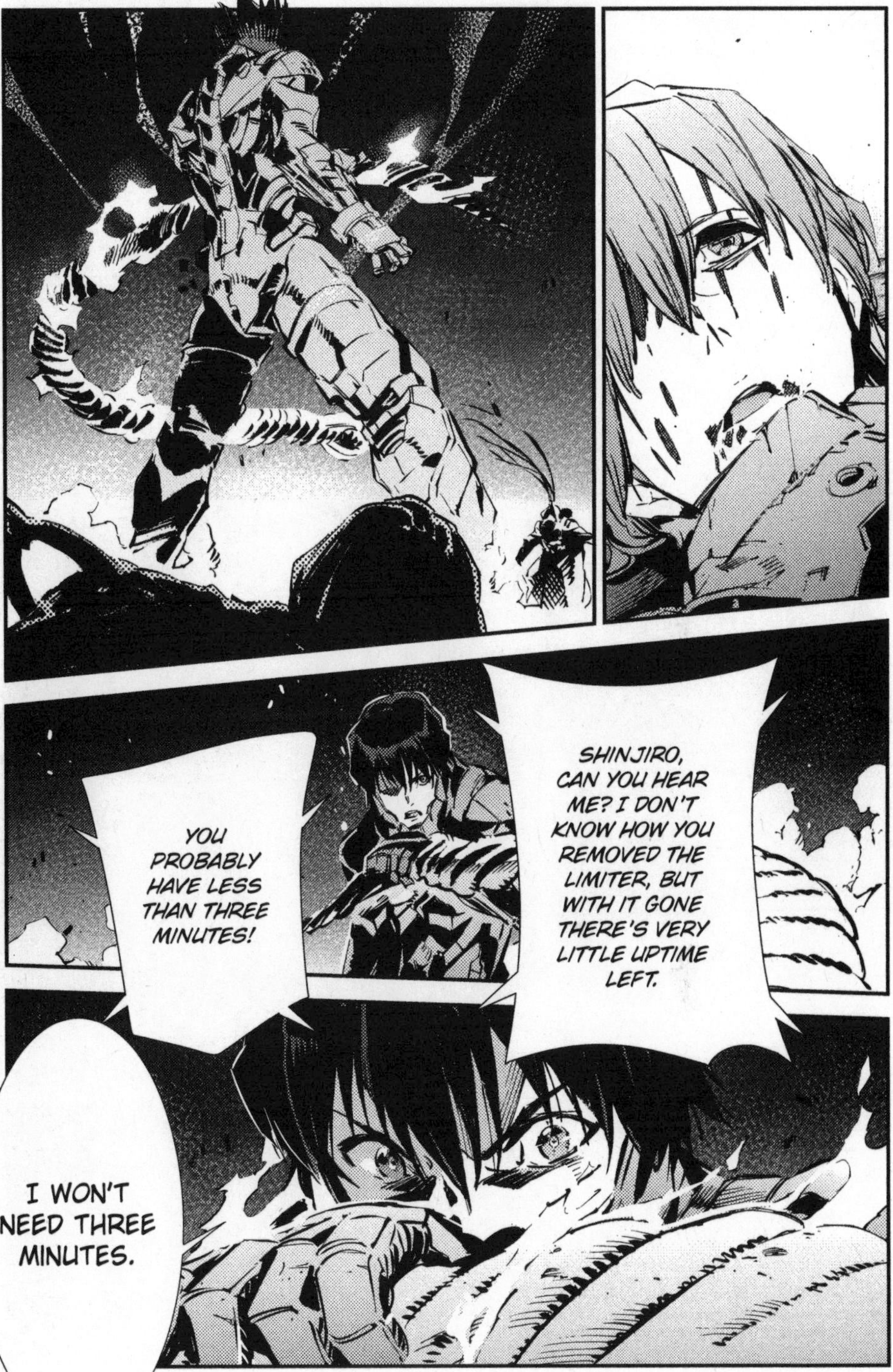
SHINJIRO, CAN YOU HEAR ME? I DON'T KNOW HOW YOU REMOVED THE LIMITER, BUT WITH IT GONE THERE'S VERY LITTLE UPTIME LEFT.
YOU PROBABLY HAVE LESS THAN THREE MINUTES!
I WON'T NEED THREE MINUTES.

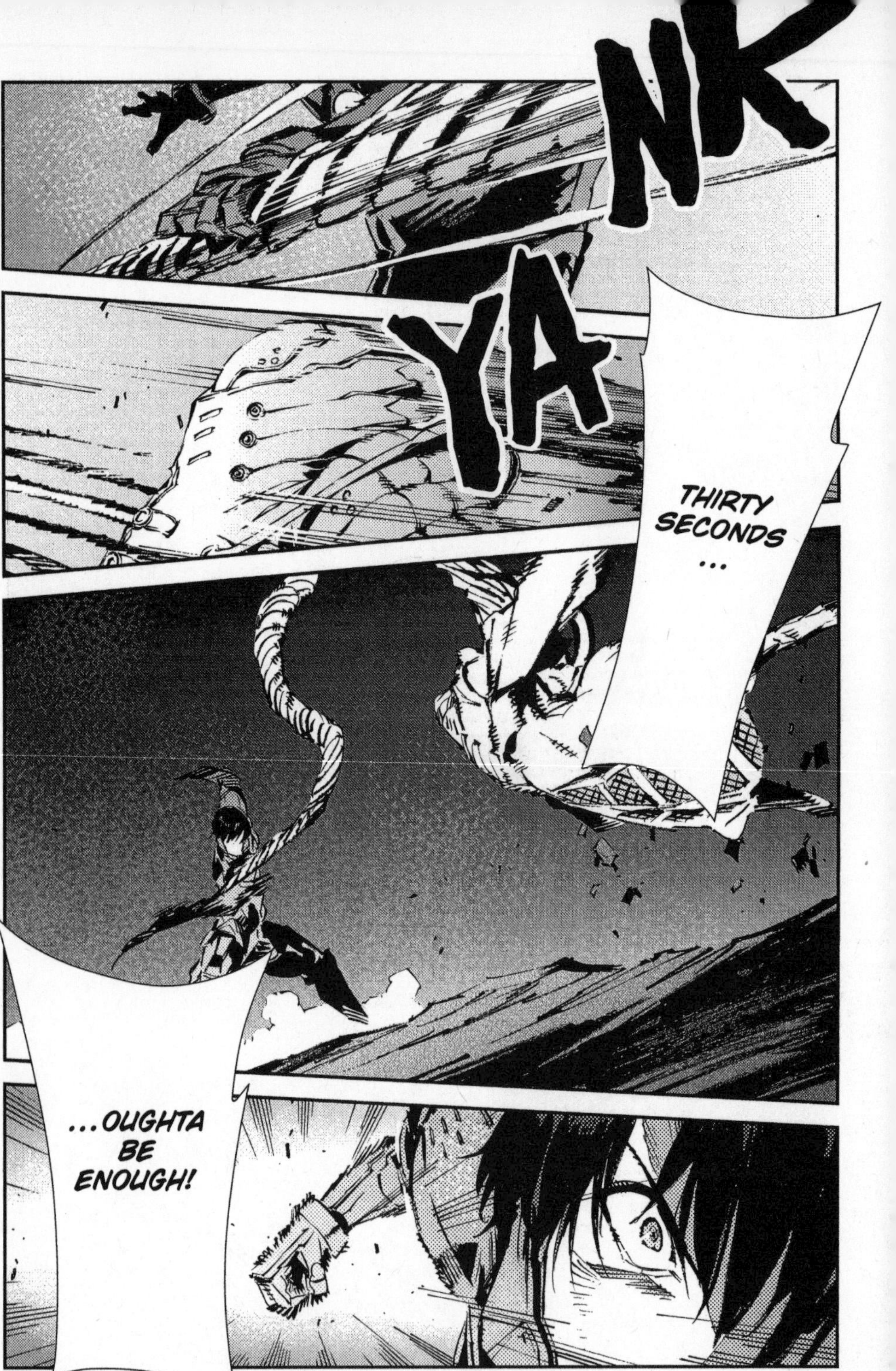
YANK
THIRTY SECONDS ...
...OUGHTA BE ENOUGH!

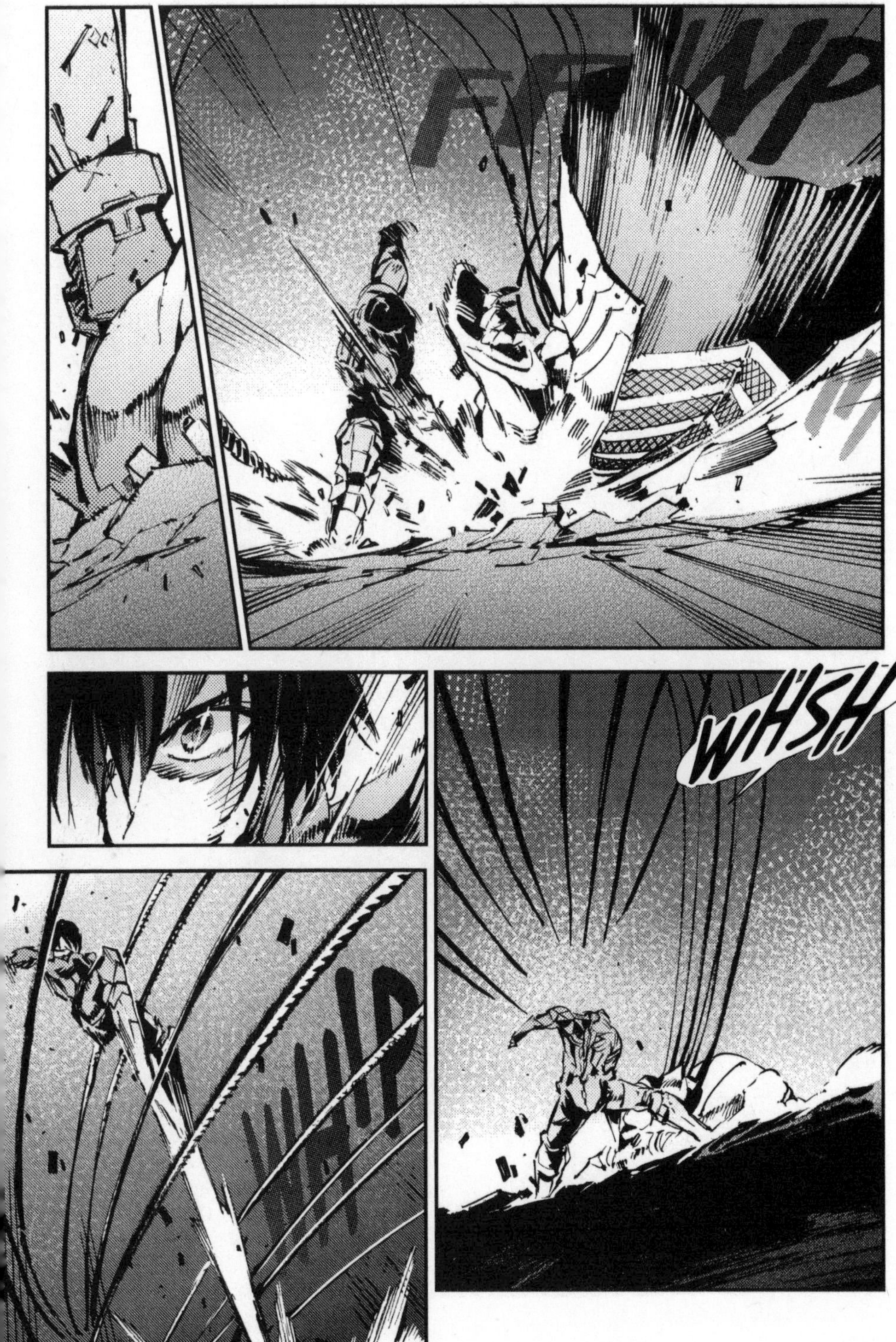
WHSH
WHIP

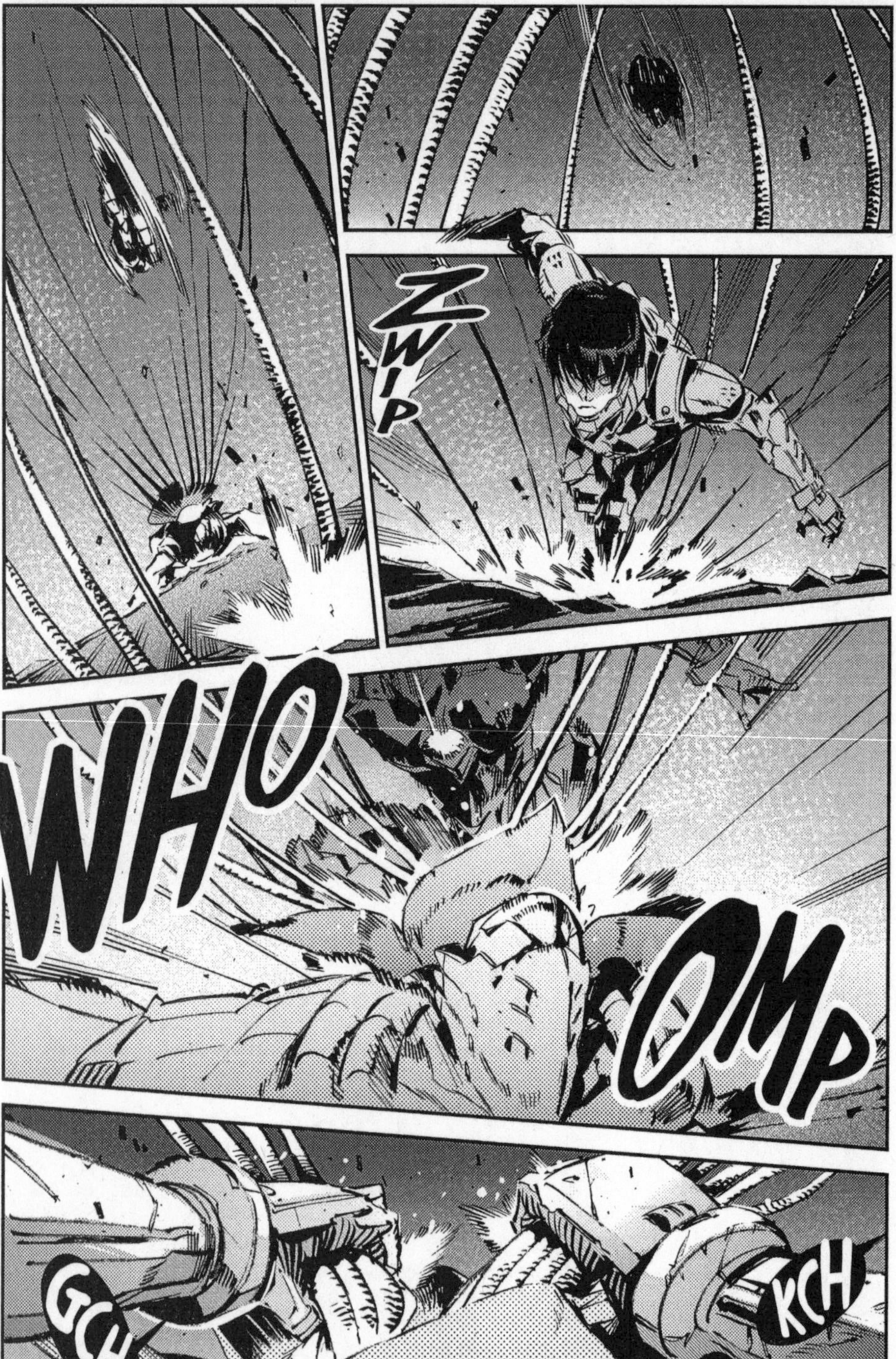
ZWIP
WHOOMP
KCH
GCH

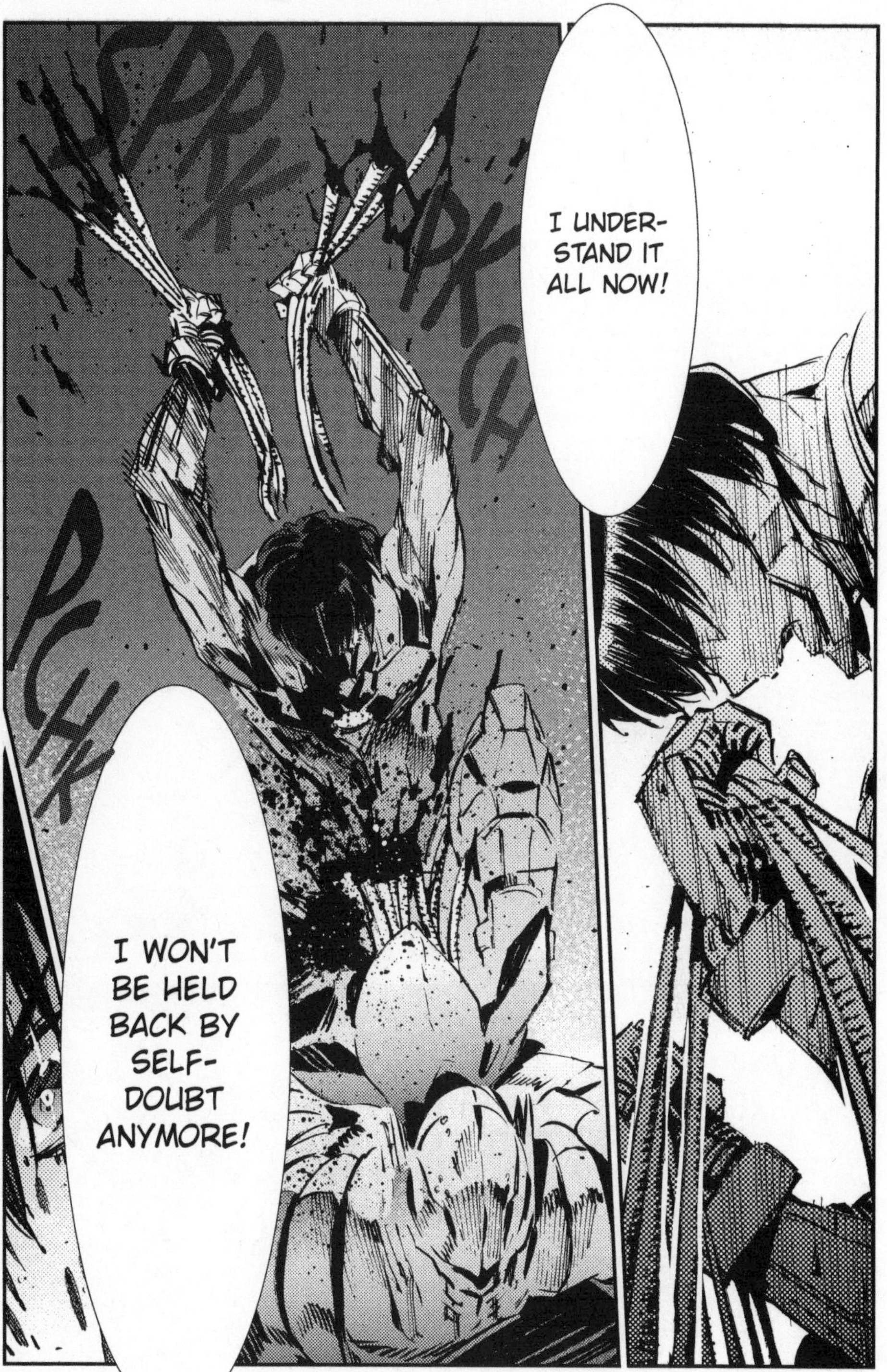
I UNDER-
STAND IT
ALL NOW!
I WON'T
BE HELD
BACK BY
SELF-
DOUBT
ANYMORE!

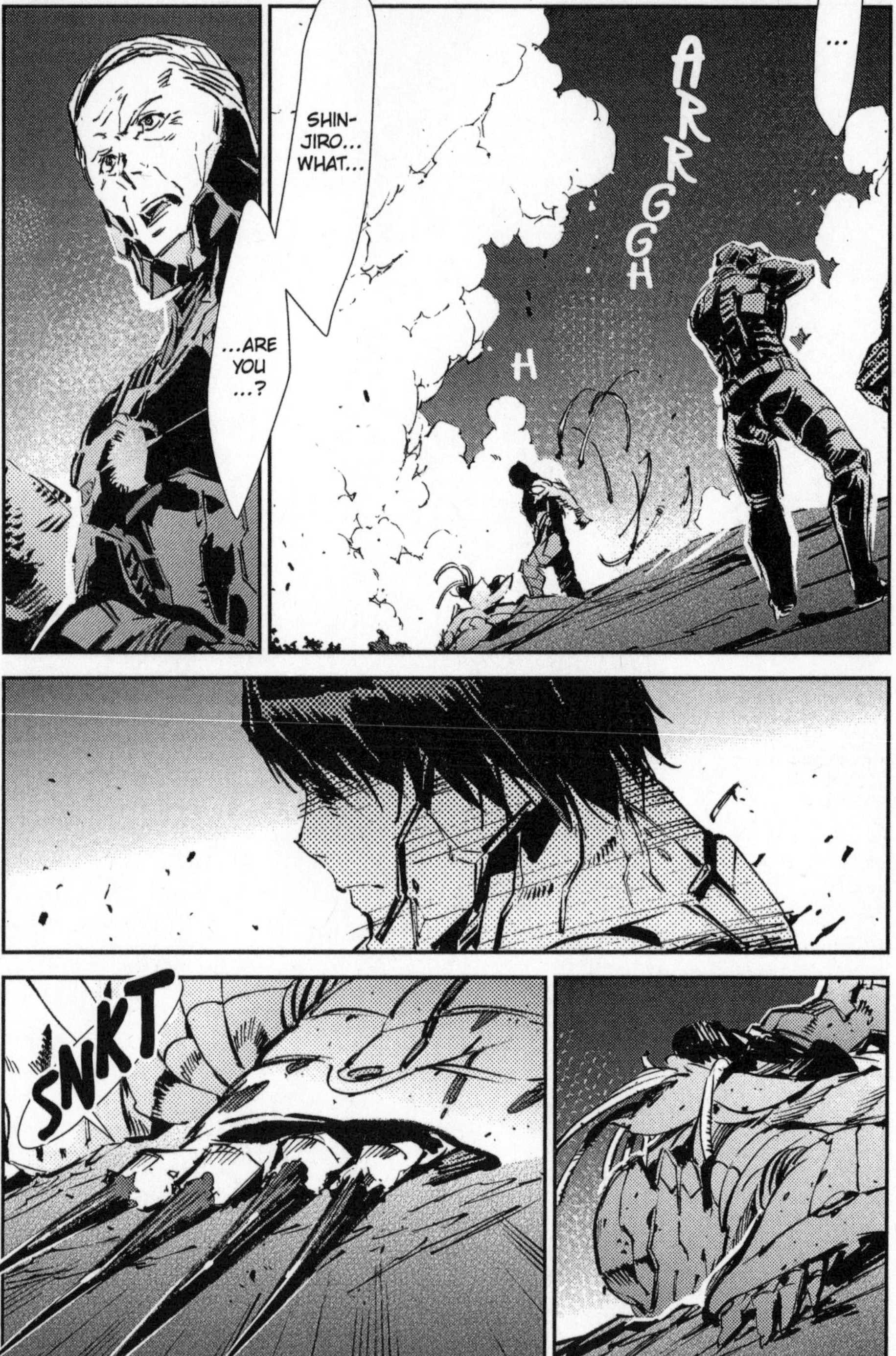
...
ARRRGGHH
SHIN-JIRO... WHAT...
...ARE YOU ...?
SNKT

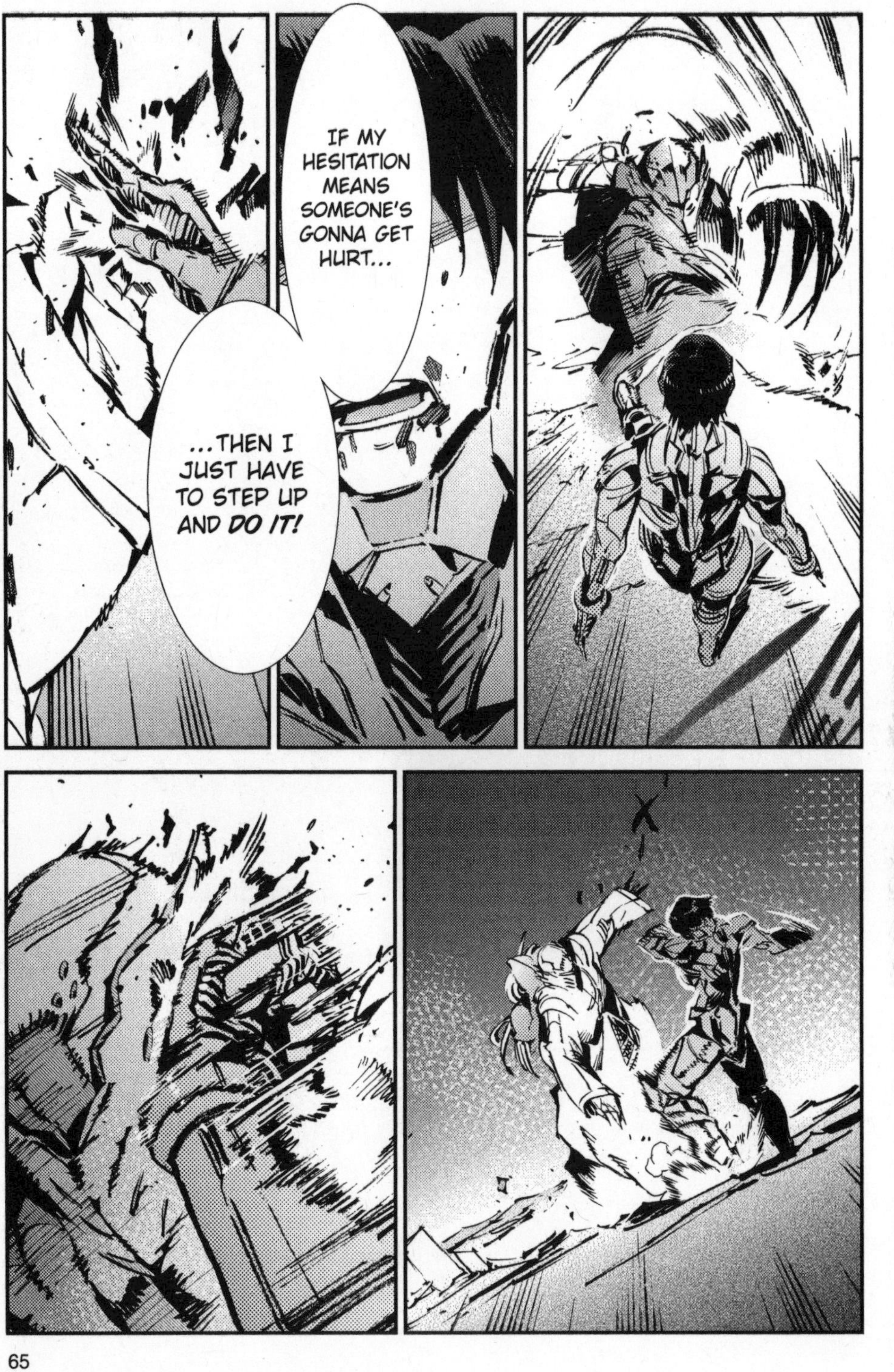
IF MY HESITATION MEANS SOMEONE'S GONNA GET HURT...
...THEN I JUST HAVE TO STEP UP AND DO IT!

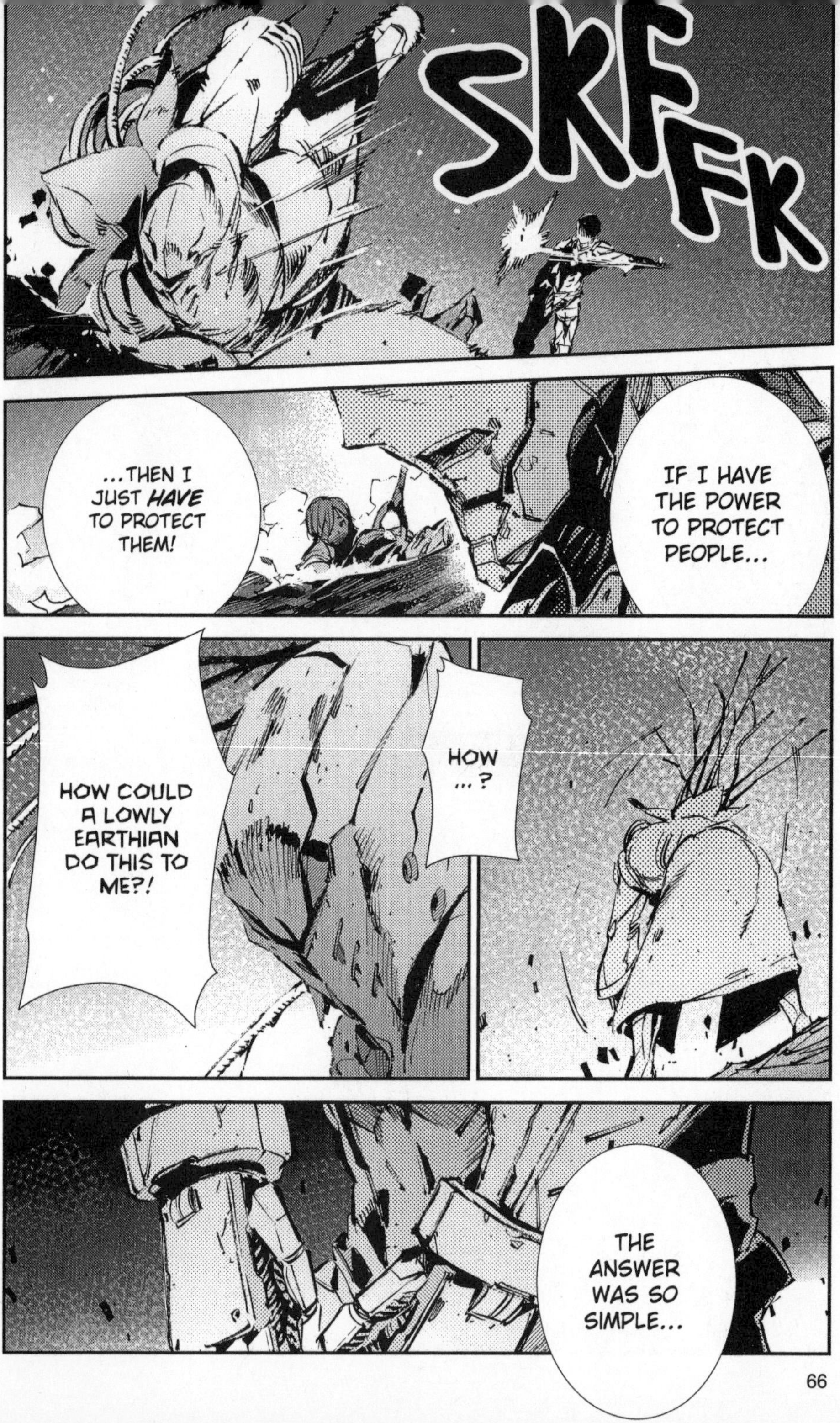
SKFFK
IF I HAVE THE POWER TO PROTECT PEOPLE...
...THEN I JUST *HAVE* TO PROTECT THEM!
HOW ...?
HOW COULD A LOWLY EARTHIAN DO THIS TO ME?!
THE ANSWER WAS SO SIMPLE...

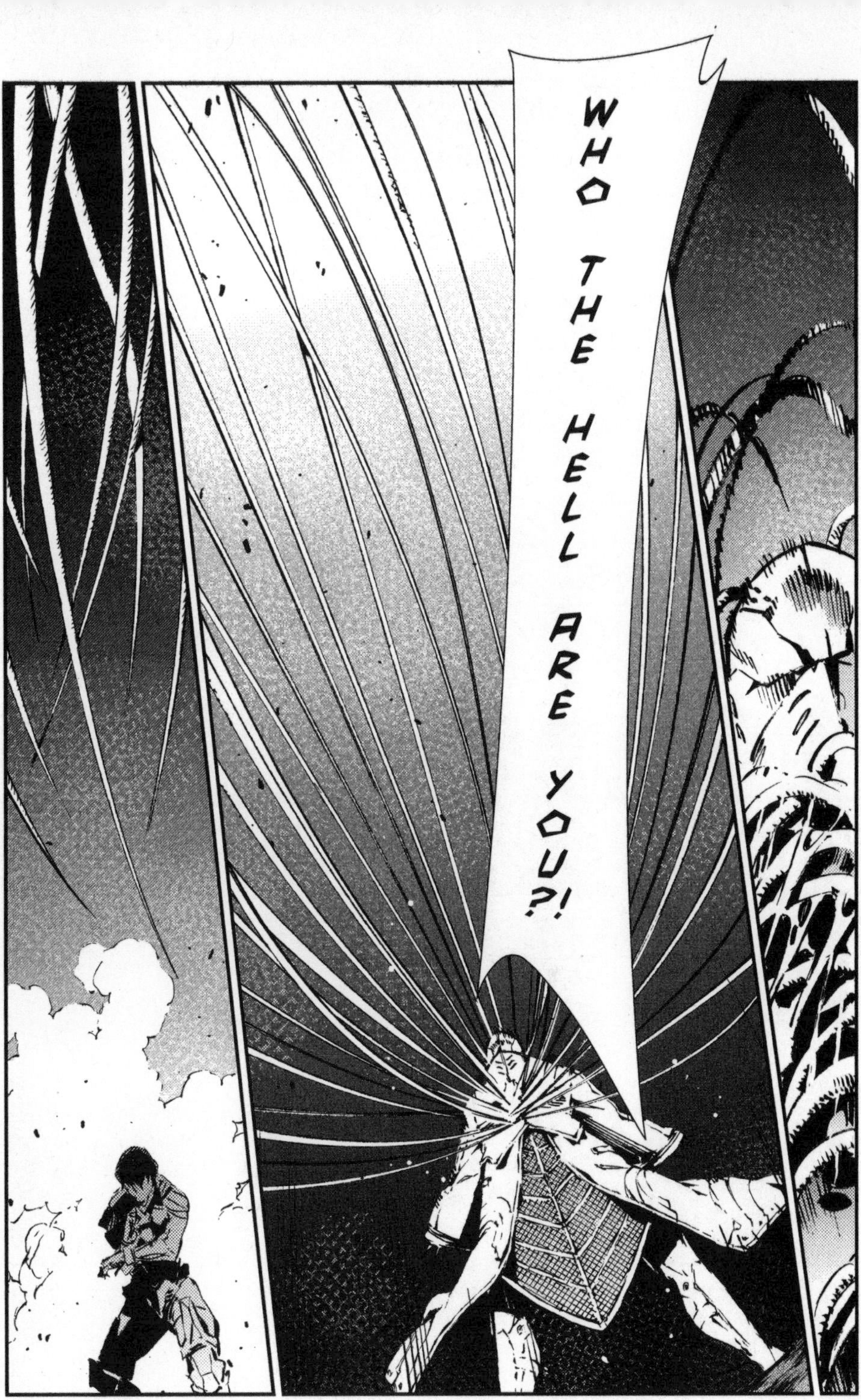
WHO THE HELL ARE YOU?!

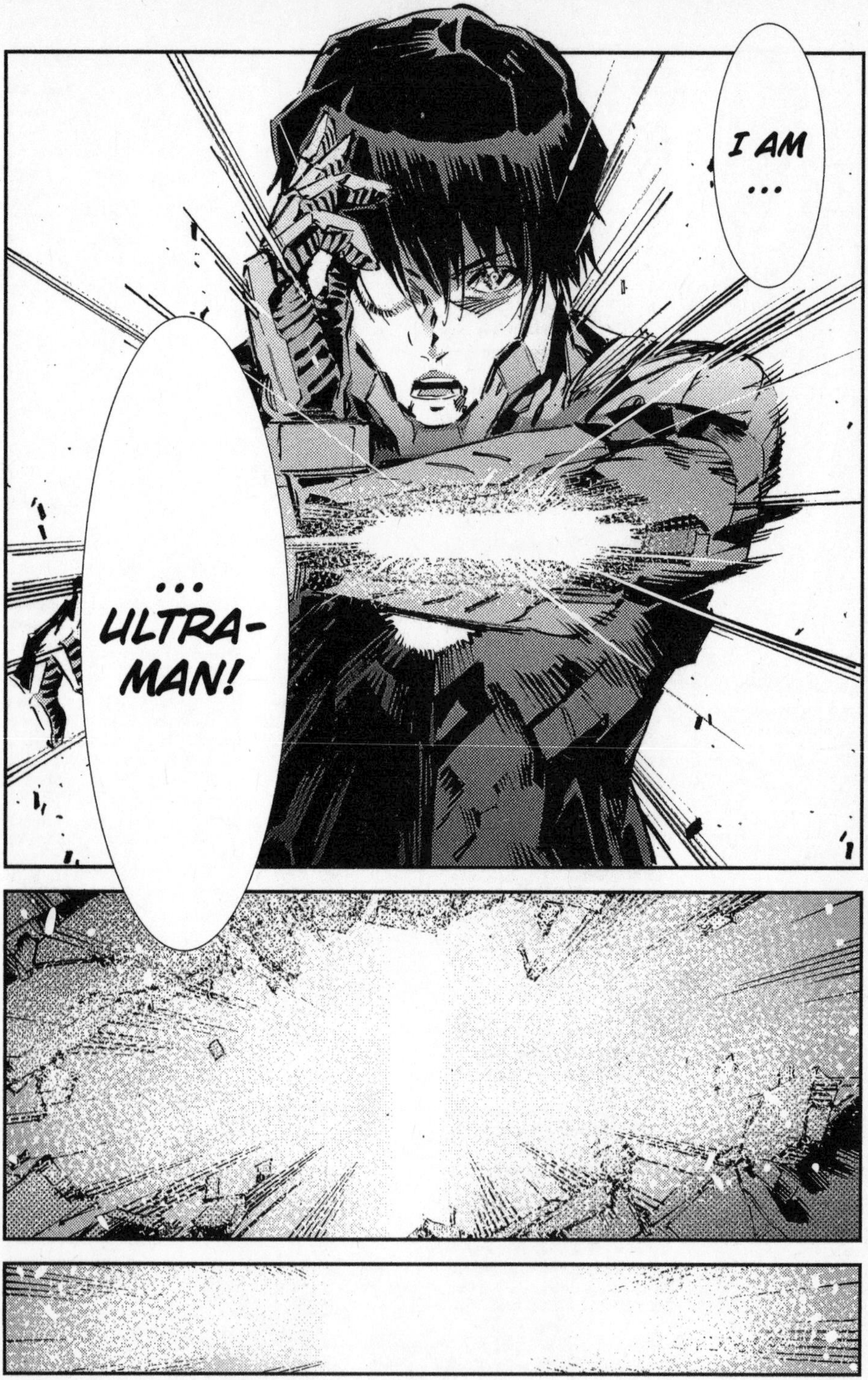
I AM ...
... ULTRA-MAN!

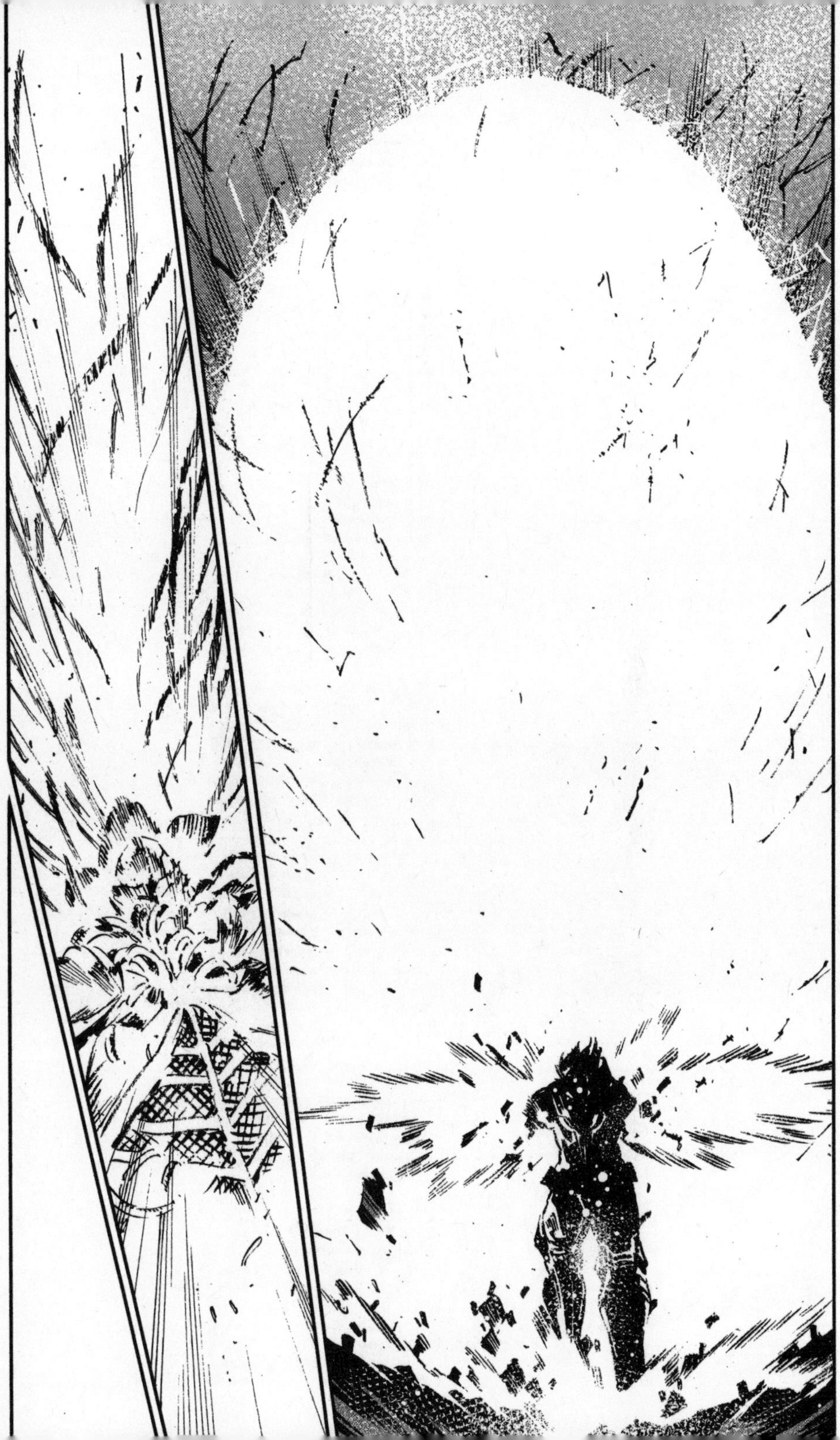

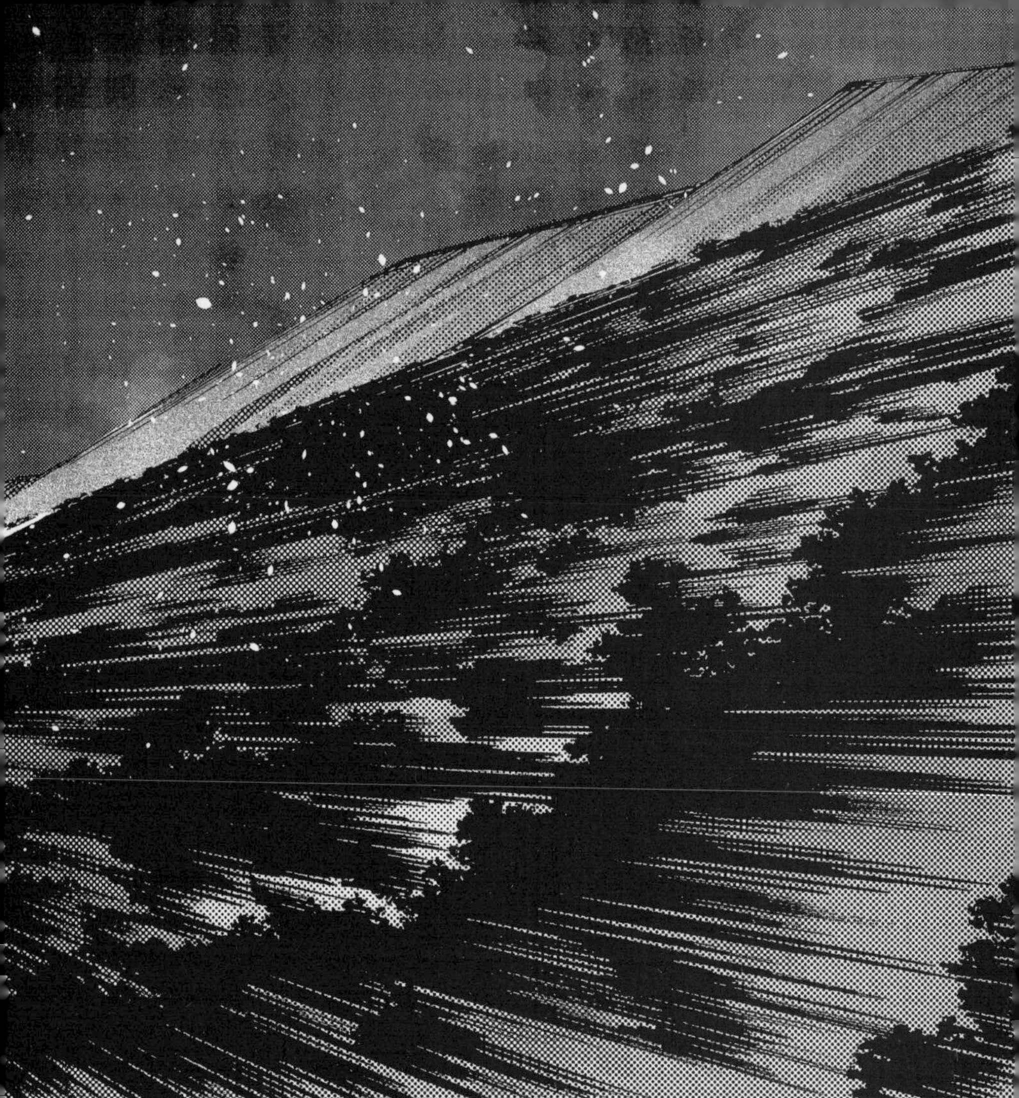
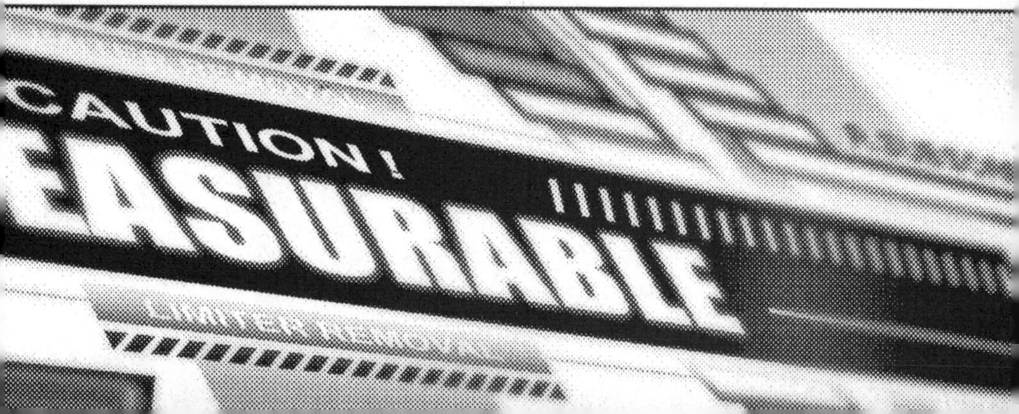
CAUTION!
EASURABLE

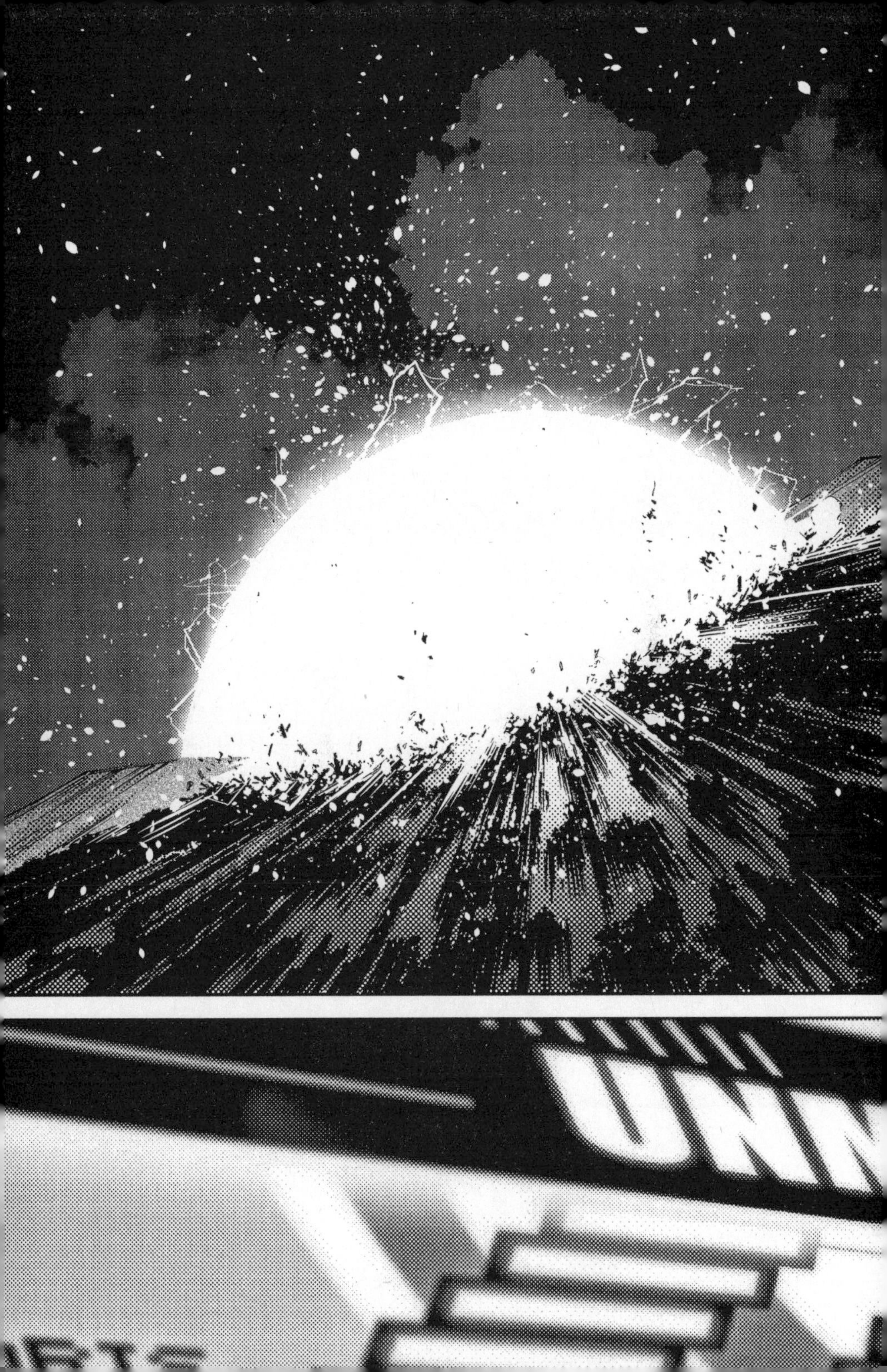

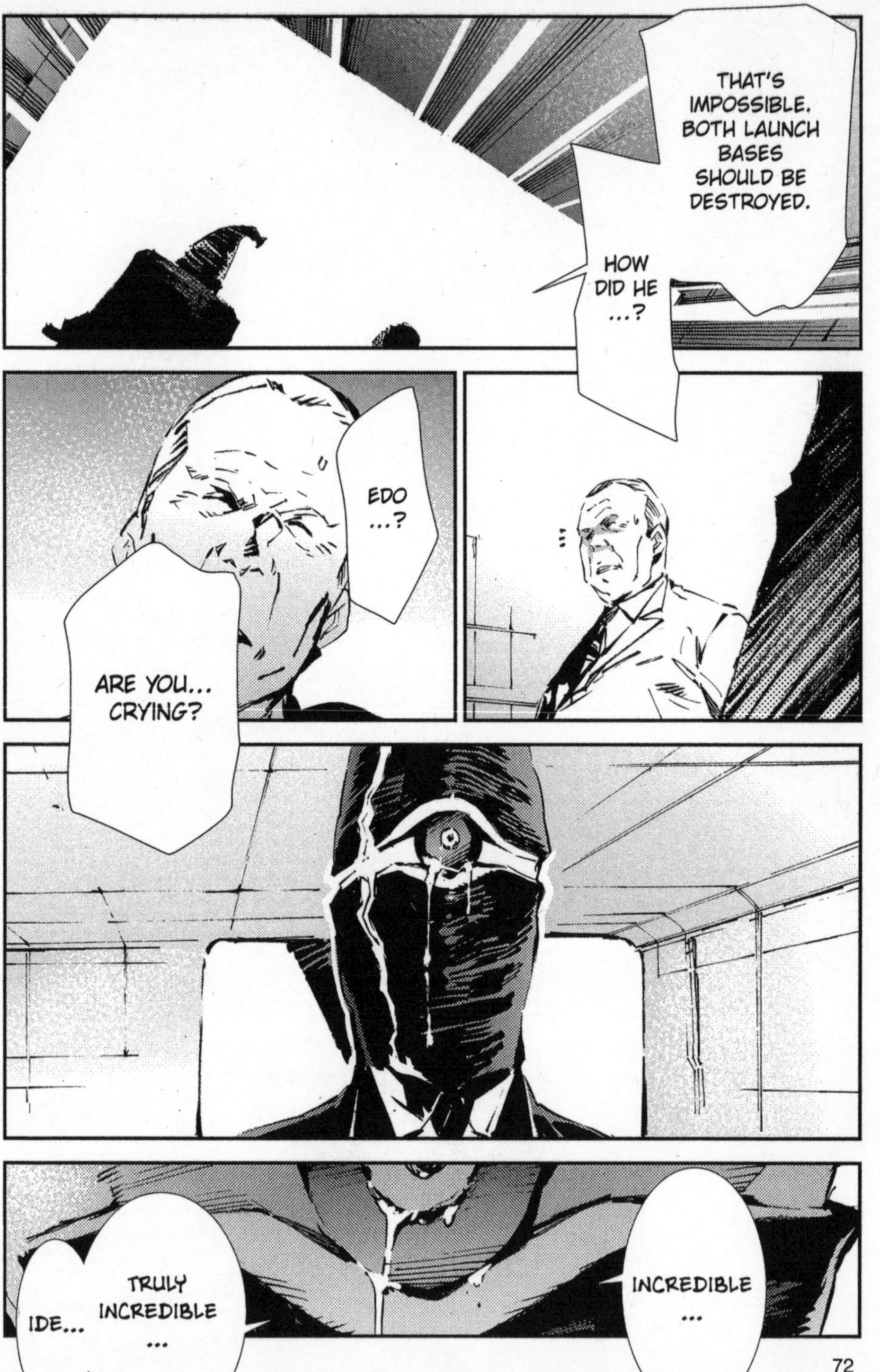
THAT'S IMPOSSIBLE. BOTH LAUNCH BASES SHOULD BE DESTROYED.
HOW DID HE ...?
EDO ...?
ARE YOU... CRYING?
INCREDIBLE ...
TRULY INCREDIBLE ...
IDE...

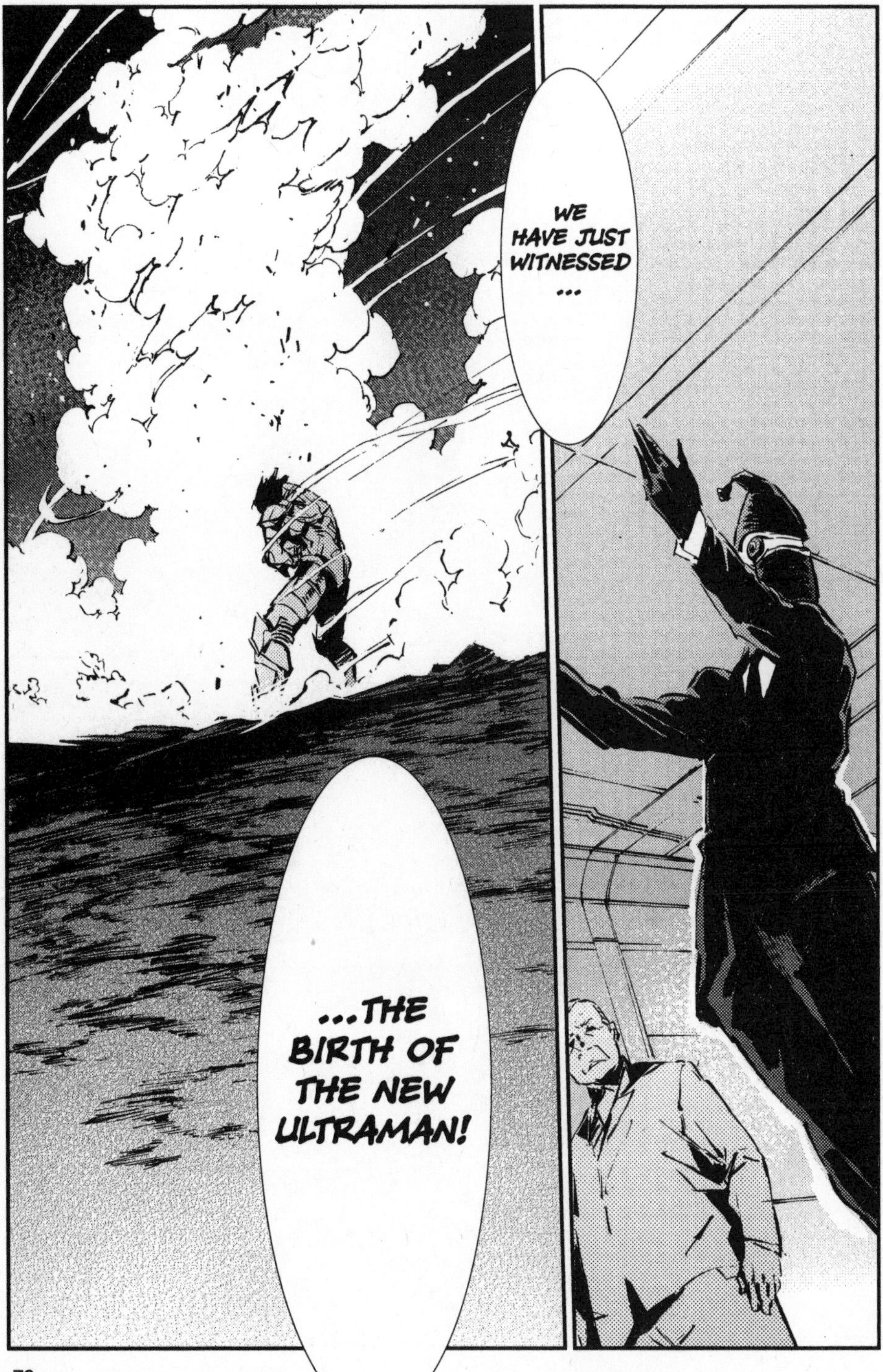
WE HAVE JUST WITNESSED ...
...THE BIRTH OF THE NEW ULTRAMAN!

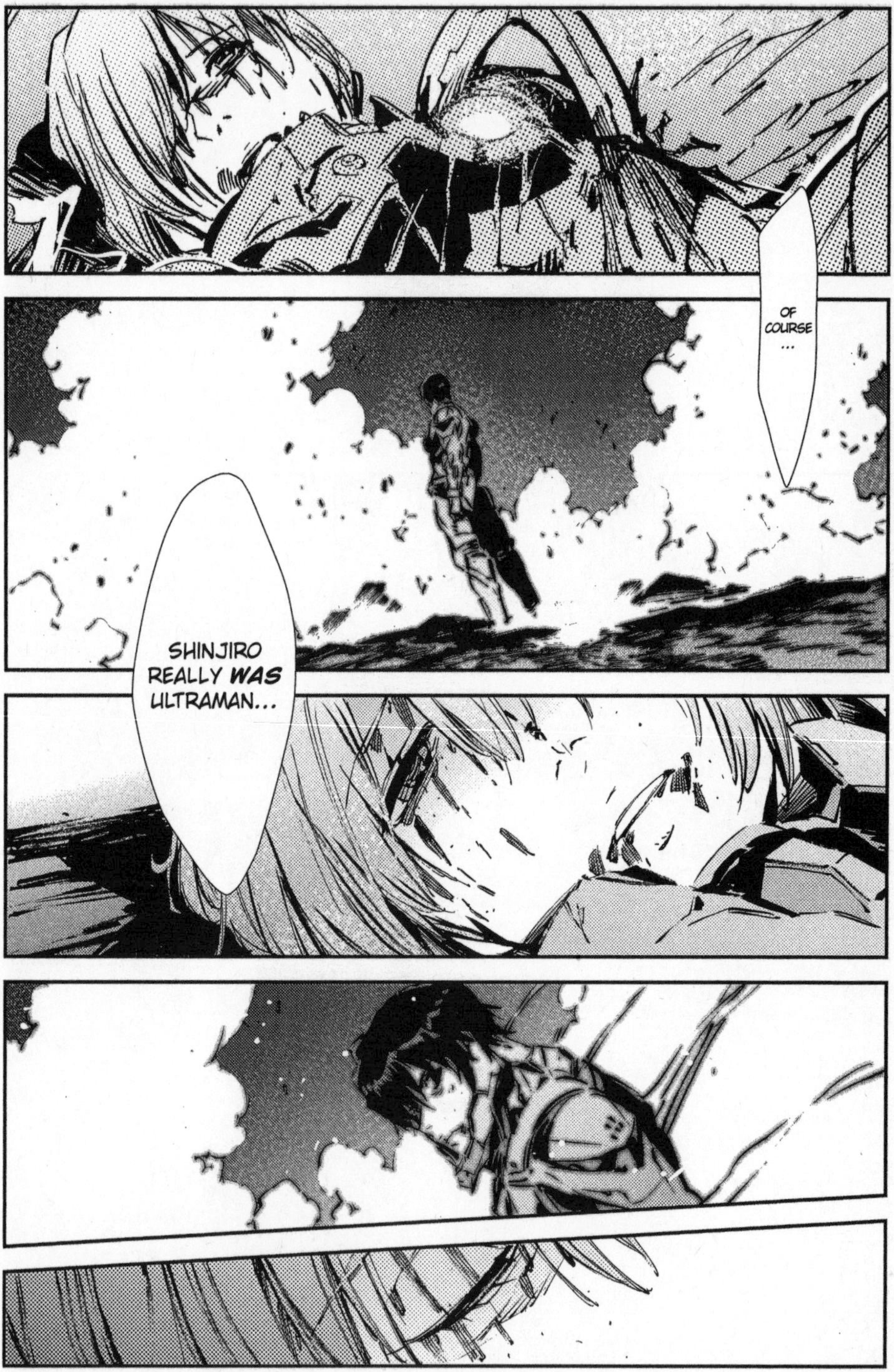
OF COURSE ...
SHINJIRO REALLY **WAS** ULTRAMAN...

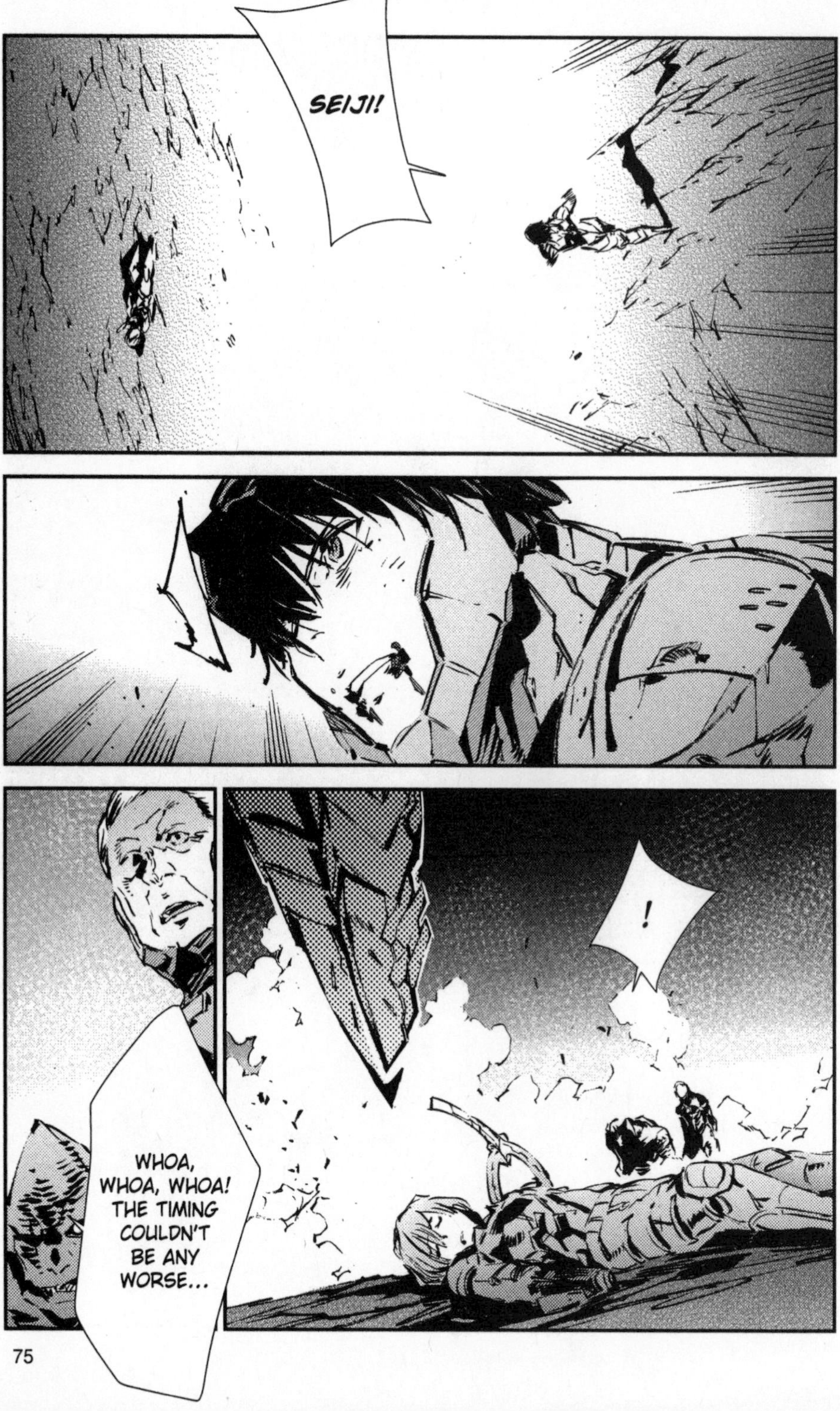
SEIJI!
!
WHOA, WHOA, WHOA! THE TIMING COULDN'T BE ANY WORSE...

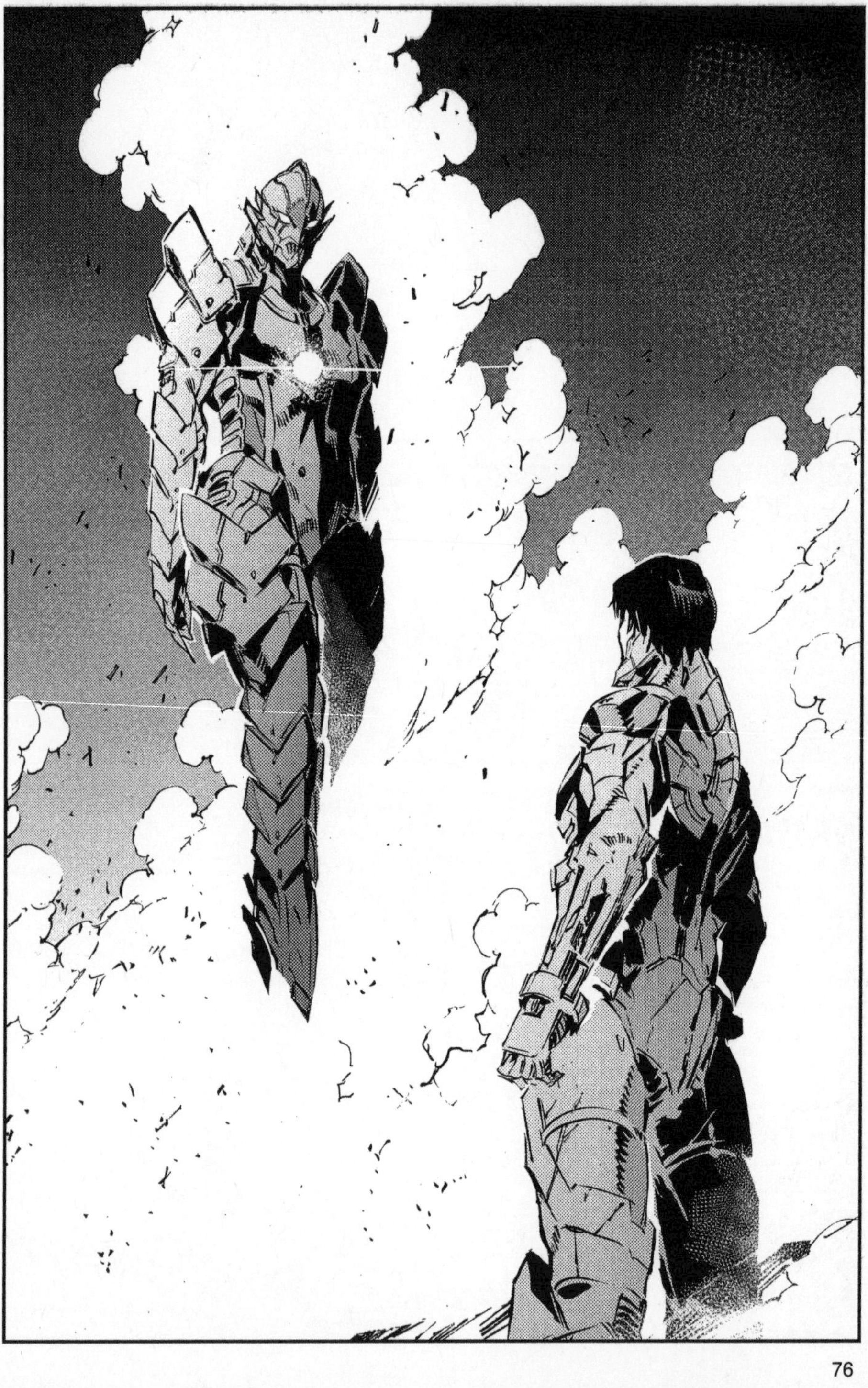

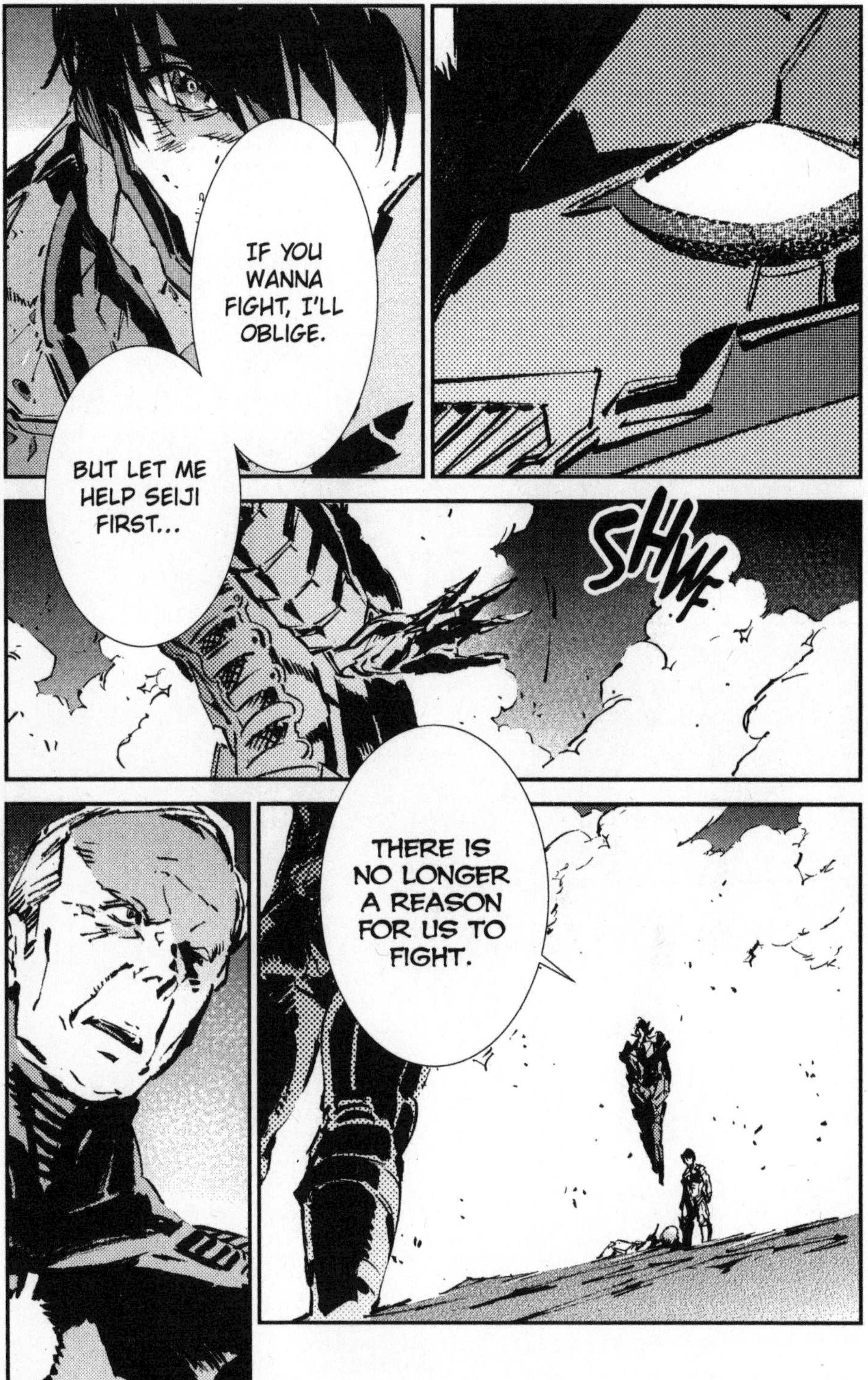
IF YOU WANNA FIGHT, I'LL OBLIGE.
BUT LET ME HELP SEIJI FIRST...
SHWF
THERE IS NO LONGER A REASON FOR US TO FIGHT.

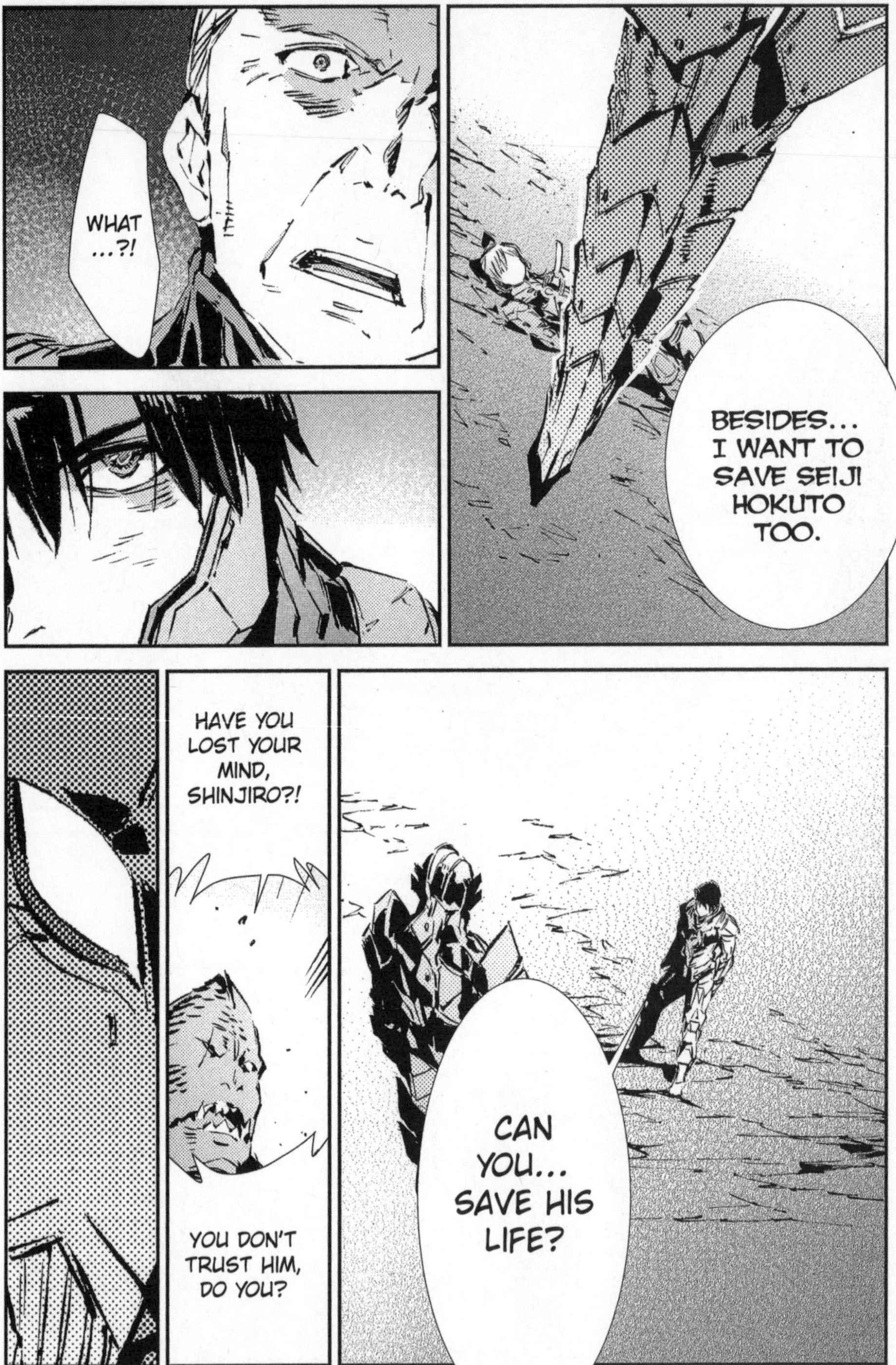
BESIDES... I WANT TO SAVE SEIJI HOKUTO TOO.
WHAT ...?!
CAN YOU... SAVE HIS LIFE?
HAVE YOU LOST YOUR MIND, SHINJIRO?!
YOU DON'T TRUST HIM, DO YOU?

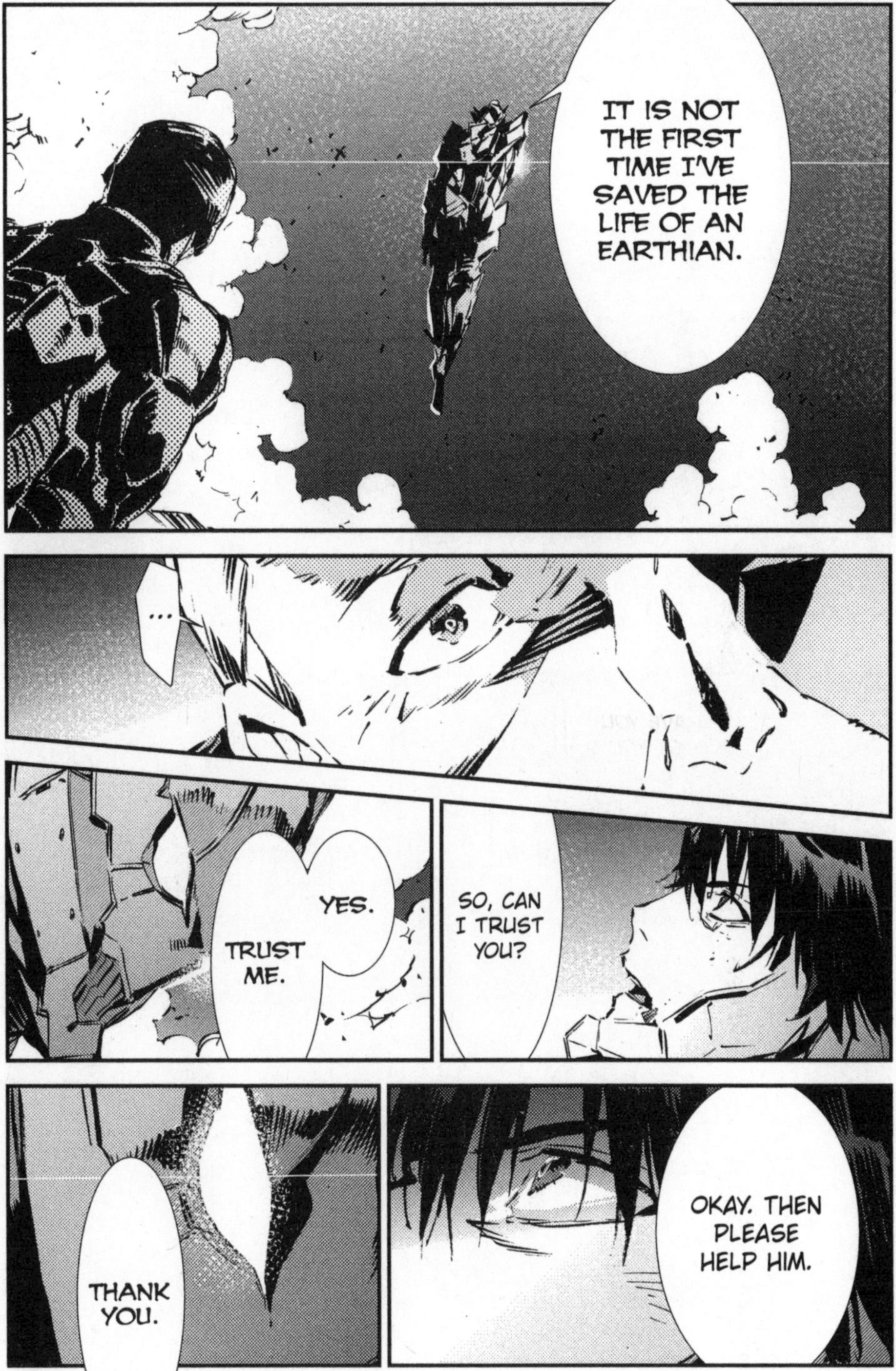
IT IS NOT THE FIRST TIME I'VE SAVED THE LIFE OF AN EARTHIAN.
...
SO, CAN I TRUST YOU?
YES.
TRUST ME.
OKAY. THEN PLEASE HELP HIM.
THANK YOU.

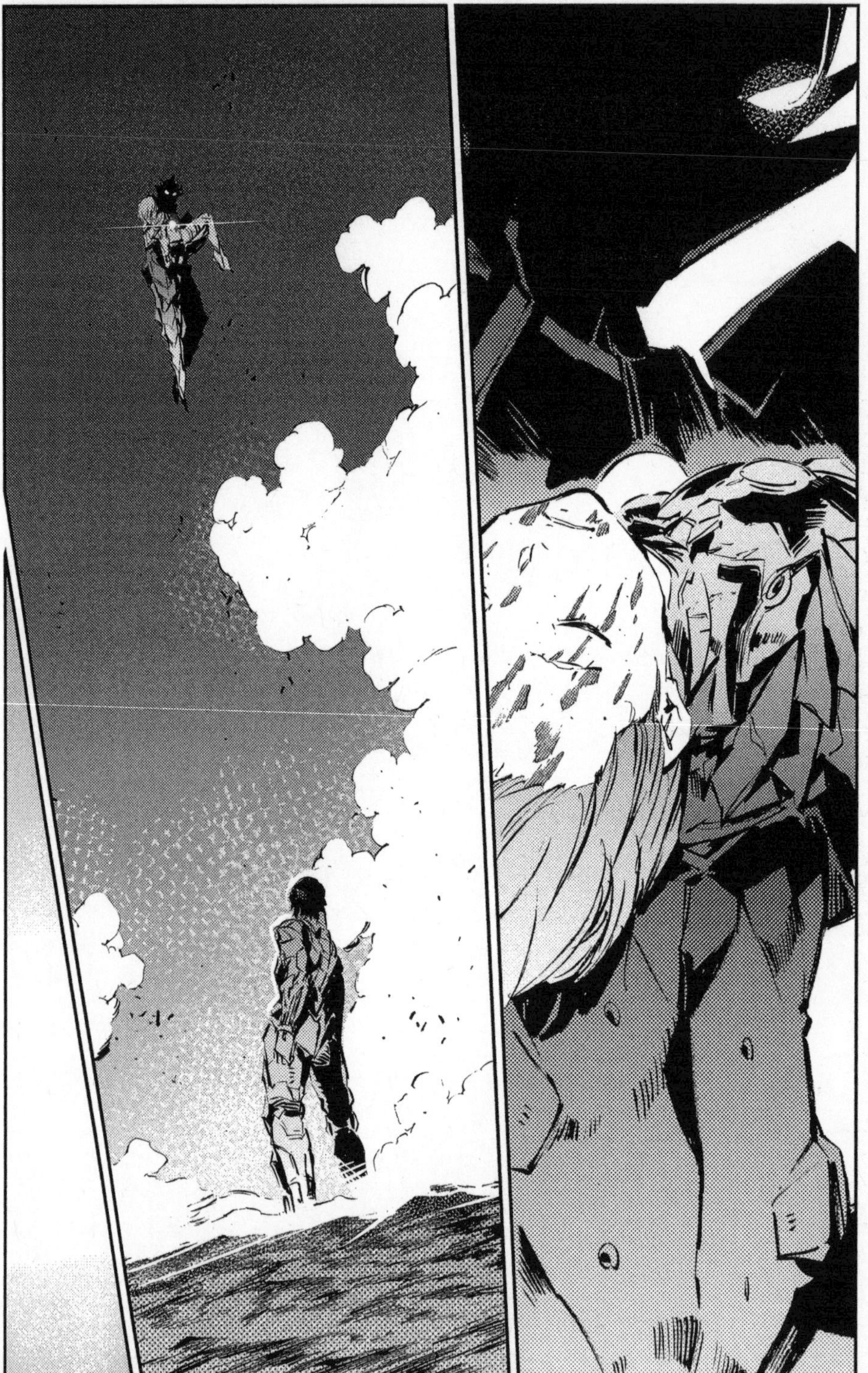

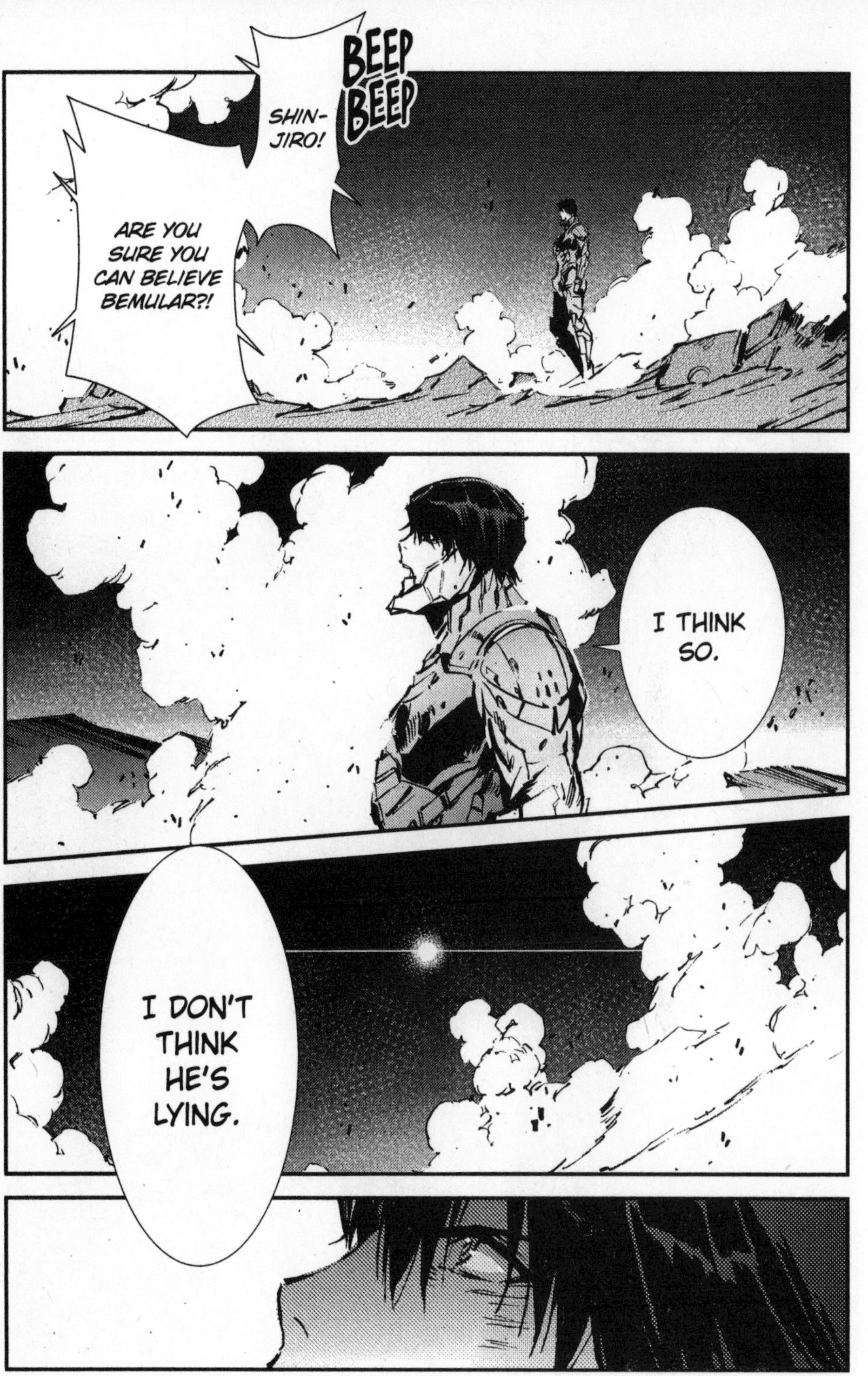
BEEP BEEP
SHIN-JIRO!
ARE YOU SURE YOU CAN BELIEVE BEMULAR?!
I THINK SO.
I DON'T THINK HE'S LYING.

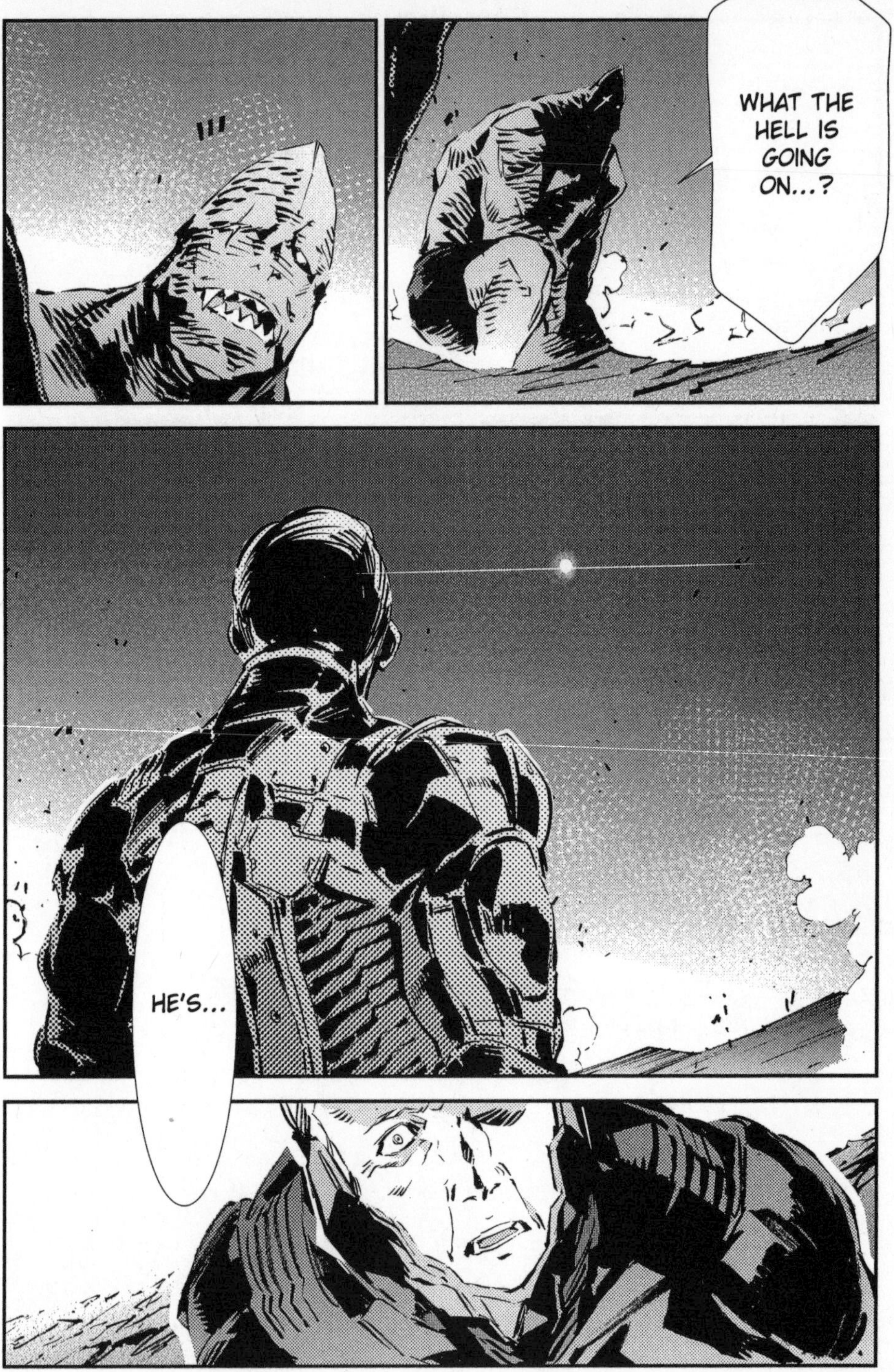
WHAT THE HELL IS GOING ON...?
HE'S...

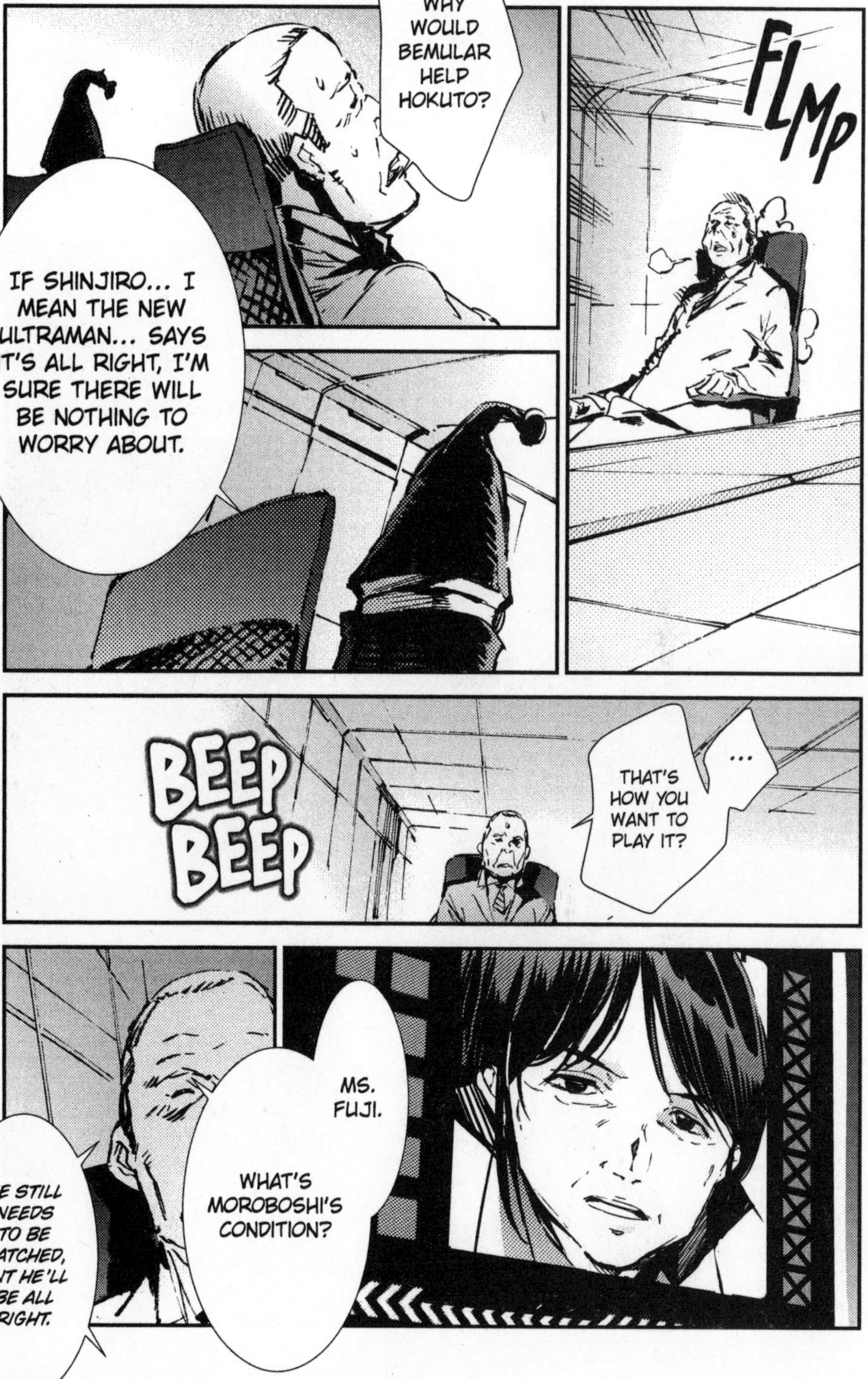
FLMP
WHY WOULD BEMULAR HELP HOKUTO?
IF SHINJIRO... I MEAN THE NEW ULTRAMAN... SAYS IT'S ALL RIGHT, I'M SURE THERE WILL BE NOTHING TO WORRY ABOUT.
...
THAT'S HOW YOU WANT TO PLAY IT?
BEEP BEEP
MS. FUJI.
WHAT'S MOROBOSHI'S CONDITION?
HE STILL NEEDS TO BE WATCHED, BUT HE'LL BE ALL RIGHT.

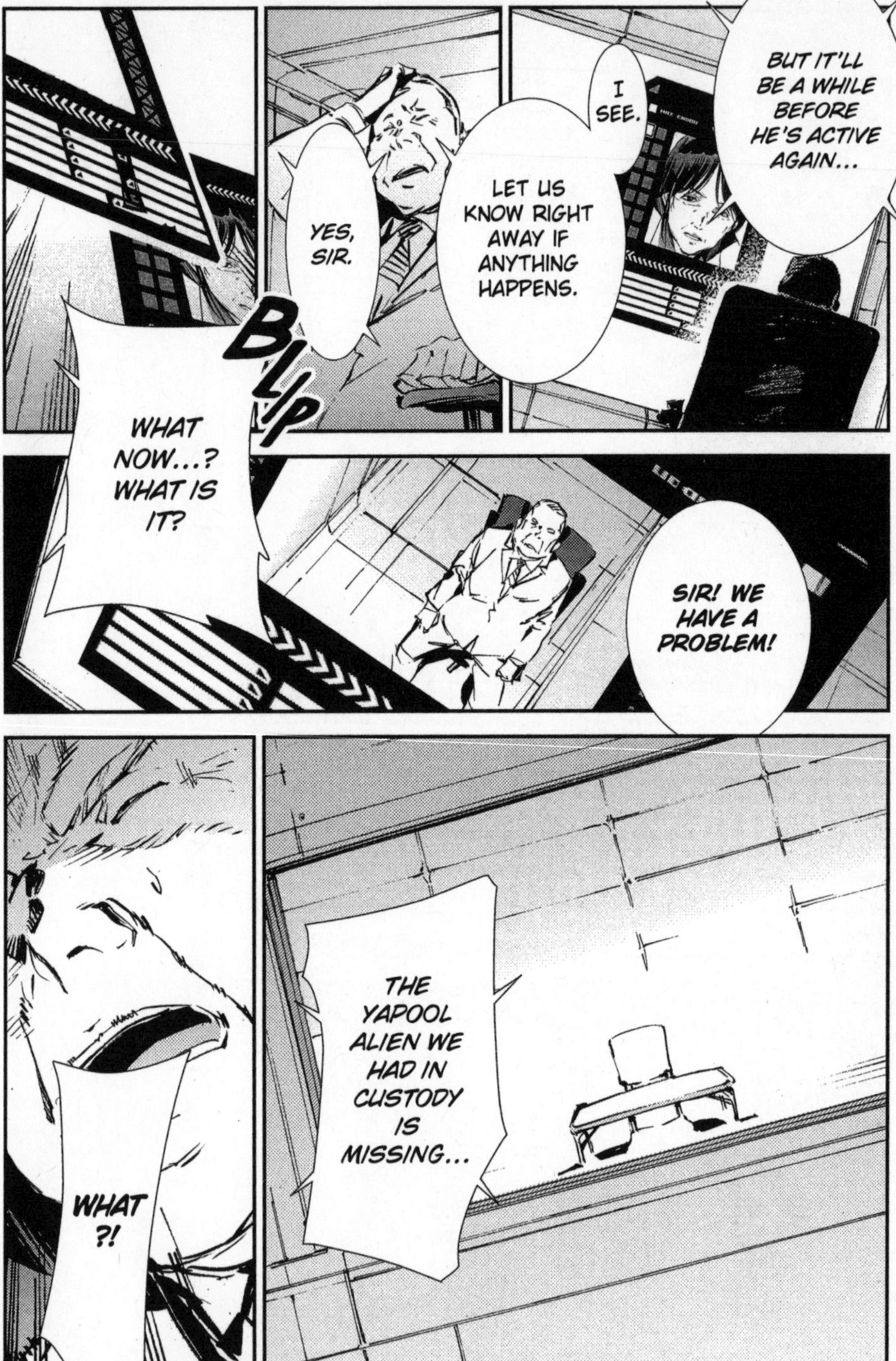
BUT IT'LL BE A WHILE BEFORE HE'S ACTIVE AGAIN...
I SEE.
LET US KNOW RIGHT AWAY IF ANYTHING HAPPENS.
YES, SIR.
BLIP
SIR! WE HAVE A PROBLEM!
WHAT NOW...? WHAT IS IT?
THE YAPOOL ALIEN WE HAD IN CUSTODY IS MISSING...
WHAT ?!

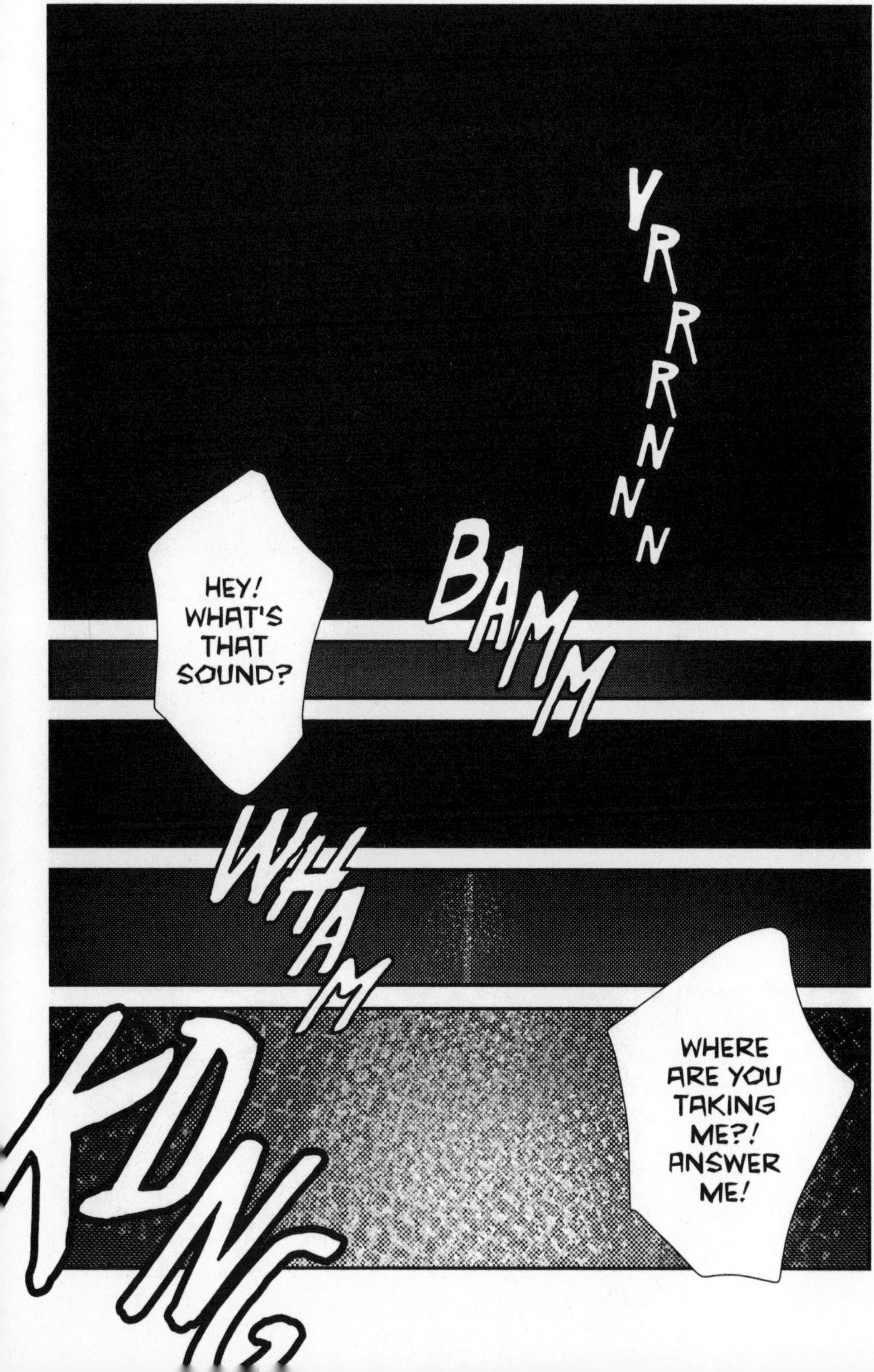
VRRRNNN
BAMM
HEY! WHAT'S THAT SOUND?
WHAM
WHERE ARE YOU TAKING ME?! ANSWER ME!

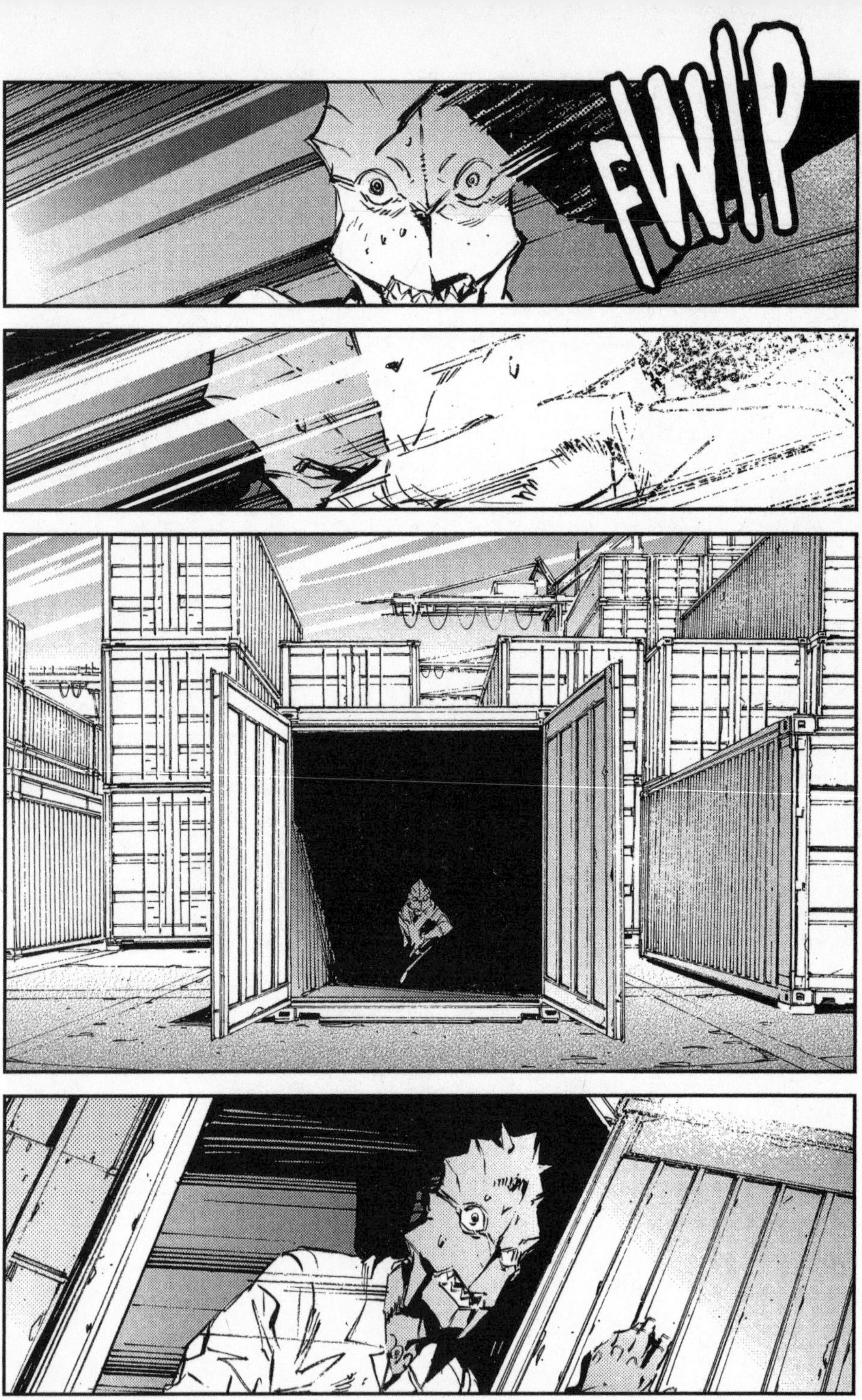
FWIP

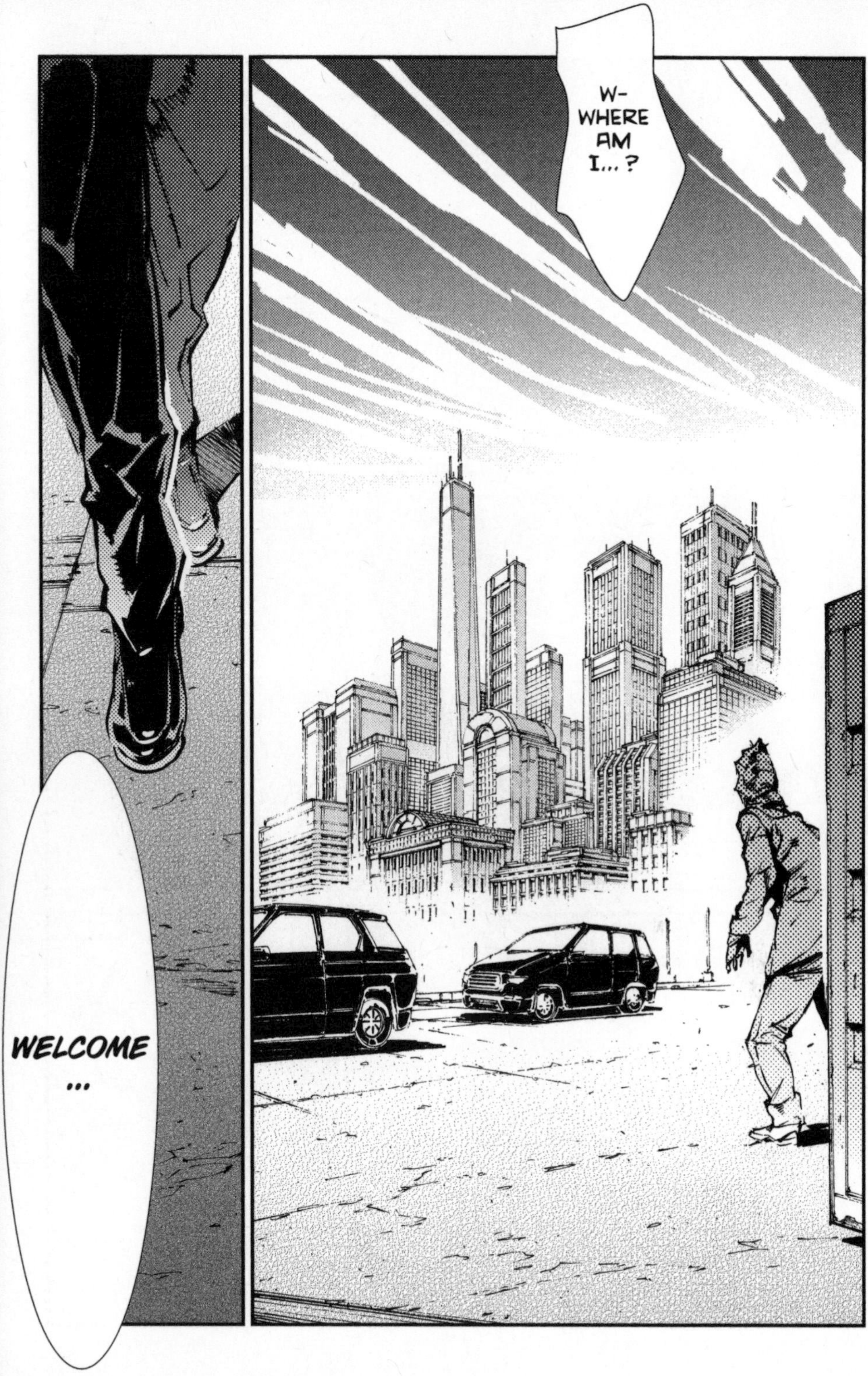
W-WHERE AM I...?
WELCOME ...

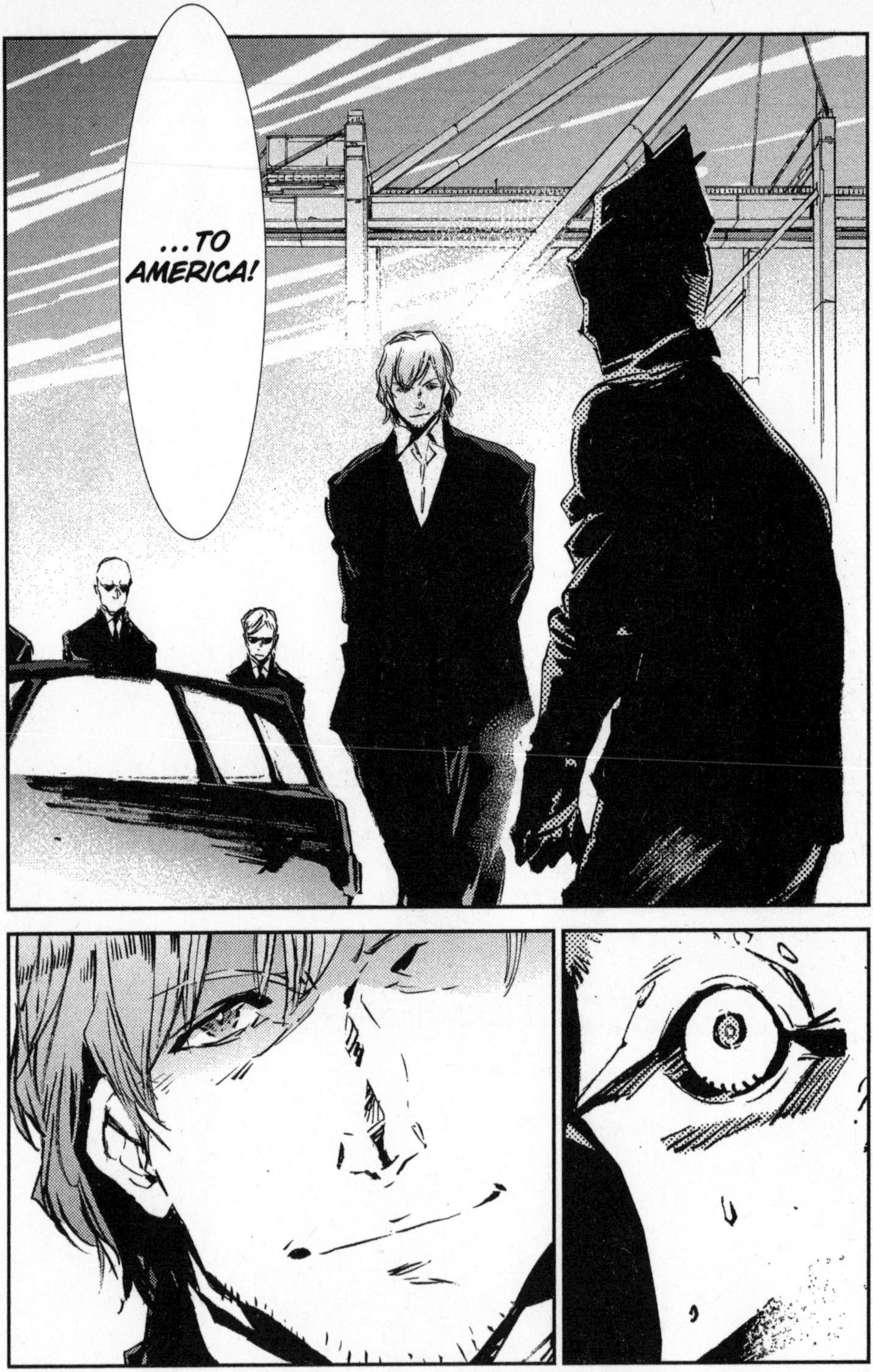
...TO AMERICA!

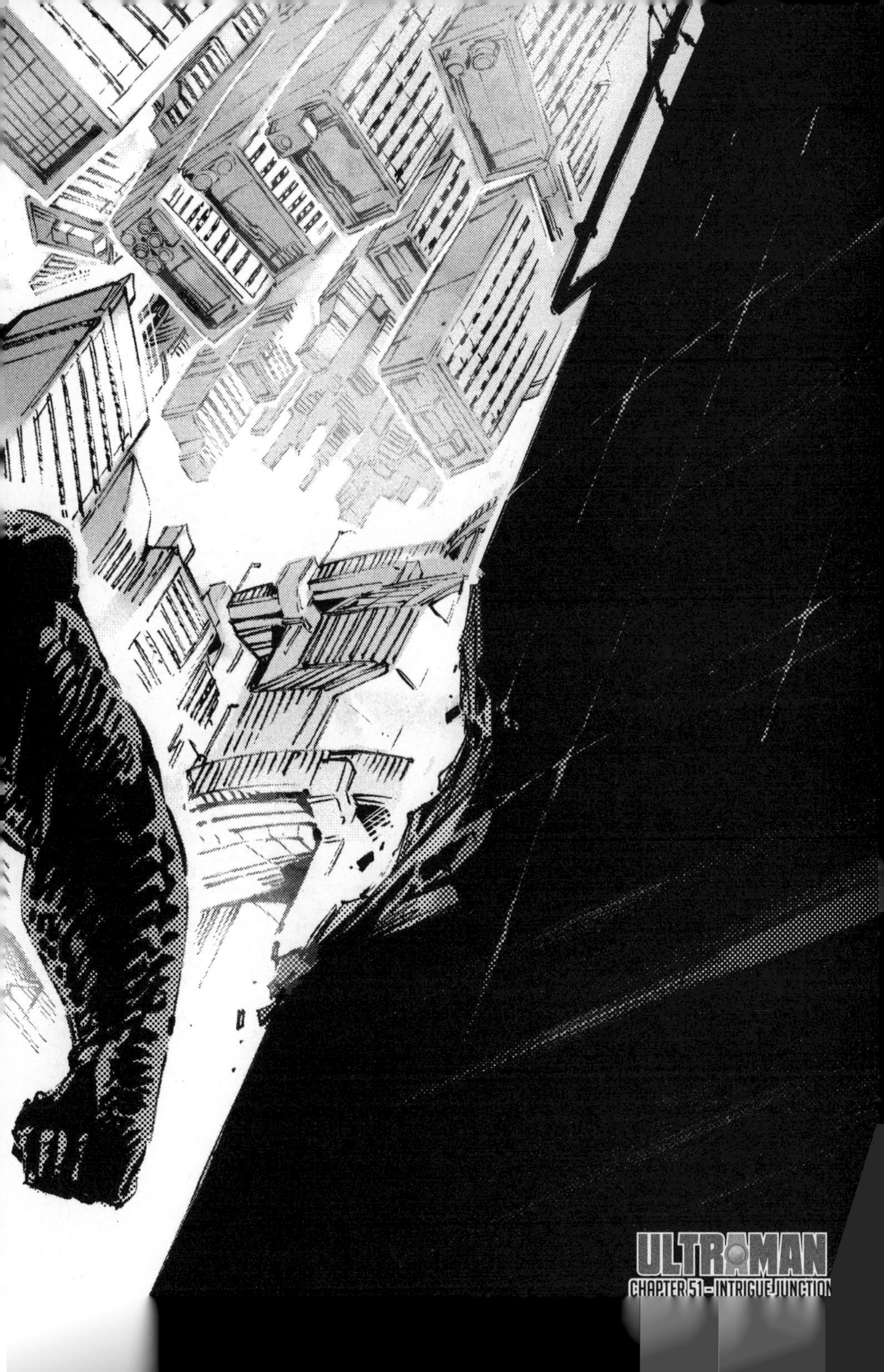
ULTRAMAN
CHAPTER 51 – INTRIGUE JUNCTION

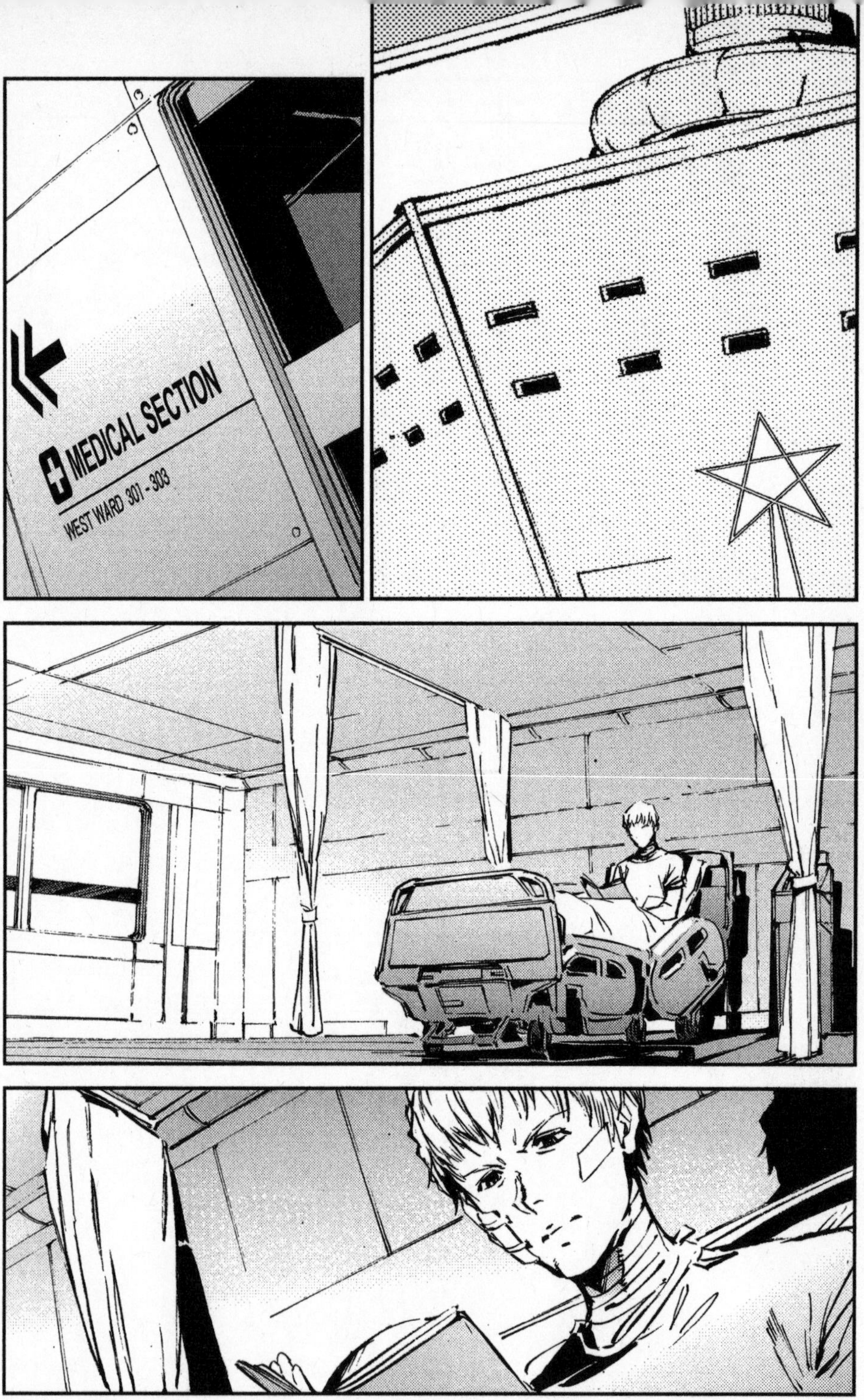
MEDICAL SECTION
WEST WARD 301 - 303

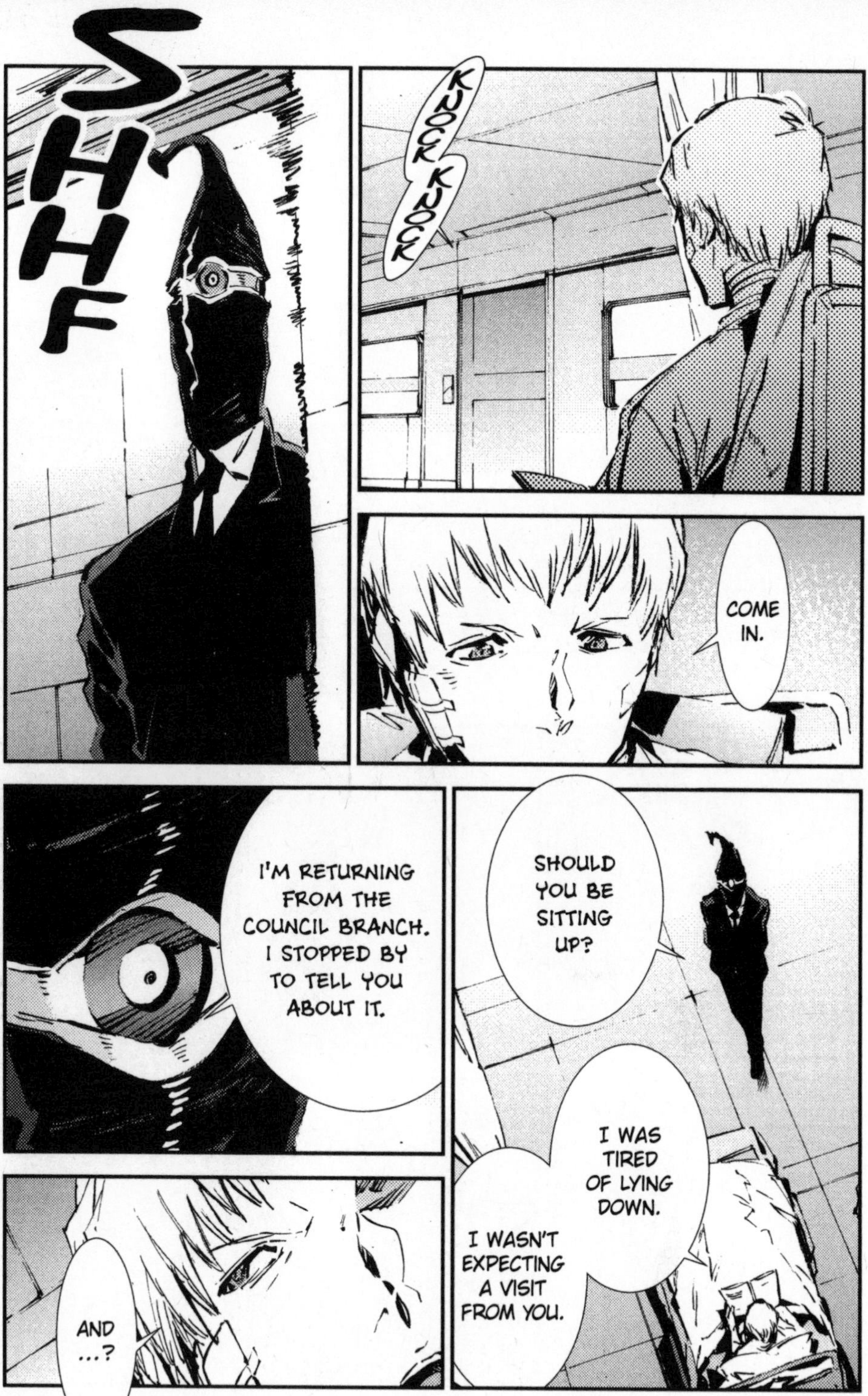
KNOCK KNOCK
COME IN.
SHHF
SHOULD YOU BE SITTING UP?
I WAS TIRED OF LYING DOWN.
I WASN'T EXPECTING A VISIT FROM YOU.
I'M RETURNING FROM THE COUNCIL BRANCH. I STOPPED BY TO TELL YOU ABOUT IT.
AND ...?

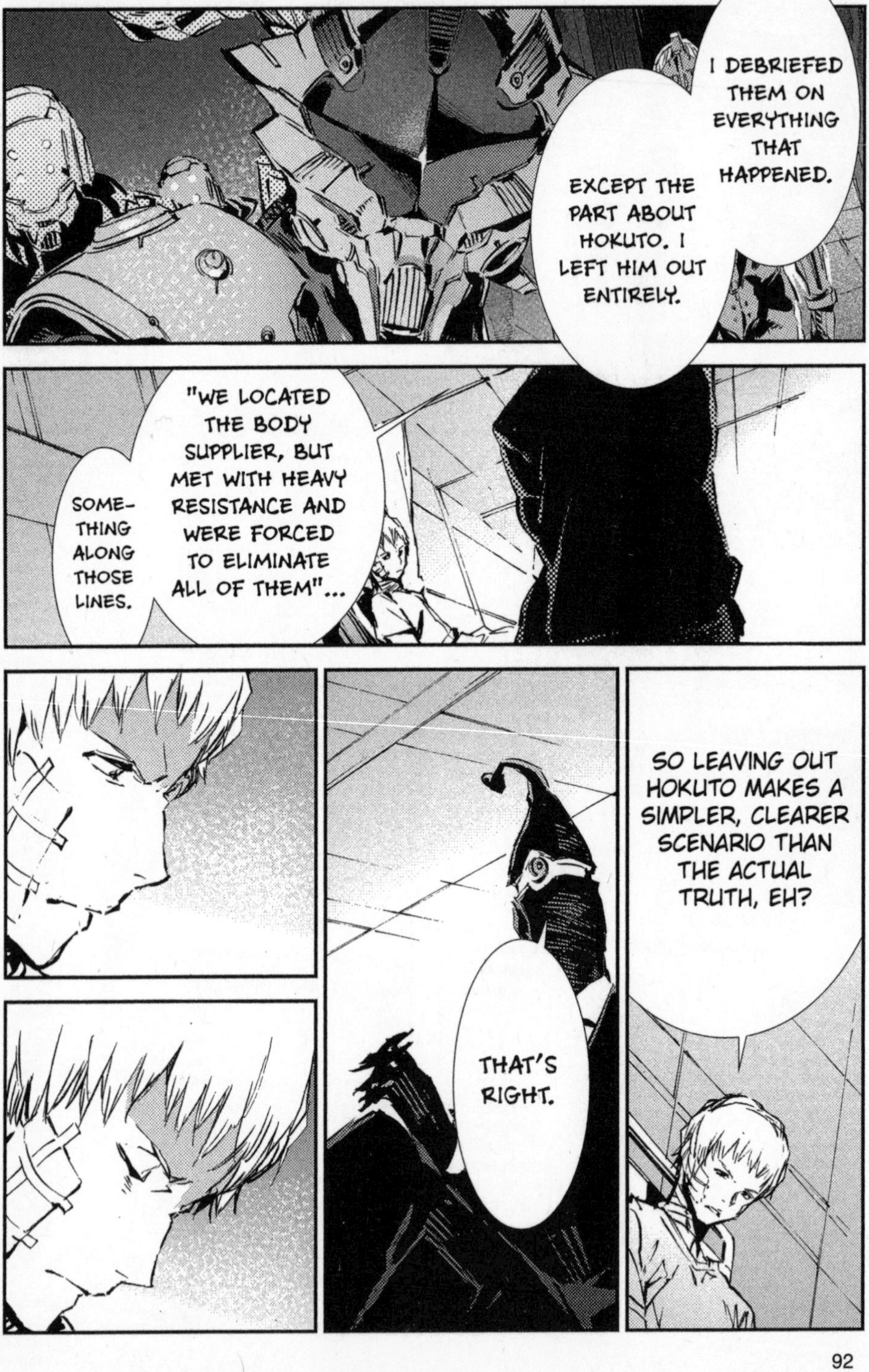
I DEBRIEFED THEM ON EVERYTHING THAT HAPPENED.
EXCEPT THE PART ABOUT HOKUTO. I LEFT HIM OUT ENTIRELY.
"WE LOCATED THE BODY SUPPLIER, BUT MET WITH HEAVY RESISTANCE AND WERE FORCED TO ELIMINATE ALL OF THEM"...
SOME-THING ALONG THOSE LINES.
SO LEAVING OUT HOKUTO MAKES A SIMPLER, CLEARER SCENARIO THAN THE ACTUAL TRUTH, EH?
THAT'S RIGHT.

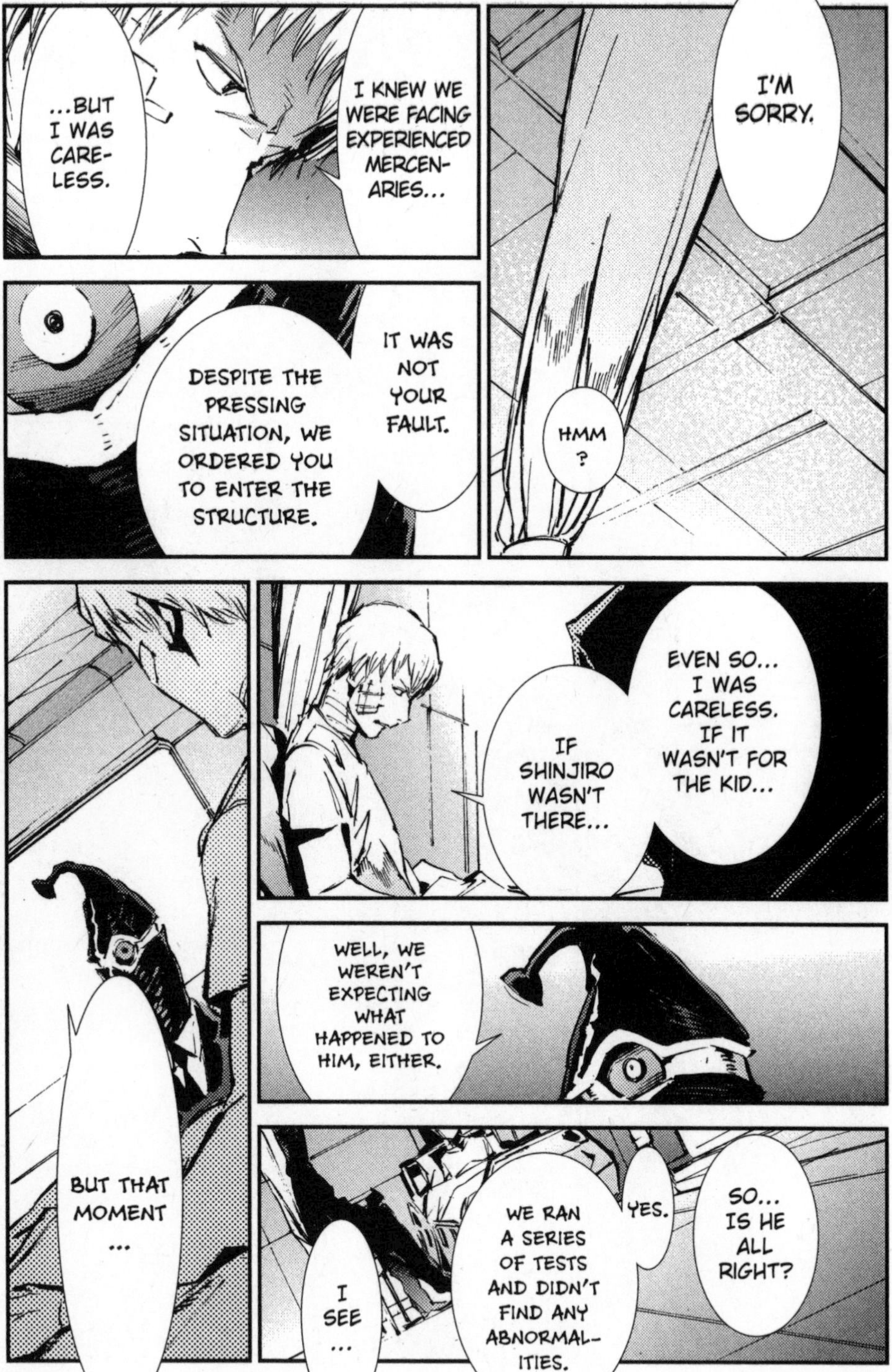
I'M SORRY.
HMM?
I KNEW WE WERE FACING EXPERIENCED MERCEN-ARIES...
...BUT I WAS CARE-LESS.
IT WAS NOT YOUR FAULT.
DESPITE THE PRESSING SITUATION, WE ORDERED YOU TO ENTER THE STRUCTURE.
EVEN SO... I WAS CARELESS. IF IT WASN'T FOR THE KID...
IF SHINJIRO WASN'T THERE...
WELL, WE WEREN'T EXPECTING WHAT HAPPENED TO HIM, EITHER.
SO... IS HE ALL RIGHT?
YES.
WE RAN A SERIES OF TESTS AND DIDN'T FIND ANY ABNORMAL-ITIES.
I SEE...
BUT THAT MOMENT...

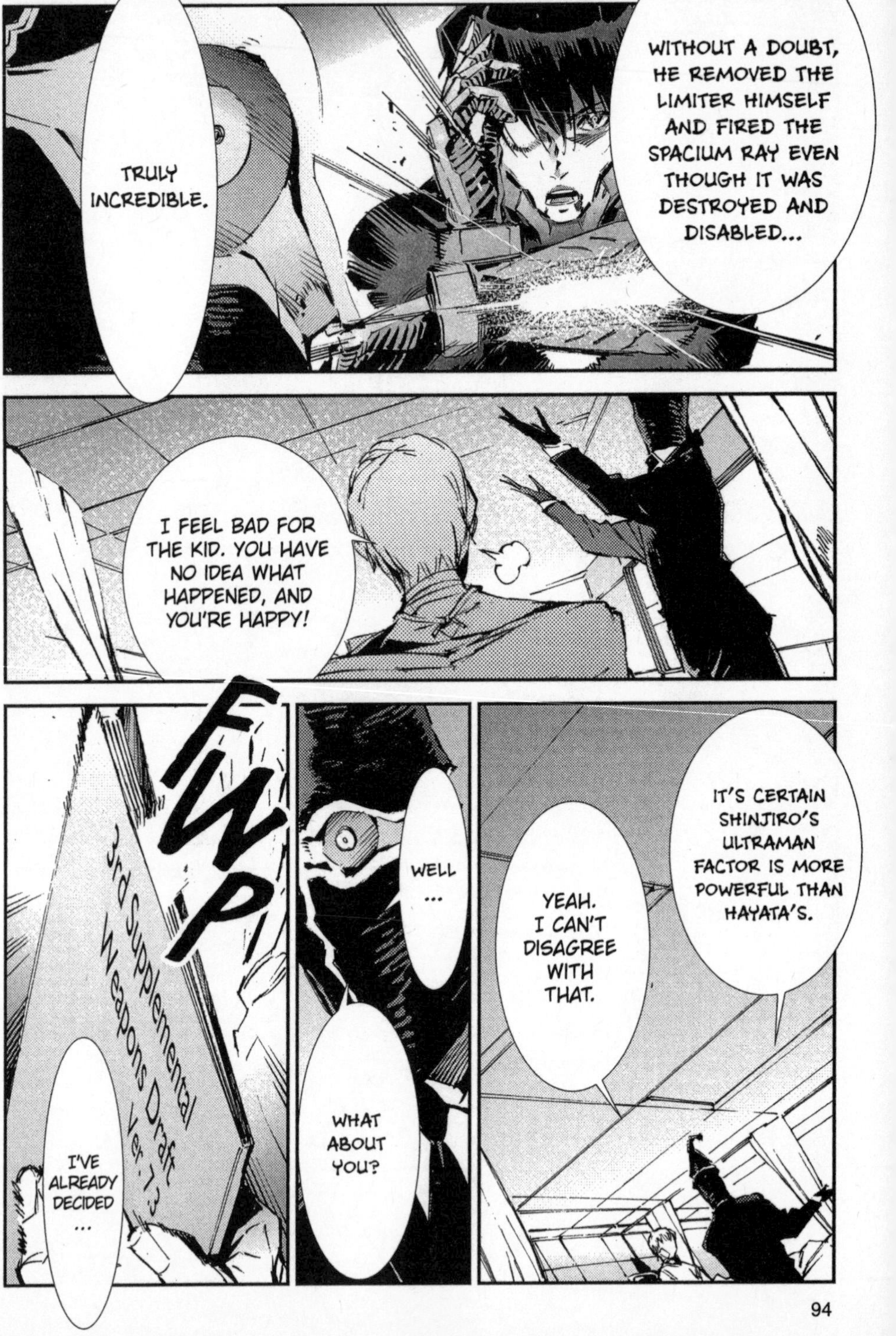
WITHOUT A DOUBT, HE REMOVED THE LIMITER HIMSELF AND FIRED THE SPACIUM RAY EVEN THOUGH IT WAS DESTROYED AND DISABLED...
TRULY INCREDIBLE.
I FEEL BAD FOR THE KID. YOU HAVE NO IDEA WHAT HAPPENED, AND YOU'RE HAPPY!
IT'S CERTAIN SHINJIRO'S ULTRAMAN FACTOR IS MORE POWERFUL THAN HAYATA'S.
YEAH. I CAN'T DISAGREE WITH THAT.
WELL ...
WHAT ABOUT YOU?
FWP
3rd Supplemental Weapons Draft Ver.7.3
I'VE ALREADY DECIDED ...

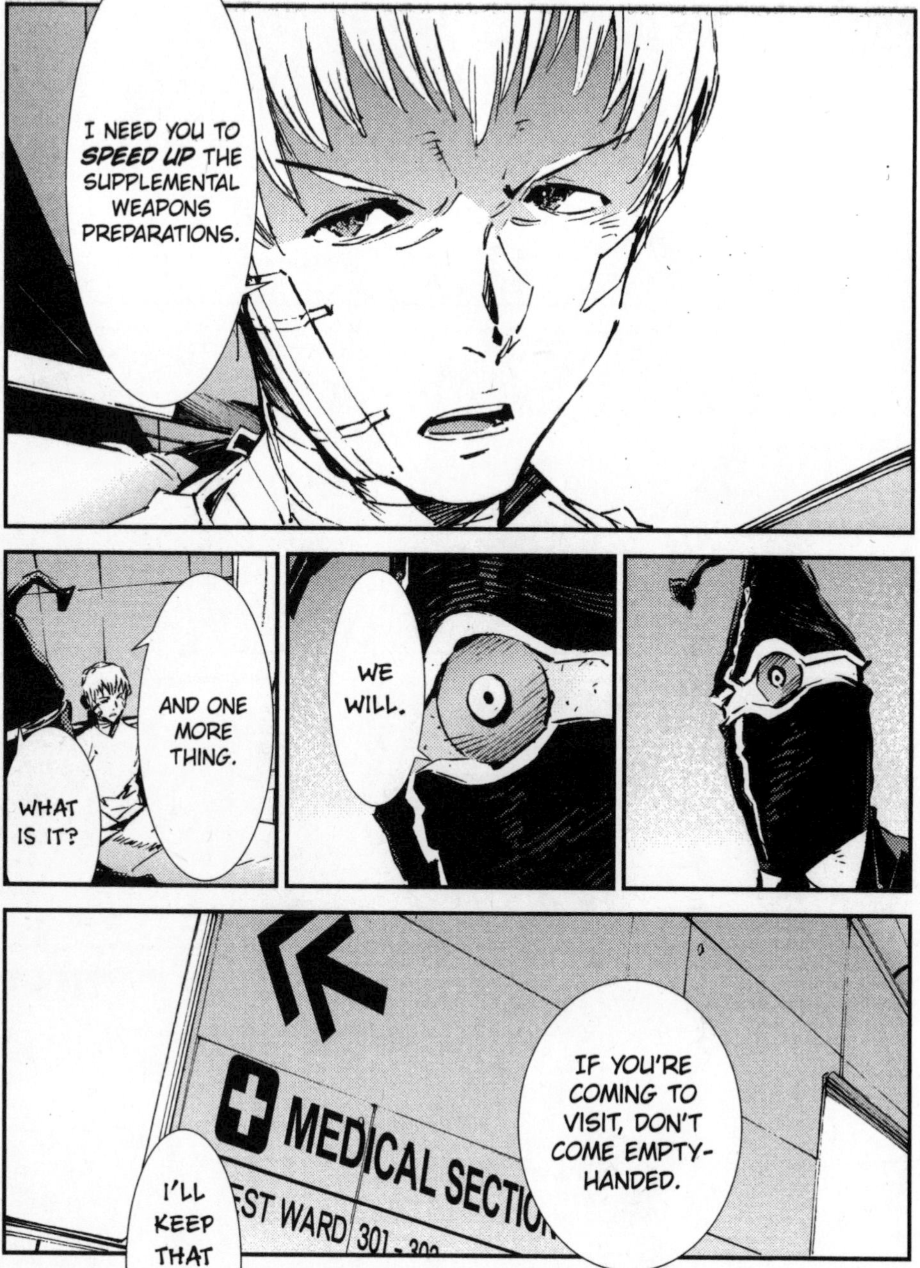
I NEED YOU TO **SPEED UP** THE SUPPLEMENTAL WEAPONS PREPARATIONS.
WE WILL.
AND ONE MORE THING.
WHAT IS IT?
MEDICAL SECTIO
EST WARD 301 -
IF YOU'RE COMING TO VISIT, DON'T COME EMPTY-HANDED.
I'LL KEEP THAT IN MIND.

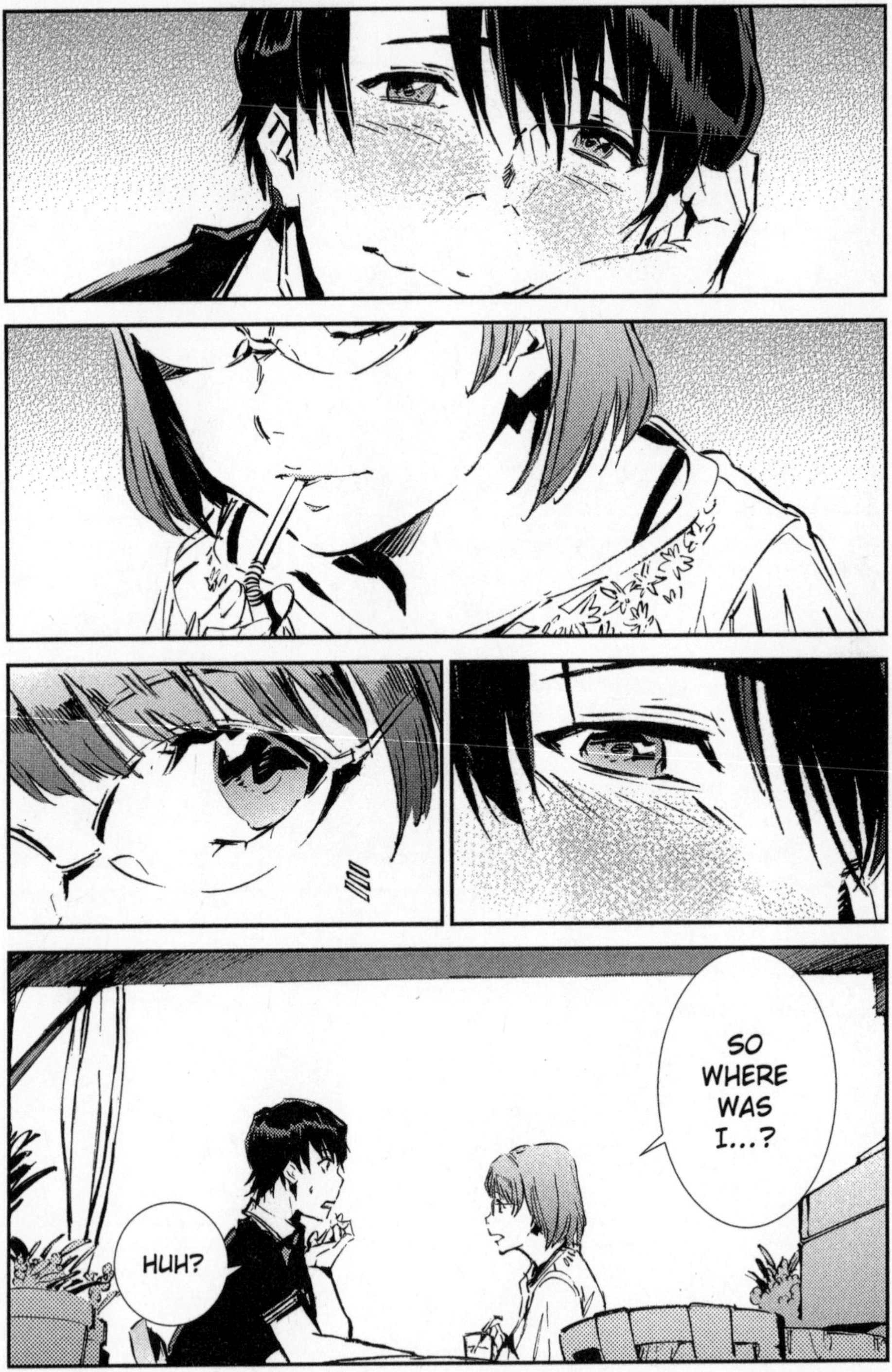
SO WHERE WAS I...?
HUH?

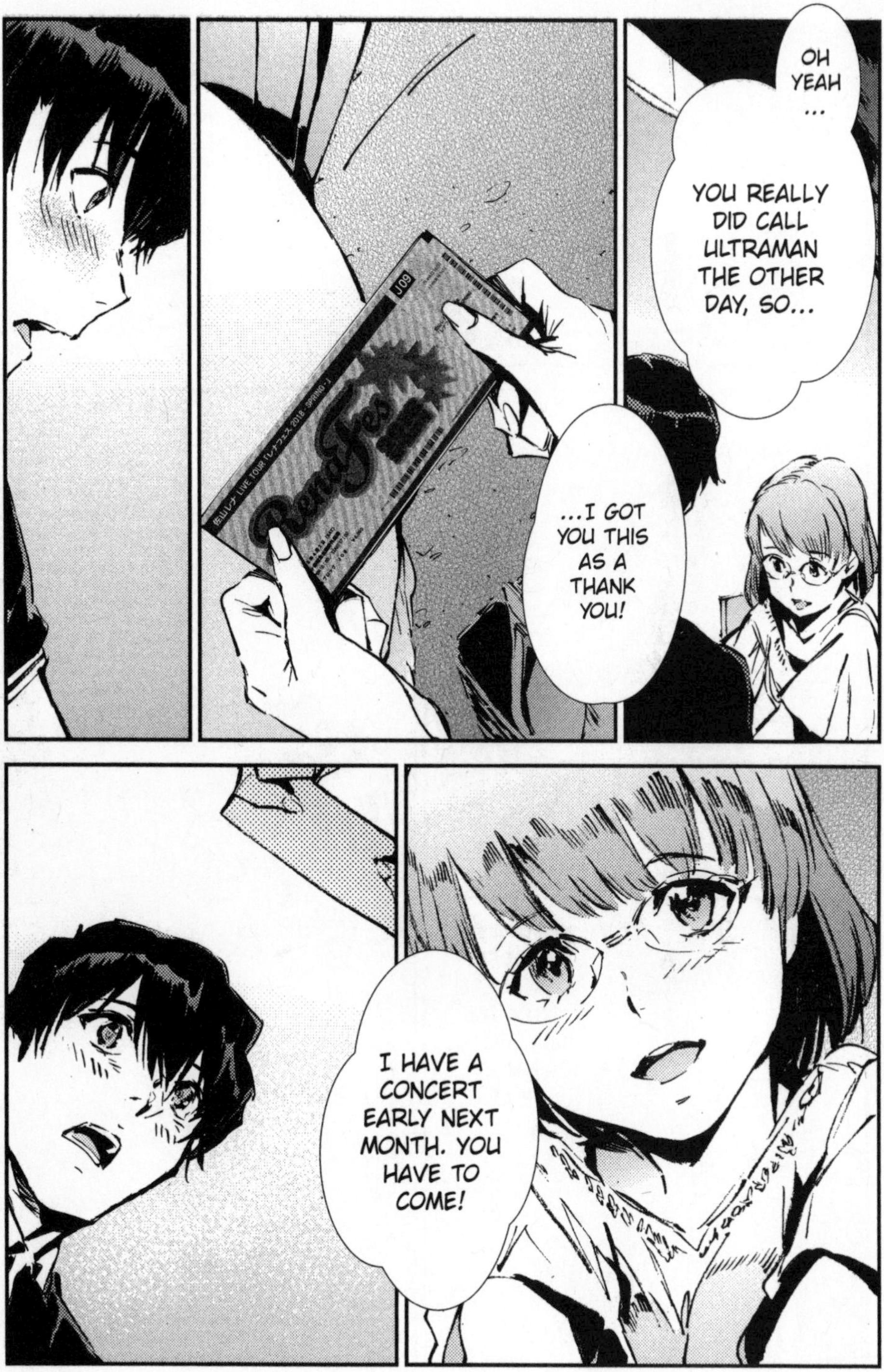

OH YEAH ...
YOU REALLY DID CALL ULTRAMAN THE OTHER DAY, SO...
...I GOT YOU THIS AS A THANK YOU!
J09
RenaFes
I HAVE A CONCERT EARLY NEXT MONTH. YOU HAVE TO COME!

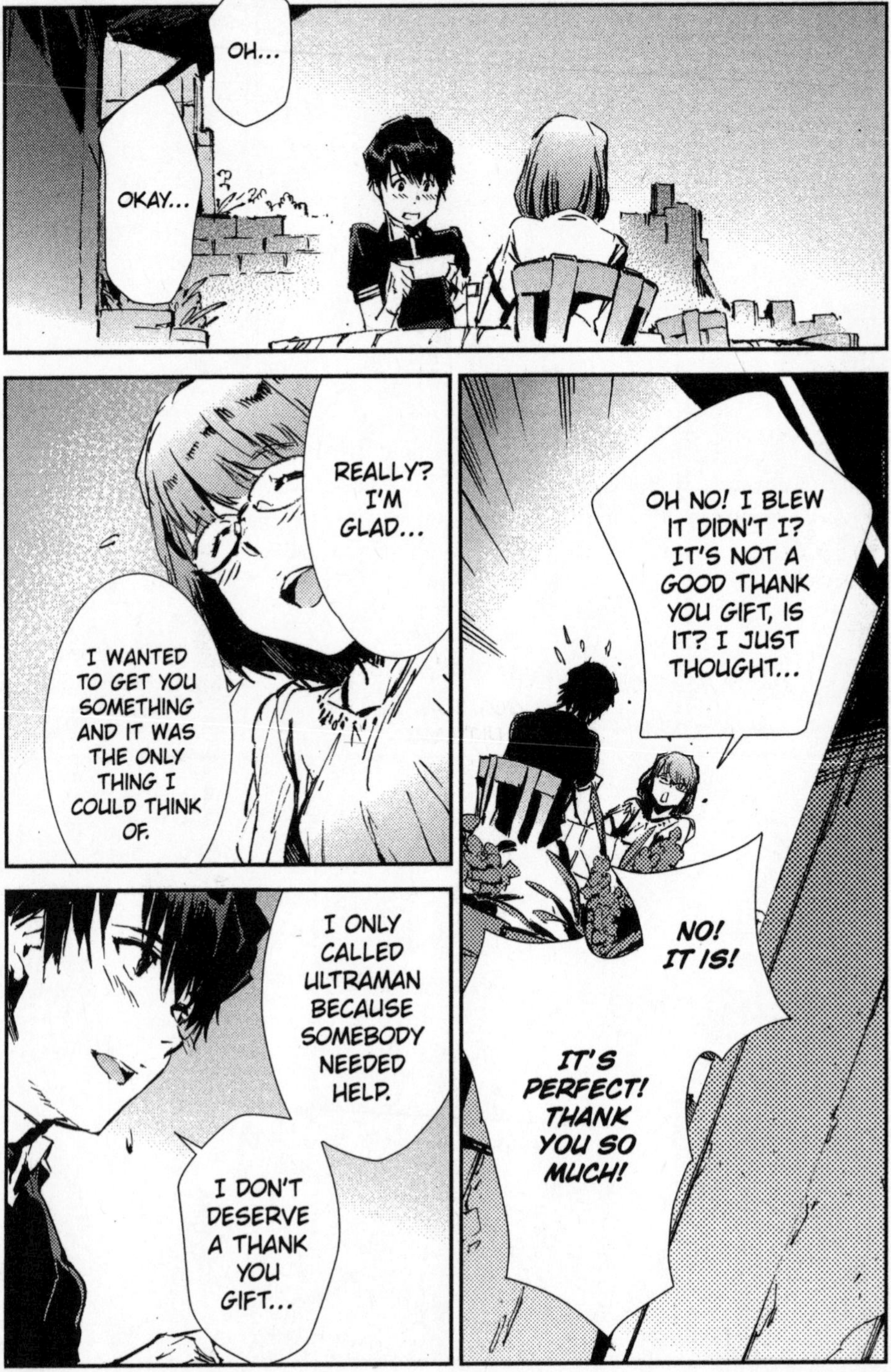
OH...
OKAY...
OH NO! I BLEW IT DIDN'T I? IT'S NOT A GOOD THANK YOU GIFT, IS IT? I JUST THOUGHT...
NO! IT IS!
IT'S PERFECT! THANK YOU SO MUCH!
REALLY? I'M GLAD...
I WANTED TO GET YOU SOMETHING AND IT WAS THE ONLY THING I COULD THINK OF.
I ONLY CALLED ULTRAMAN BECAUSE SOMEBODY NEEDED HELP.
I DON'T DESERVE A THANK YOU GIFT...

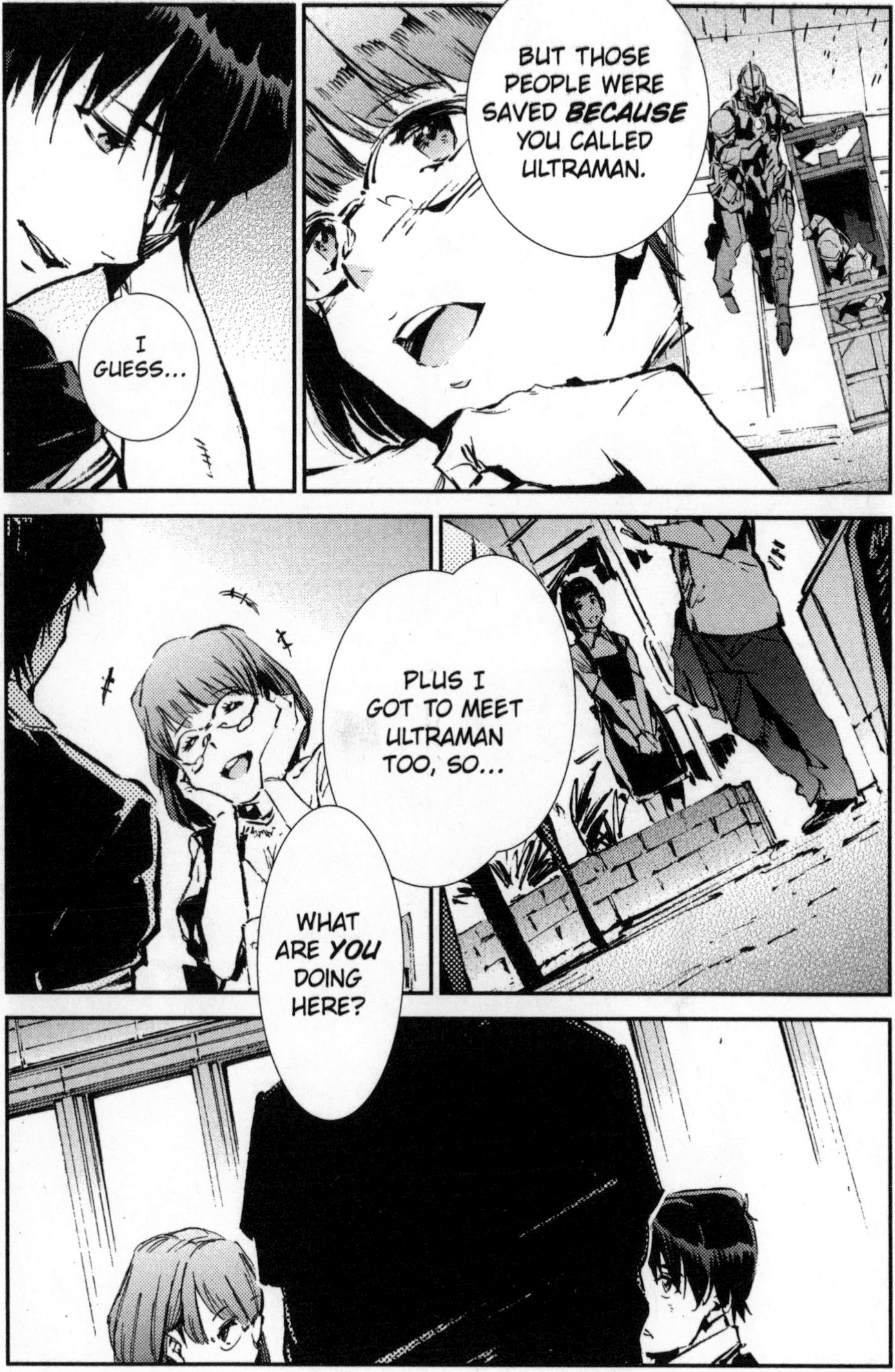
BUT THOSE PEOPLE WERE SAVED *BECAUSE* YOU CALLED ULTRAMAN.
I GUESS...
PLUS I GOT TO MEET ULTRAMAN TOO, SO...
WHAT ARE *YOU* DOING HERE?

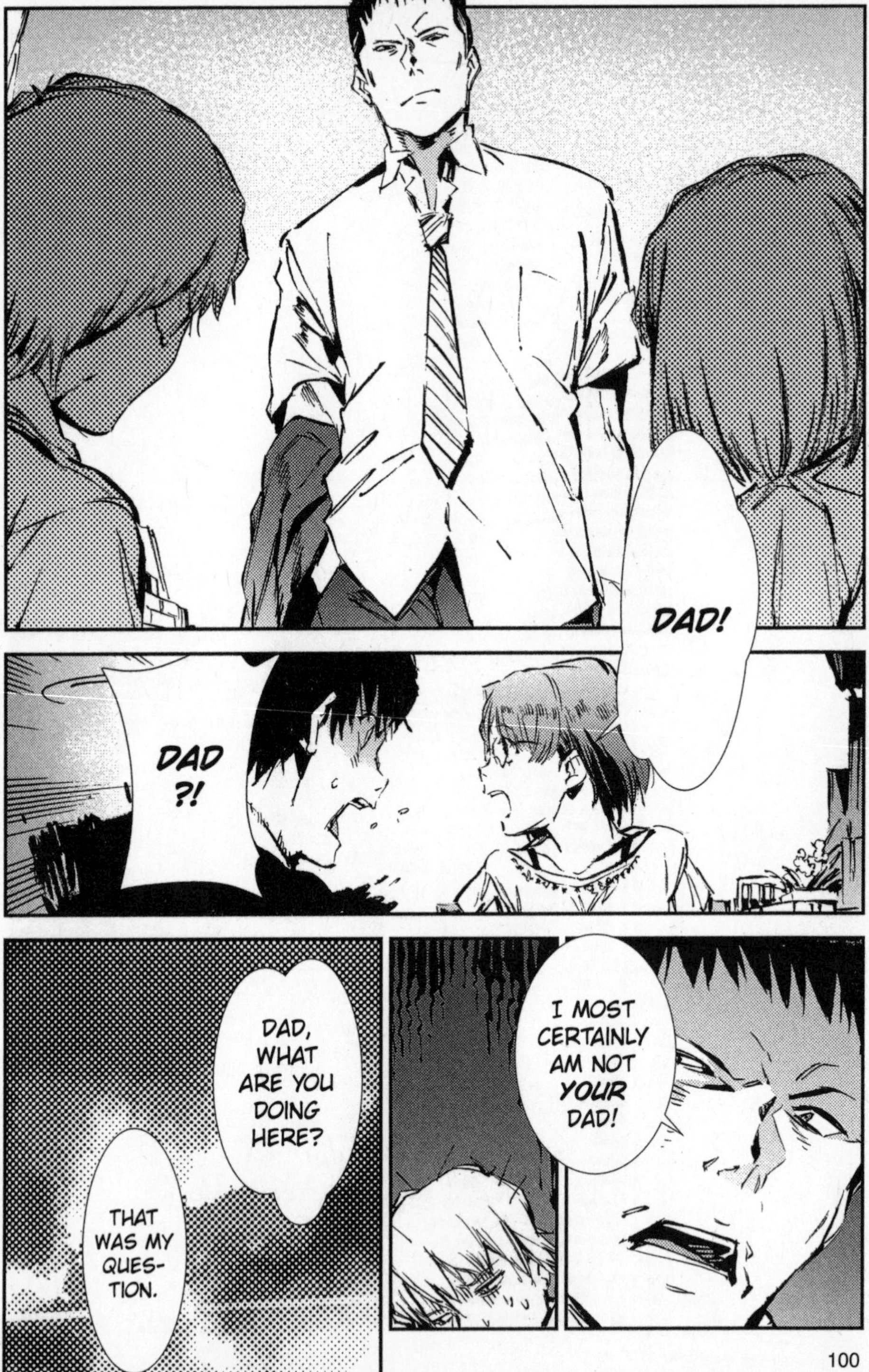
DAD!
DAD ?!
I MOST CERTAINLY AM NOT YOUR DAD!
DAD, WHAT ARE YOU DOING HERE?
THAT WAS MY QUES-TION.

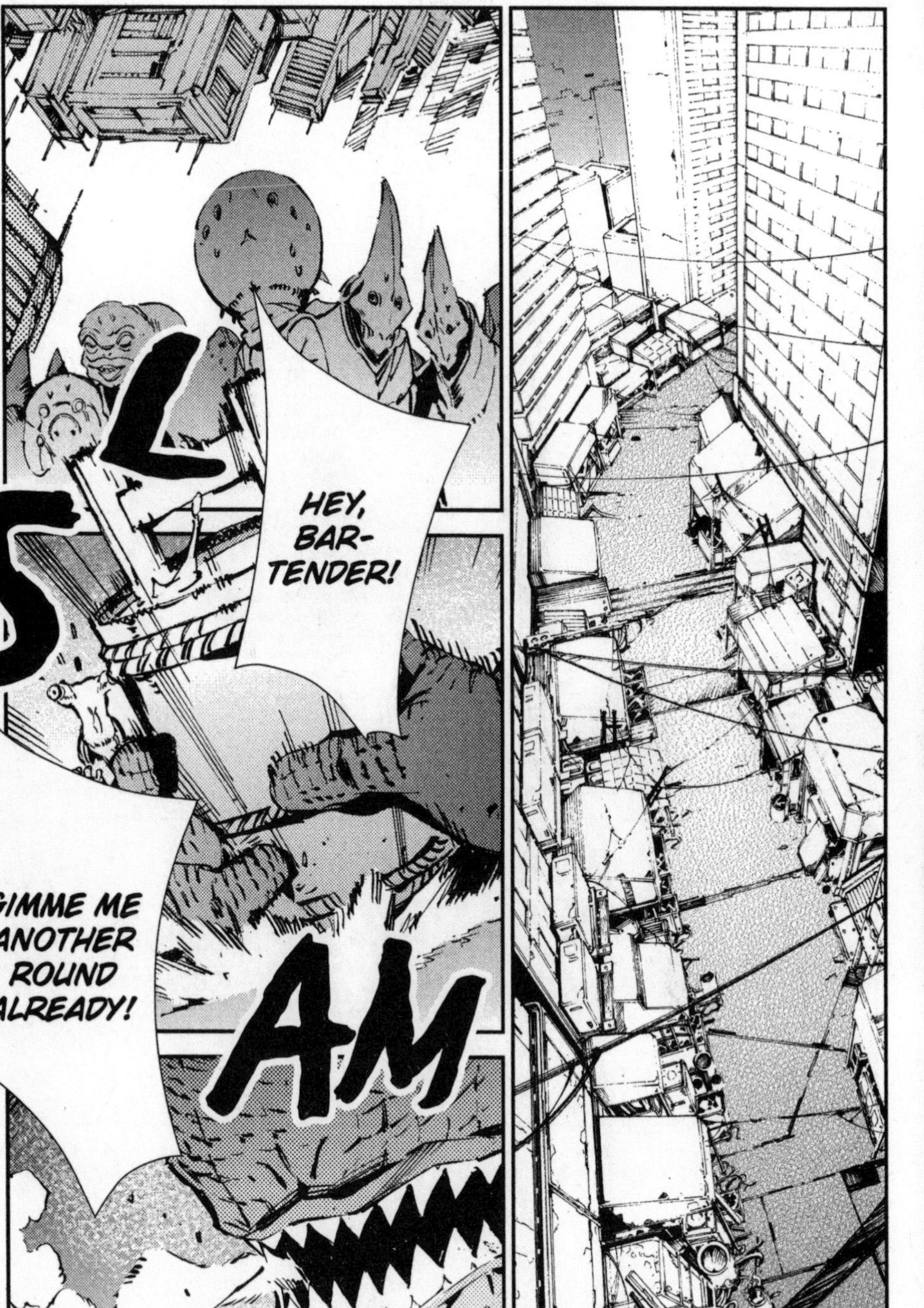
HEY, BAR-TENDER!
GIMME ME ANOTHER ROUND ALREADY!
SLAM

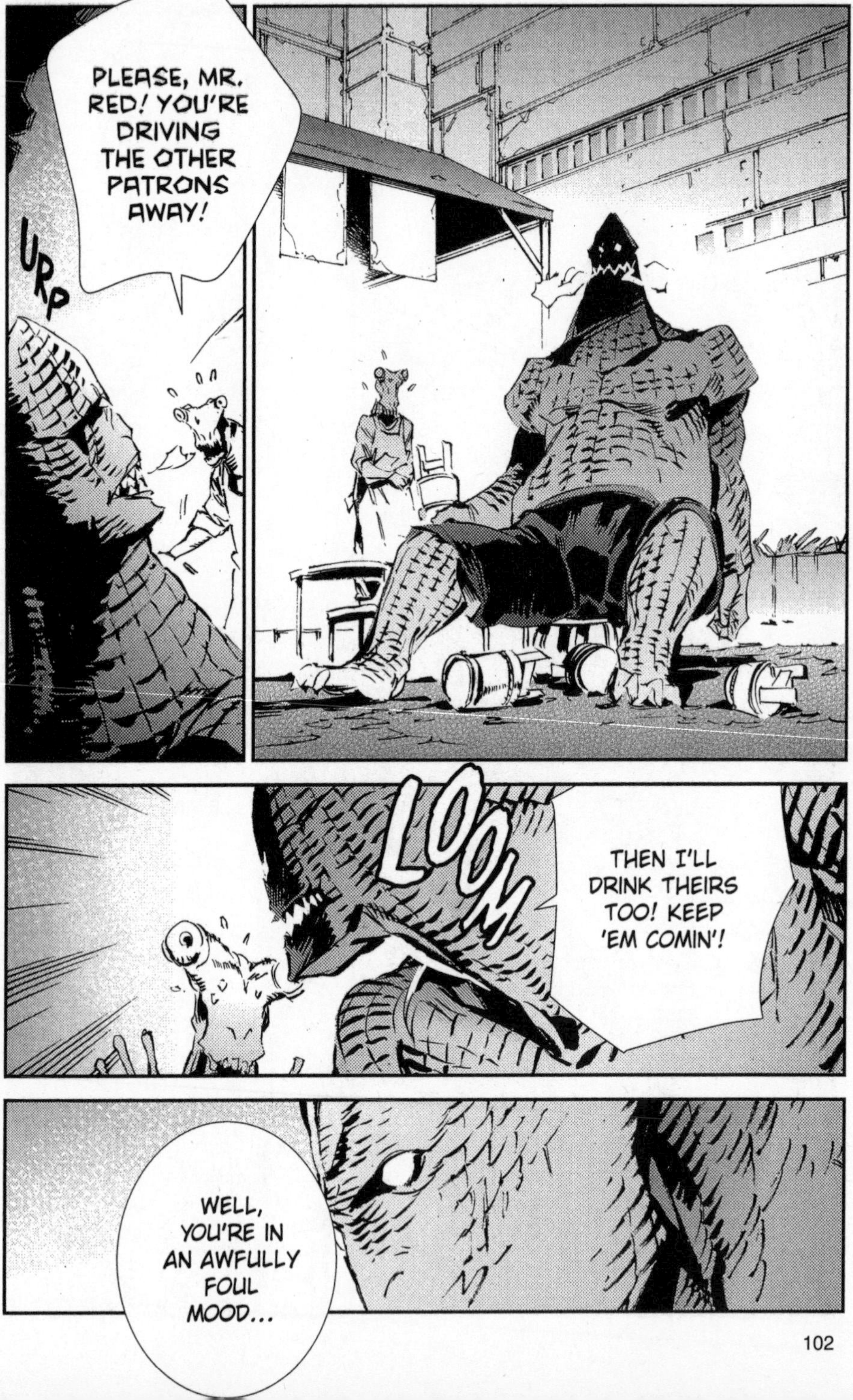
PLEASE, MR. RED! YOU'RE DRIVING THE OTHER PATRONS AWAY!
URP
LOOM
THEN I'LL DRINK THEIRS TOO! KEEP 'EM COMIN'!
WELL, YOU'RE IN AN AWFULLY FOUL MOOD...

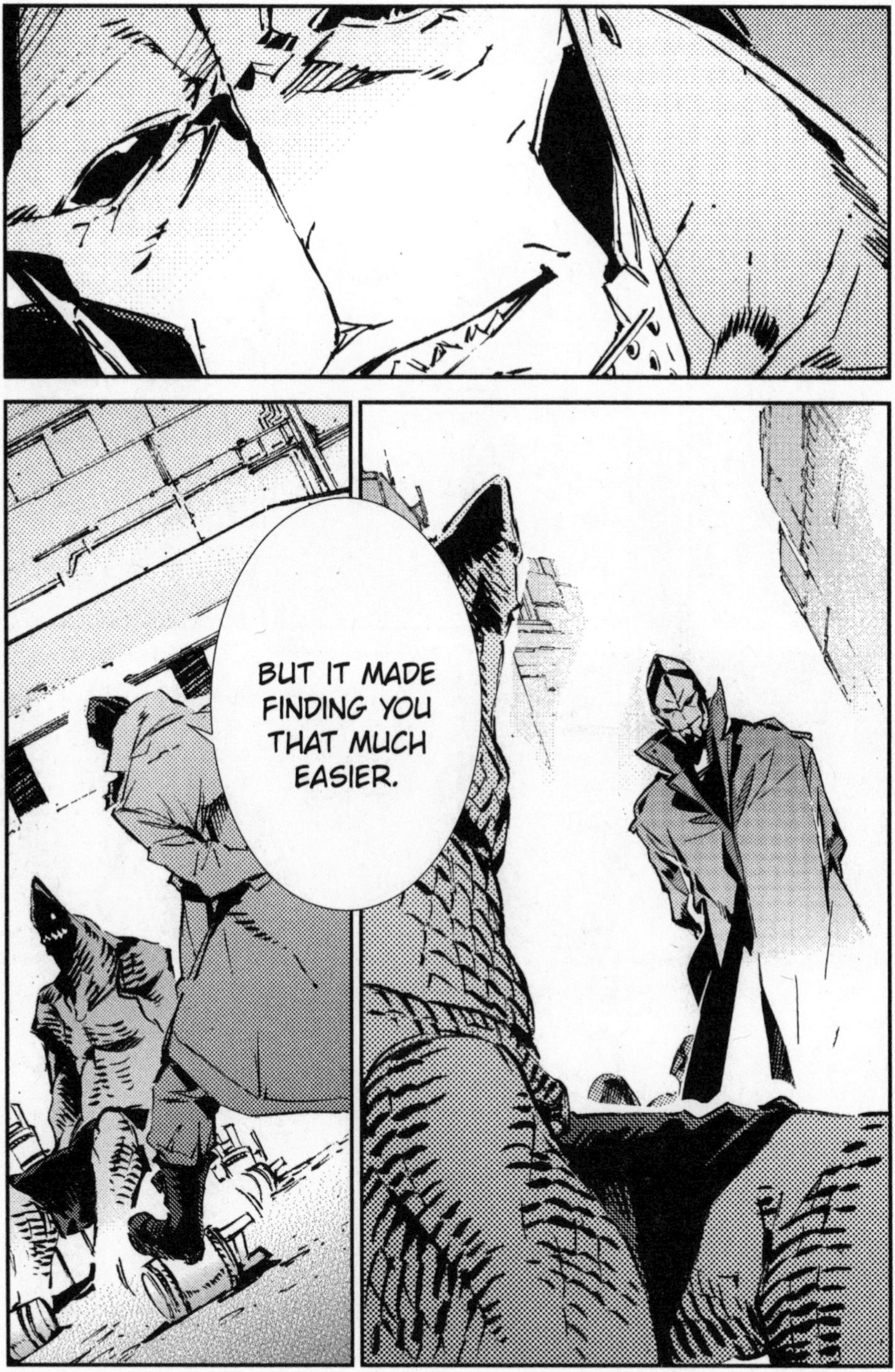
BUT IT MADE FINDING YOU THAT MUCH EASIER.

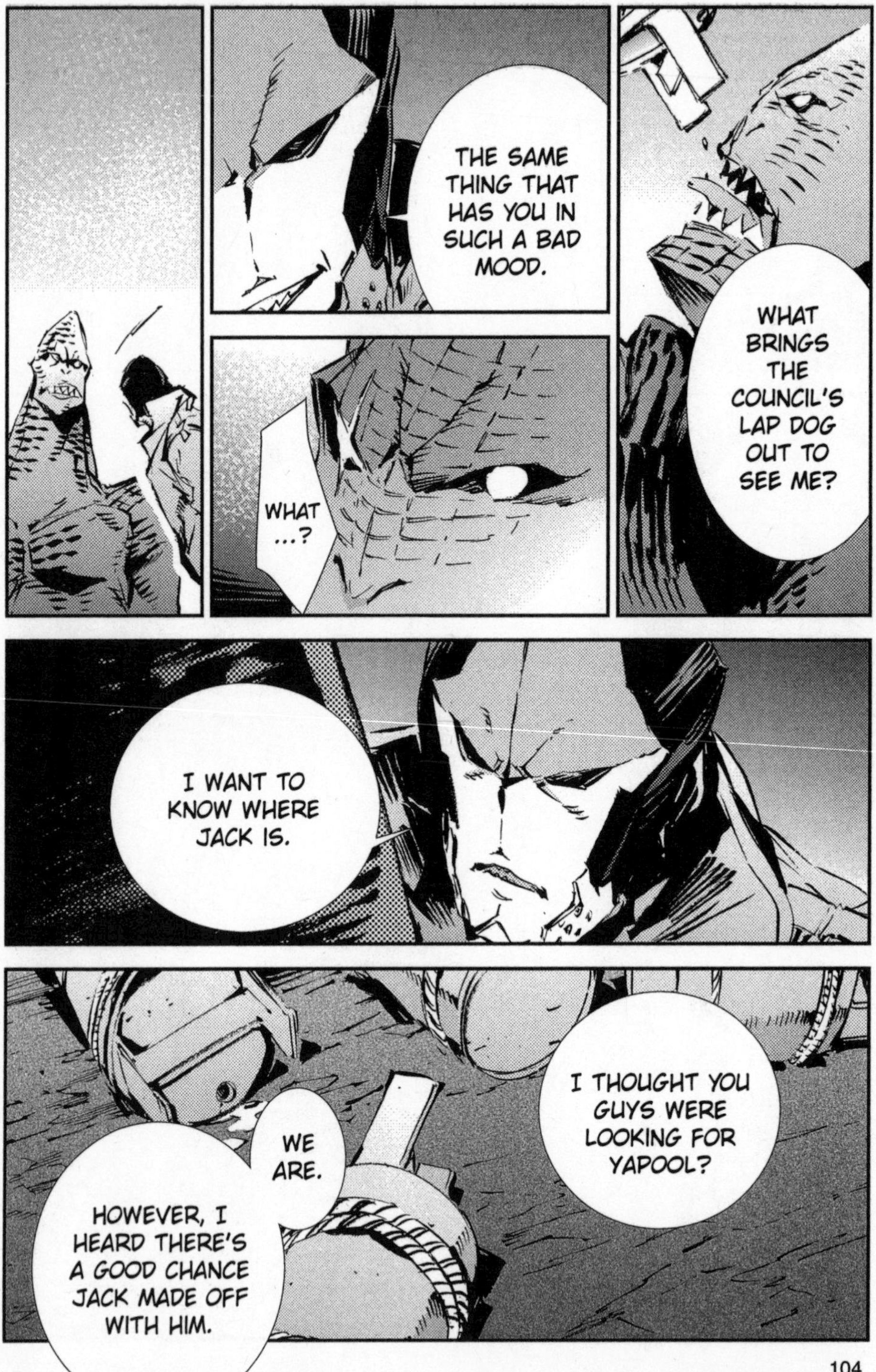
WHAT BRINGS THE COUNCIL'S LAP DOG OUT TO SEE ME?
THE SAME THING THAT HAS YOU IN SUCH A BAD MOOD.
WHAT ...?
I WANT TO KNOW WHERE JACK IS.
I THOUGHT YOU GUYS WERE LOOKING FOR YAPOOL?
WE ARE.
HOWEVER, I HEARD THERE'S A GOOD CHANCE JACK MADE OFF WITH HIM.

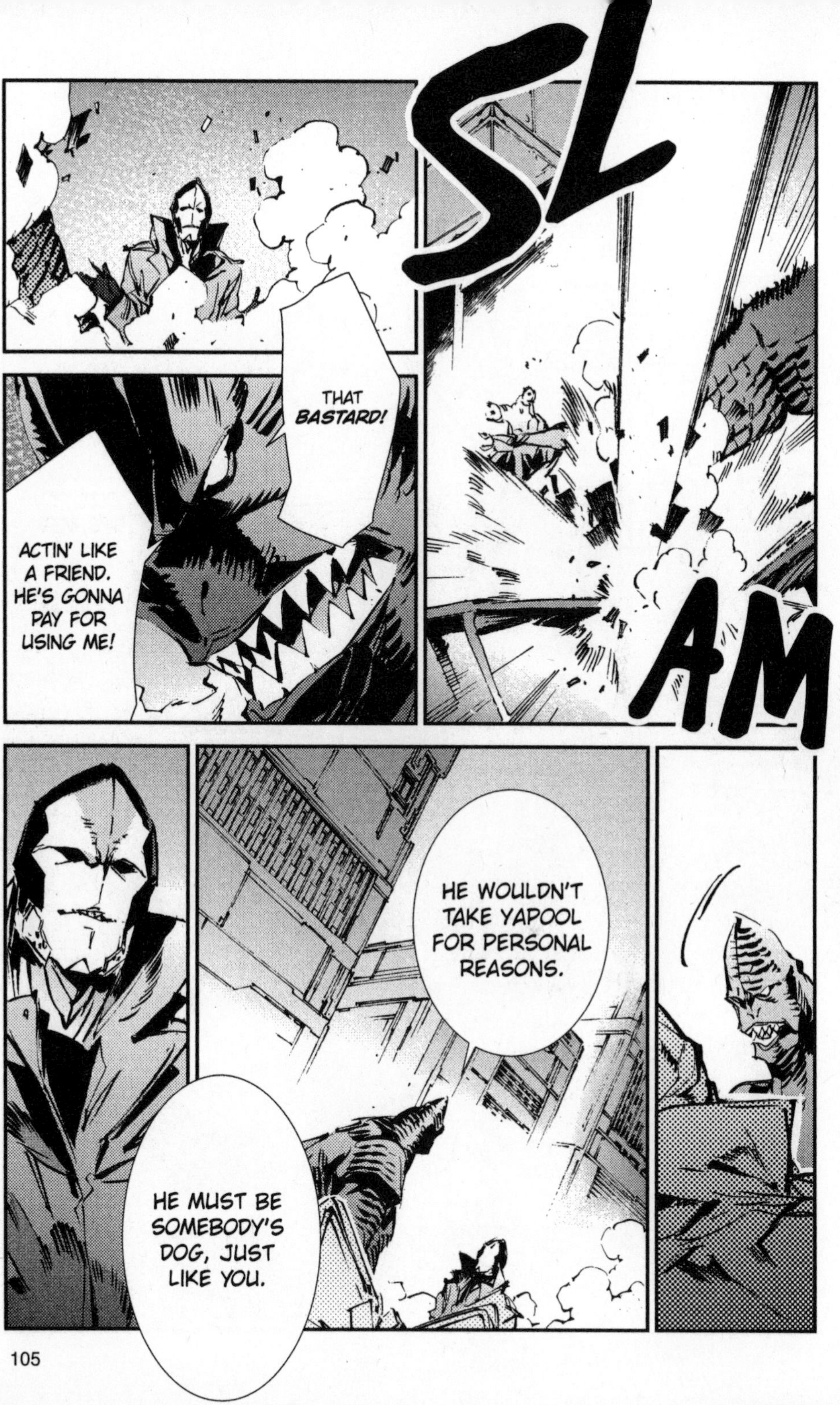
SL
AM
THAT BASTARD!
ACTIN' LIKE A FRIEND. HE'S GONNA PAY FOR USING ME!
HE WOULDN'T TAKE YAPOOL FOR PERSONAL REASONS.
HE MUST BE SOMEBODY'S DOG, JUST LIKE YOU.

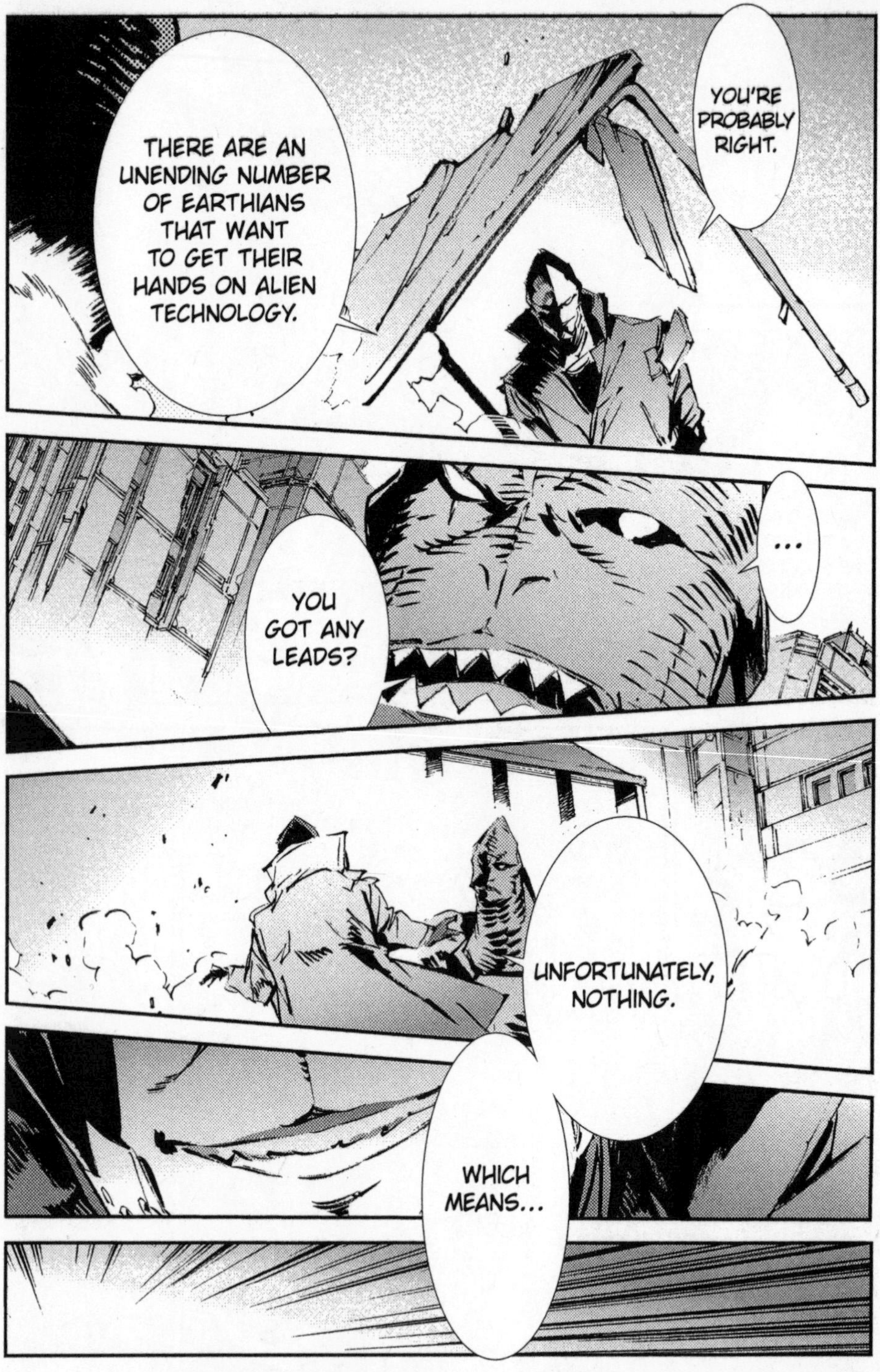
YOU'RE PROBABLY RIGHT.
THERE ARE AN UNENDING NUMBER OF EARTHIANS THAT WANT TO GET THEIR HANDS ON ALIEN TECHNOLOGY.
...
YOU GOT ANY LEADS?
UNFORTUNATELY, NOTHING.
WHICH MEANS...

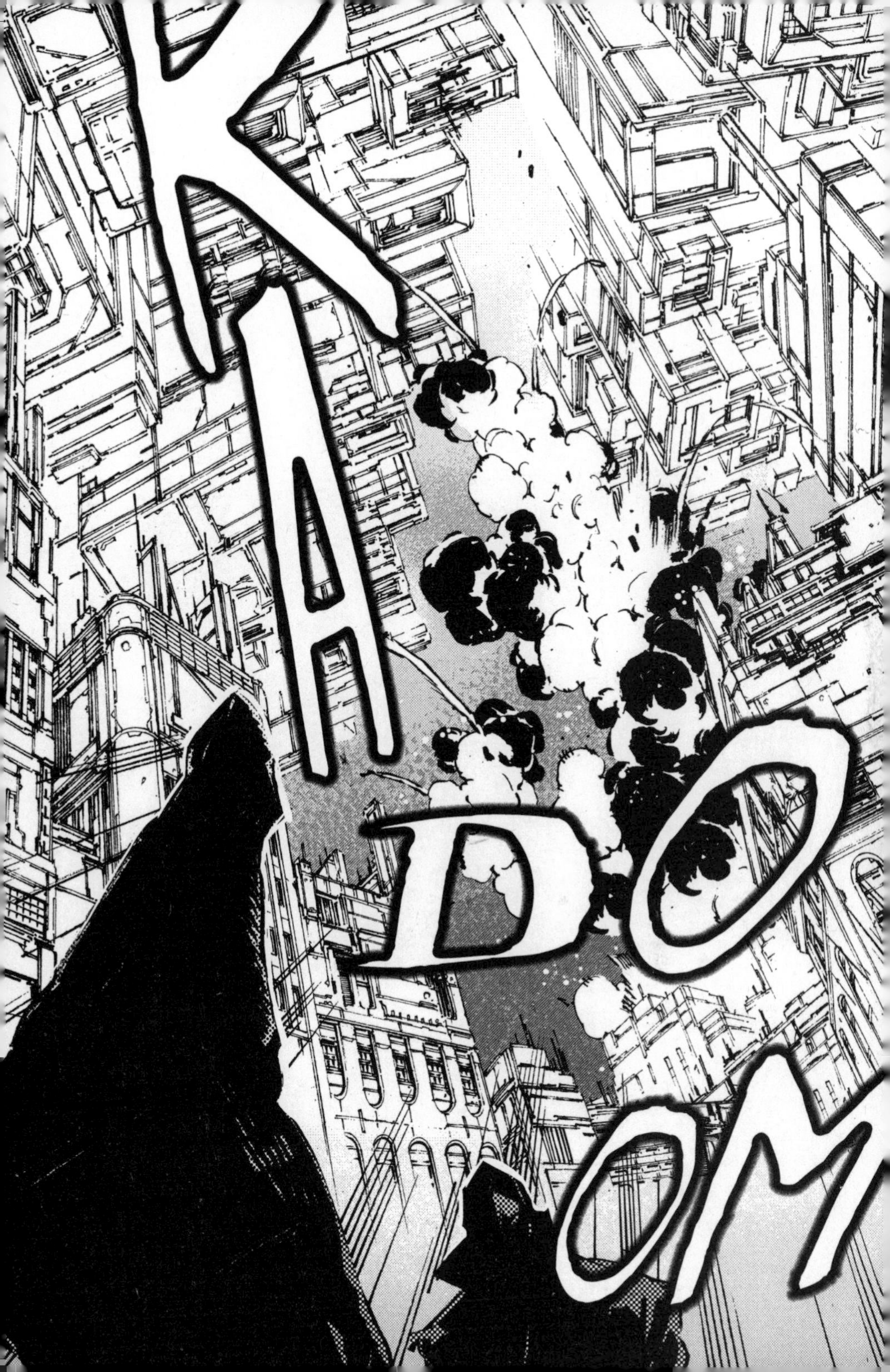
KADOOM

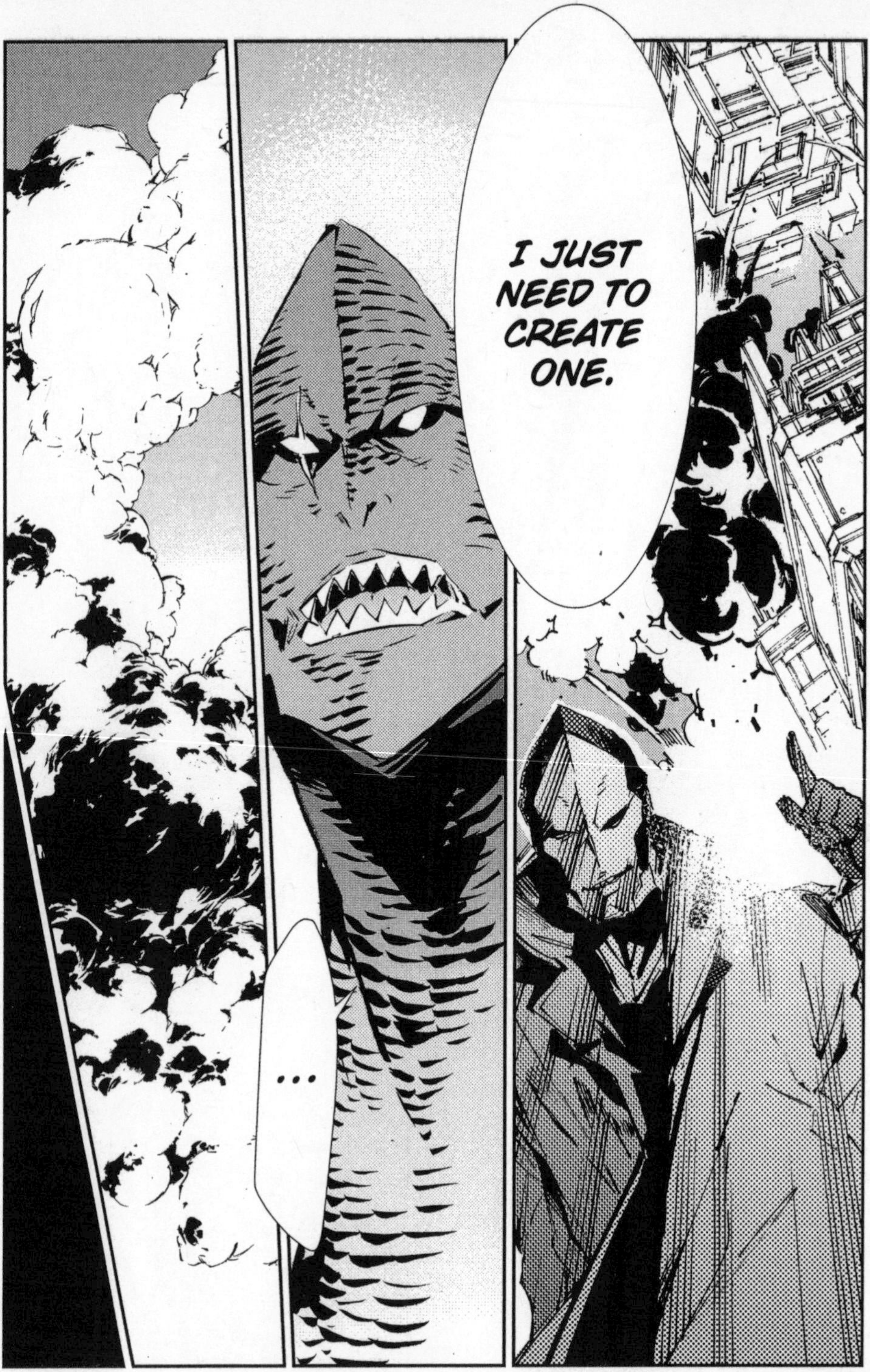
I JUST NEED TO CREATE ONE.
...

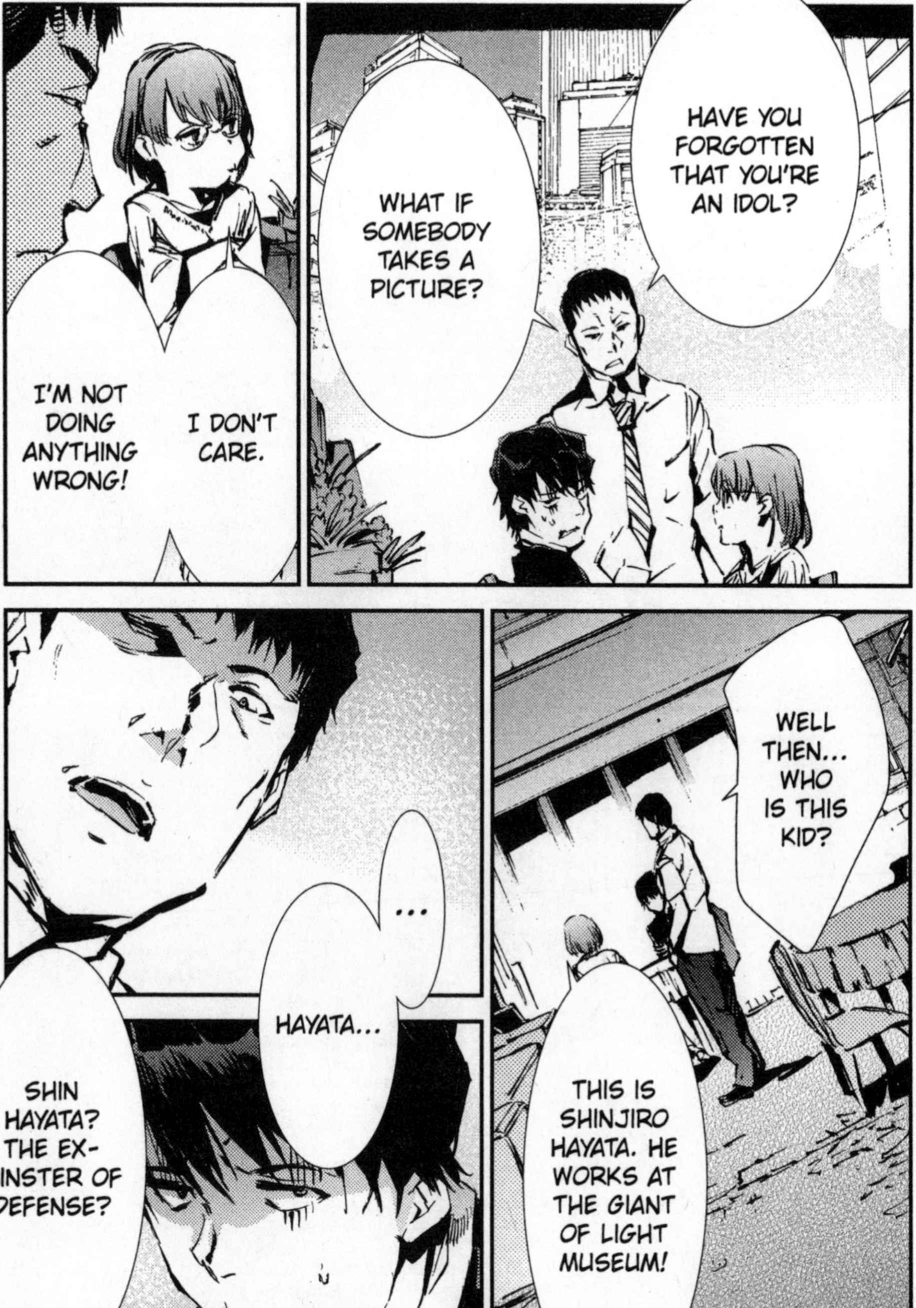
HAVE YOU FORGOTTEN THAT YOU'RE AN IDOL?
WHAT IF SOMEBODY TAKES A PICTURE?
I DON'T CARE.
I'M NOT DOING ANYTHING WRONG!
WELL THEN... WHO IS THIS KID?
THIS IS SHINJIRO HAYATA. HE WORKS AT THE GIANT OF LIGHT MUSEUM!
...
HAYATA...
SHIN HAYATA? THE EX-MINSTER OF DEFENSE?

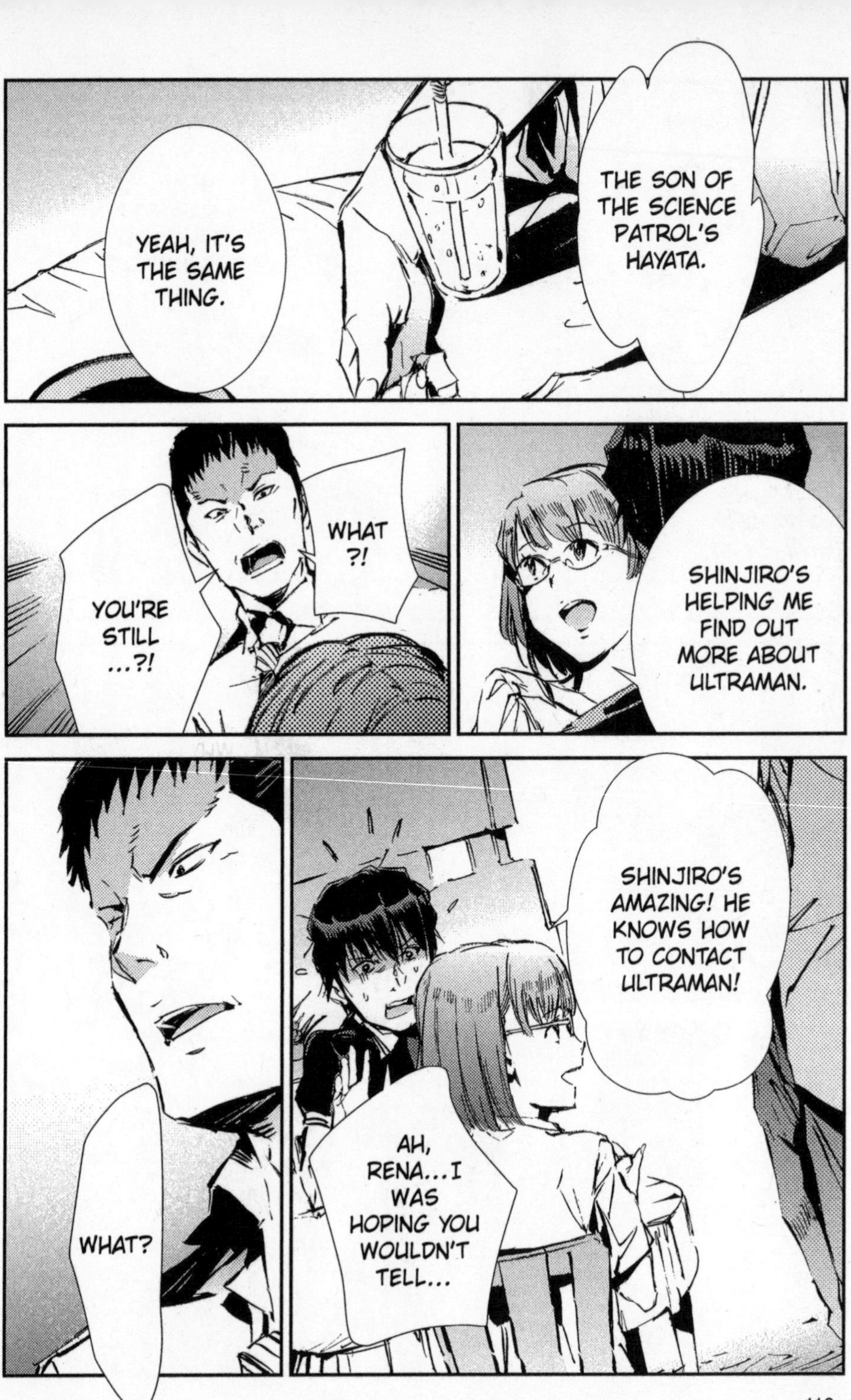
THE SON OF THE SCIENCE PATROL'S HAYATA.
YEAH, IT'S THE SAME THING.
SHINJIRO'S HELPING ME FIND OUT MORE ABOUT ULTRAMAN.
WHAT ?!
YOU'RE STILL ...?!
SHINJIRO'S AMAZING! HE KNOWS HOW TO CONTACT ULTRAMAN!
AH, RENA...I WAS HOPING YOU WOULDN'T TELL...
WHAT?

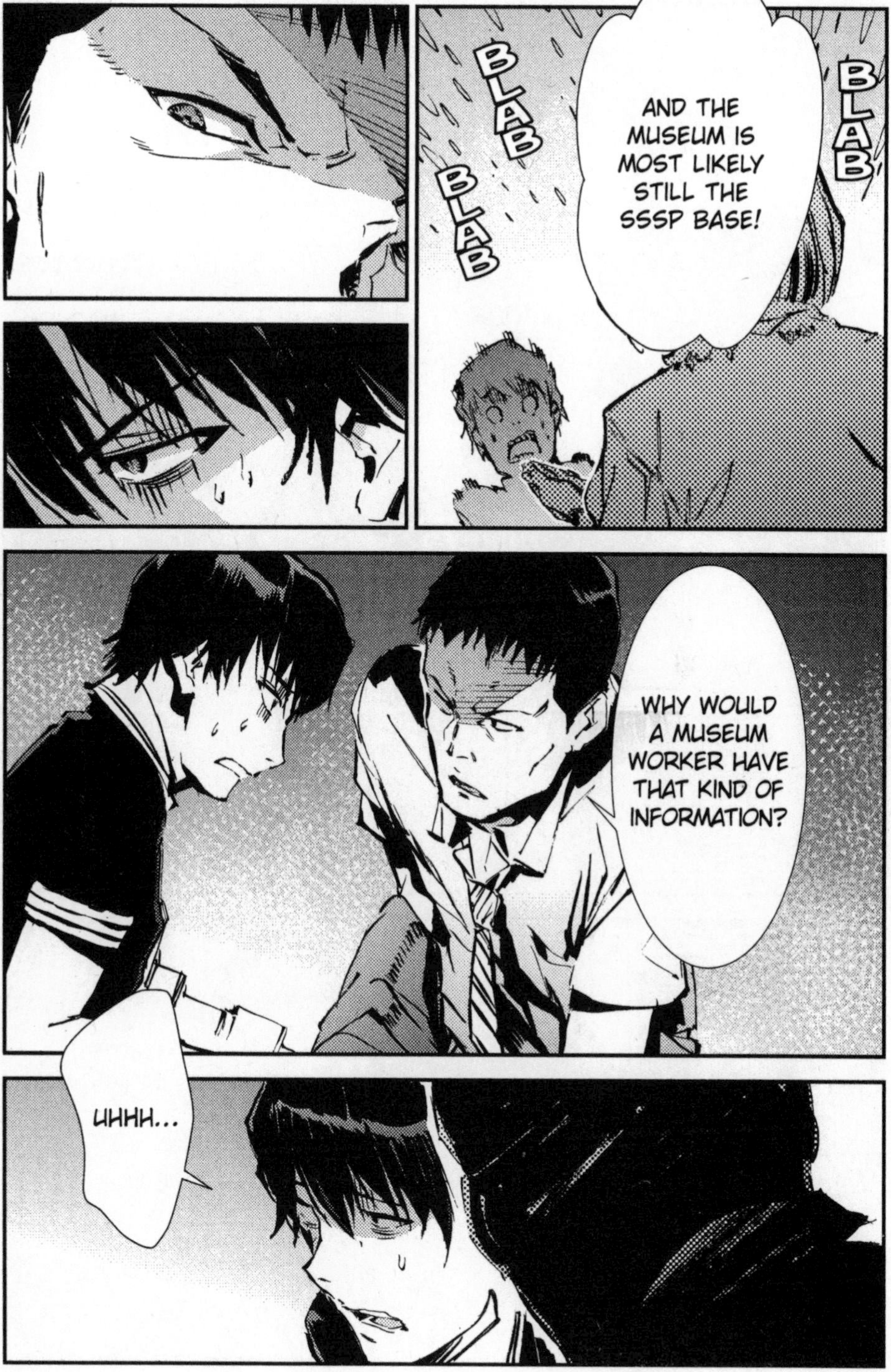
BLAB
AND THE MUSEUM IS MOST LIKELY STILL THE SSSP BASE!
BLAB
BLAB
WHY WOULD A MUSEUM WORKER HAVE THAT KIND OF INFORMATION?
UHHH...

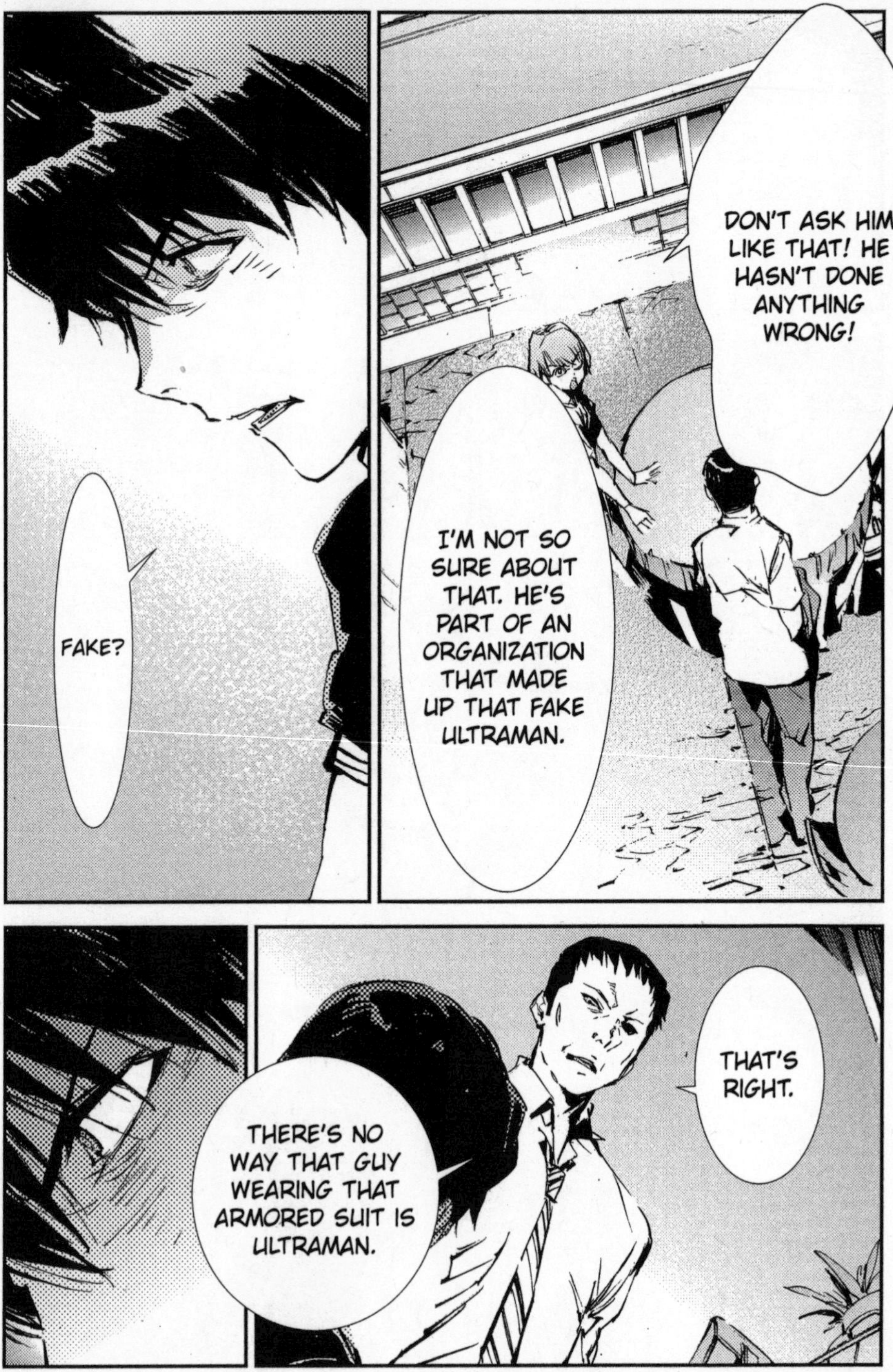
DON'T ASK HIM LIKE THAT! HE HASN'T DONE ANYTHING WRONG!
I'M NOT SO SURE ABOUT THAT. HE'S PART OF AN ORGANIZATION THAT MADE UP THAT FAKE ULTRAMAN.
FAKE?
THAT'S RIGHT.
THERE'S NO WAY THAT GUY WEARING THAT ARMORED SUIT IS ULTRAMAN.

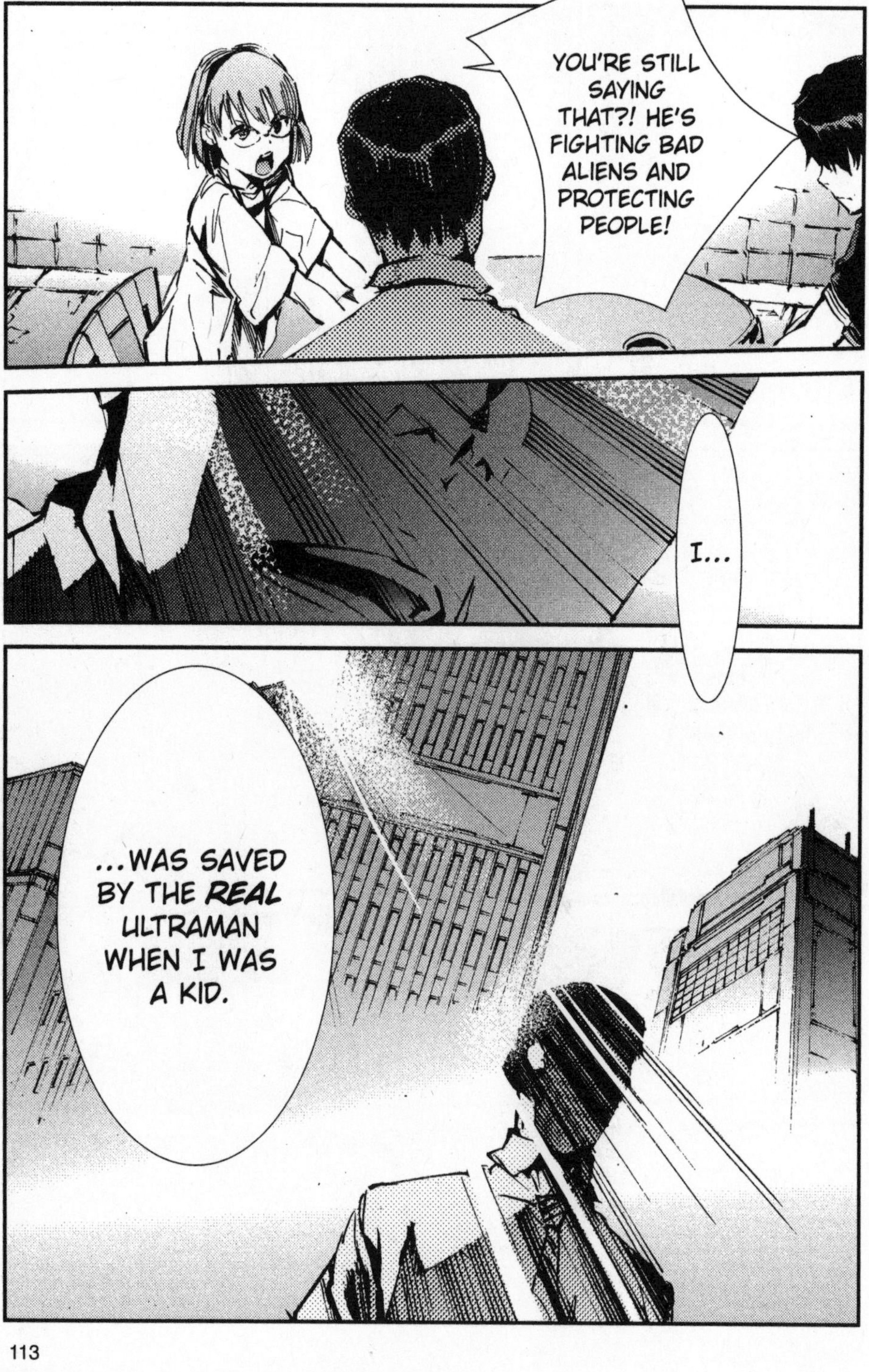
YOU'RE STILL SAYING THAT?! HE'S FIGHTING BAD ALIENS AND PROTECTING PEOPLE!
I...
...WAS SAVED BY THE *REAL* ULTRAMAN WHEN I WAS A KID.

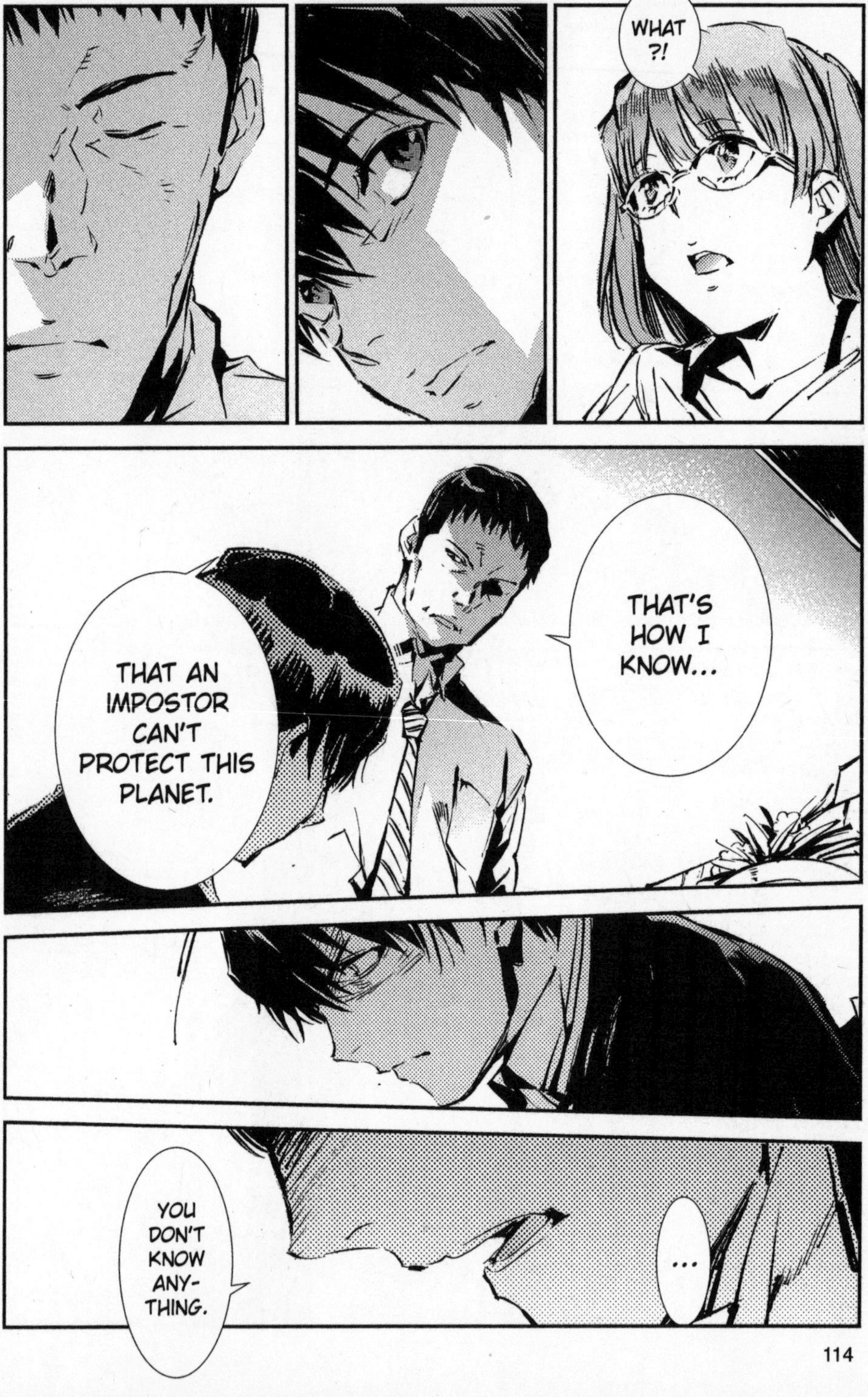
WHAT ?!
THAT'S HOW I KNOW...
THAT AN IMPOSTOR CAN'T PROTECT THIS PLANET.
...
YOU DON'T KNOW ANYTHING.

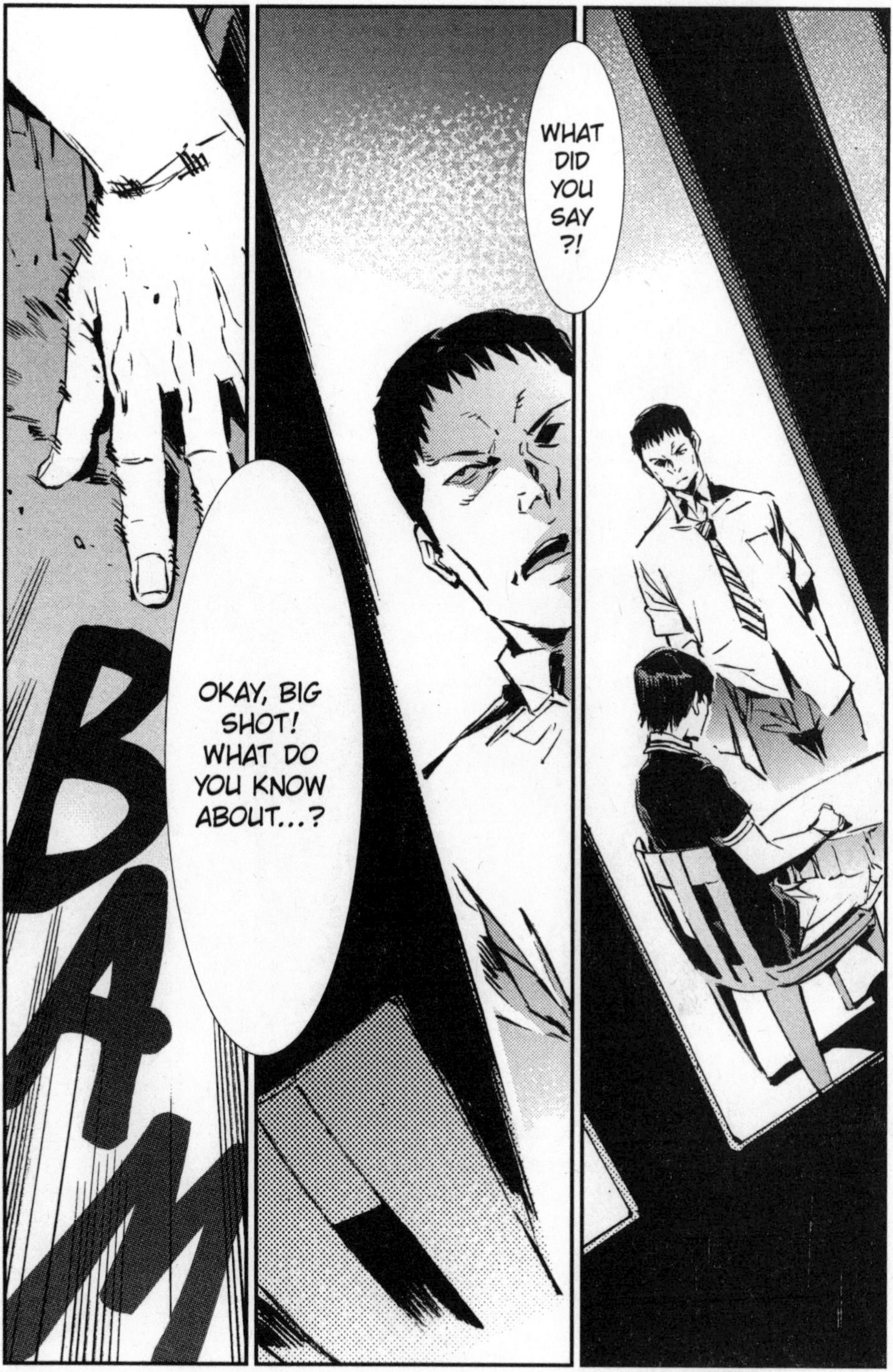
WHAT DID YOU SAY ?!
OKAY, BIG SHOT! WHAT DO YOU KNOW ABOUT...?
BAM

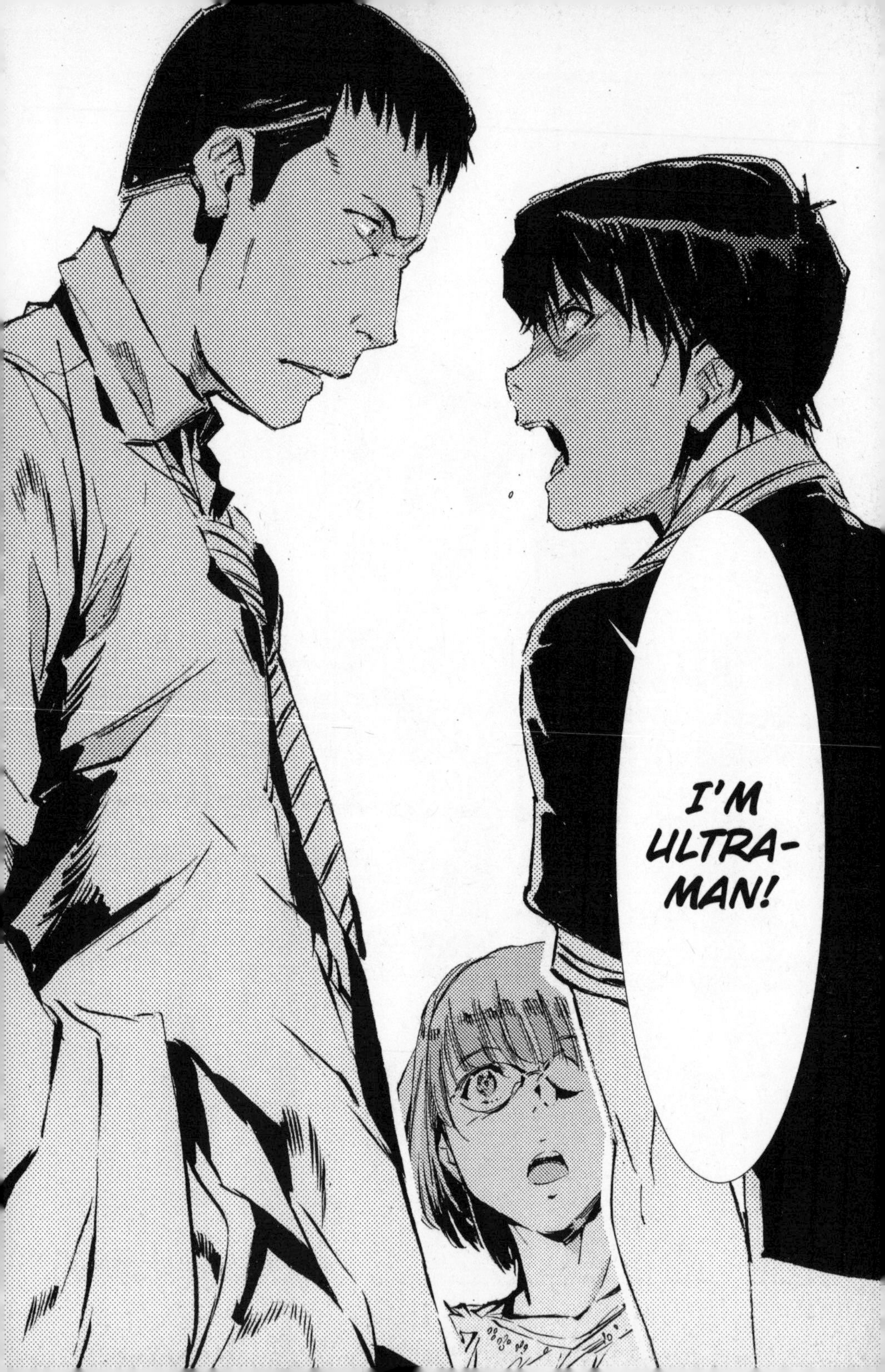
I'M ULTRA-MAN!

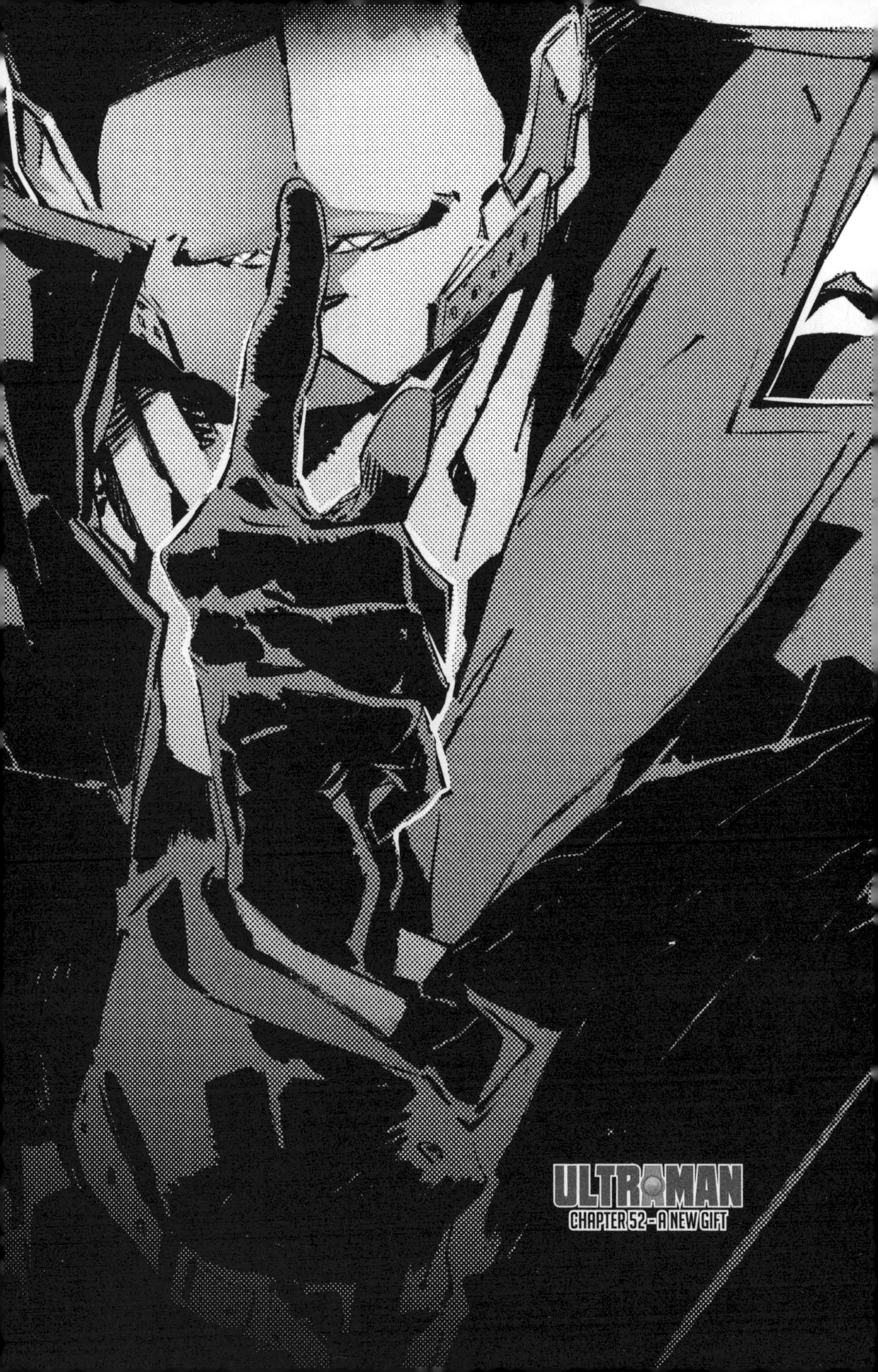
ULTRAMAN
CHAPTER 52 - A NEW GIFT

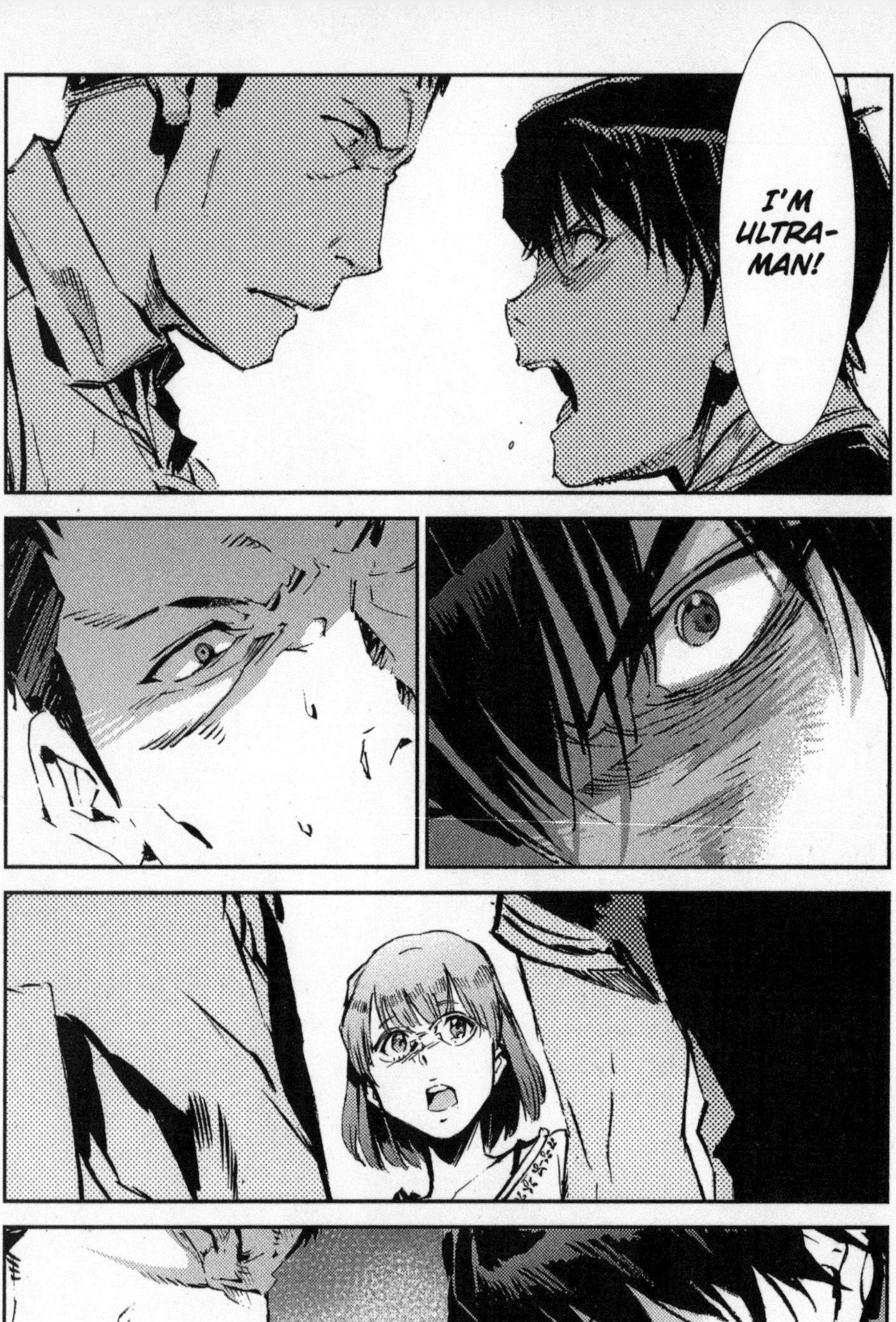
I'M ULTRA-MAN!

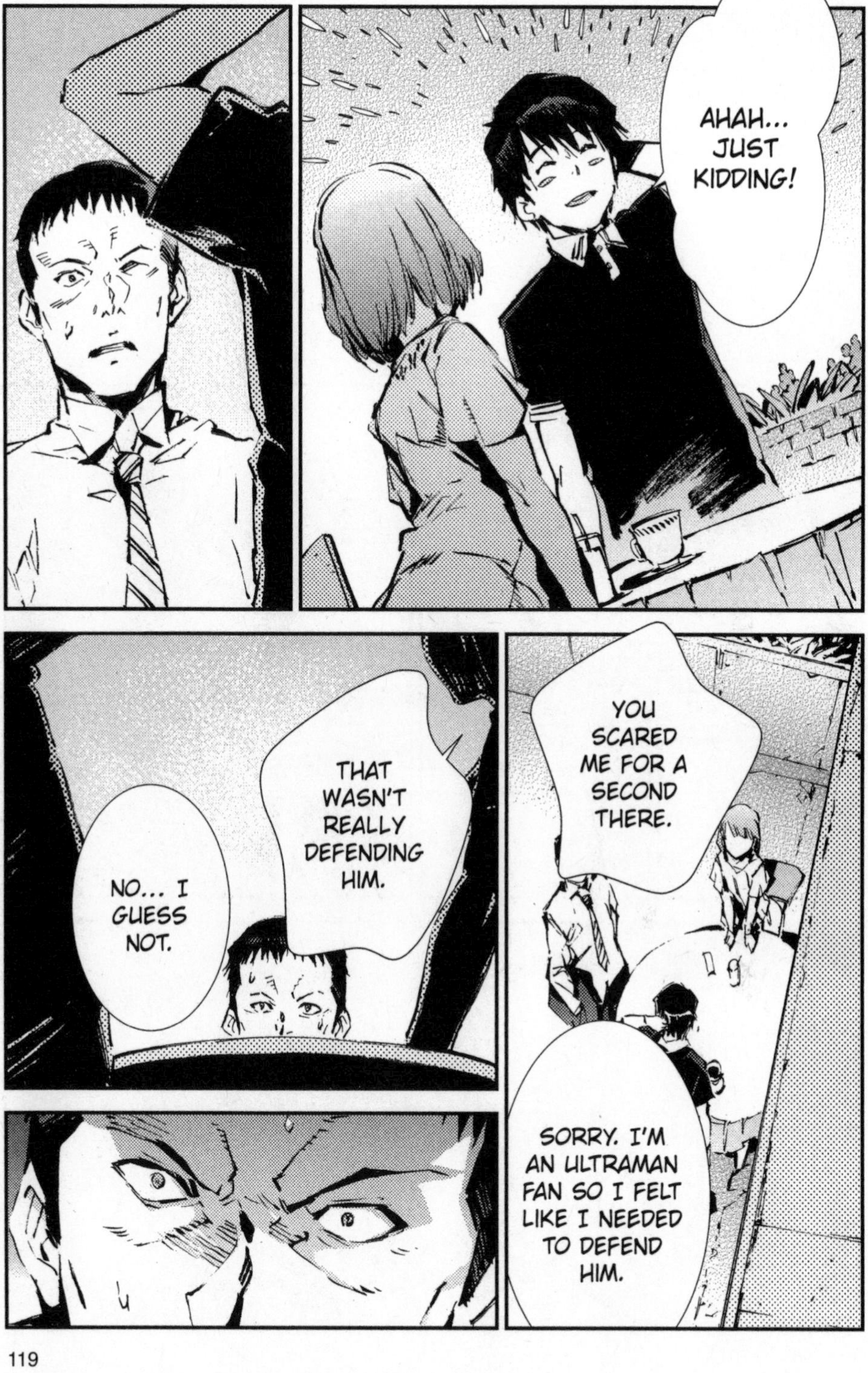
AHAH... JUST KIDDING!
YOU SCARED ME FOR A SECOND THERE.
SORRY. I'M AN ULTRAMAN FAN SO I FELT LIKE I NEEDED TO DEFEND HIM.
THAT WASN'T REALLY DEFENDING HIM.
NO... I GUESS NOT.

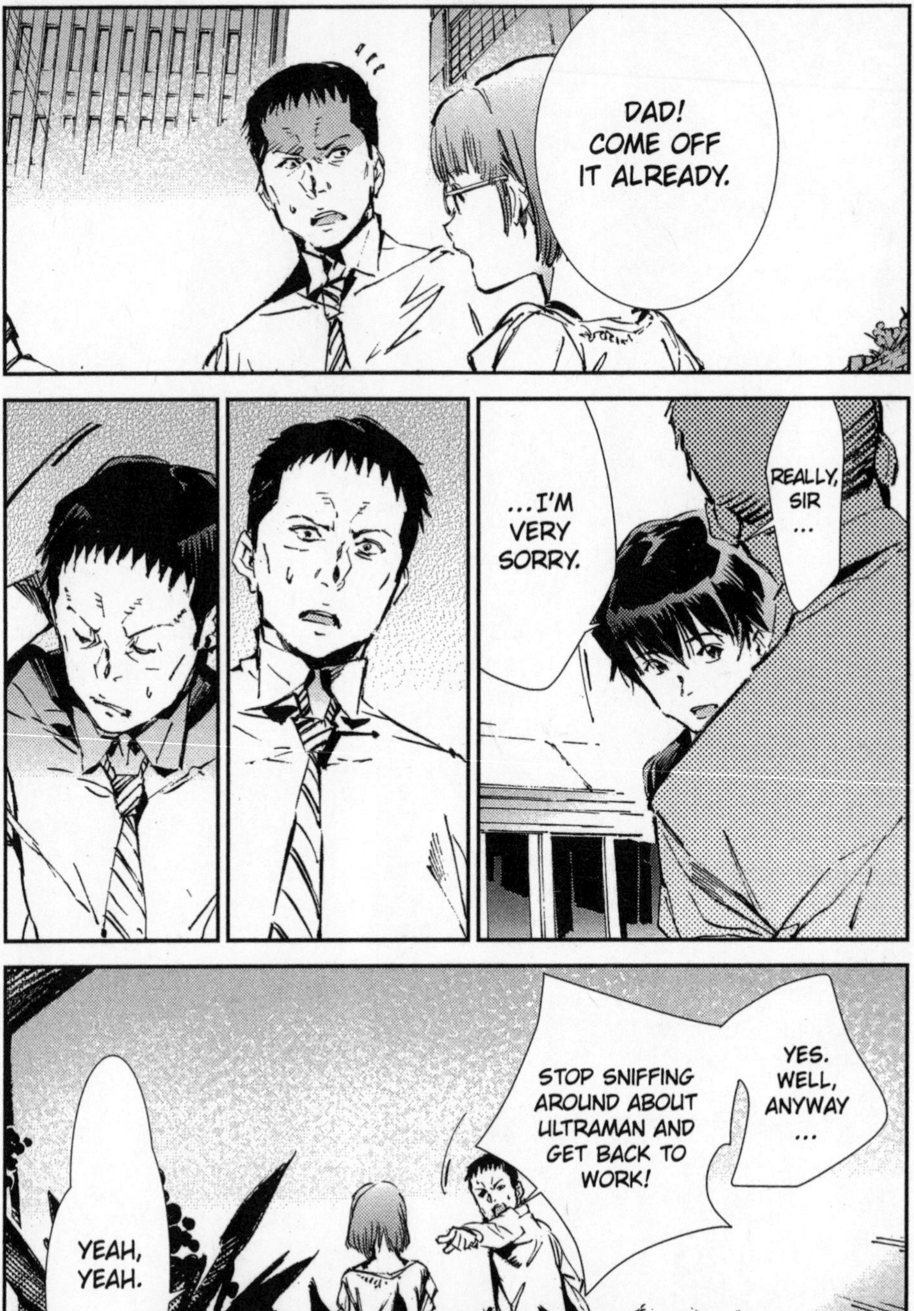
DAD! COME OFF IT ALREADY.
REALLY, SIR ...
...I'M VERY SORRY.
YES. WELL, ANYWAY ...
STOP SNIFFING AROUND ABOUT ULTRAMAN AND GET BACK TO WORK!
YEAH, YEAH.

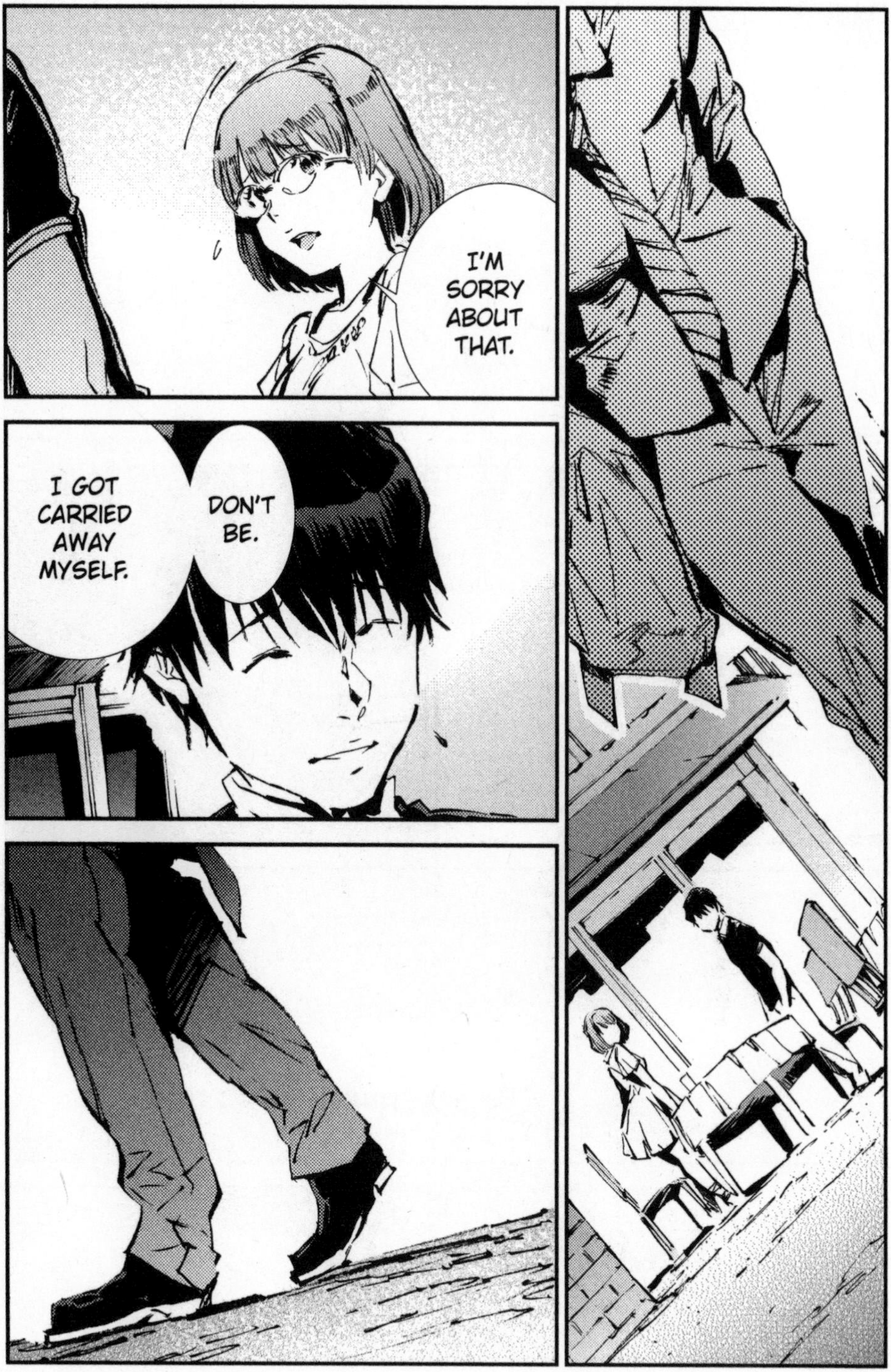
I'M SORRY ABOUT THAT.
DON'T BE.
I GOT CARRIED AWAY MYSELF.

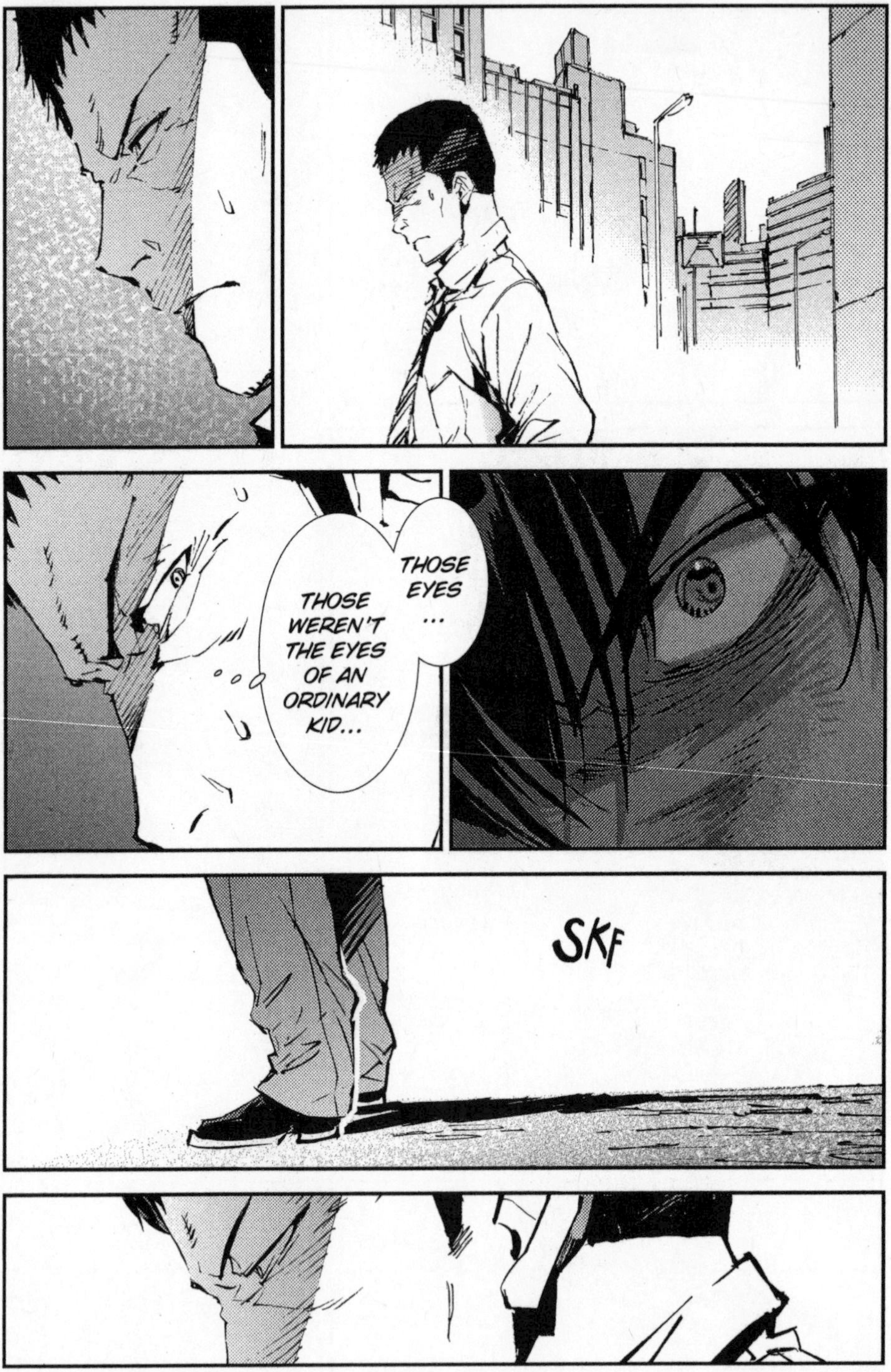
THOSE EYES...
THOSE WEREN'T THE EYES OF AN ORDINARY KID...
SKF

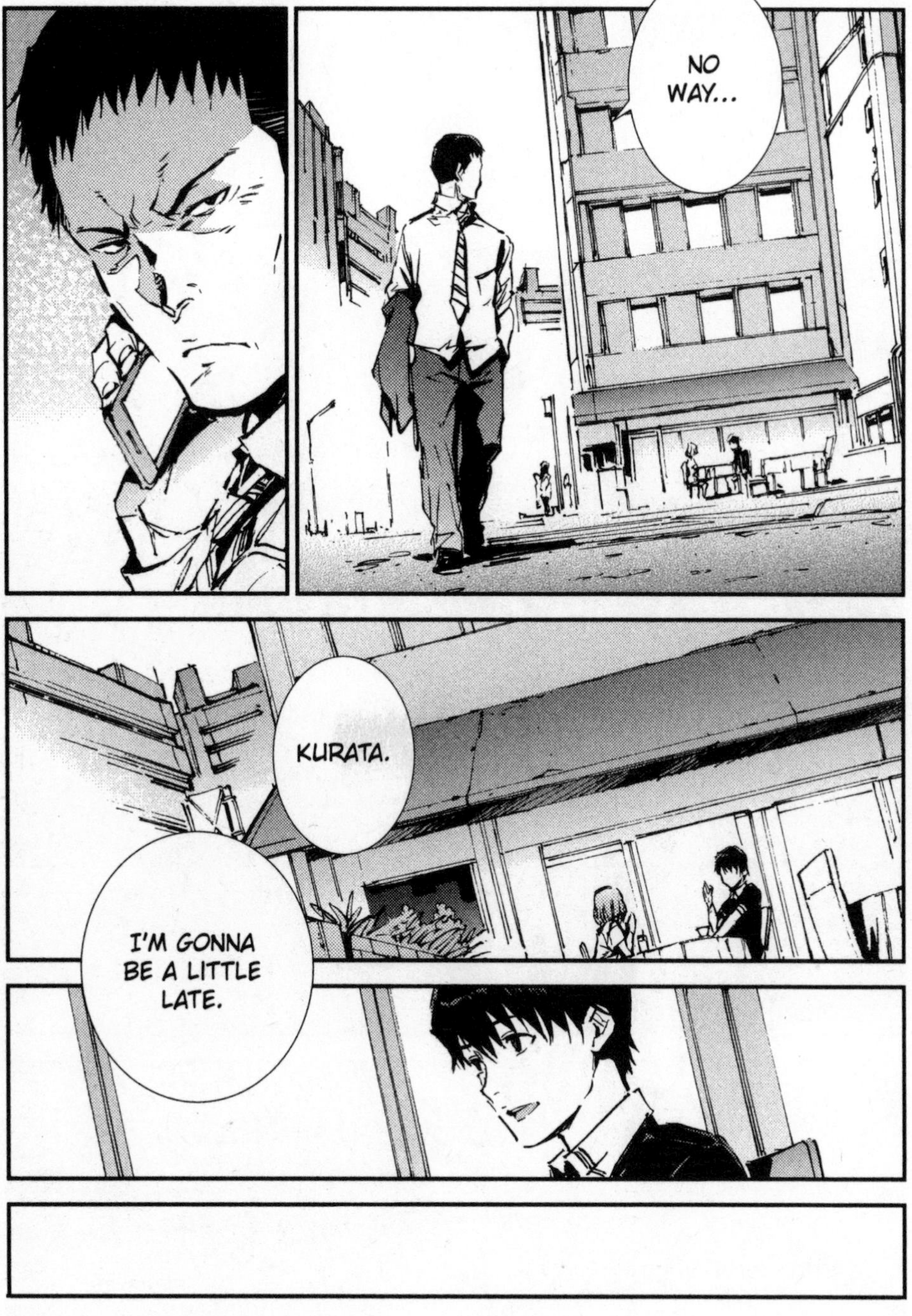
NO WAY...
KURATA.
I'M GONNA BE A LITTLE LATE.

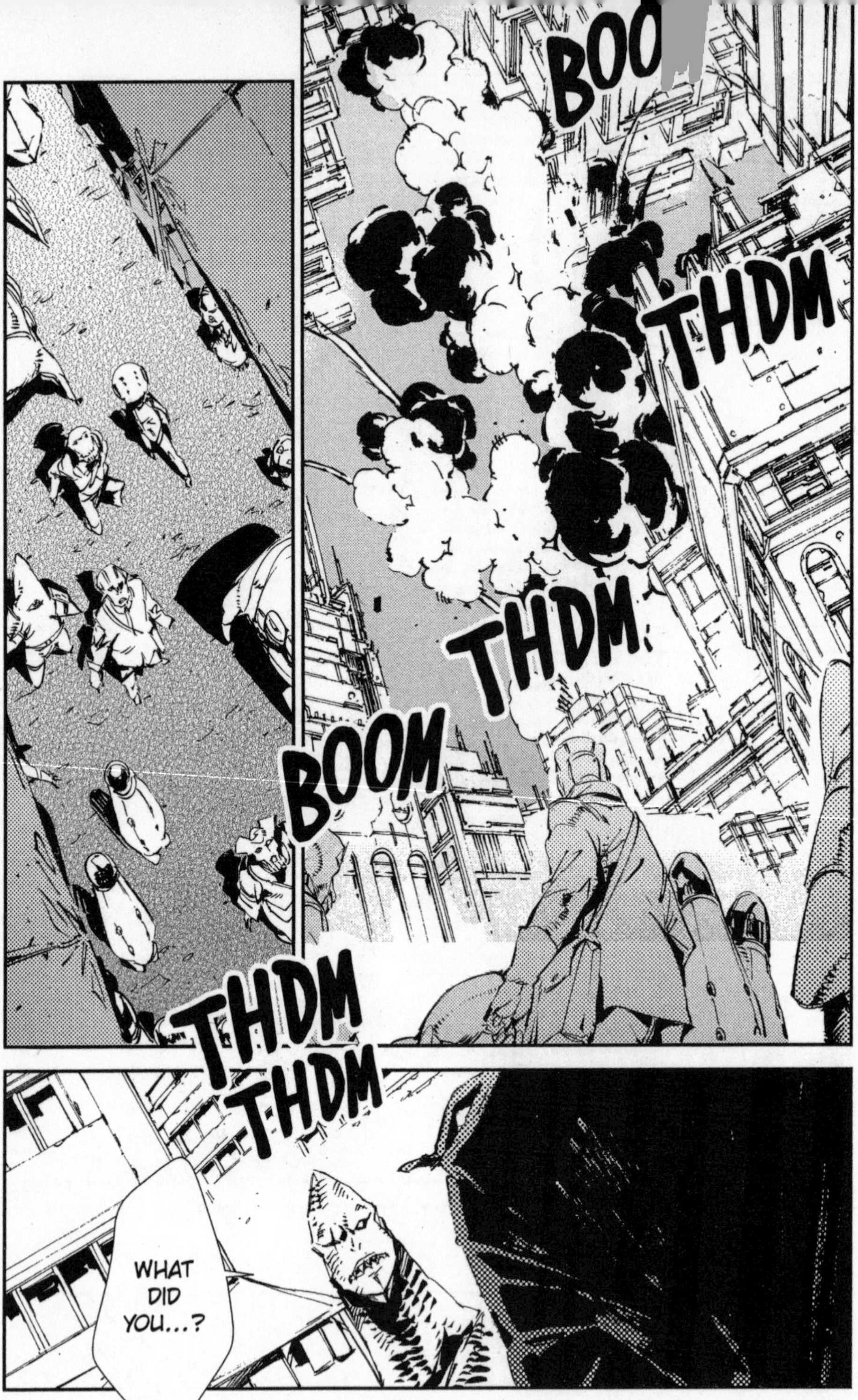
BOO
THDM
THDM
BOOM
THDM
THDM
WHAT DID YOU...?

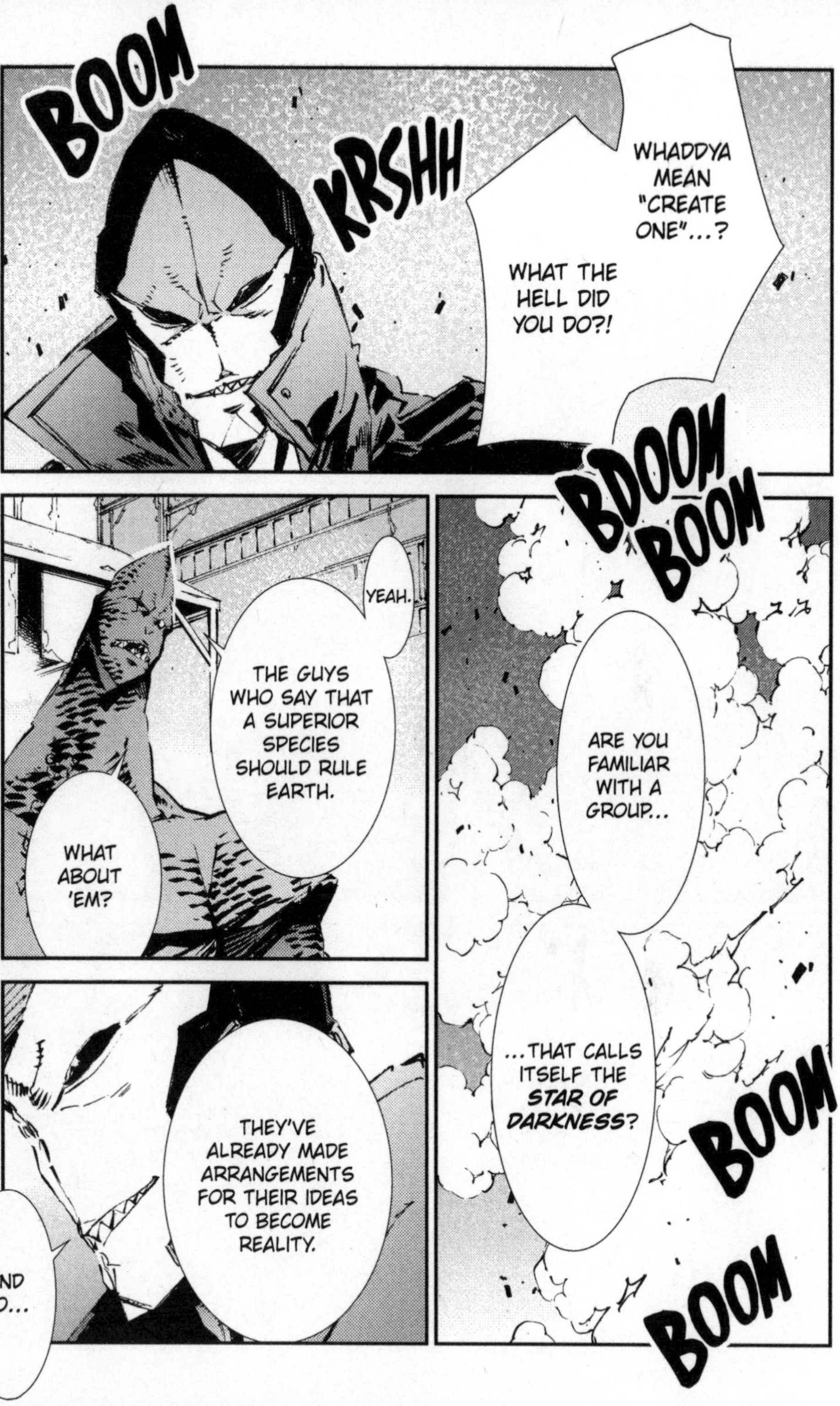
WHADDYA MEAN "CREATE ONE"...?
WHAT THE HELL DID YOU DO?!
KRSHH
BOOM
BDOOM
BOOM
ARE YOU FAMILIAR WITH A GROUP...
...THAT CALLS ITSELF THE *STAR OF DARKNESS*?
BOOM
BOOM
YEAH.
THE GUYS WHO SAY THAT A SUPERIOR SPECIES SHOULD RULE EARTH.
WHAT ABOUT 'EM?
THEY'VE ALREADY MADE ARRANGEMENTS FOR THEIR IDEAS TO BECOME REALITY.
AND SO...

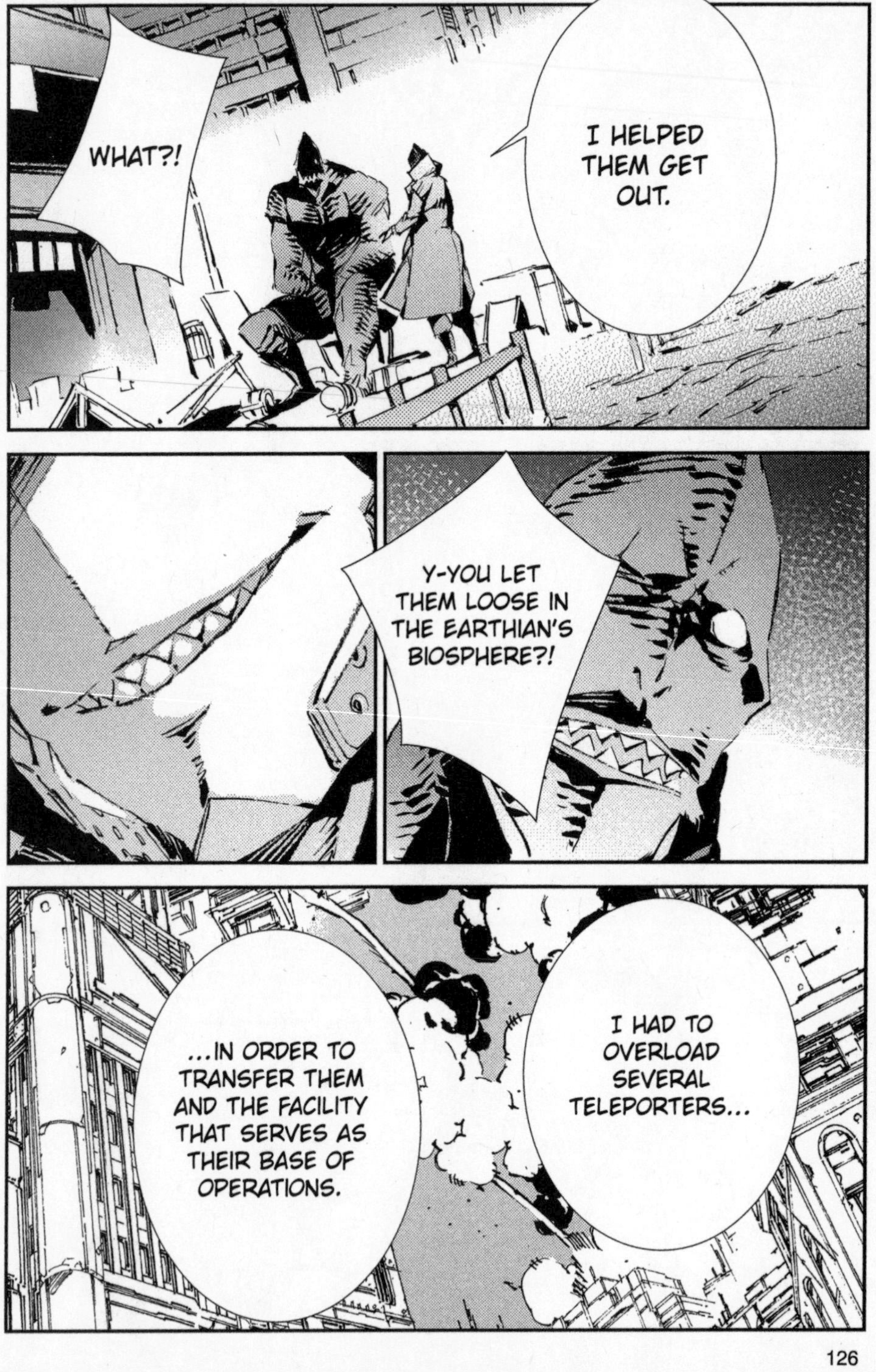
I HELPED THEM GET OUT.
WHAT?!
Y-YOU LET THEM LOOSE IN THE EARTHIAN'S BIOSPHERE?!
I HAD TO OVERLOAD SEVERAL TELEPORTERS...
...IN ORDER TO TRANSFER THEM AND THE FACILITY THAT SERVES AS THEIR BASE OF OPERATIONS.

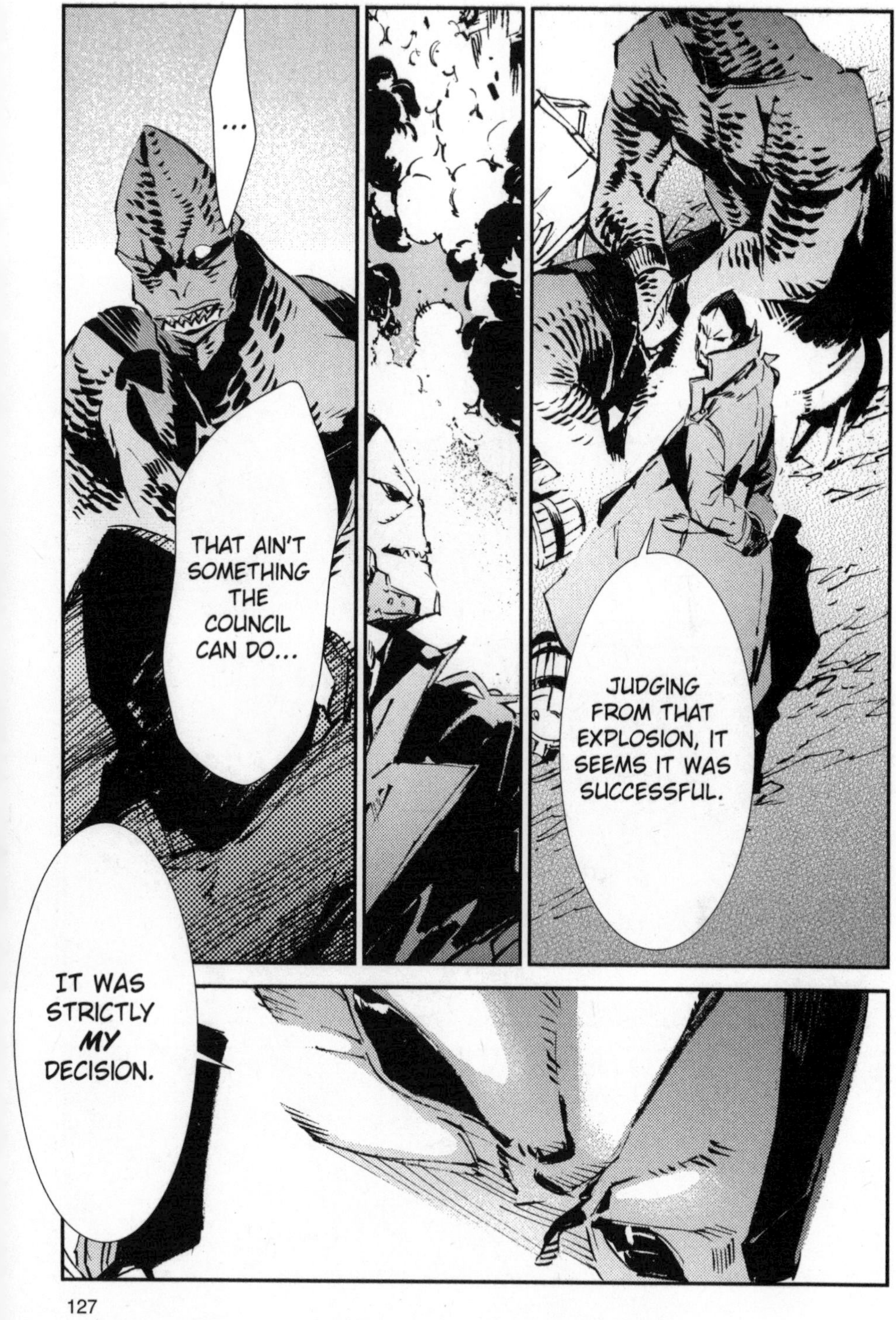
JUDGING FROM THAT EXPLOSION, IT SEEMS IT WAS SUCCESSFUL.
...
THAT AIN'T SOMETHING THE COUNCIL CAN DO...
IT WAS STRICTLY *MY* DECISION.

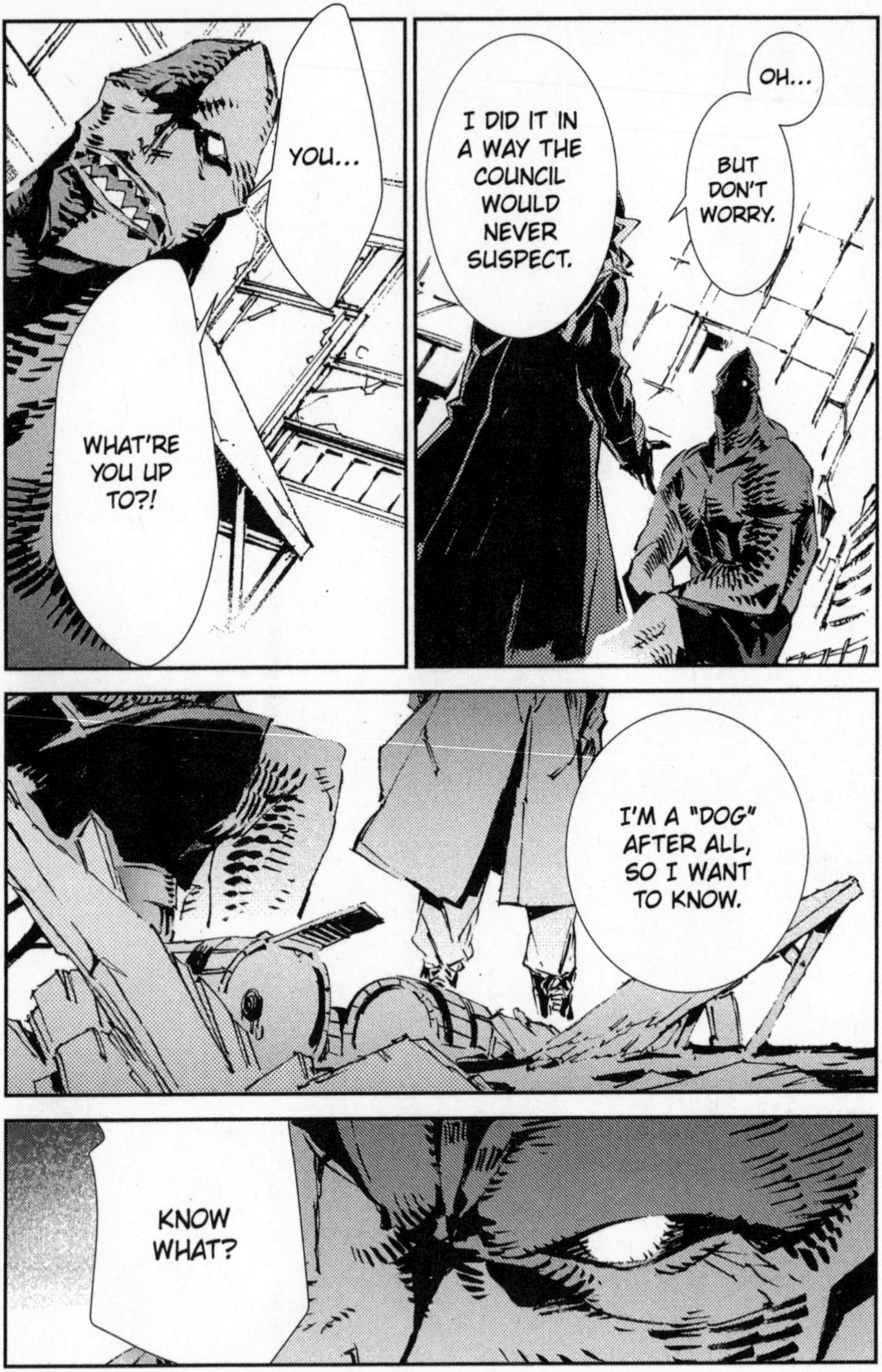
OH...
BUT DON'T WORRY.
I DID IT IN A WAY THE COUNCIL WOULD NEVER SUSPECT.
YOU...
WHAT'RE YOU UP TO?!
I'M A "DOG" AFTER ALL, SO I WANT TO KNOW.
KNOW WHAT?

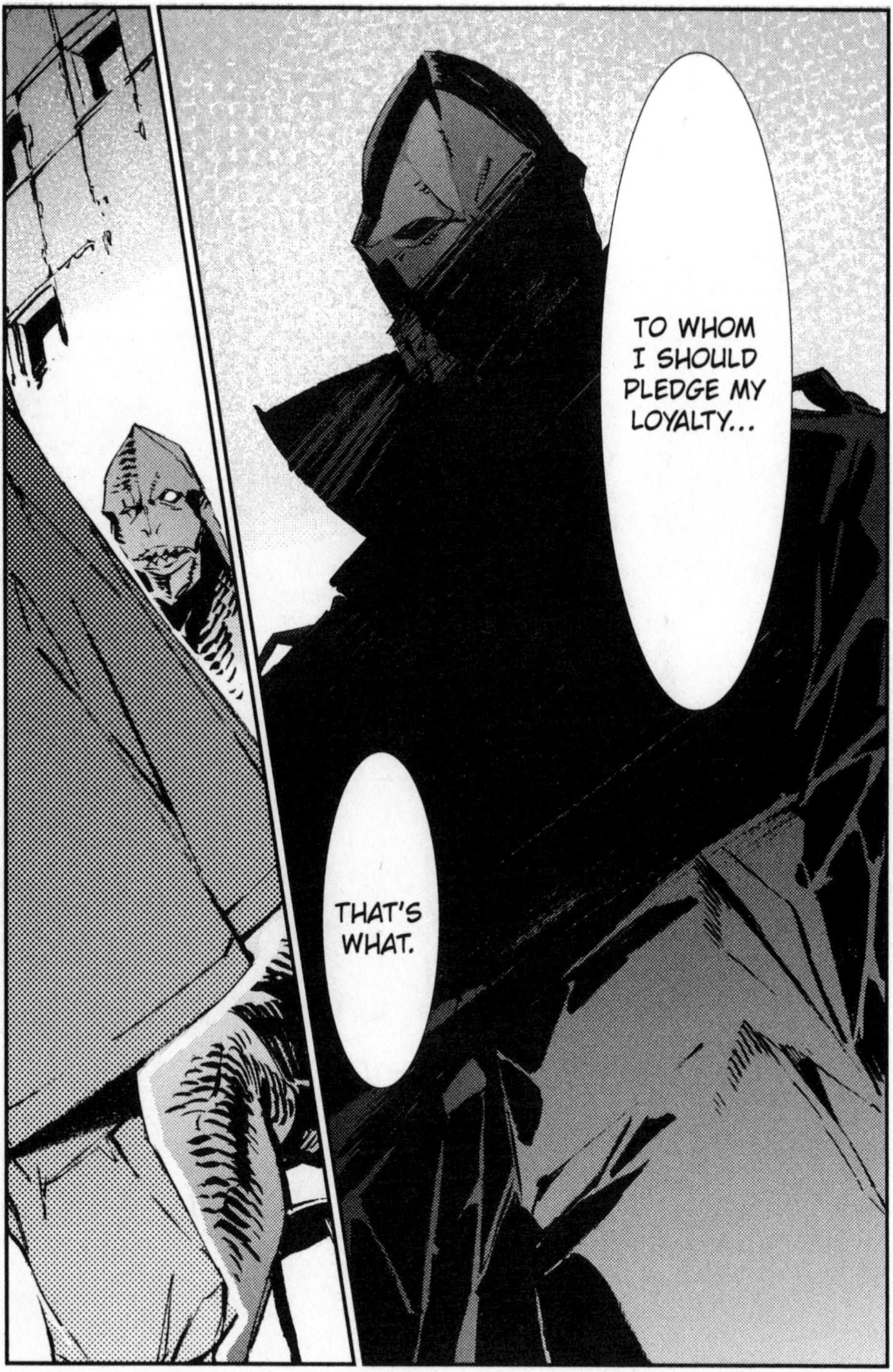
TO WHOM I SHOULD PLEDGE MY LOYALTY...
THAT'S WHAT.

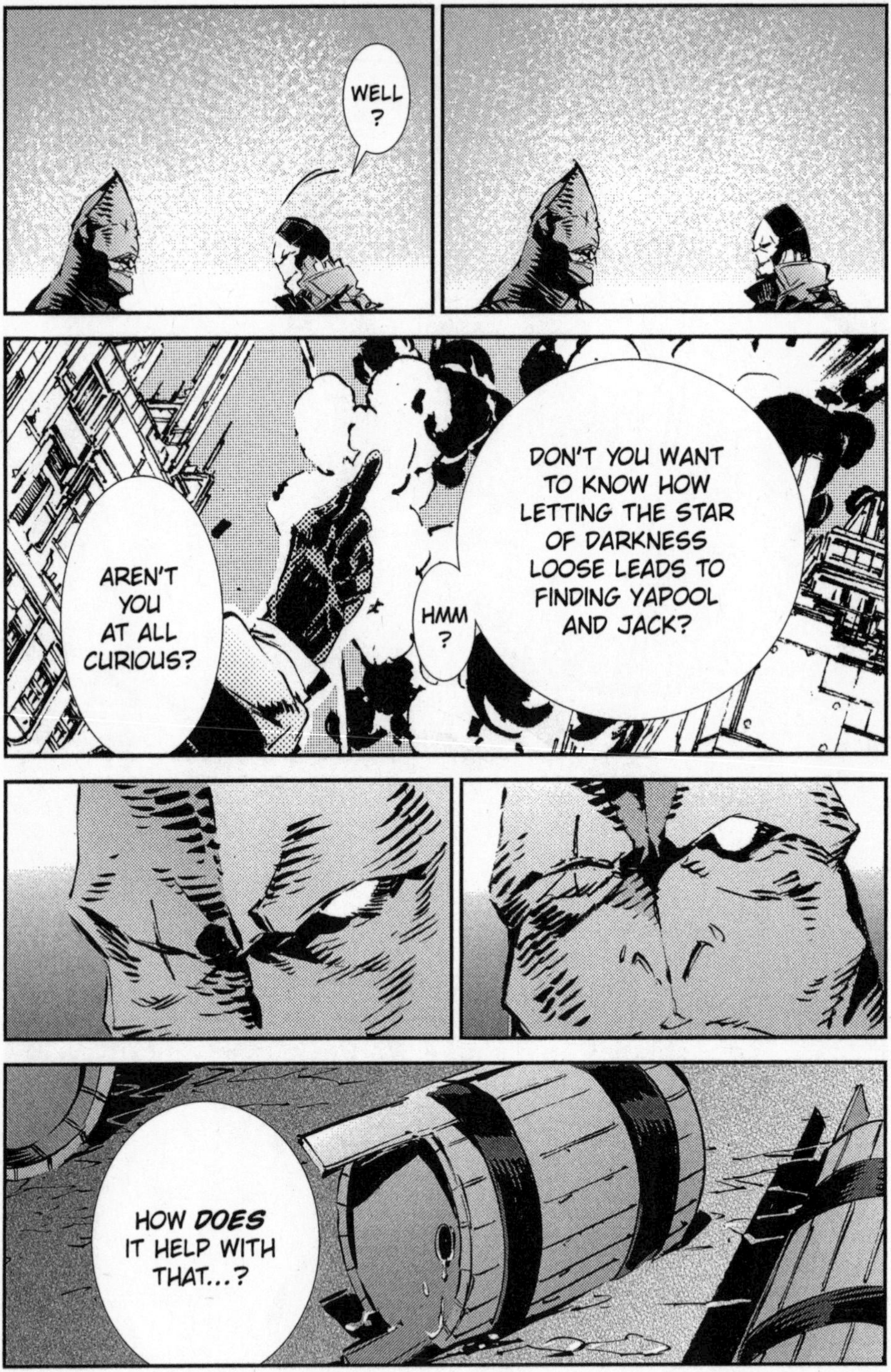
WELL ?
DON'T YOU WANT TO KNOW HOW LETTING THE STAR OF DARKNESS LOOSE LEADS TO FINDING YAPOOL AND JACK?
HMM ?
AREN'T YOU AT ALL CURIOUS?
HOW *DOES* IT HELP WITH THAT...?

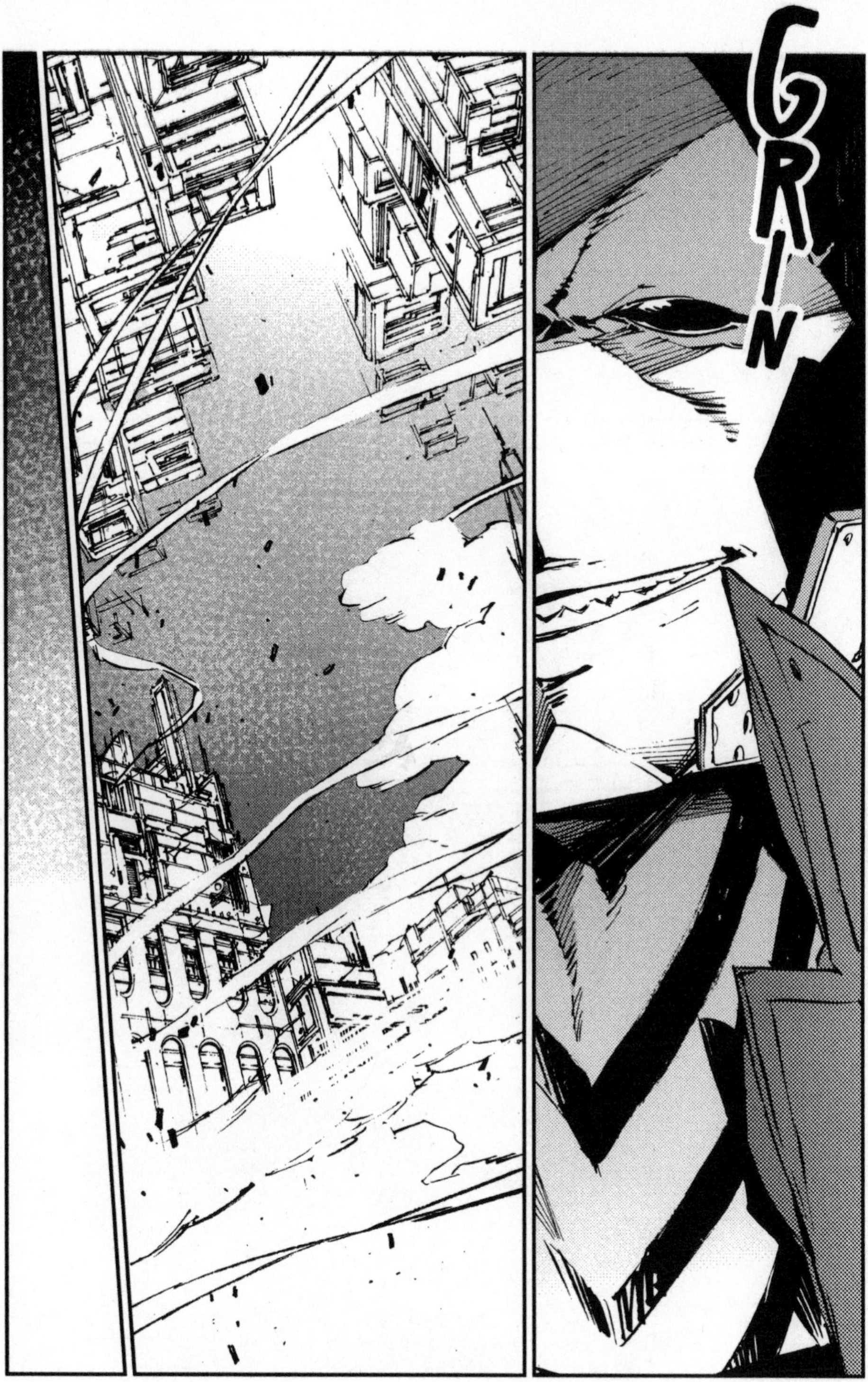
GRIN

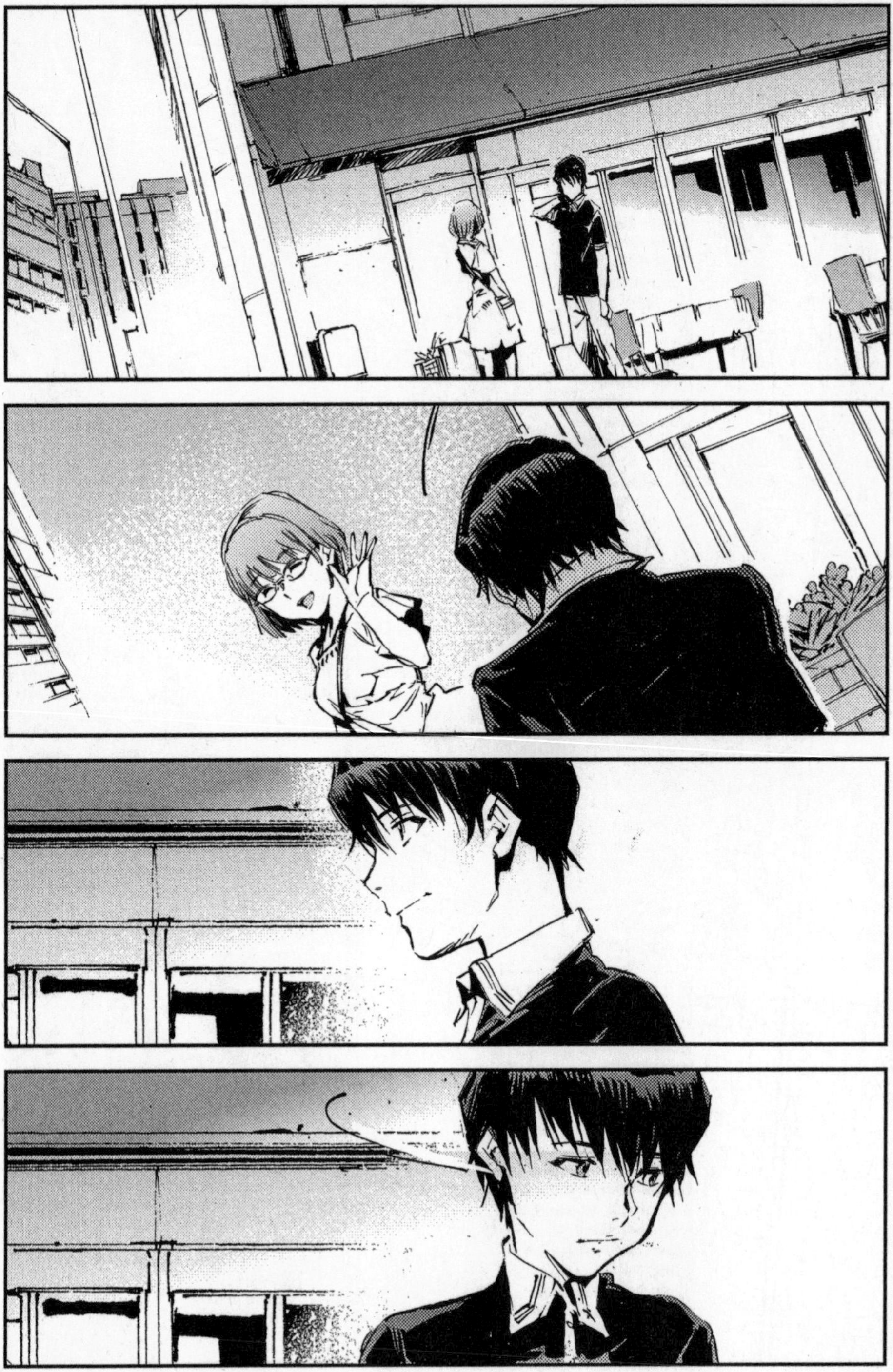

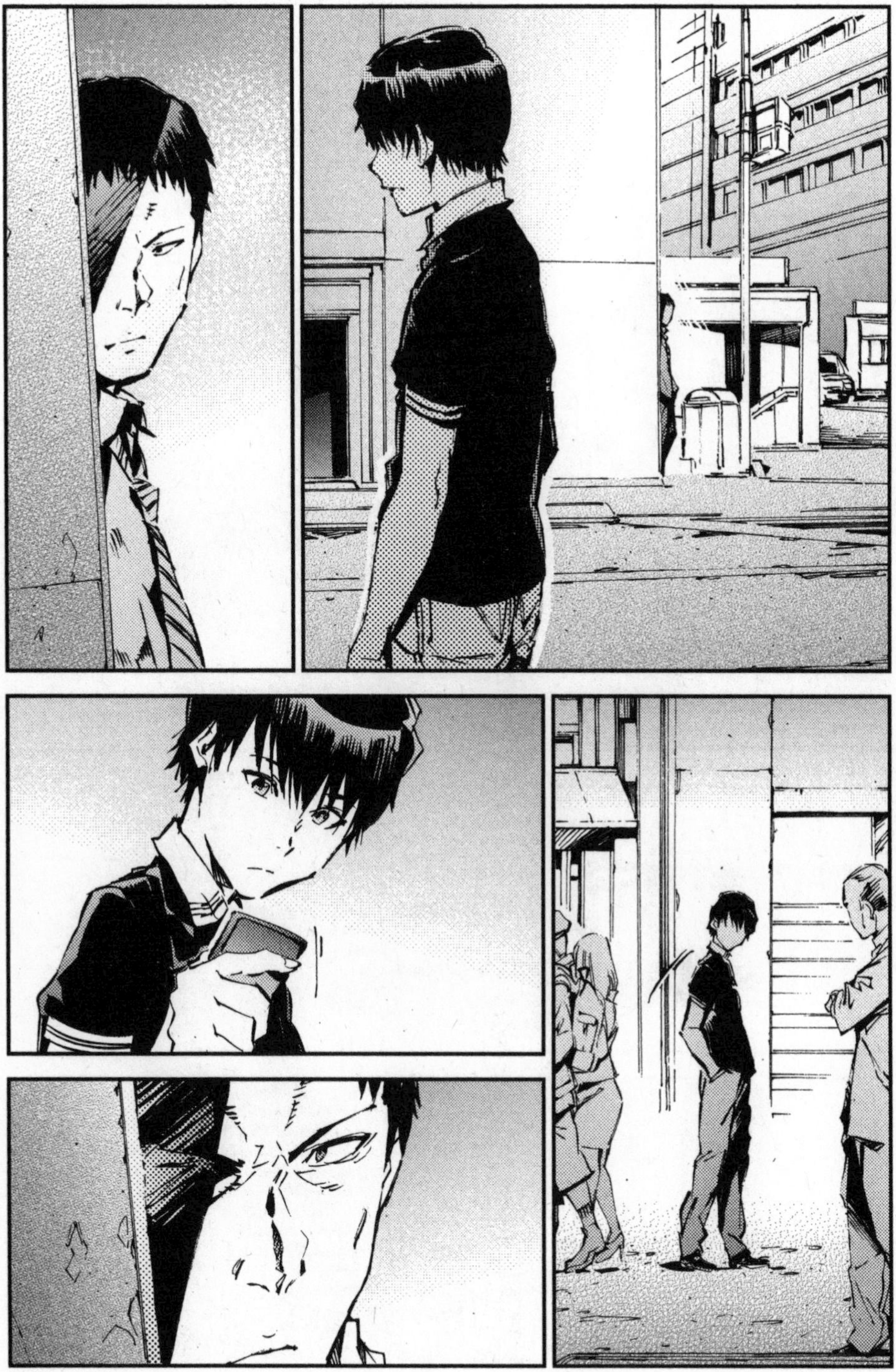

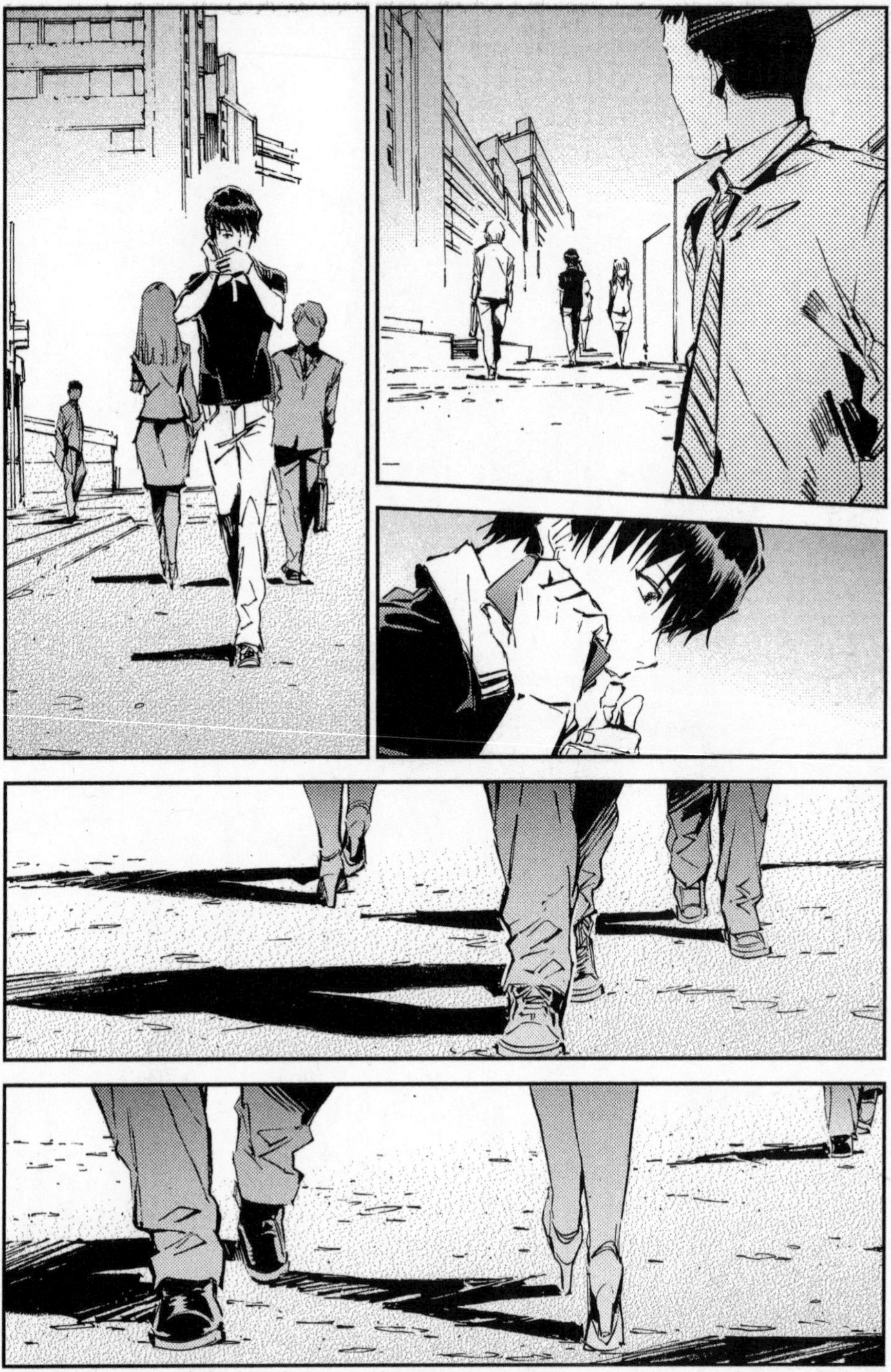

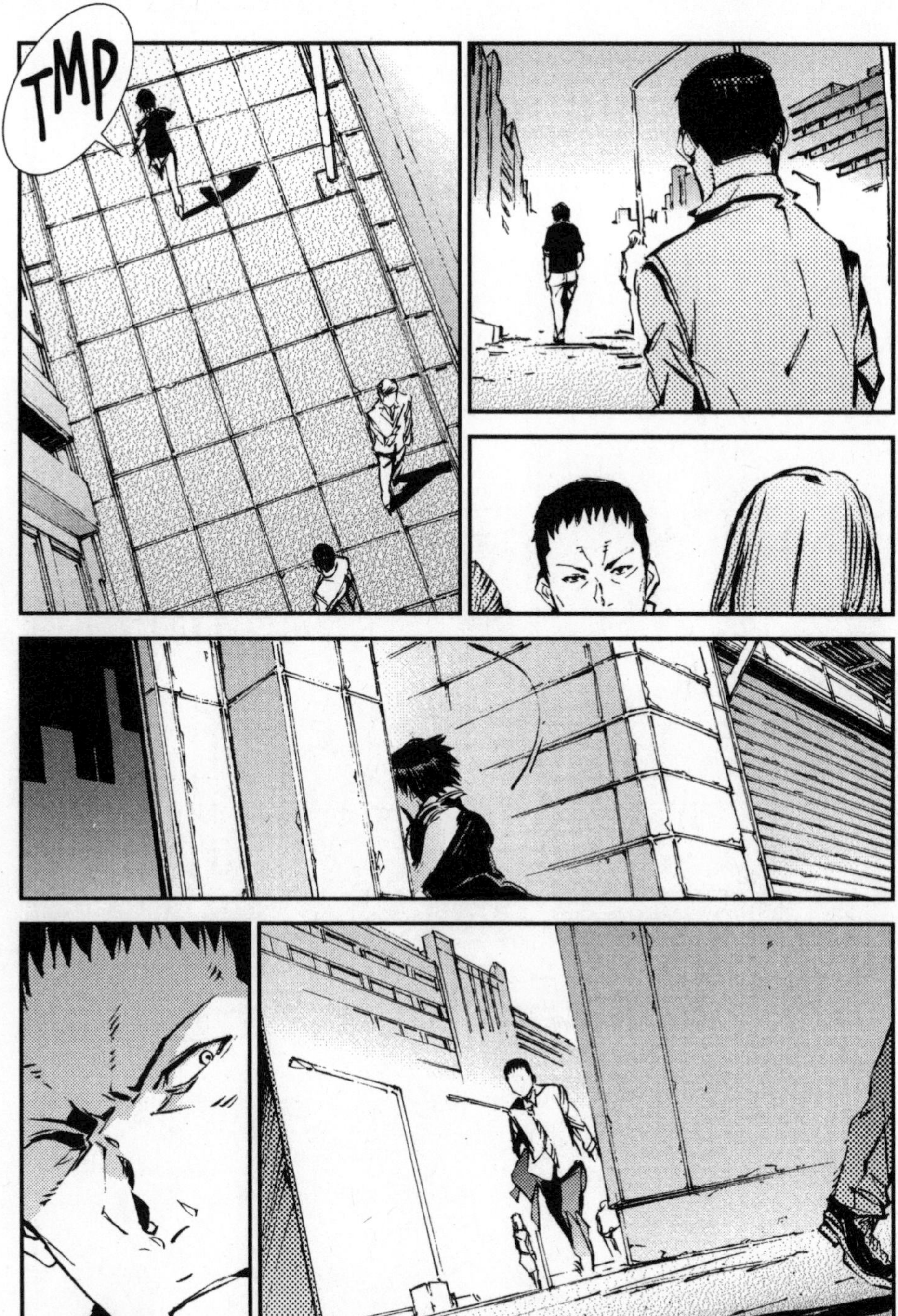
TMP

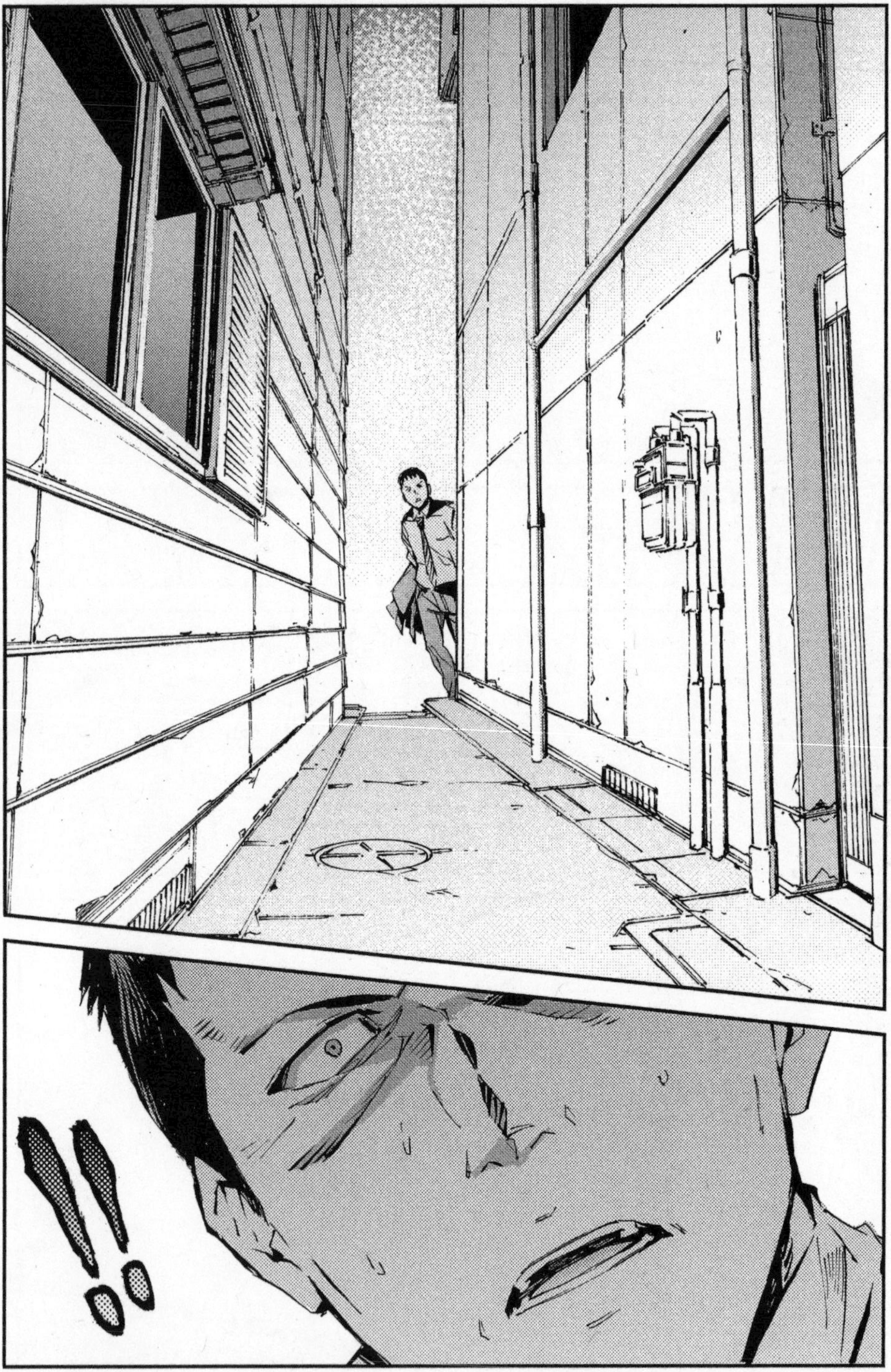
!!

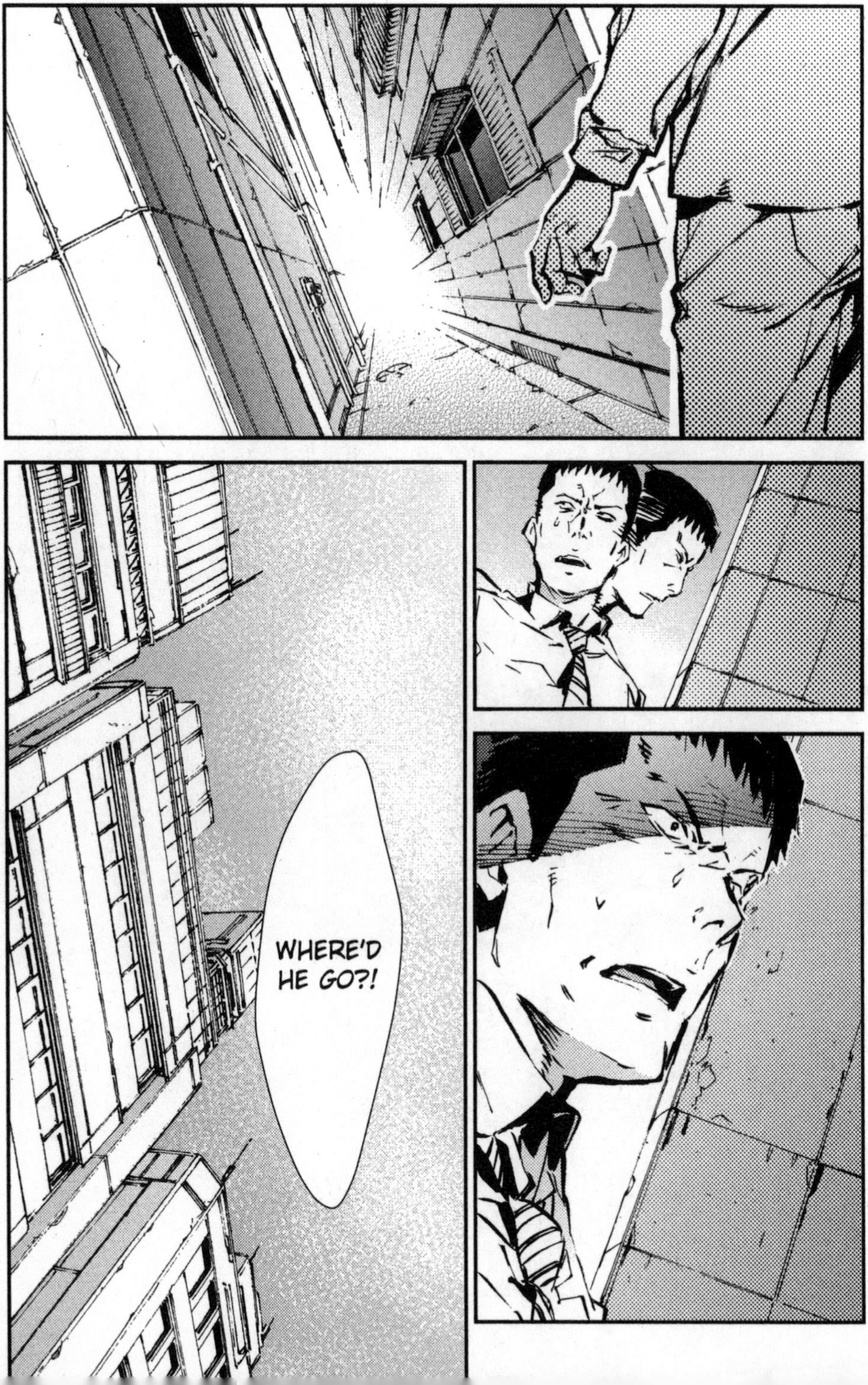
WHERE'D
HE GO?!

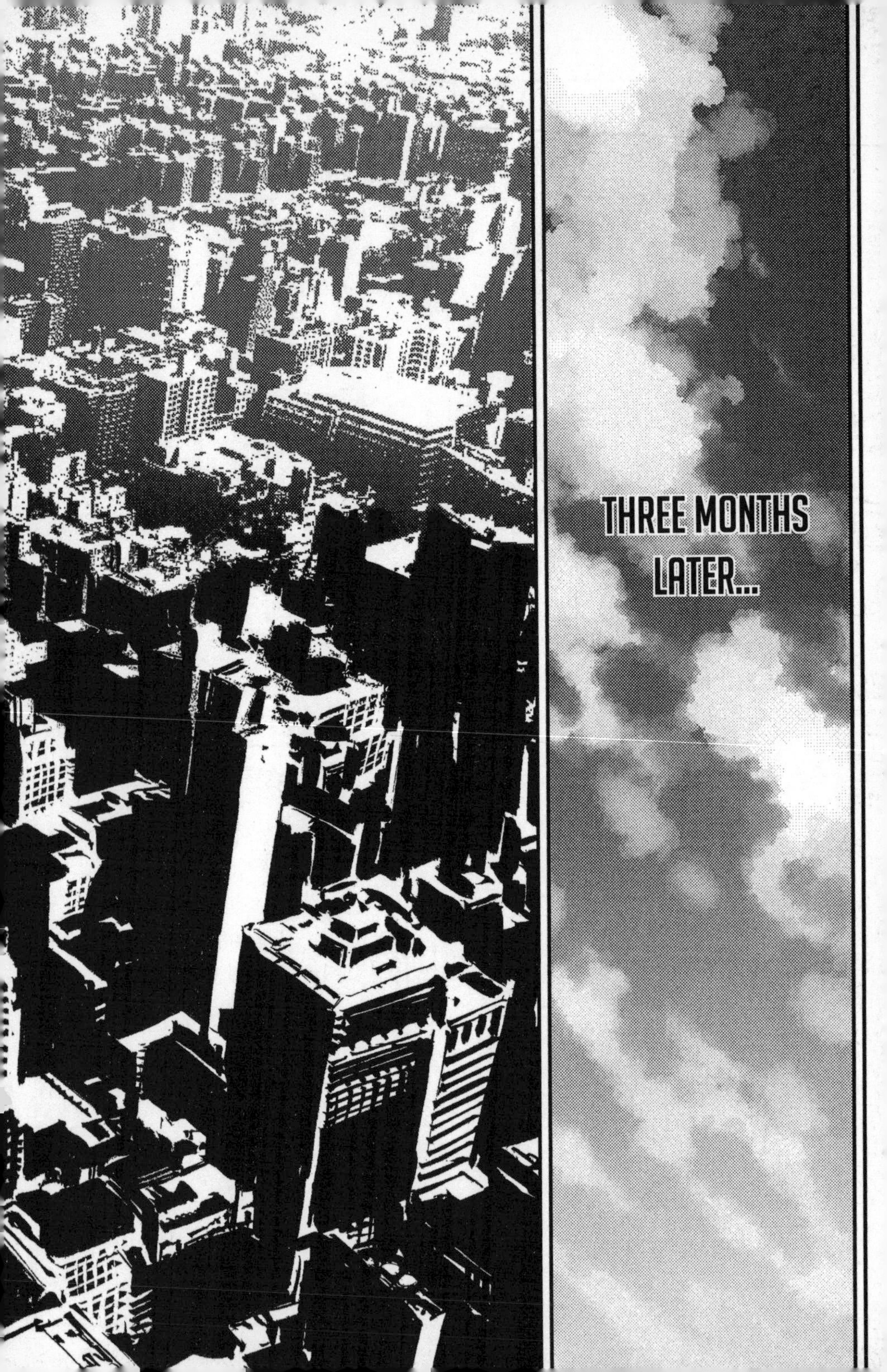
THREE MONTHS LATER...

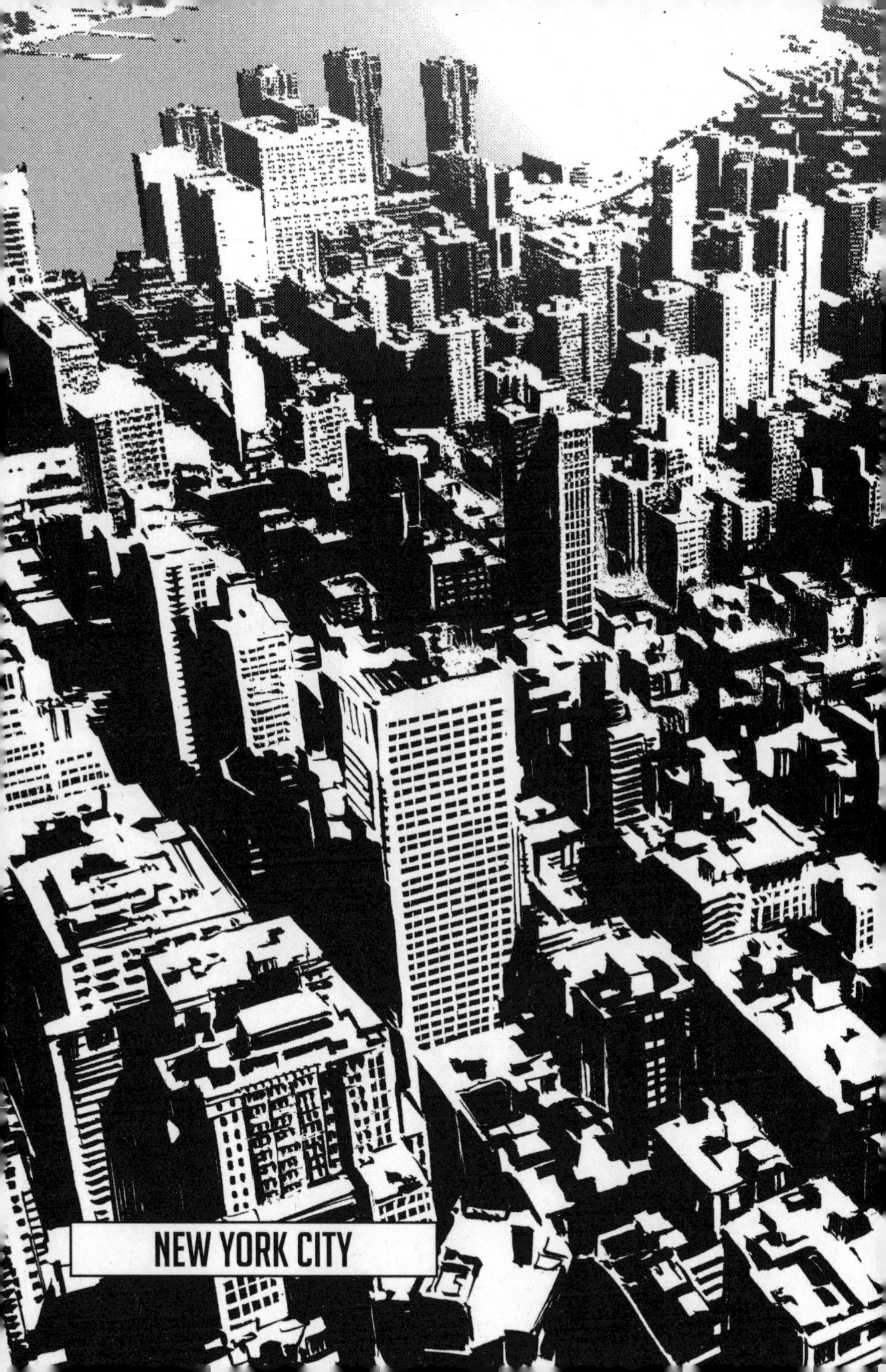
NEW YORK CITY

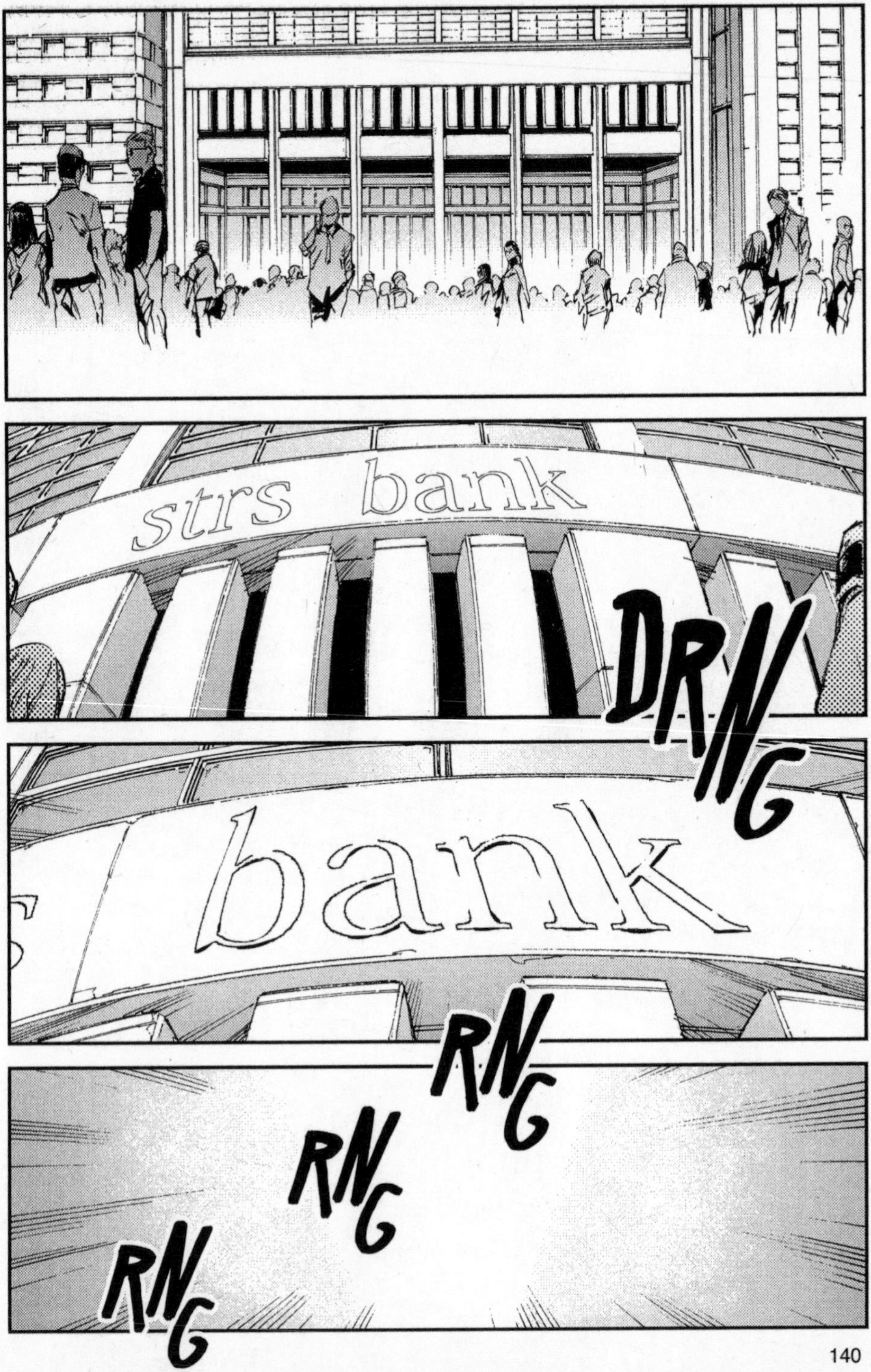
strs bank
DRNG
bank
RNG
RNG
RNG

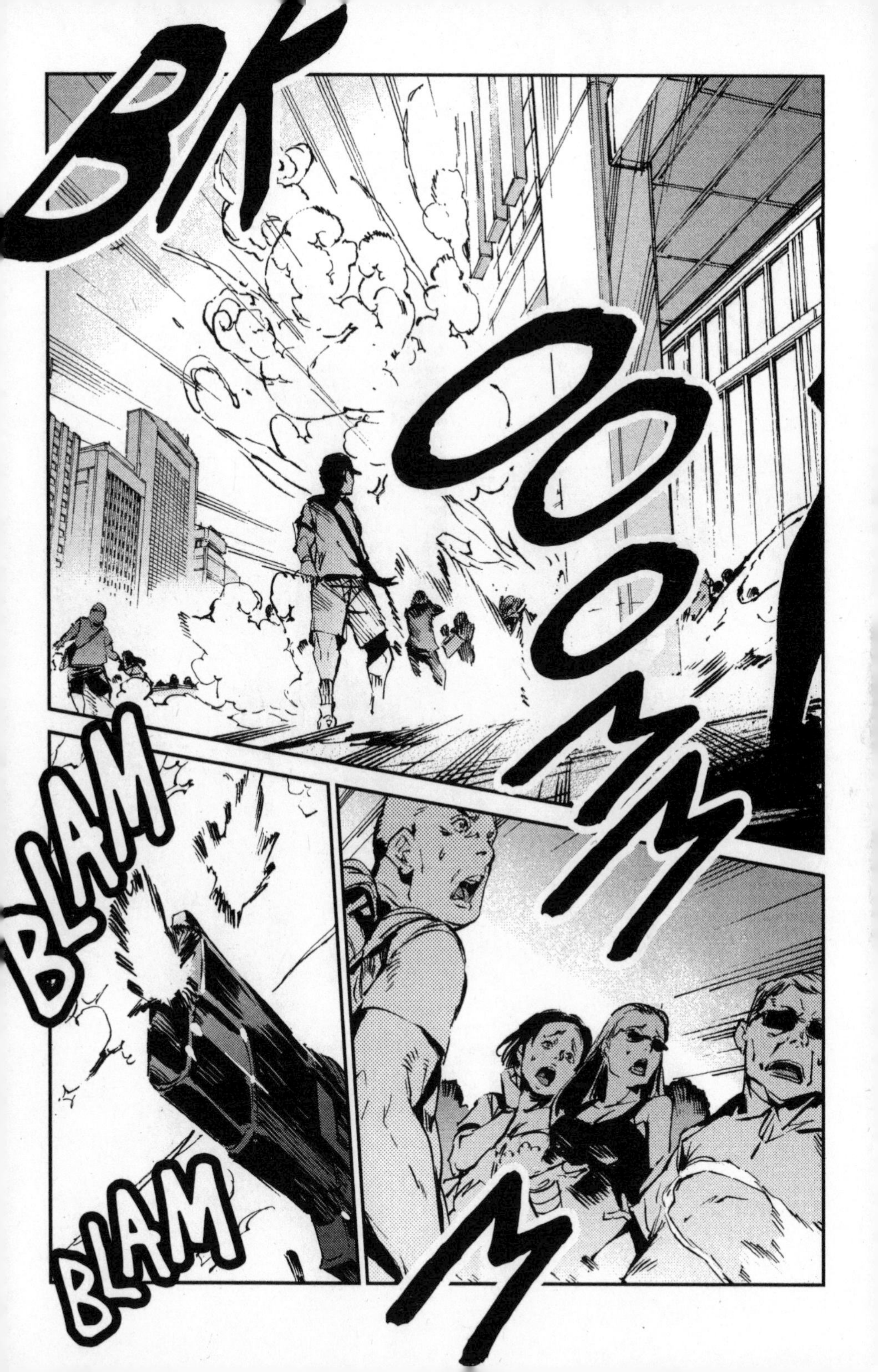
BKOOOMMM
BLAM
BLAM

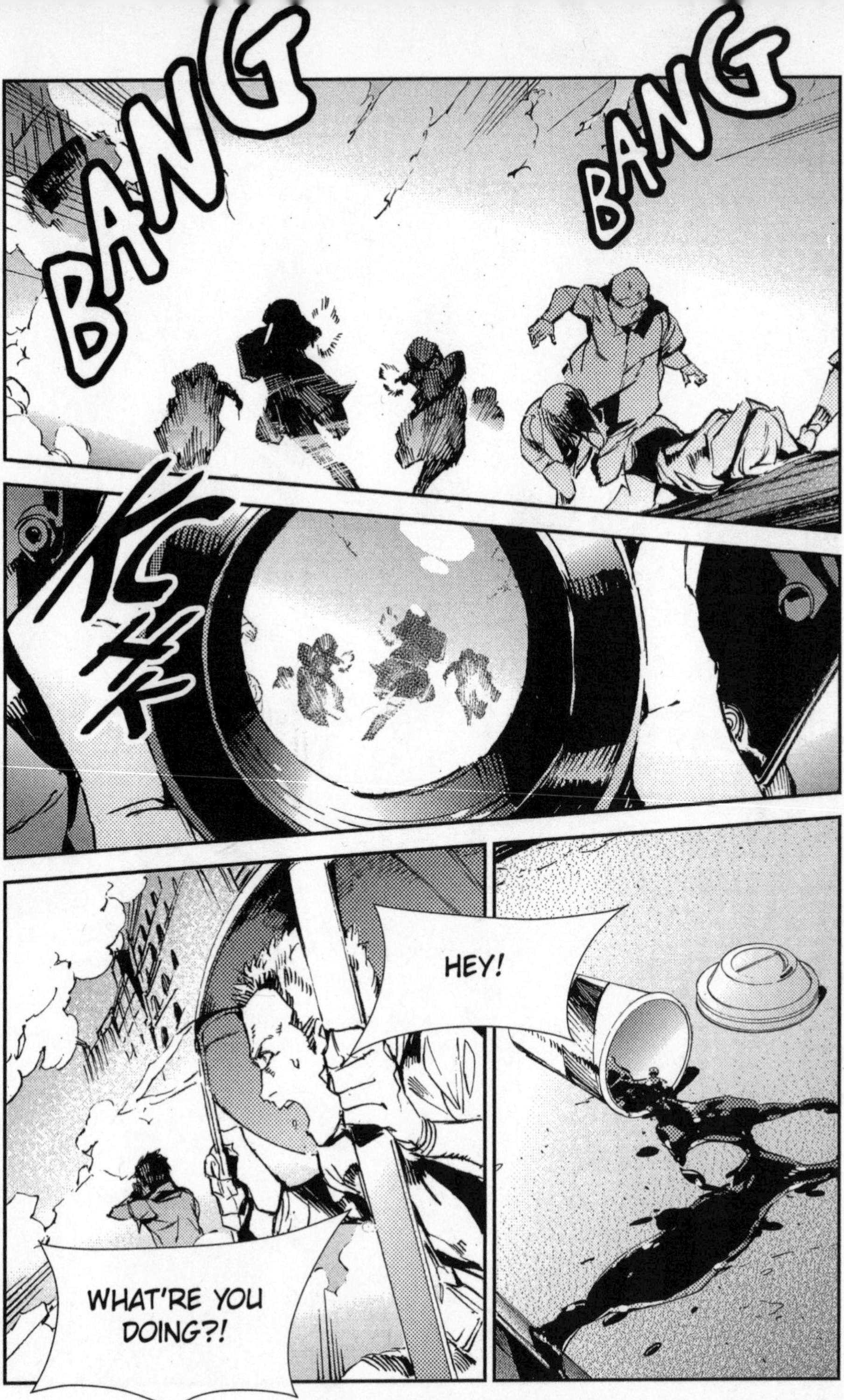
BANG
BANG
KCHK
HEY!
WHAT'RE YOU DOING?!

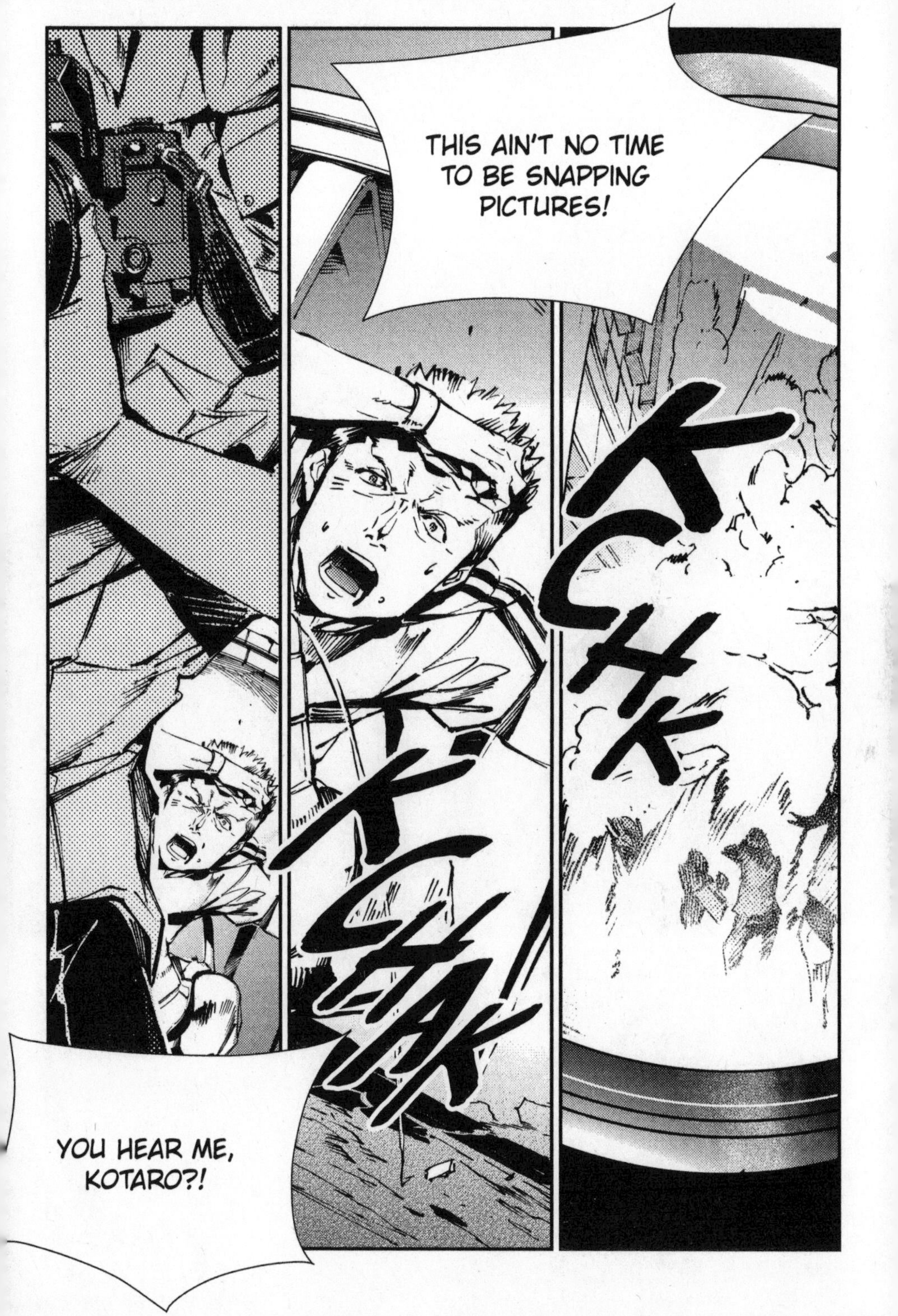
THIS AIN'T NO TIME TO BE SNAPPING PICTURES!
KCHK
KCHAK
YOU HEAR ME, KOTARO?!

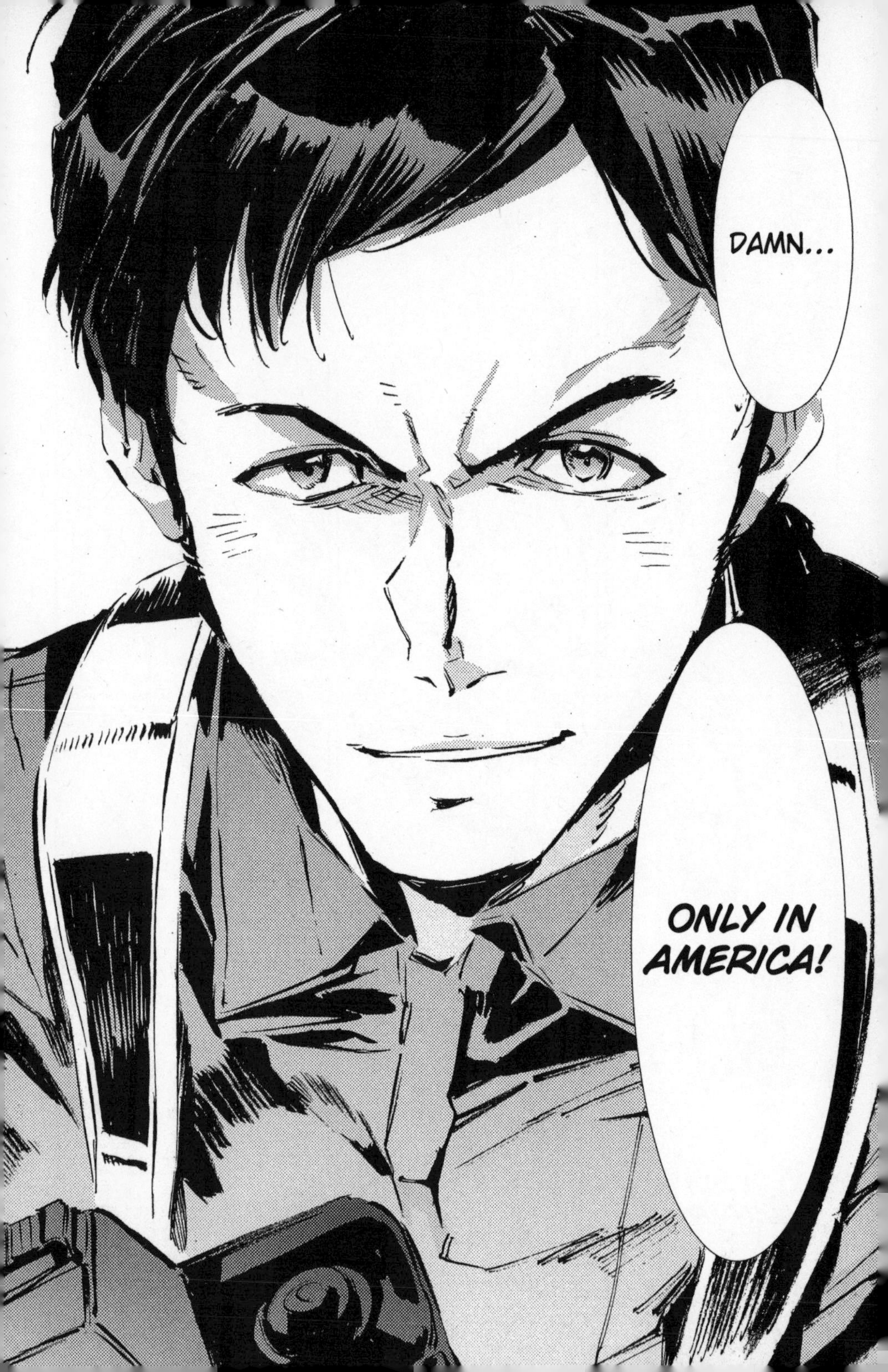
DAMN...
ONLY IN AMERICA!

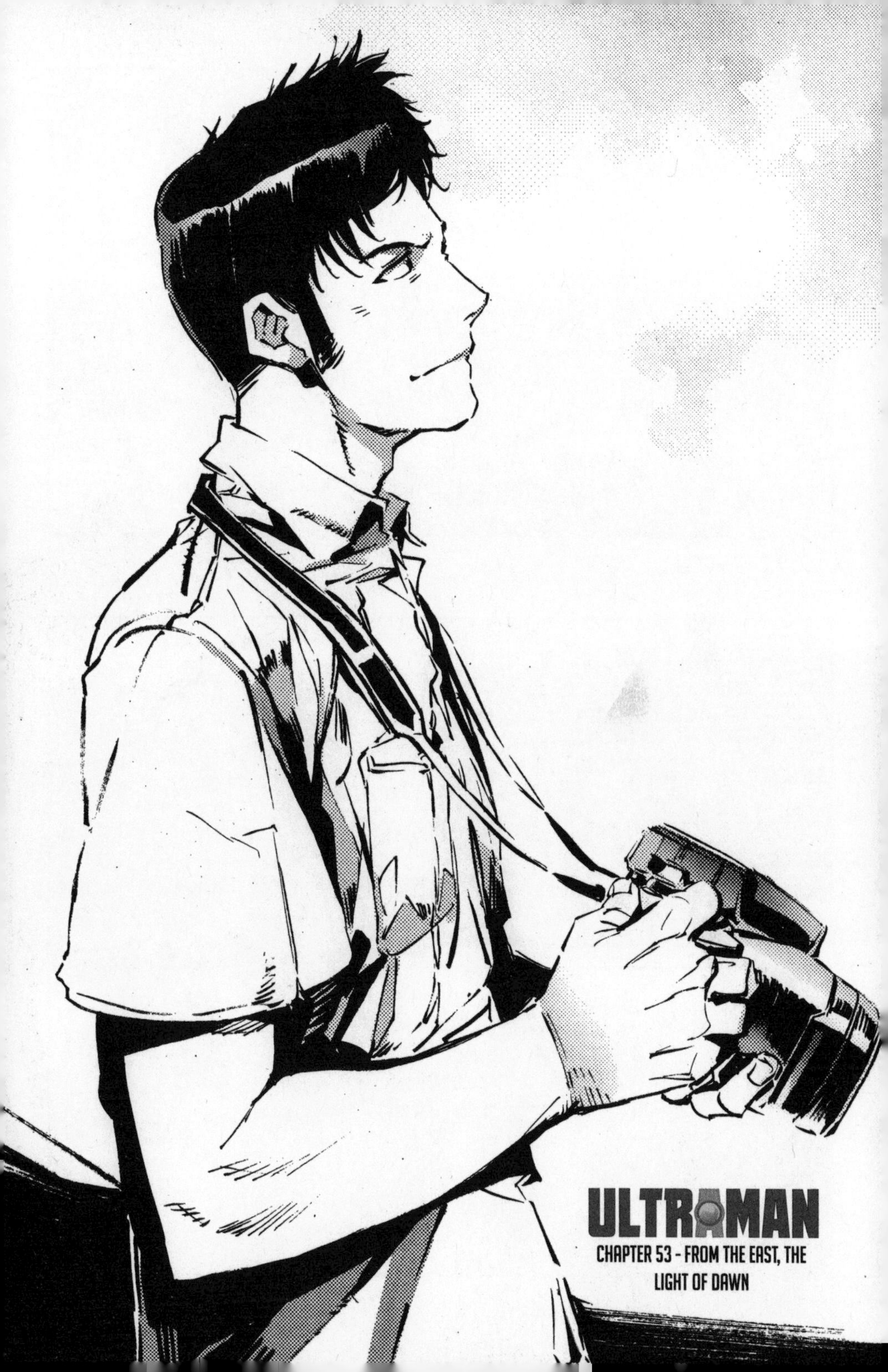
ULTRAMAN
CHAPTER 53 - FROM THE EAST, THE LIGHT OF DAWN

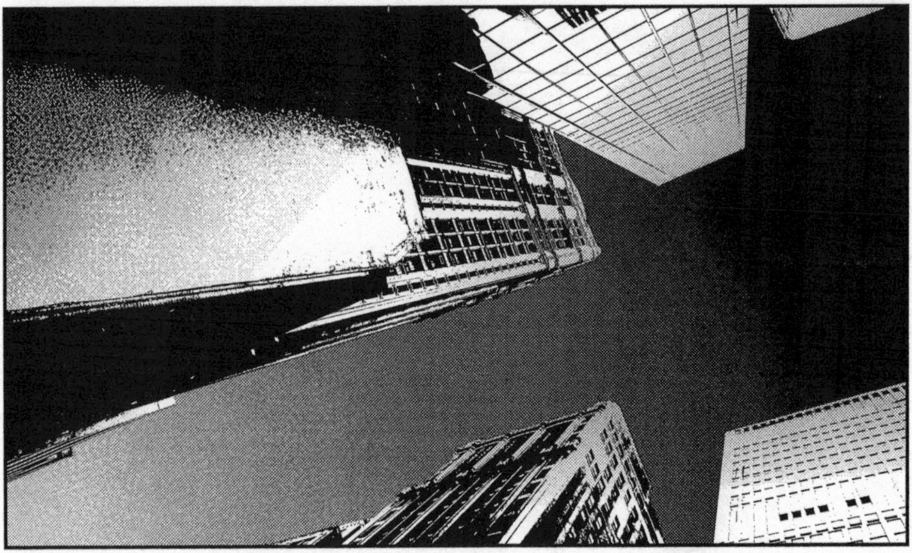

New York

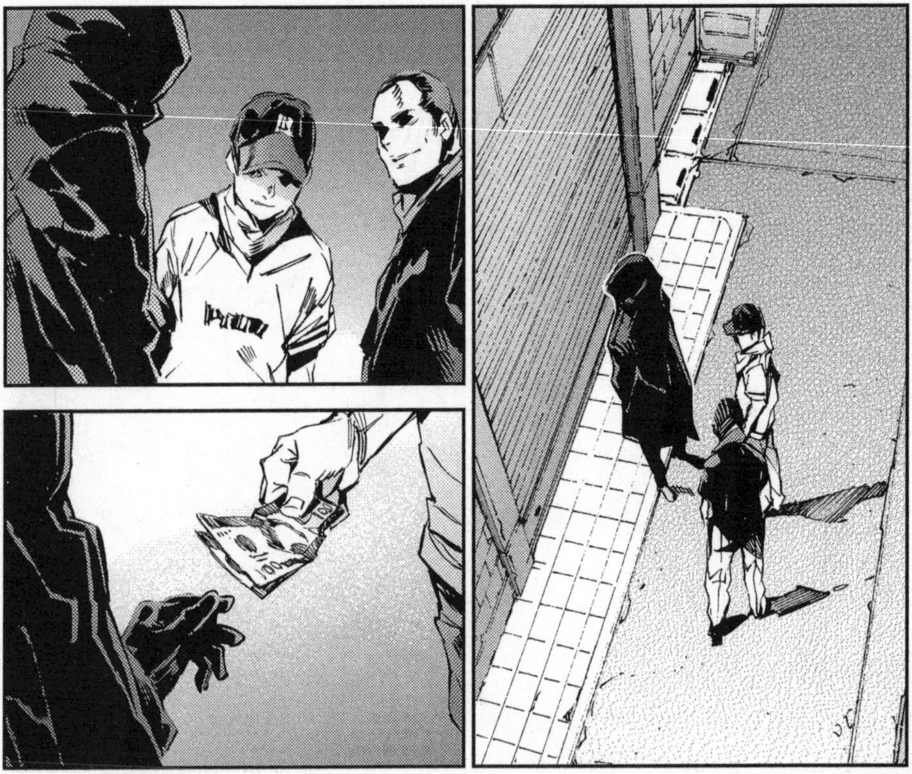

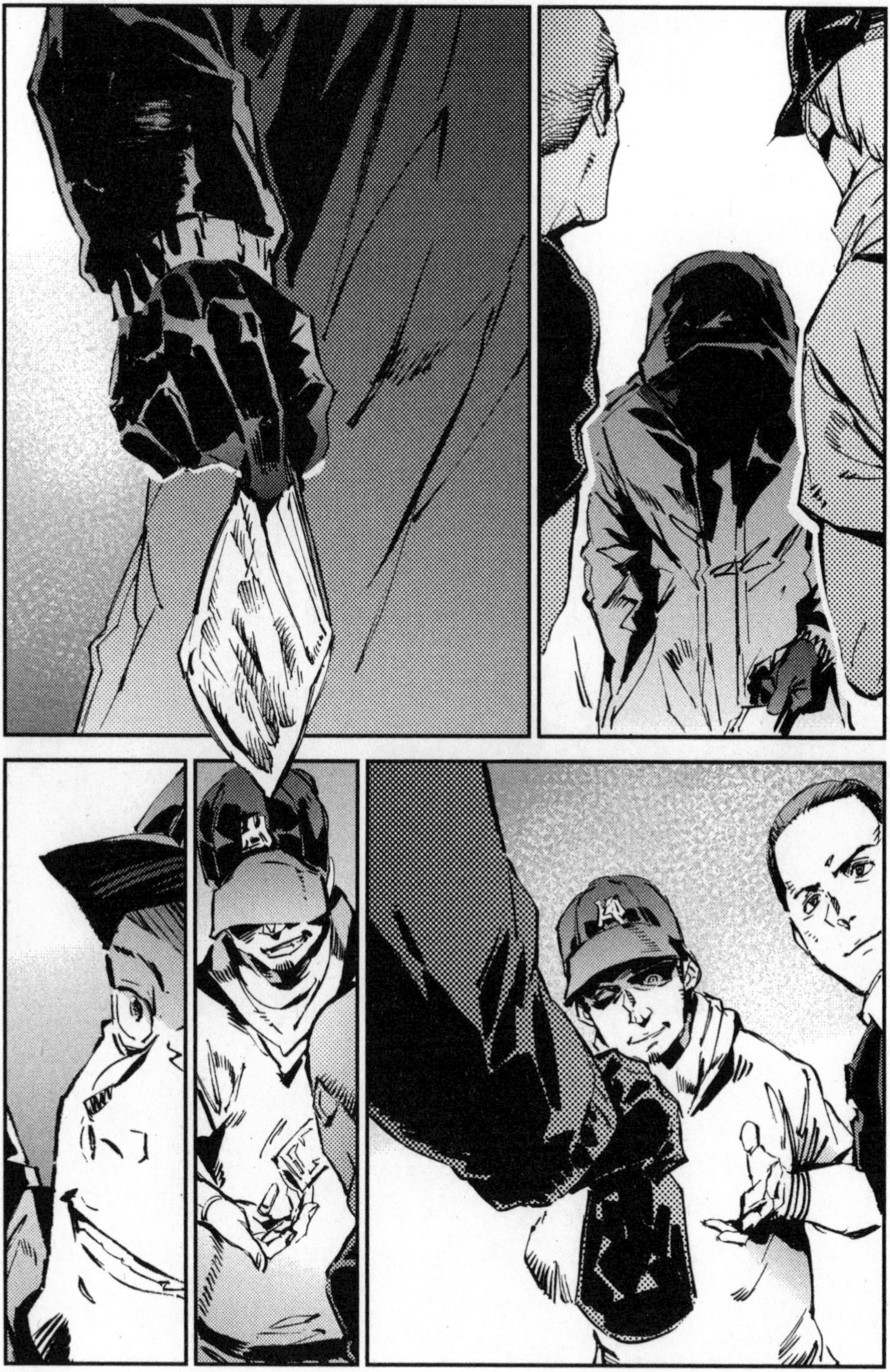

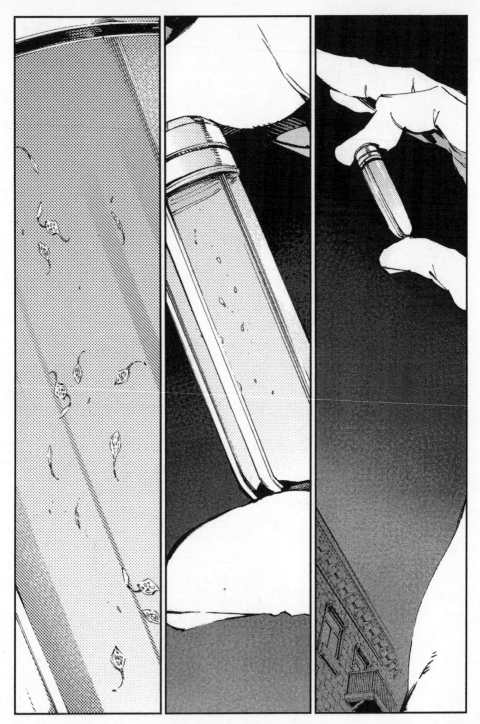

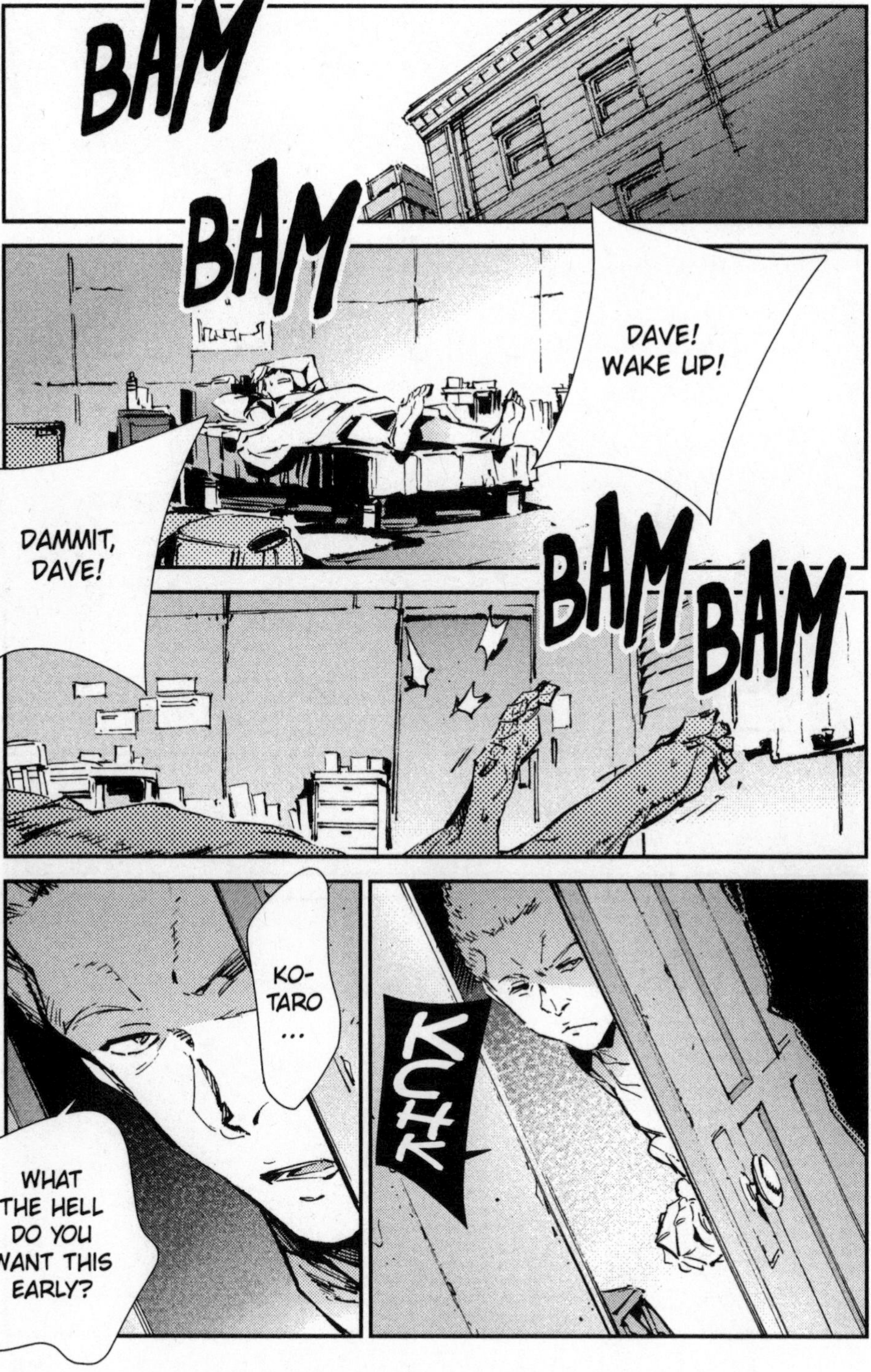
BAM
BAM
DAVE! WAKE UP!
DAMMIT, DAVE!
BAM
BAM
KCHK
KO-TARO ...
WHAT THE HELL DO YOU WANT THIS EARLY?

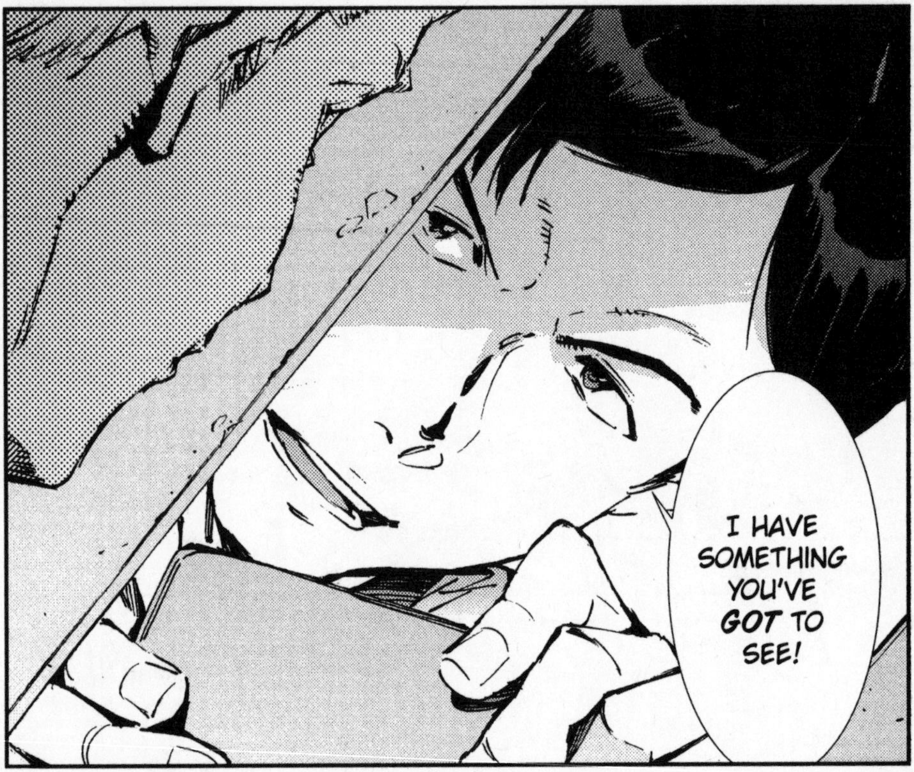
I HAVE SOMETHING YOU'VE *GOT* TO SEE!

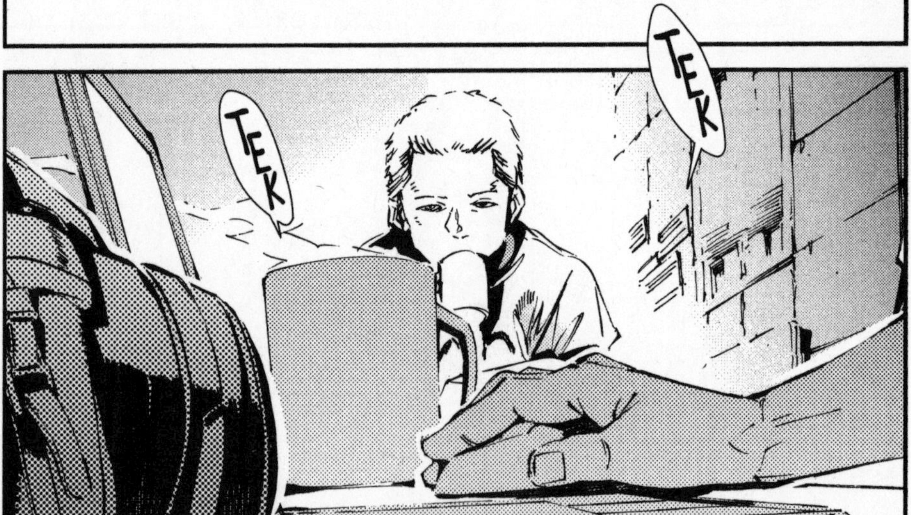
TEK
TEK

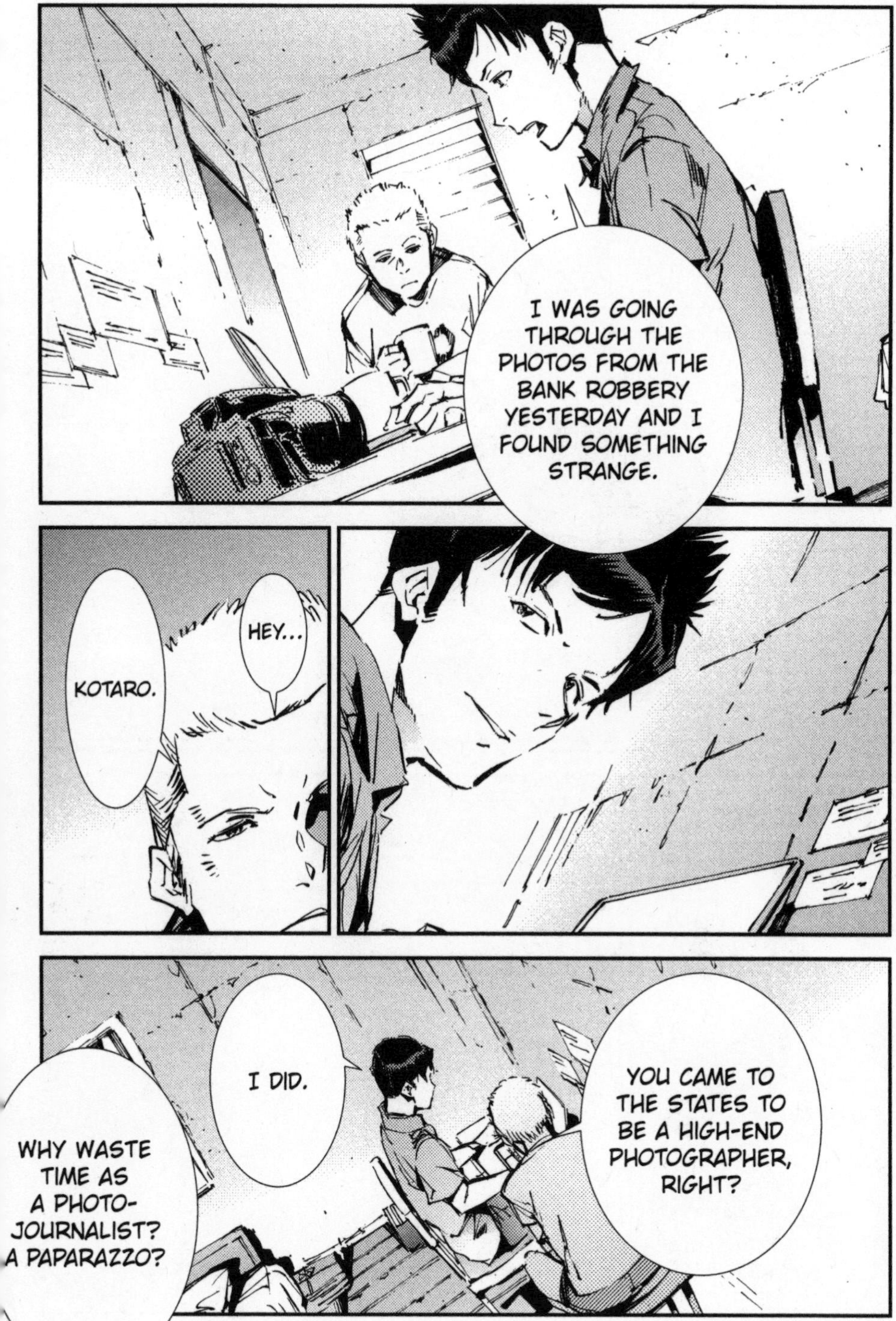
I WAS GOING THROUGH THE PHOTOS FROM THE BANK ROBBERY YESTERDAY AND I FOUND SOMETHING STRANGE.
HEY...
KOTARO.
YOU CAME TO THE STATES TO BE A HIGH-END PHOTOGRAPHER, RIGHT?
I DID.
WHY WASTE TIME AS A PHOTO-JOURNALIST? A PAPARAZZO?

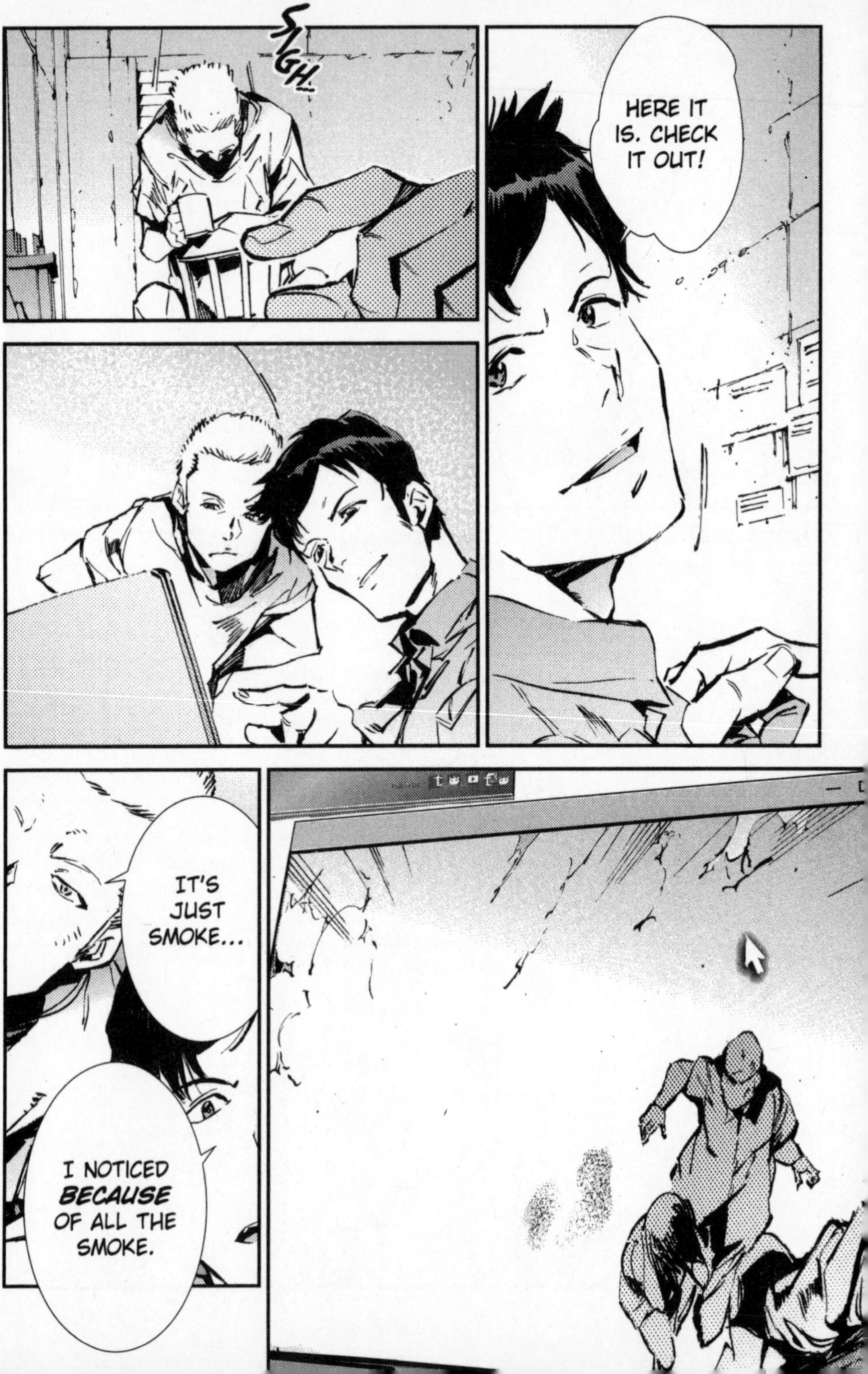
HERE IT IS. CHECK IT OUT!
SIGH
IT'S JUST SMOKE...
I NOTICED *BECAUSE* OF ALL THE SMOKE.

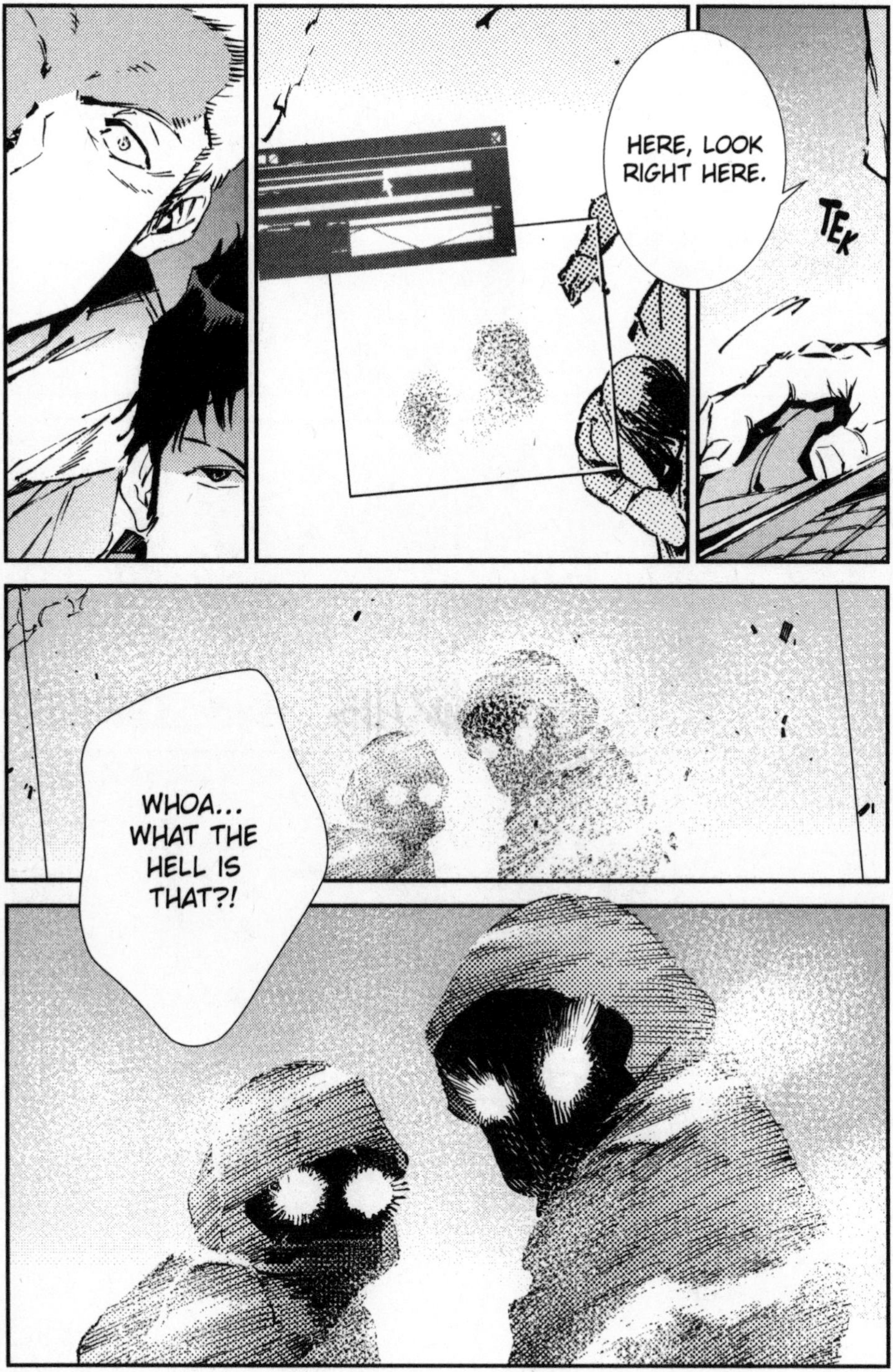
HERE, LOOK RIGHT HERE.
TEK
WHOA... WHAT THE HELL IS THAT?!

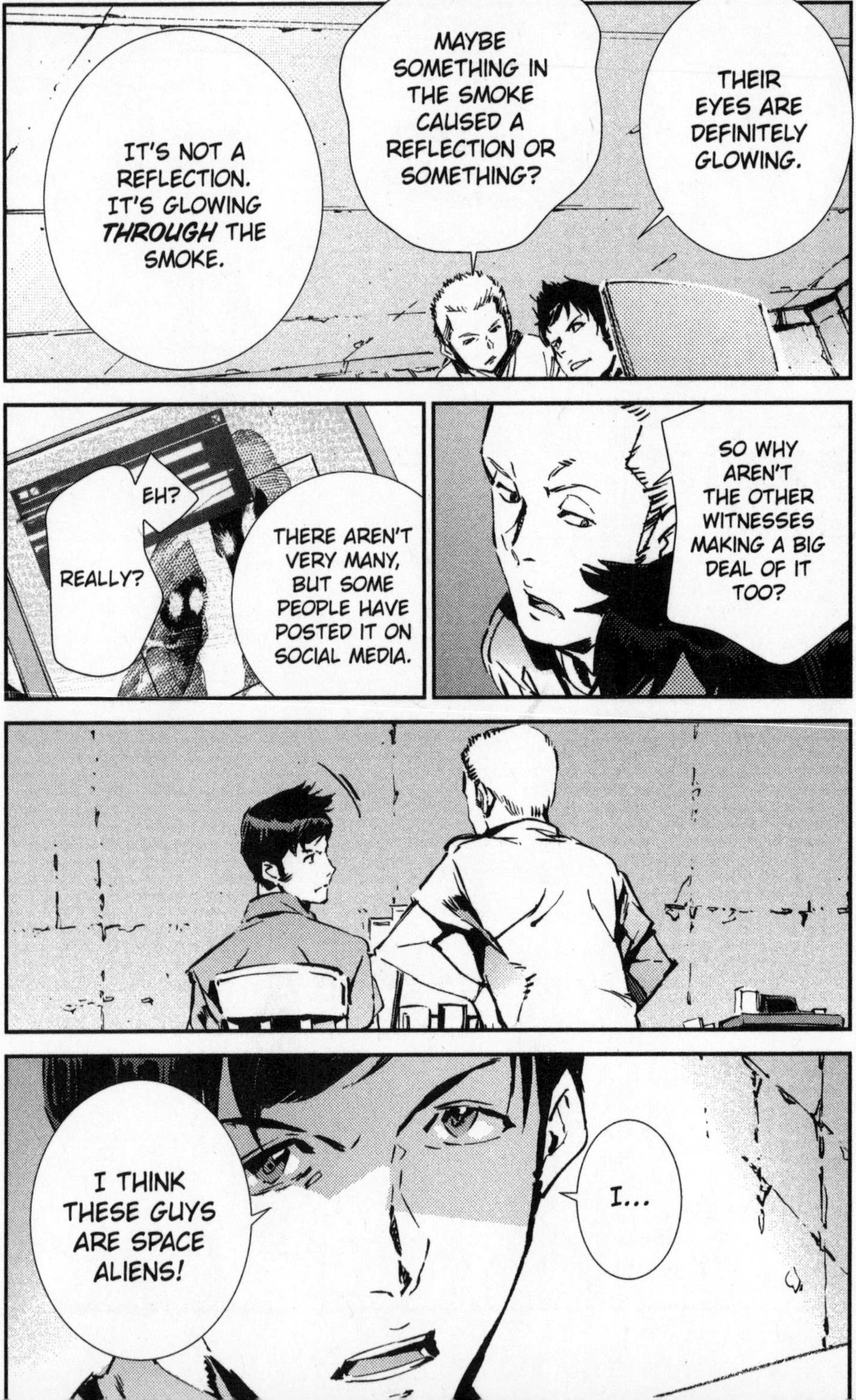
THEIR EYES ARE DEFINITELY GLOWING.
MAYBE SOMETHING IN THE SMOKE CAUSED A REFLECTION OR SOMETHING?
IT'S NOT A REFLECTION. IT'S GLOWING *THROUGH* THE SMOKE.
SO WHY AREN'T THE OTHER WITNESSES MAKING A BIG DEAL OF IT TOO?
THERE AREN'T VERY MANY, BUT SOME PEOPLE HAVE POSTED IT ON SOCIAL MEDIA.
EH?
REALLY?
I...
I THINK THESE GUYS ARE SPACE ALIENS!

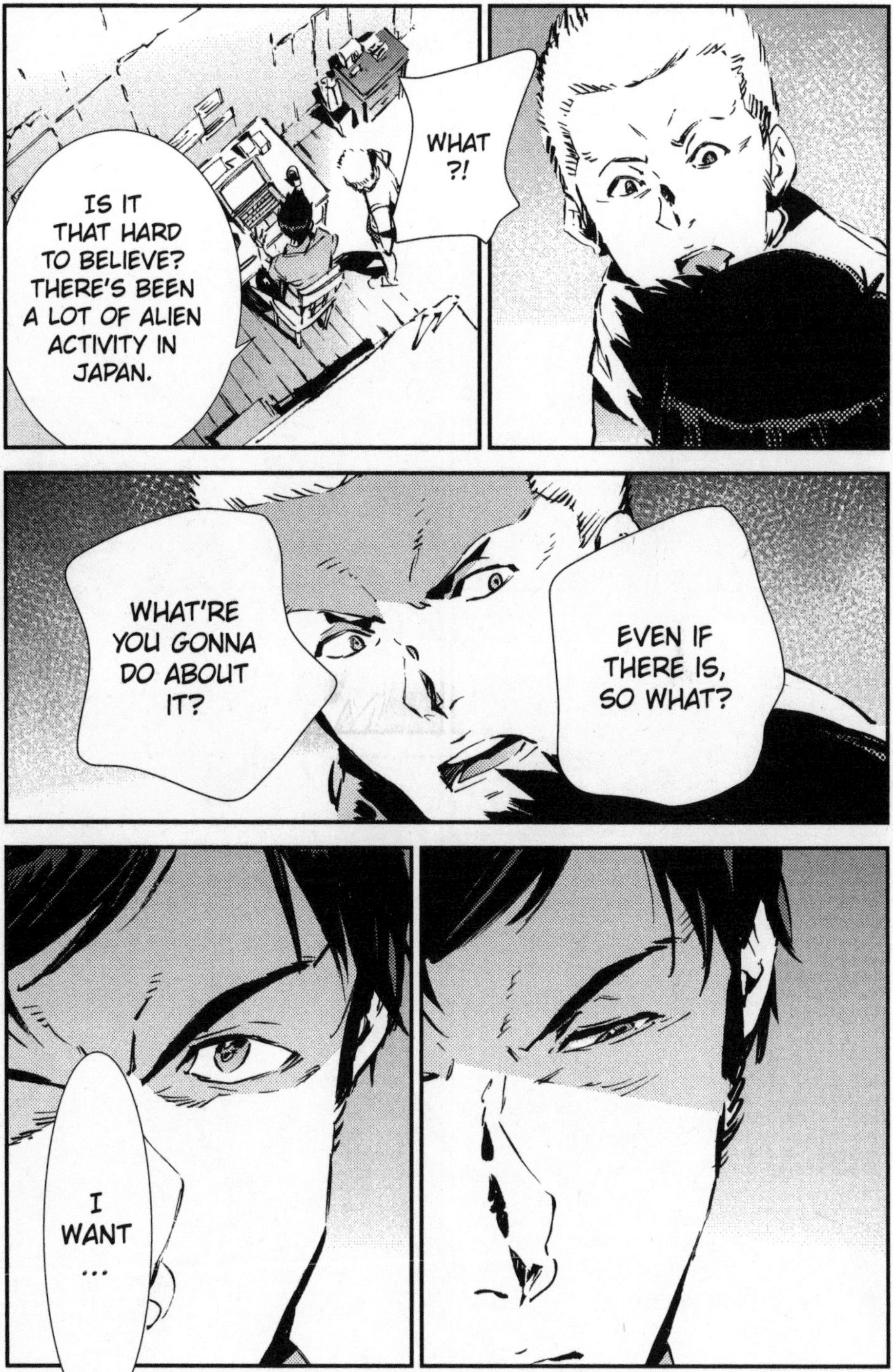
WHAT ?!
IS IT THAT HARD TO BELIEVE? THERE'S BEEN A LOT OF ALIEN ACTIVITY IN JAPAN.
EVEN IF THERE IS, SO WHAT?
WHAT'RE YOU GONNA DO ABOUT IT?
I WANT ...

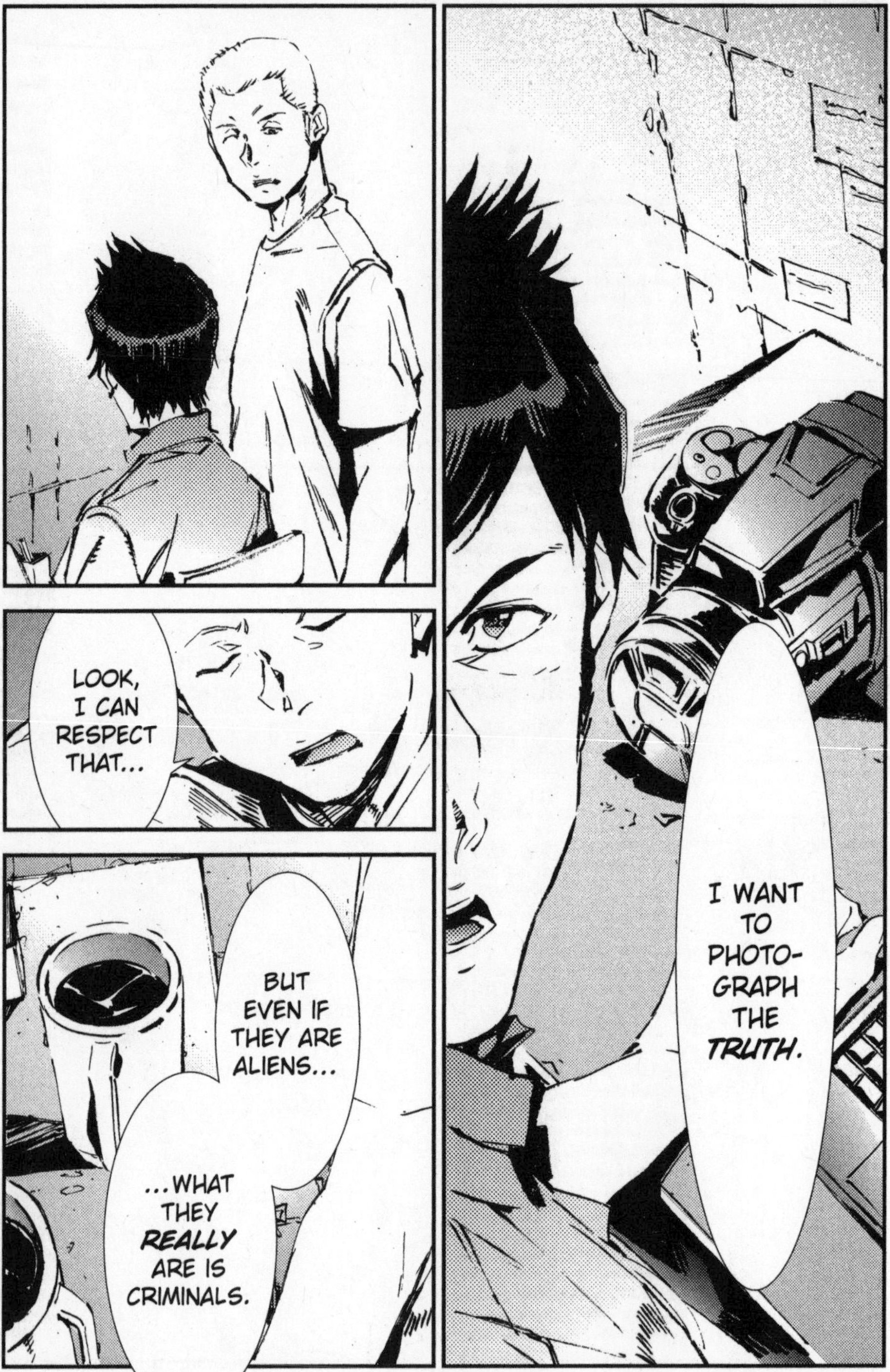
I WANT TO PHOTO-GRAPH THE *TRUTH*.
LOOK, I CAN RESPECT THAT...
BUT EVEN IF THEY ARE ALIENS...
...WHAT THEY ***REALLY*** ARE IS CRIMINALS.

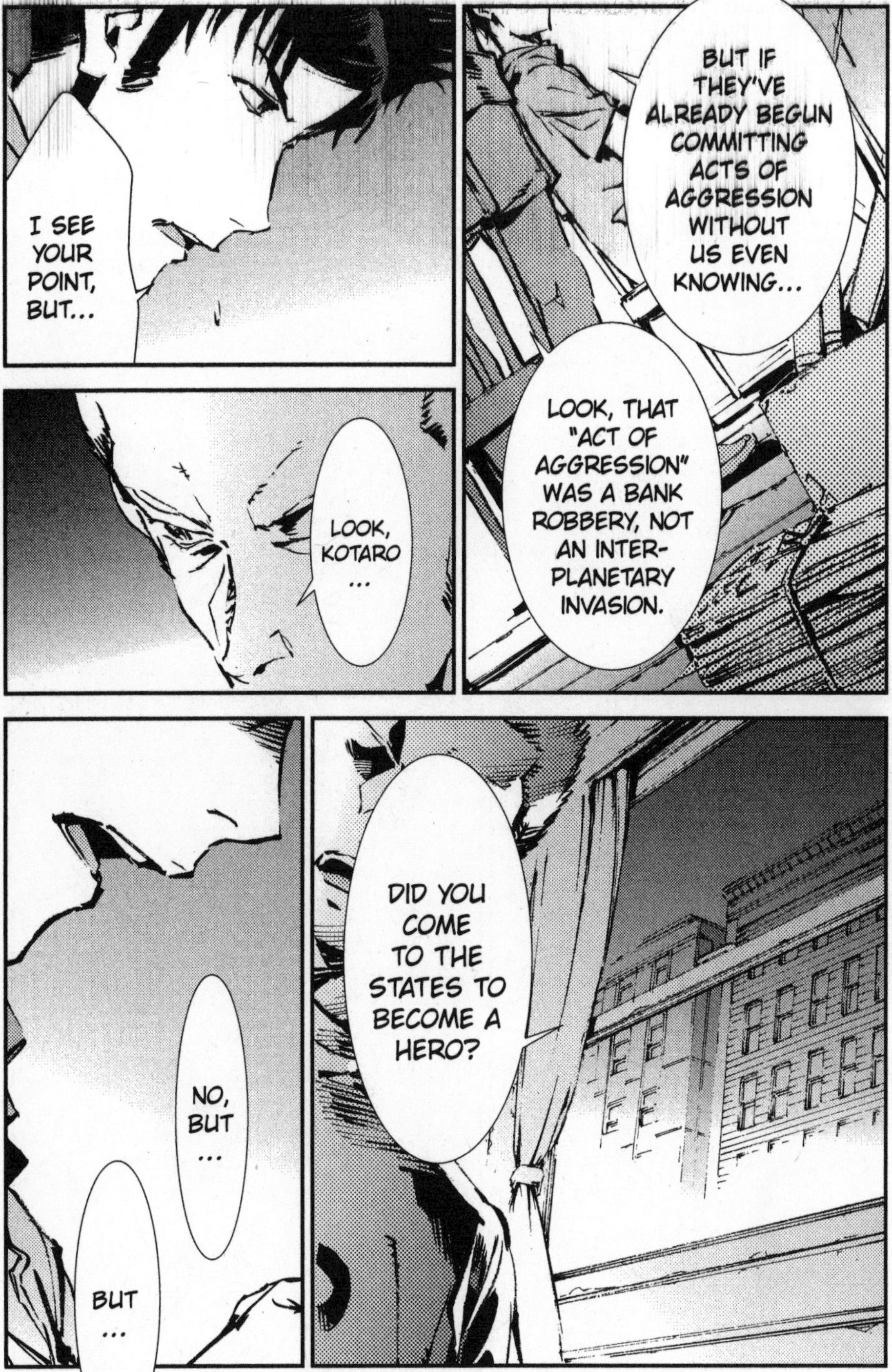
BUT IF THEY'VE ALREADY BEGUN COMMITTING ACTS OF AGGRESSION WITHOUT US EVEN KNOWING...
LOOK, THAT "ACT OF AGGRESSION" WAS A BANK ROBBERY, NOT AN INTER-PLANETARY INVASION.
I SEE YOUR POINT, BUT...
LOOK, KOTARO ...
DID YOU COME TO THE STATES TO BECOME A HERO?
NO, BUT ...
BUT ...

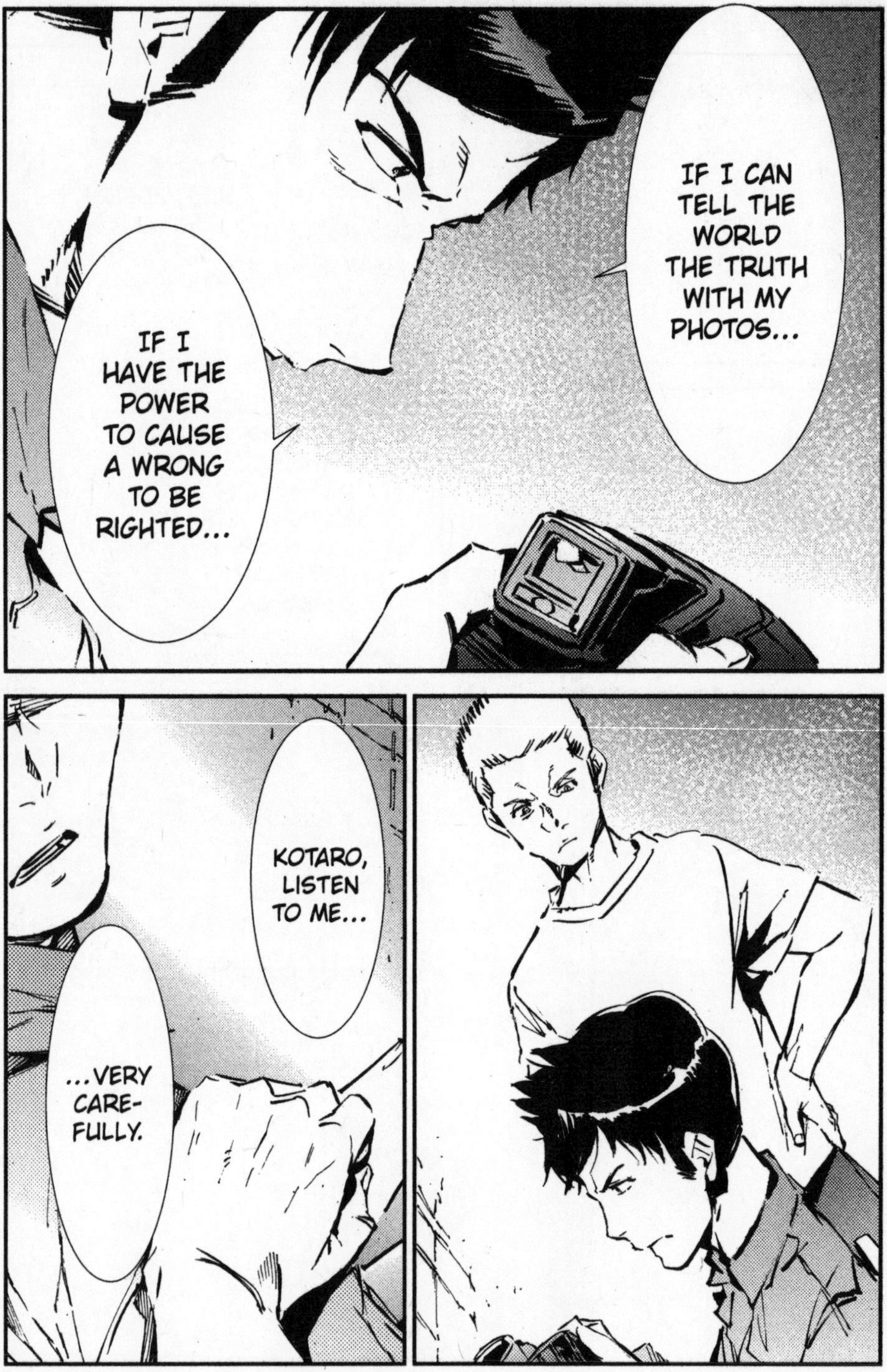
IF I CAN TELL THE WORLD THE TRUTH WITH MY PHOTOS...
IF I HAVE THE POWER TO CAUSE A WRONG TO BE RIGHTED...
KOTARO, LISTEN TO ME...
...VERY CARE-FULLY.

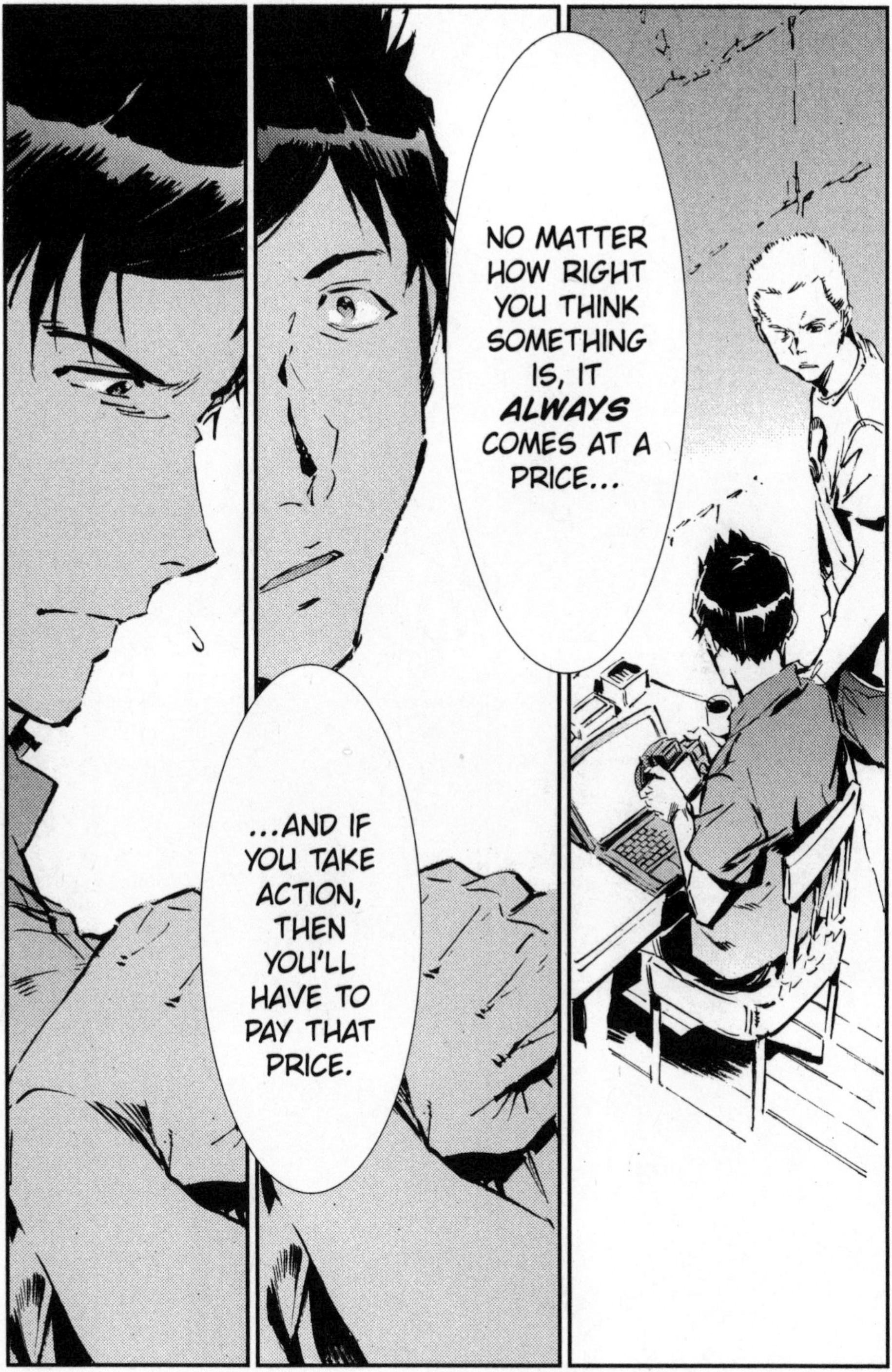
NO MATTER HOW RIGHT YOU THINK SOMETHING IS, IT ALWAYS COMES AT A PRICE...
...AND IF YOU TAKE ACTION, THEN YOU'LL HAVE TO PAY THAT PRICE.

Japan

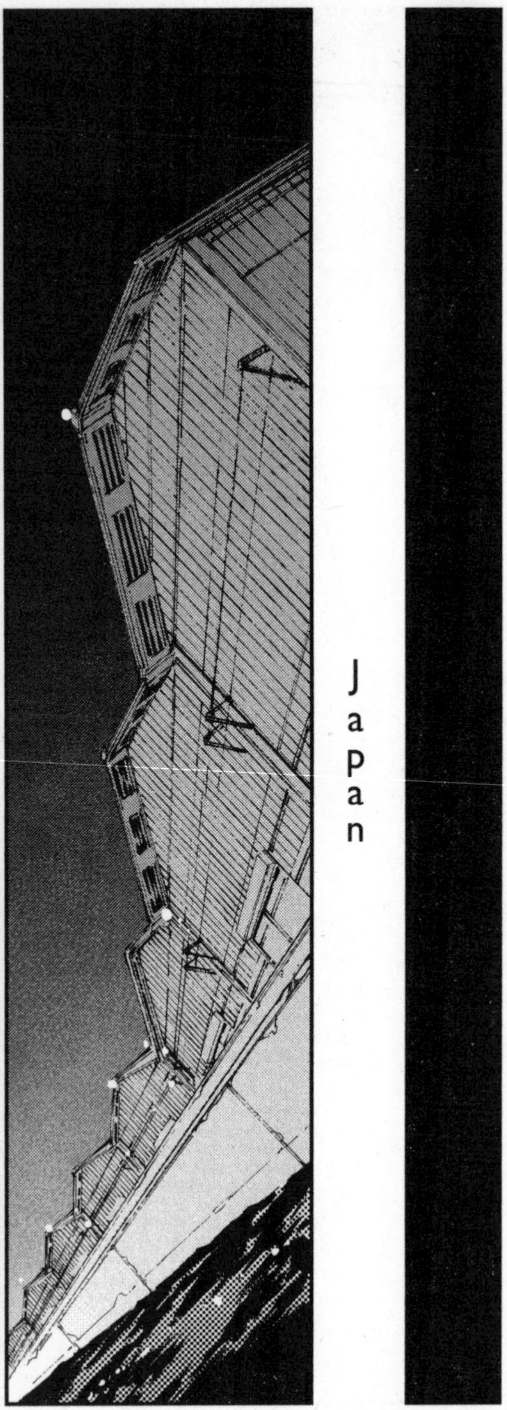

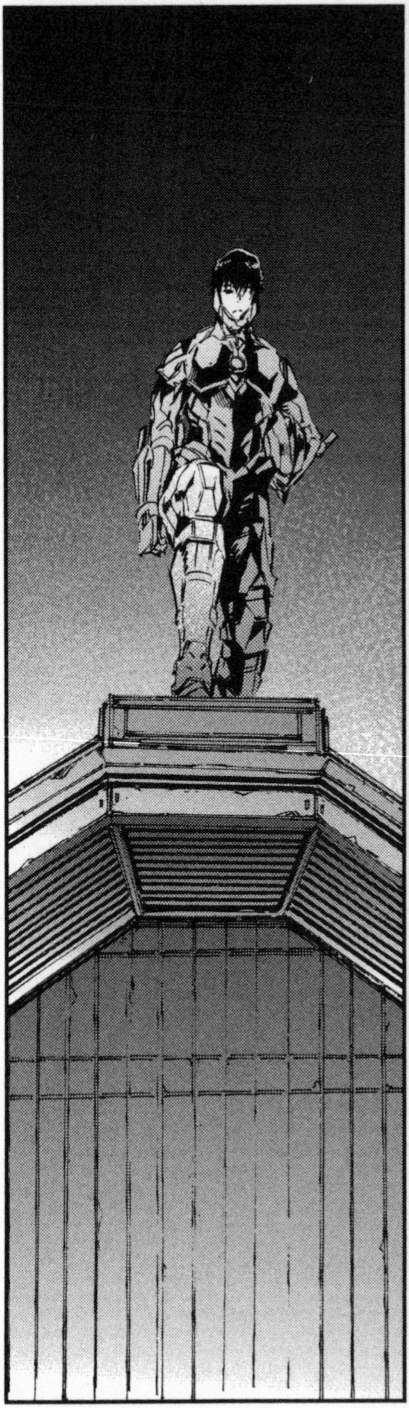

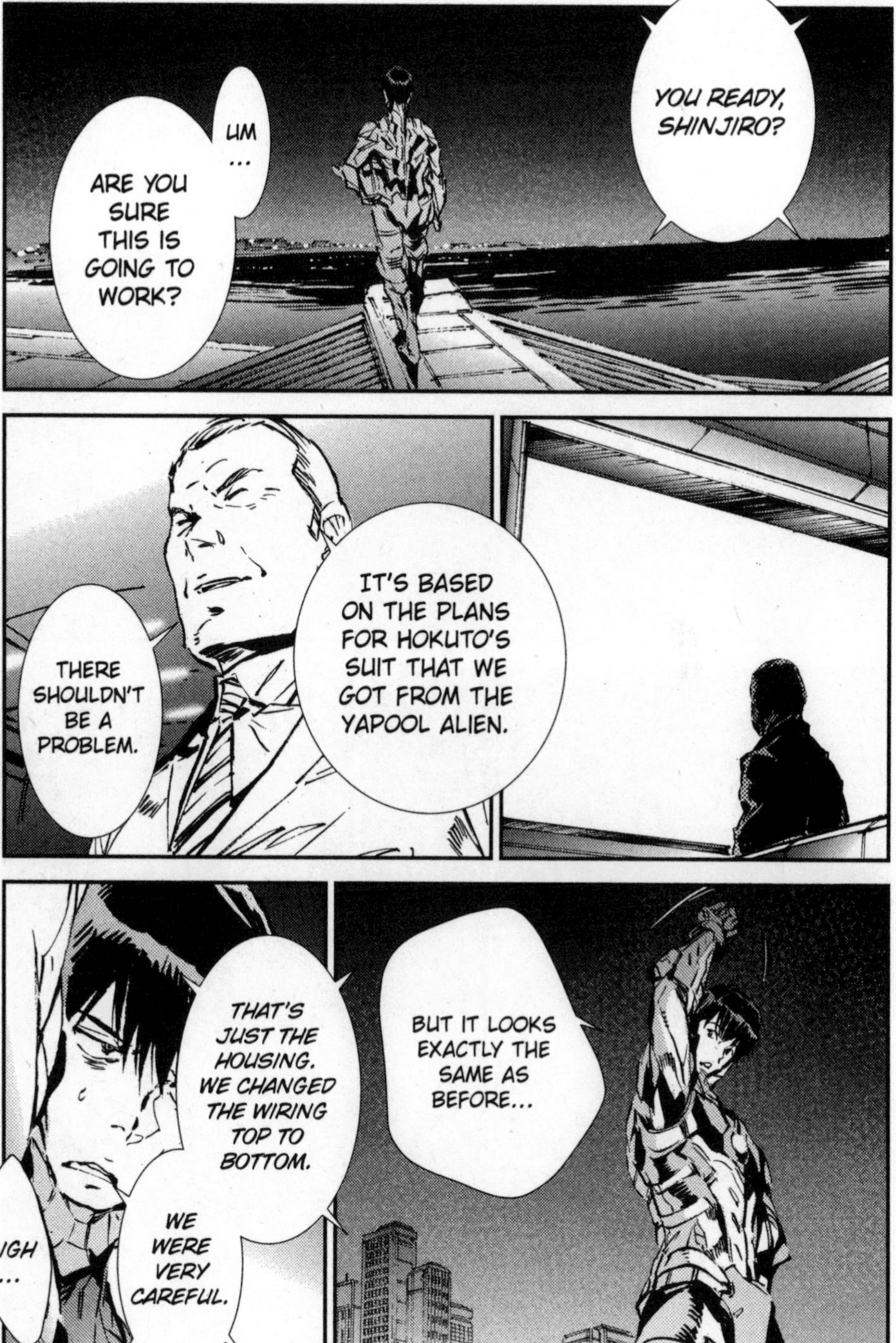
YOU READY, SHINJIRO?
UM ...
ARE YOU SURE THIS IS GOING TO WORK?
IT'S BASED ON THE PLANS FOR HOKUTO'S SUIT THAT WE GOT FROM THE YAPOOL ALIEN.
THERE SHOULDN'T BE A PROBLEM.
BUT IT LOOKS EXACTLY THE SAME AS BEFORE...
THAT'S JUST THE HOUSING. WE CHANGED THE WIRING TOP TO BOTTOM.
WE WERE VERY CAREFUL.
SIGH ...

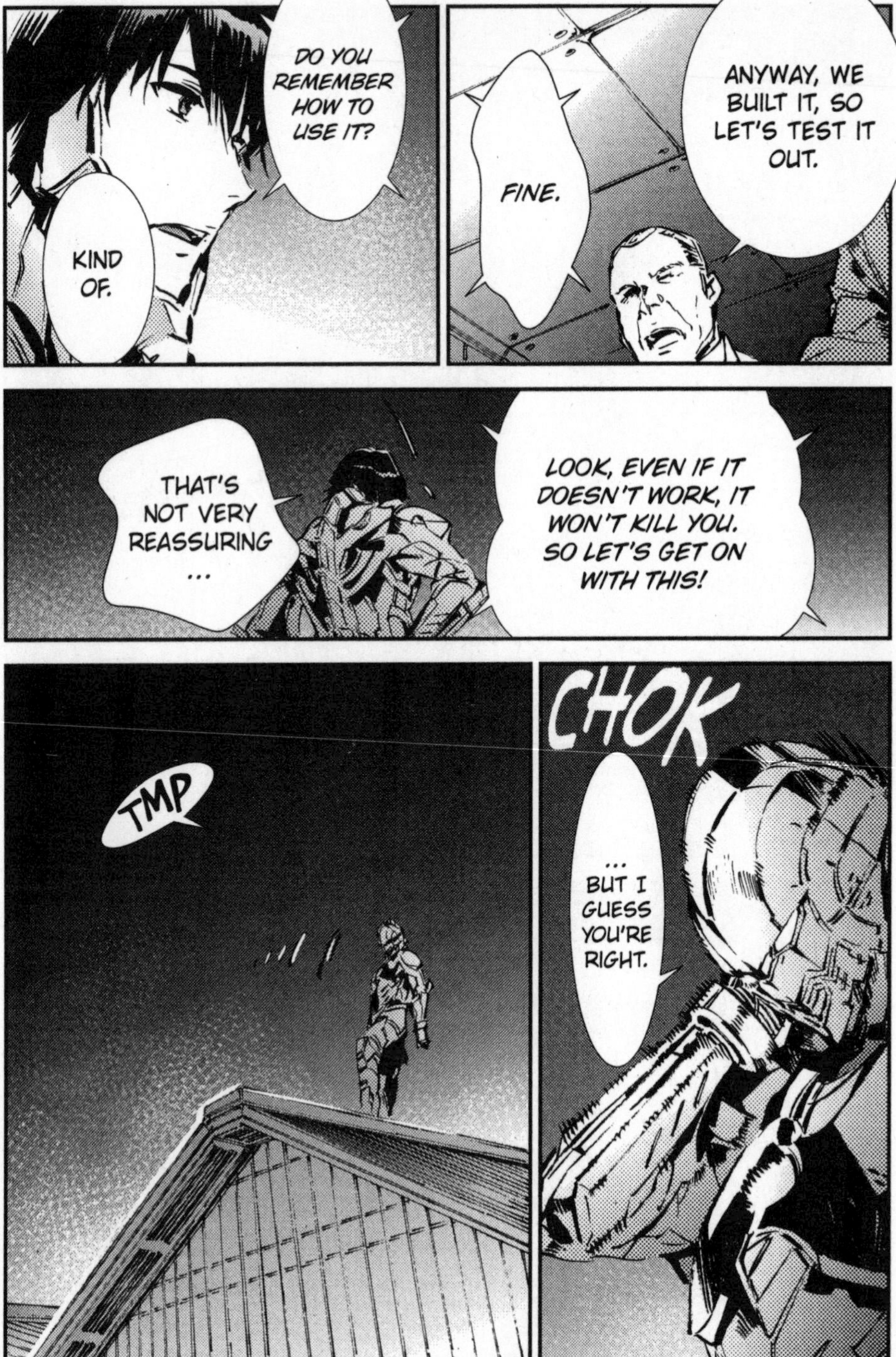
ANYWAY, WE BUILT IT, SO LET'S TEST IT OUT.
FINE.
DO YOU REMEMBER HOW TO USE IT?
KIND OF.
LOOK, EVEN IF IT DOESN'T WORK, IT WON'T KILL YOU. SO LET'S GET ON WITH THIS!
THAT'S NOT VERY REASSURING ...
CHOK
... BUT I GUESS YOU'RE RIGHT.
TMP

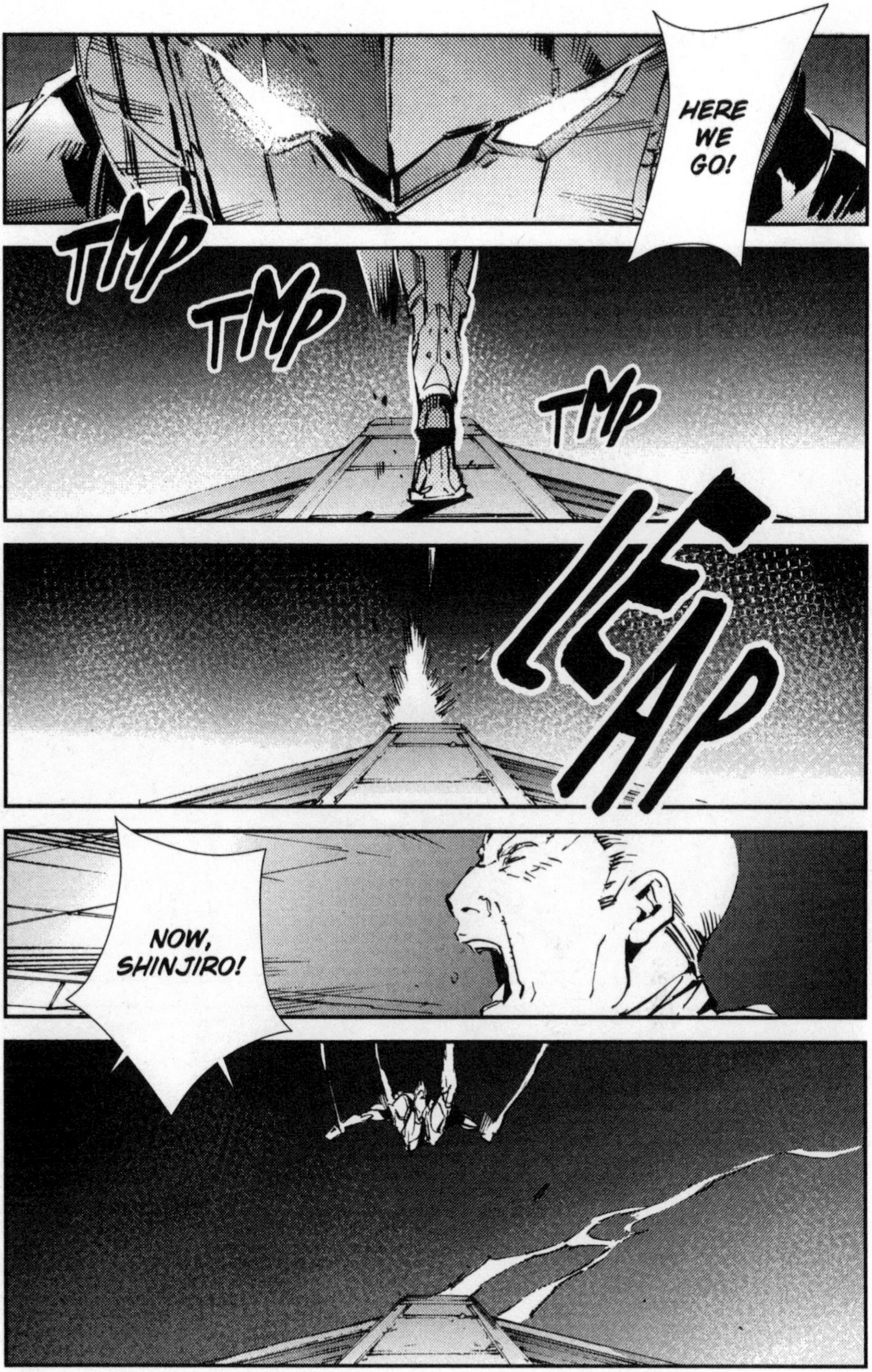
HERE WE GO!
TMP TMP
TMP
LEAP
NOW, SHINJIRO!

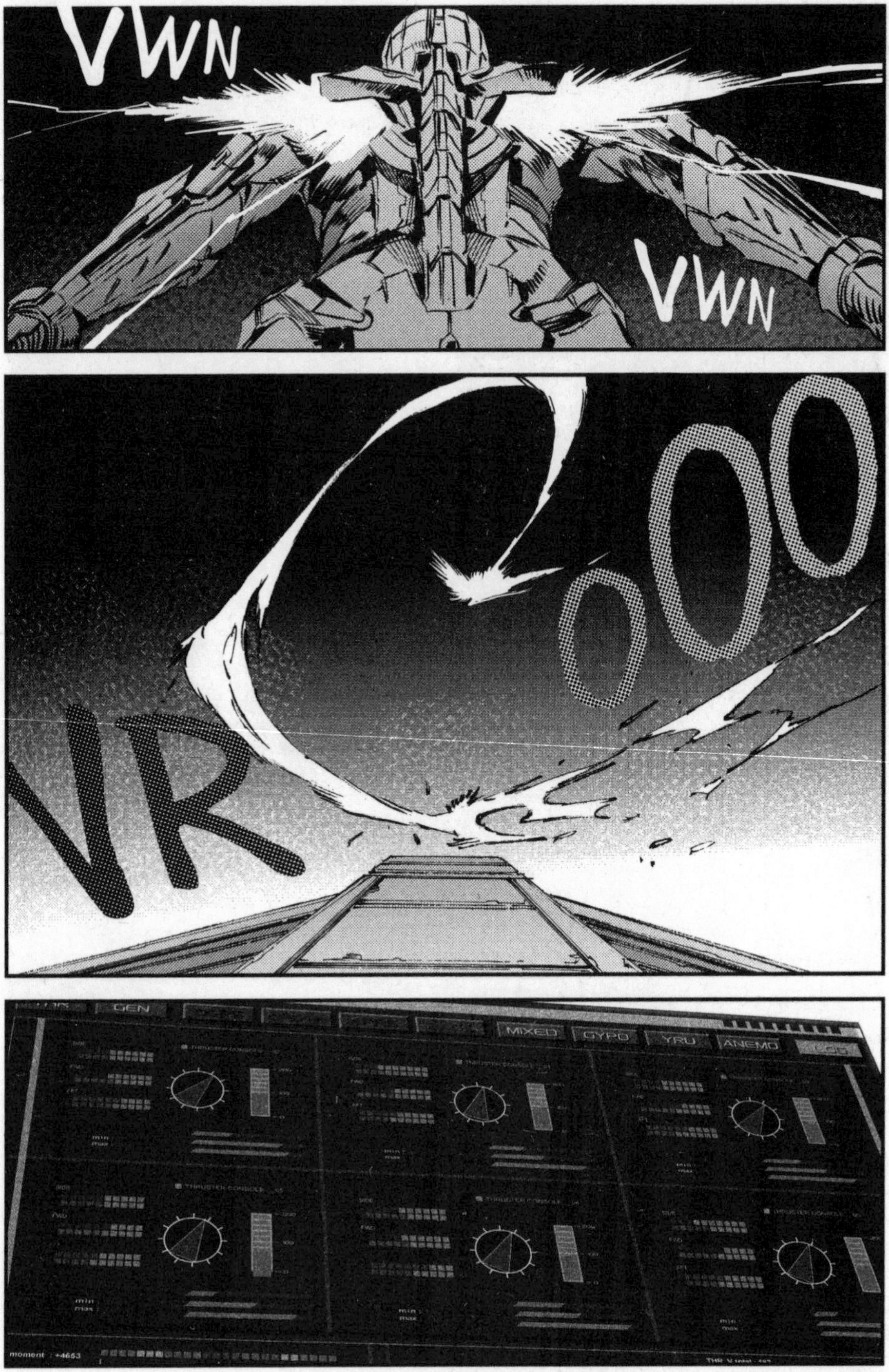
VWN
VWN
VRCOOOO
GEN
MIXED
GYPO
YRU
ANEMO
THRUSTER CONSOLE
min
max
moment : +4653

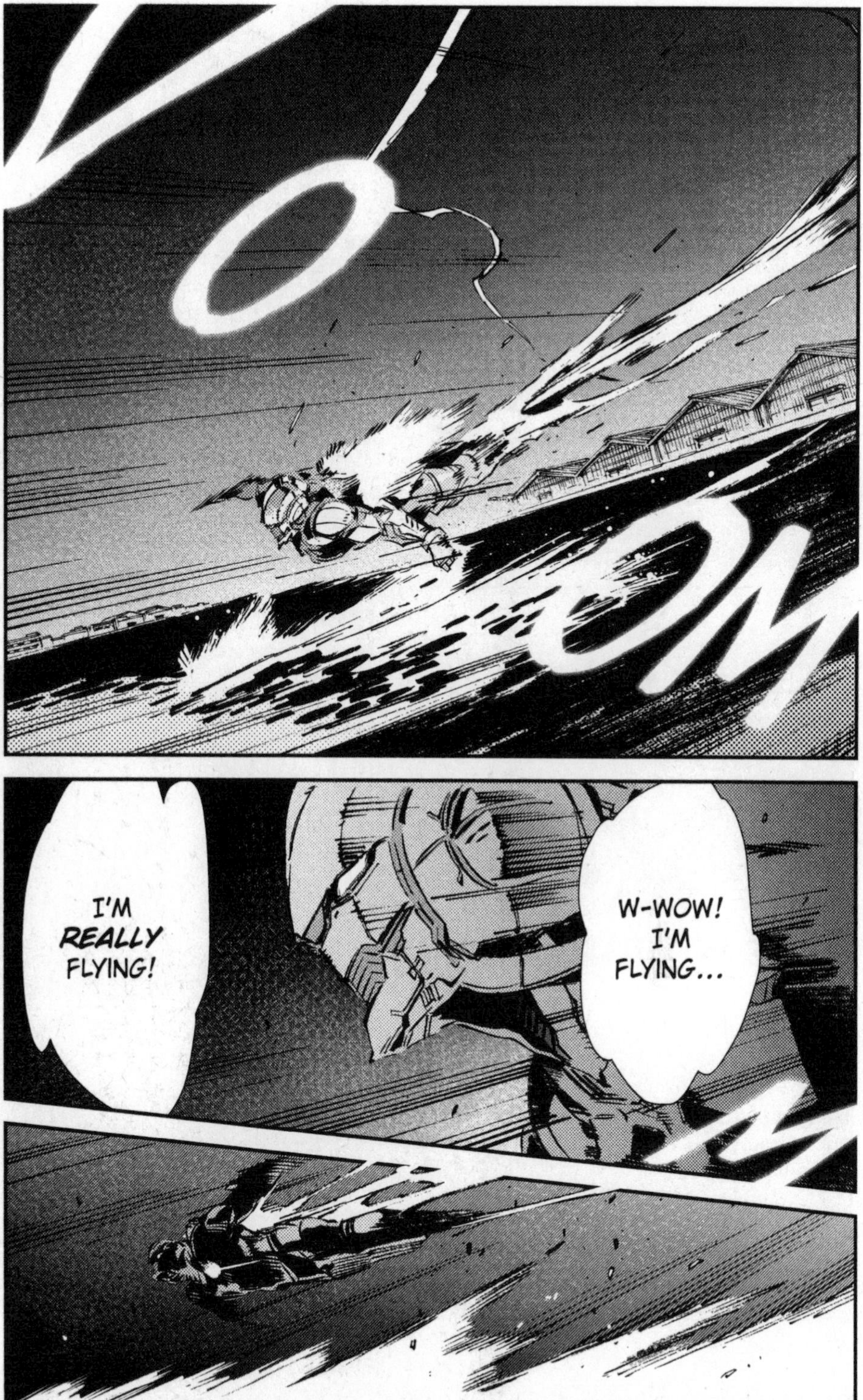
W-WOW! I'M FLYING...
I'M *REALLY* FLYING!

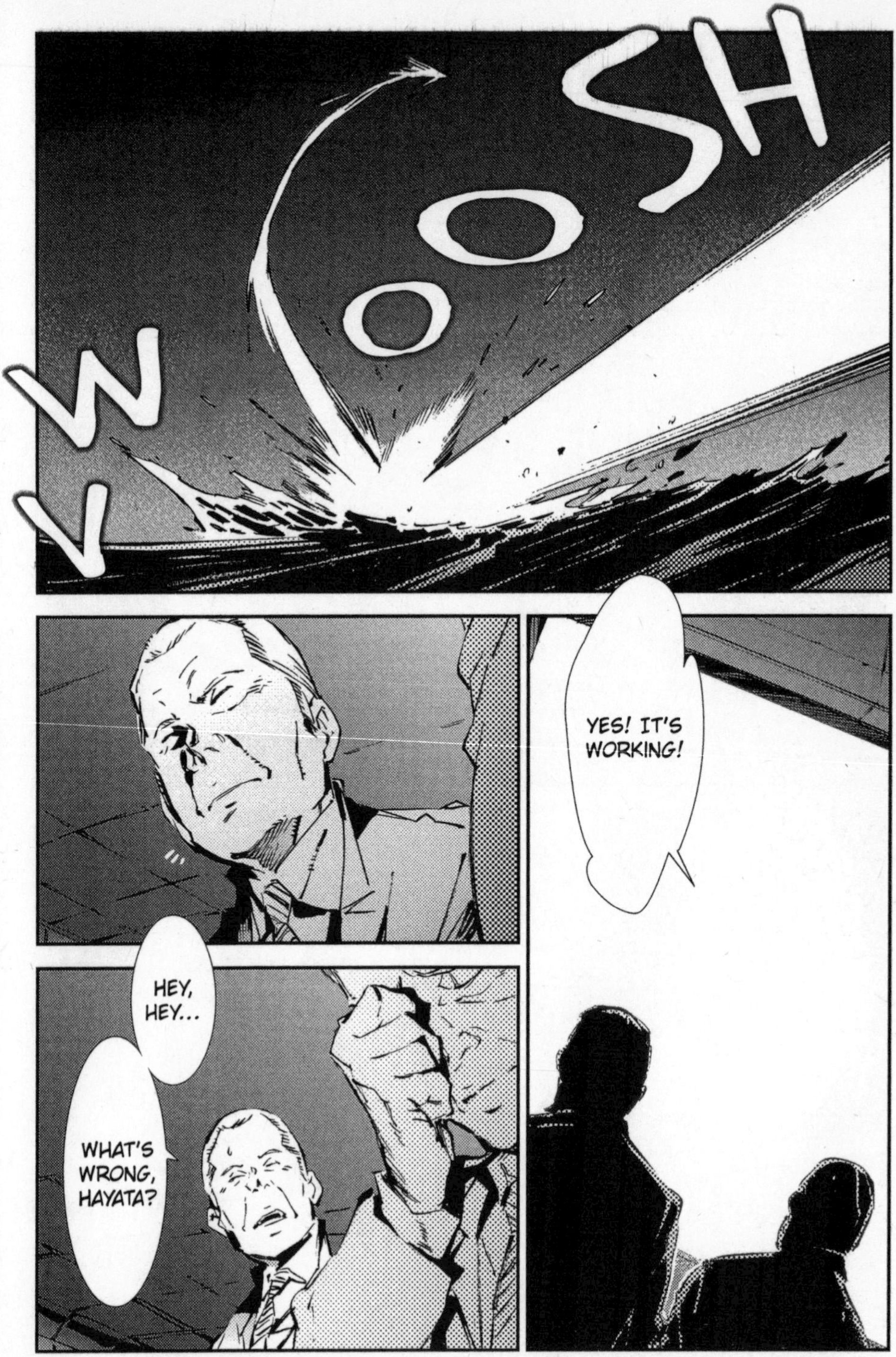
WOOSH
YES! IT'S WORKING!
HEY, HEY...
WHAT'S WRONG, HAYATA?

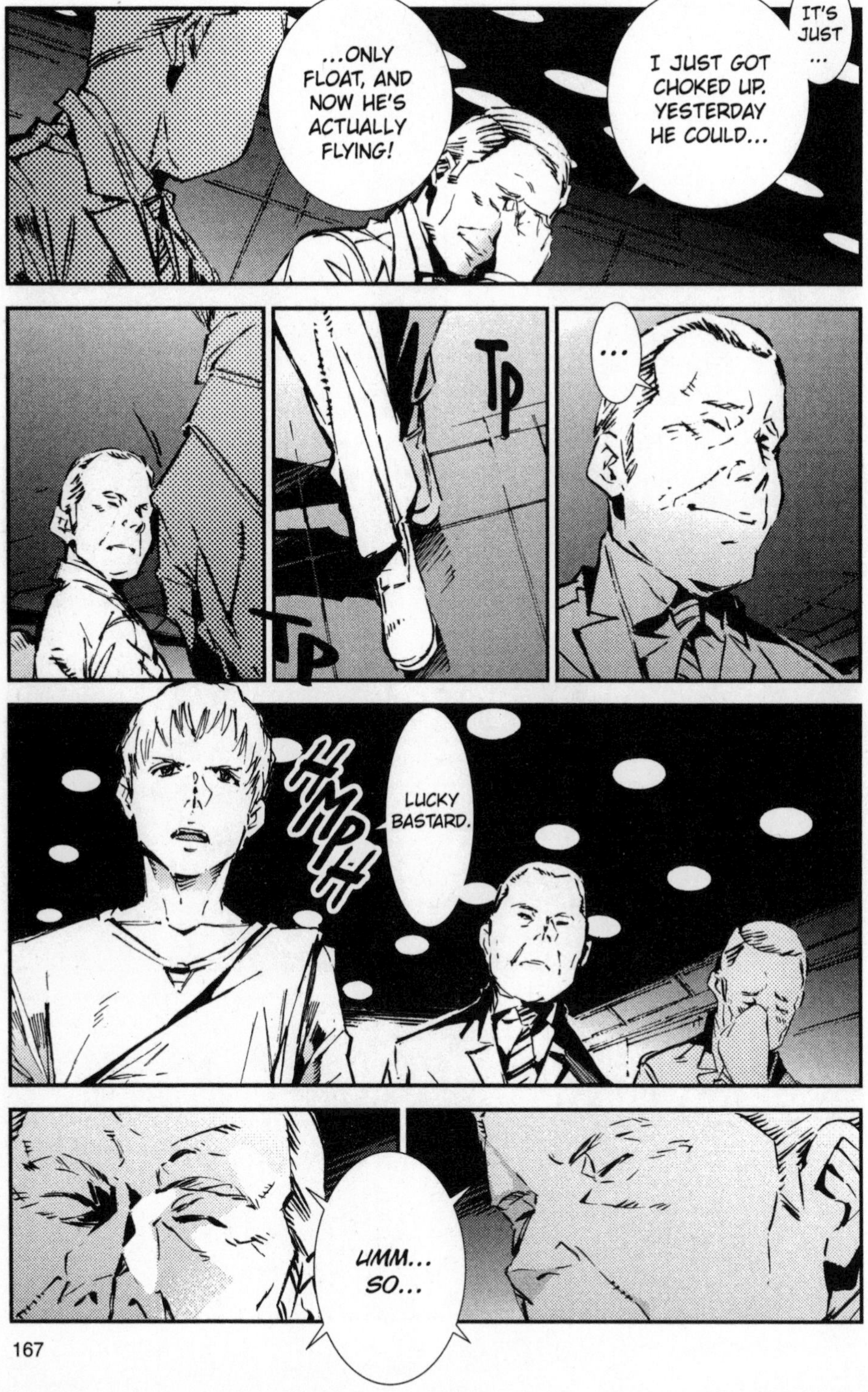
IT'S JUST ...
I JUST GOT CHOKED UP. YESTERDAY HE COULD...
...ONLY FLOAT, AND NOW HE'S ACTUALLY FLYING!
...
TP
TP
HMPH
LUCKY BASTARD.
UMM... SO...

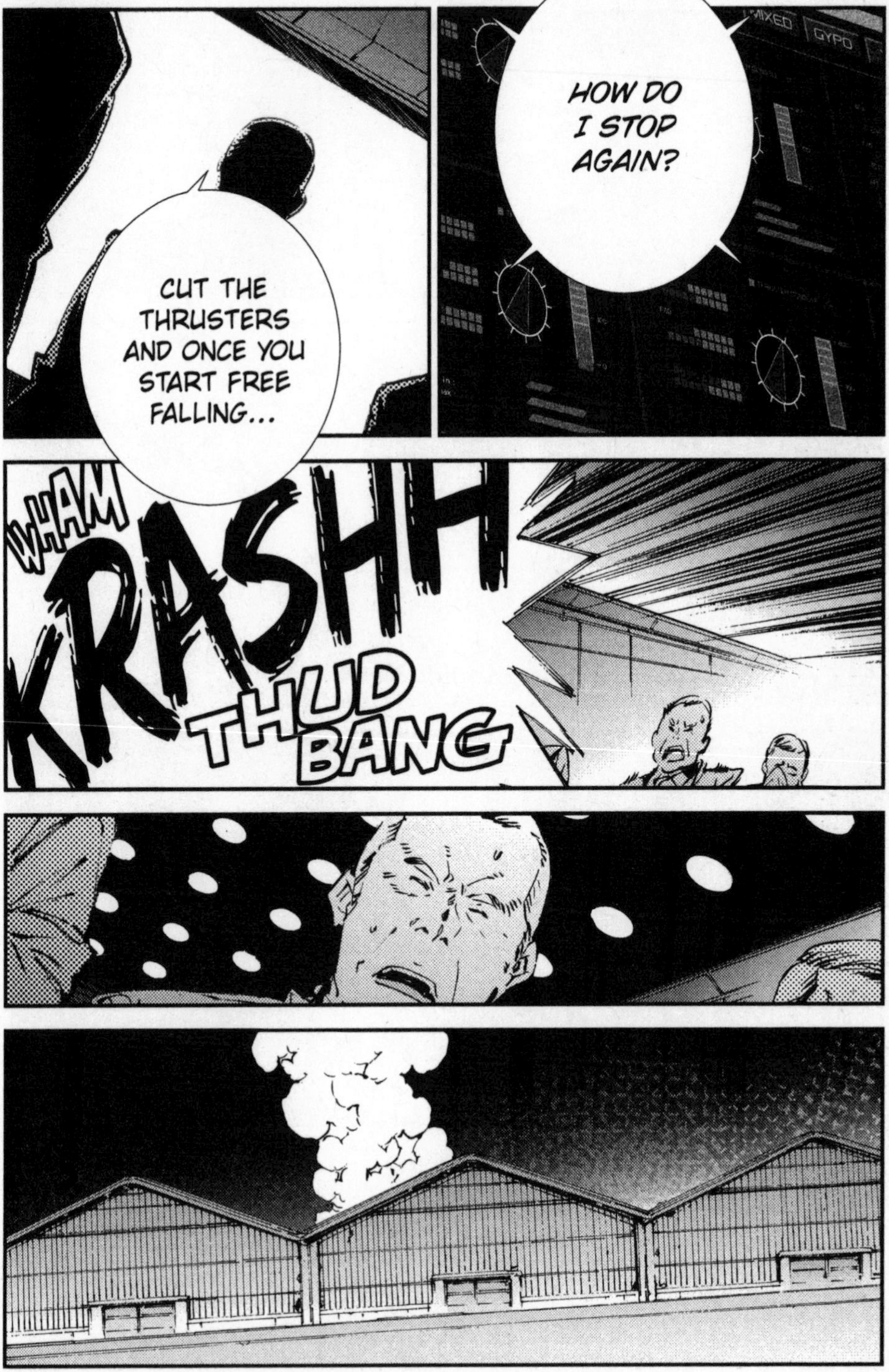
MIXED
GYPO
HOW DO I STOP AGAIN?
CUT THE THRUSTERS AND ONCE YOU START FREE FALLING...
KRASHH
WHAM
THUD
BANG

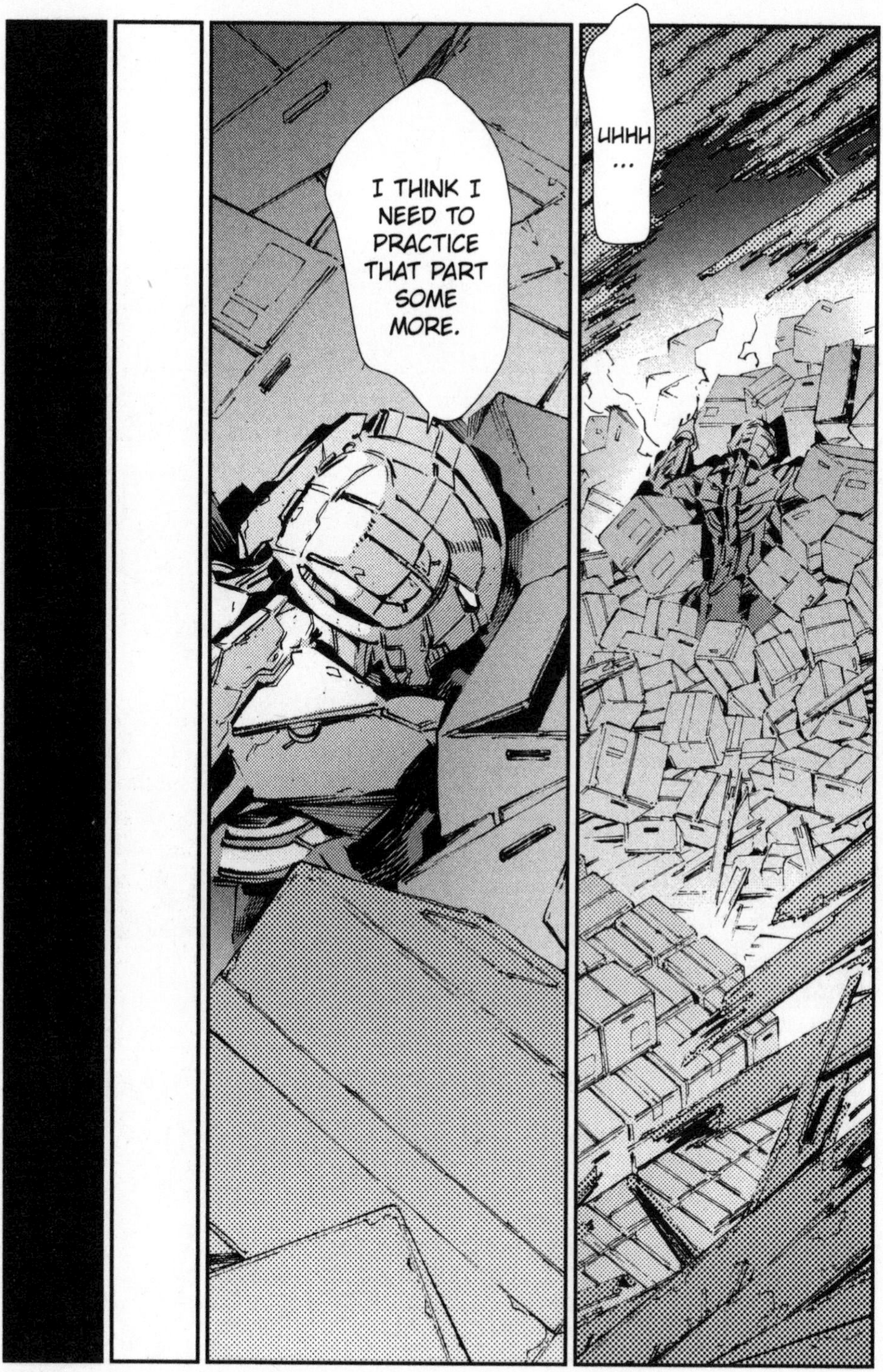
UHHH ...
I THINK I NEED TO PRACTICE THAT PART SOME MORE.

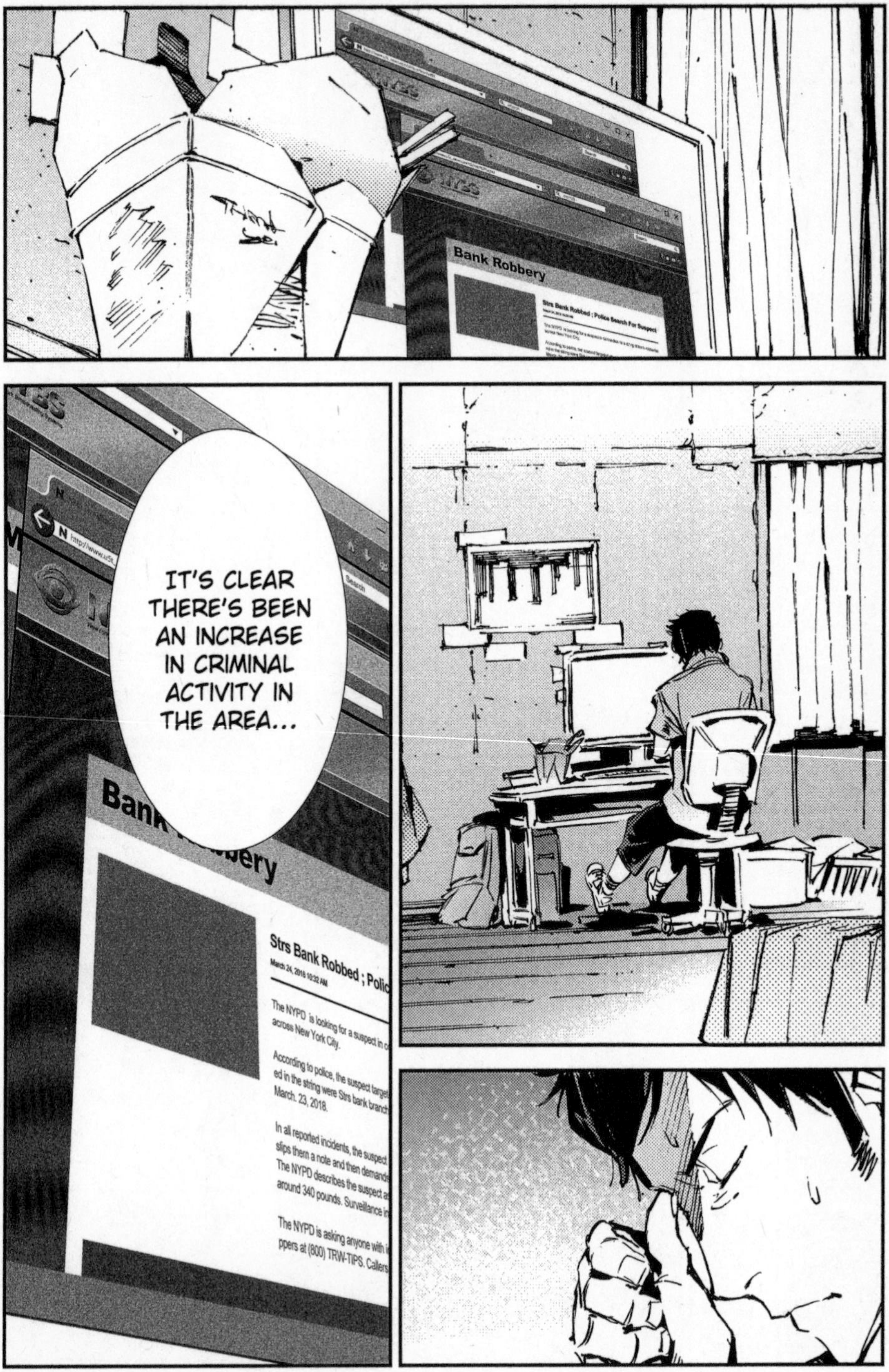
Bank Robbery
Strs Bank Robbed ; Police Search For Suspect
IT'S CLEAR THERE'S BEEN AN INCREASE IN CRIMINAL ACTIVITY IN THE AREA...
Bank Robbery
Strs Bank Robbed ; Polic
March 24, 2018 10:32 AM
The NYPD is looking for a suspect in c
across New York City.
According to police, the suspect target
ed in the string were Strs bank branch
March. 23, 2018.
In all reported incidents, the suspect
slips them a note and then demands
The NYPD describes the suspect a
around 340 pounds. Surveillance in
The NYPD is asking anyone with i
ppers at (800) TRW-TIPS. Callers

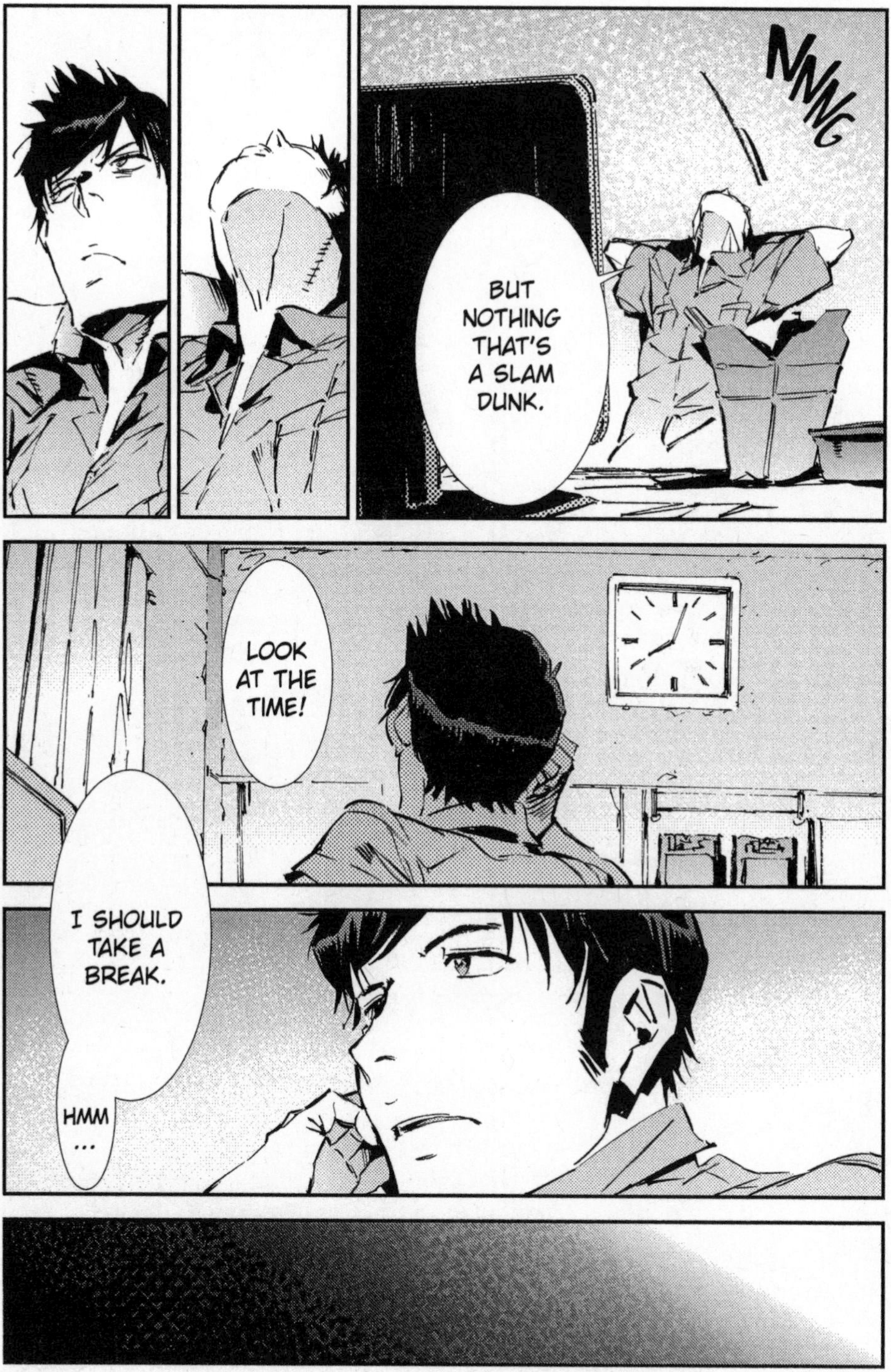
NNNG
BUT NOTHING THAT'S A SLAM DUNK.
LOOK AT THE TIME!
I SHOULD TAKE A BREAK.
HMM...

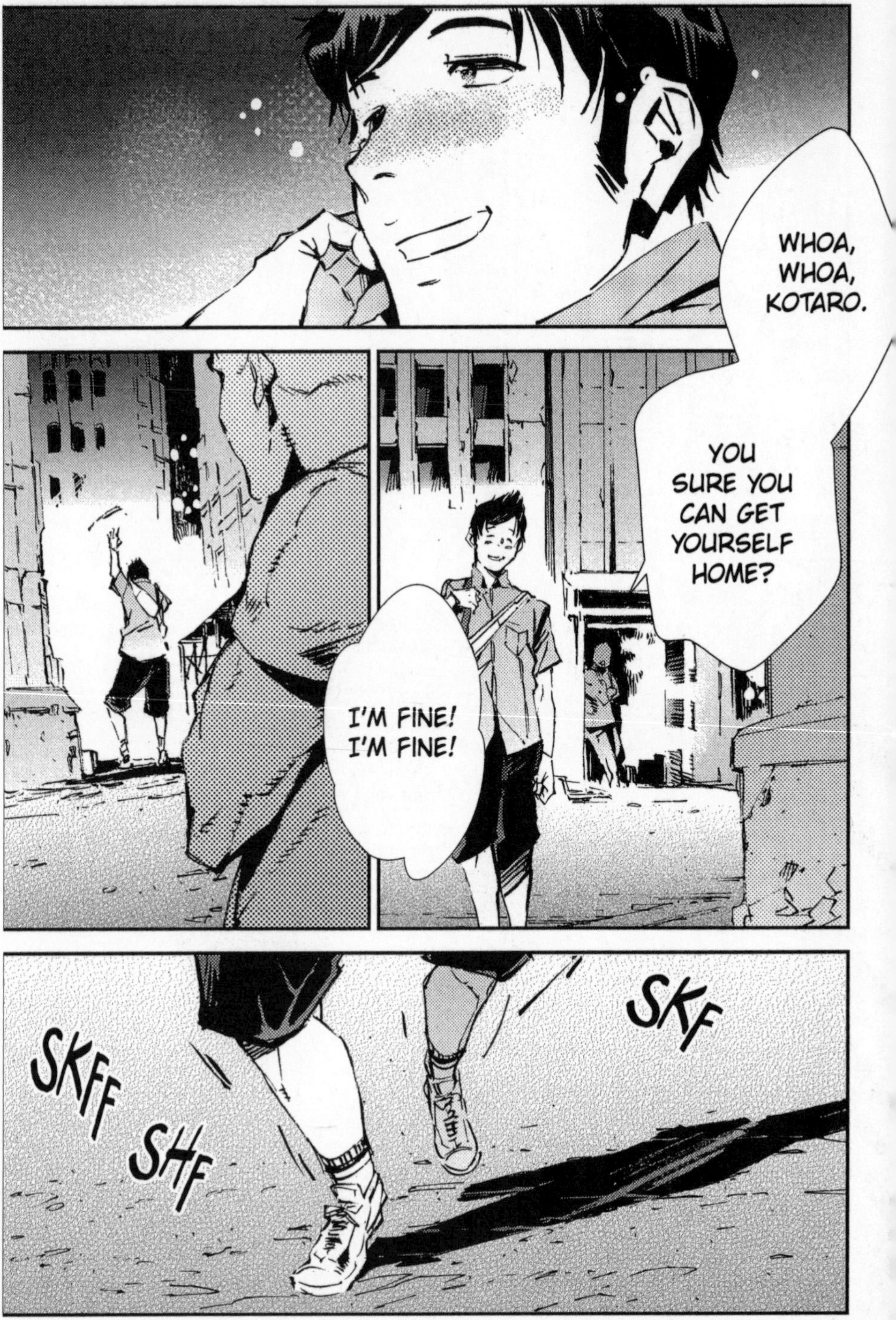
WHOA, WHOA, KOTARO.
YOU SURE YOU CAN GET YOURSELF HOME?
I'M FINE! I'M FINE!
SKF
SKFF
SHF

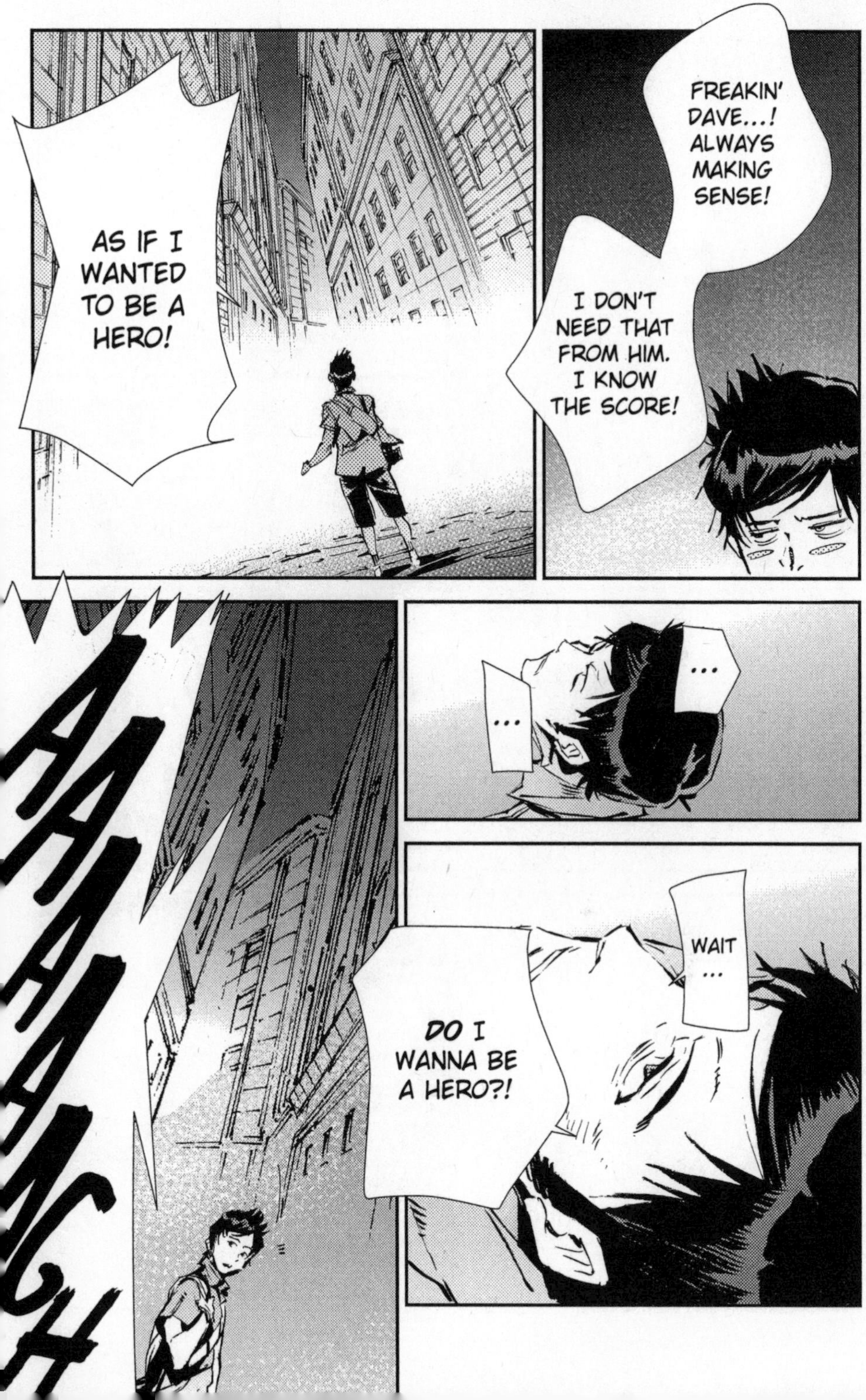
FREAKIN' DAVE...! ALWAYS MAKING SENSE!
I DON'T NEED THAT FROM HIM. I KNOW THE SCORE!
AS IF I WANTED TO BE A HERO!
...
...
WAIT...
DO I WANNA BE A HERO?!
AAAAAGH

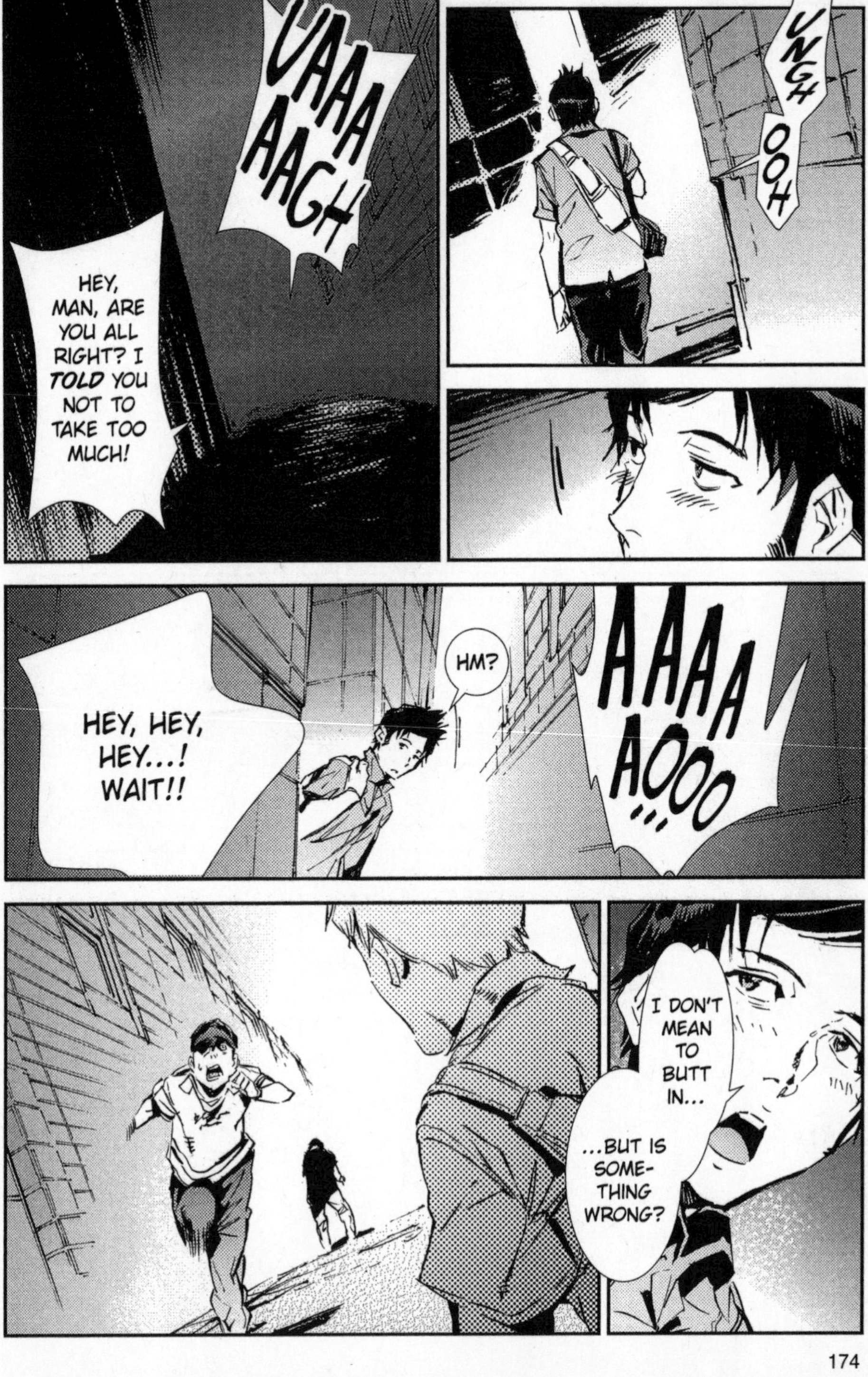
UNGH OOH
UAAAA AAGH
HEY, MAN, ARE YOU ALL RIGHT? I *TOLD* YOU NOT TO TAKE TOO MUCH!
AAAAAOOO...
HM?
HEY, HEY, HEY...! WAIT!!
I DON'T MEAN TO BUTT IN...
...BUT IS SOME-THING WRONG?

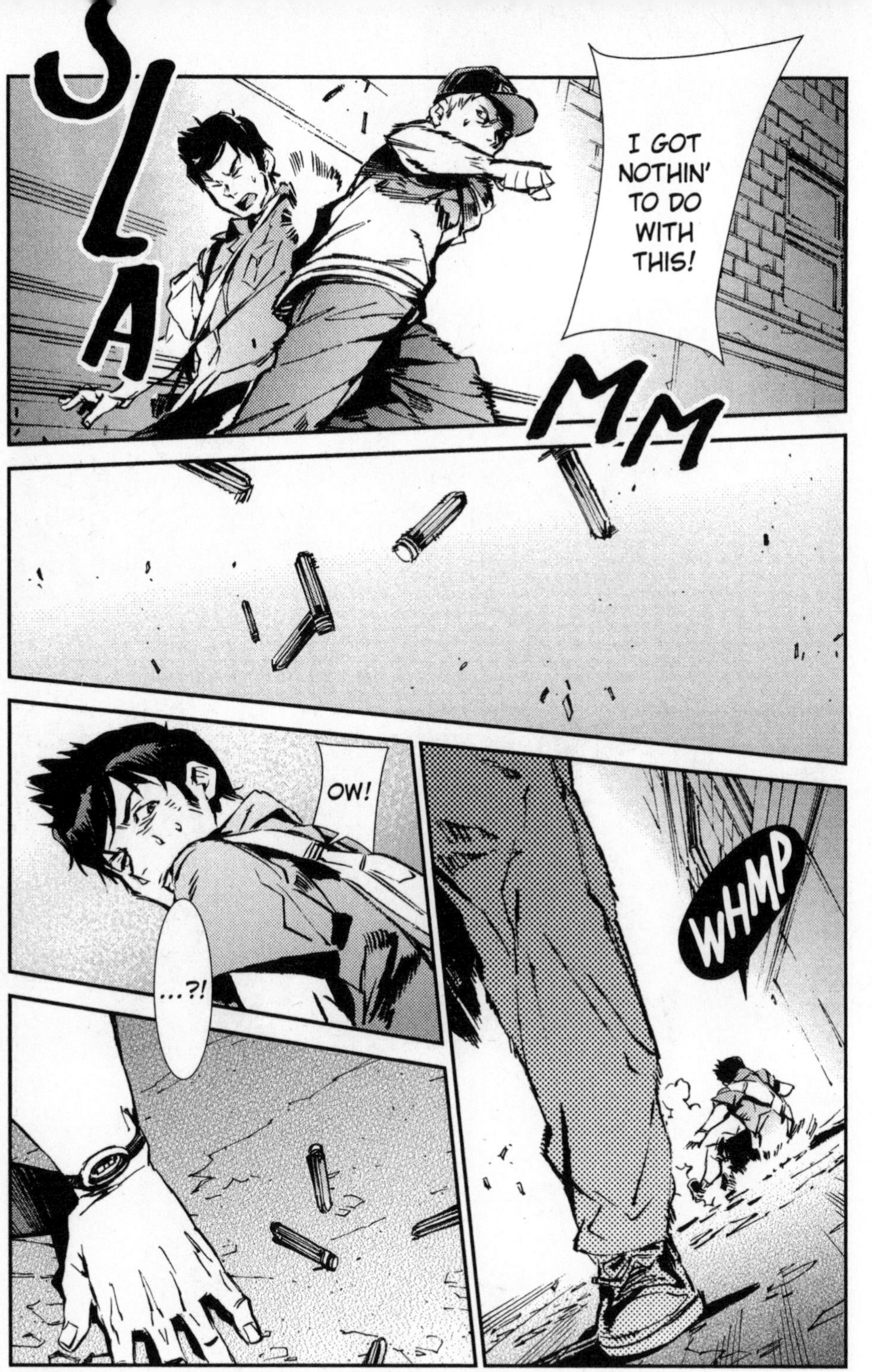
I GOT NOTHIN' TO DO WITH THIS!
SLAMM
WHMP
OW!
...?!

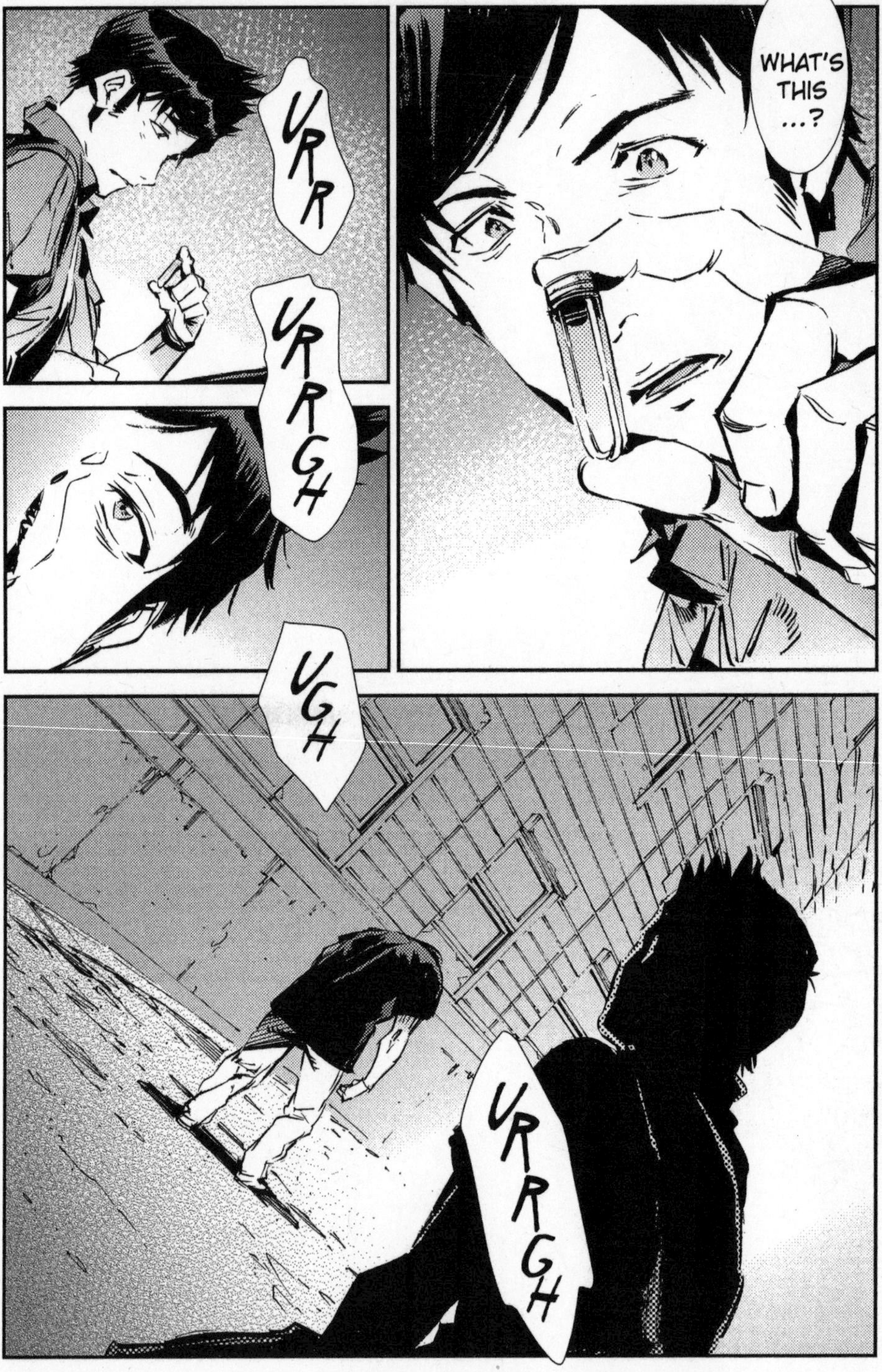
WHAT'S THIS ...?
URR
URRGH
UGH
URRGH

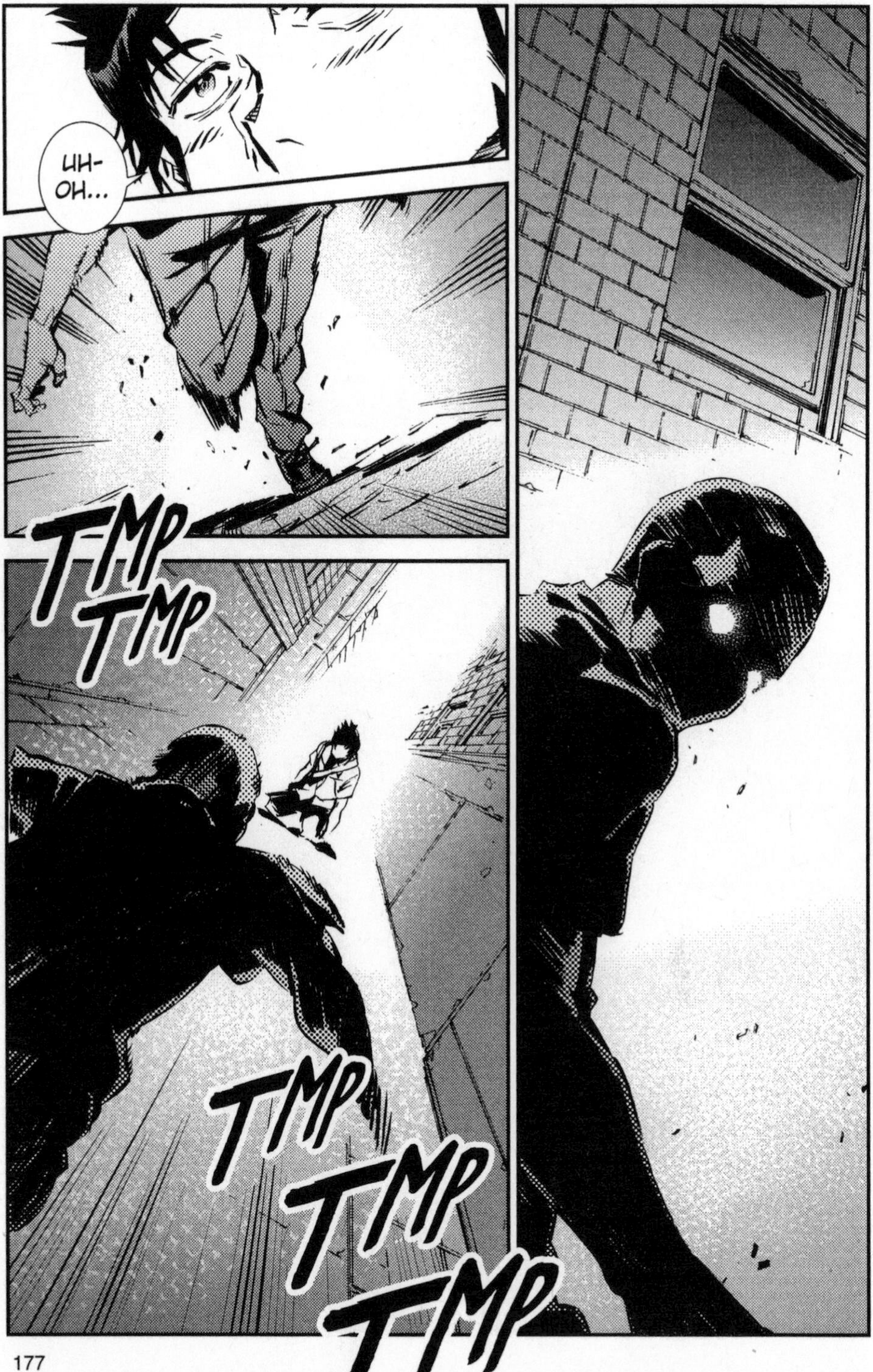
UH-OH...
TMP TMP
TMP TMP TMP

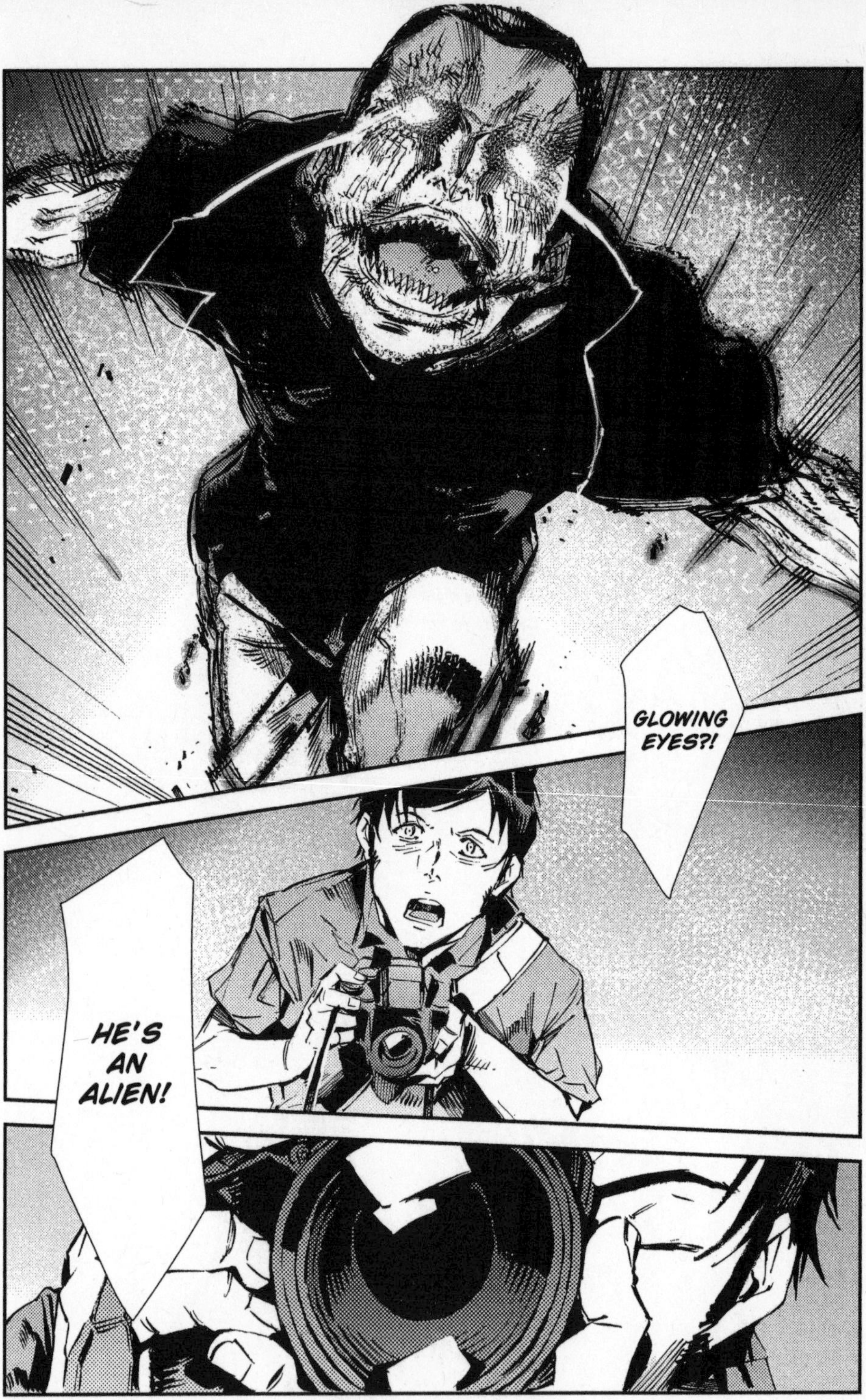
GLOWING EYES?!
HE'S AN ALIEN!

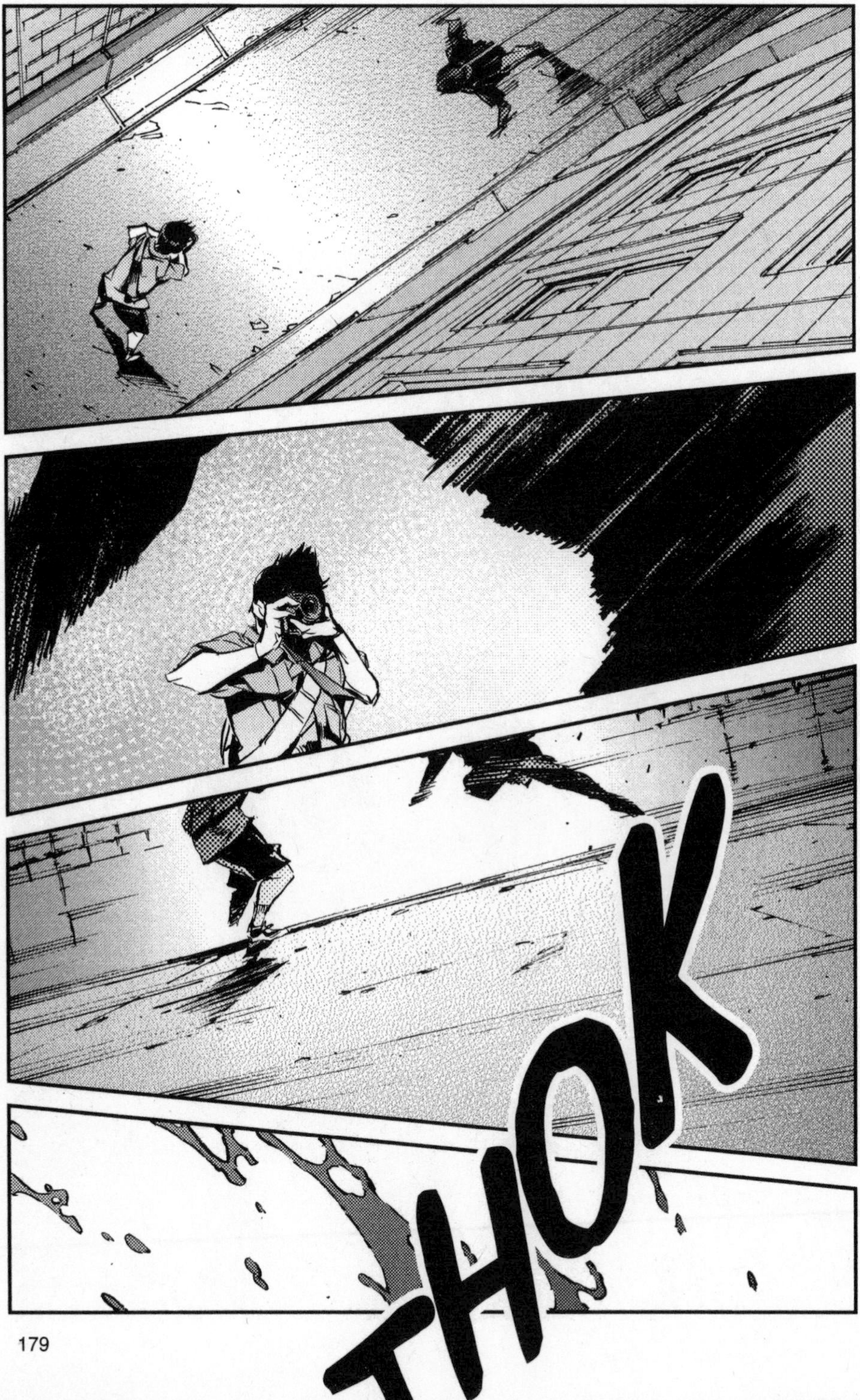
THOK

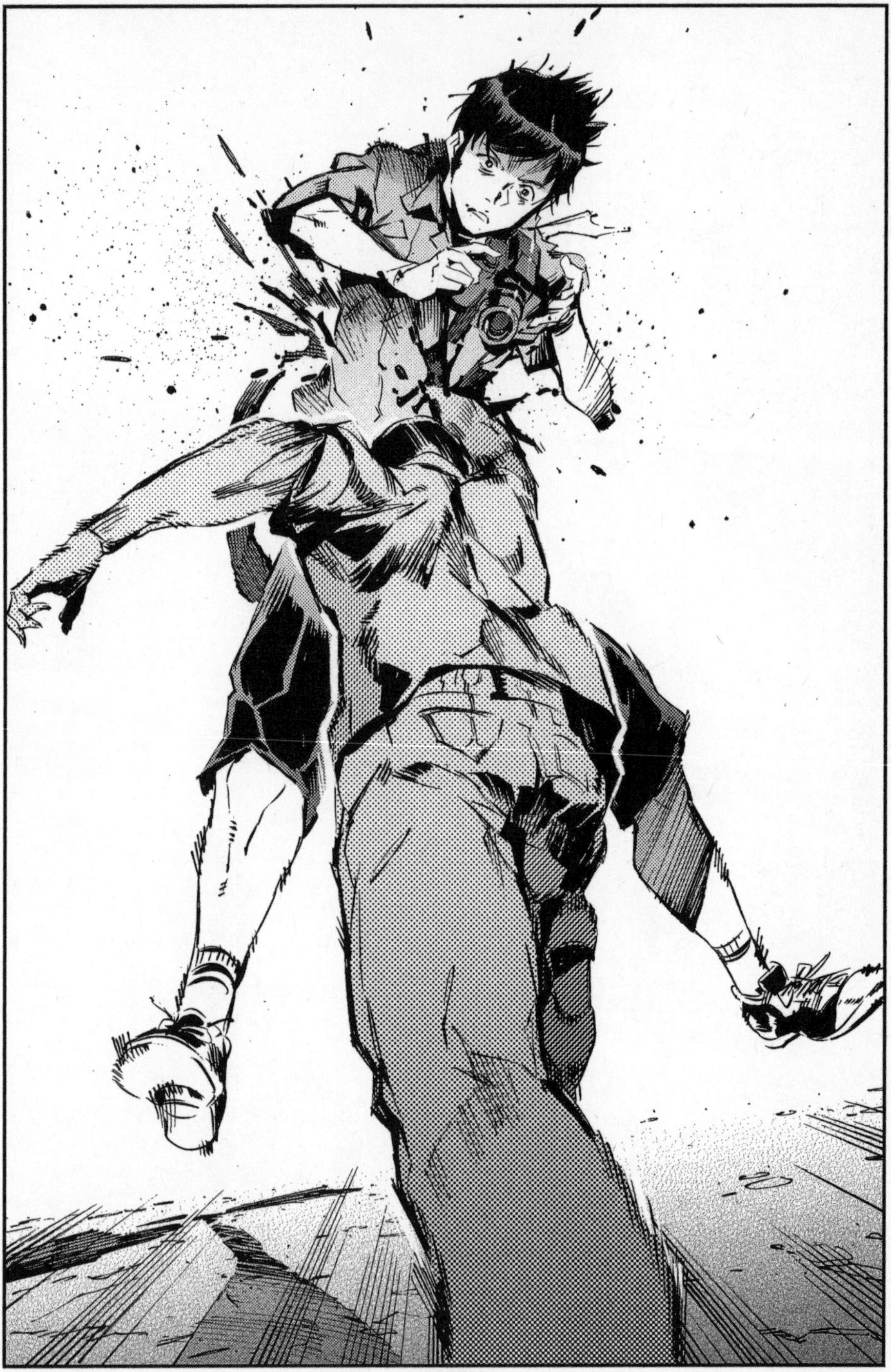

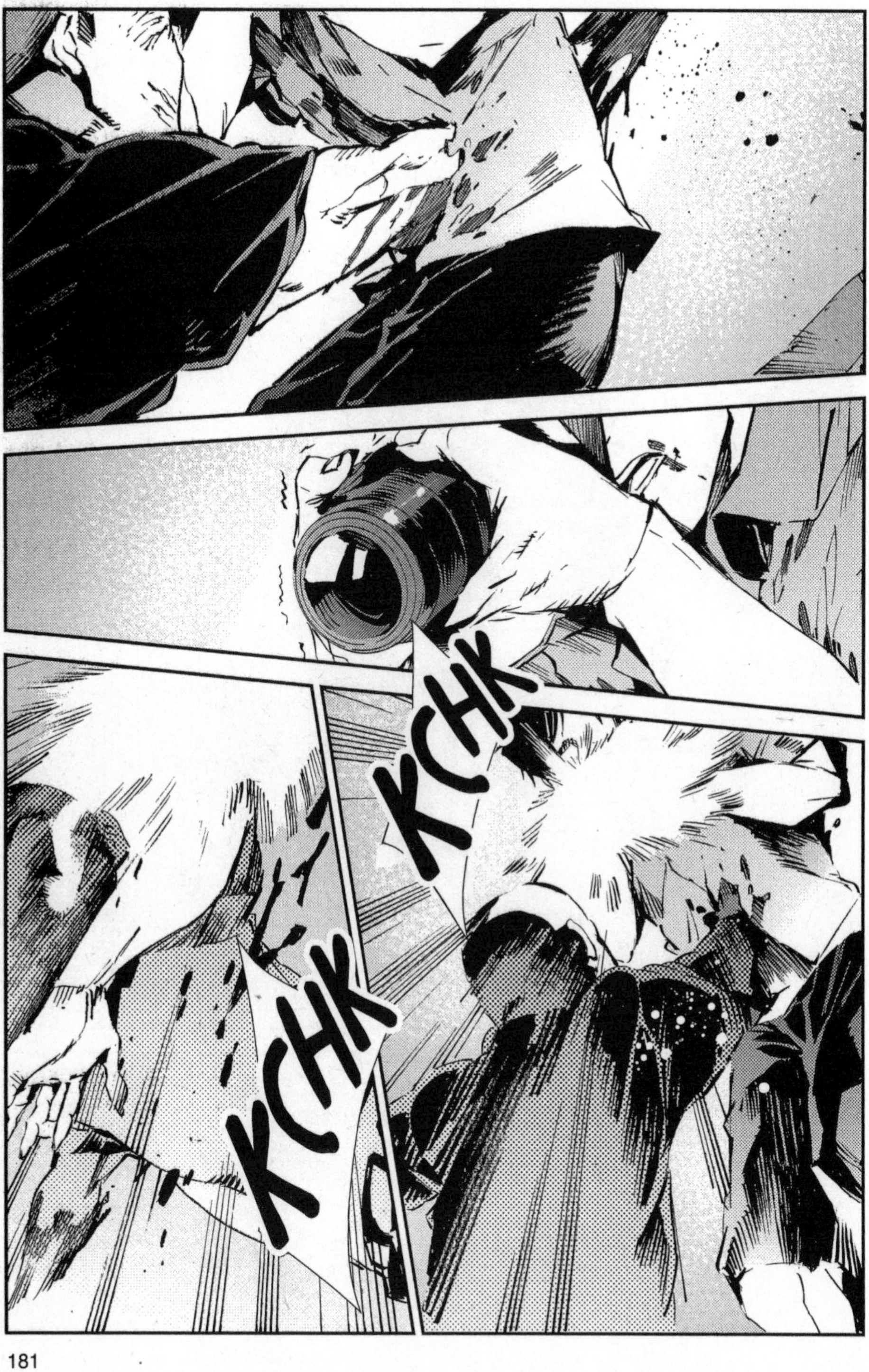
KCHK
KCHK

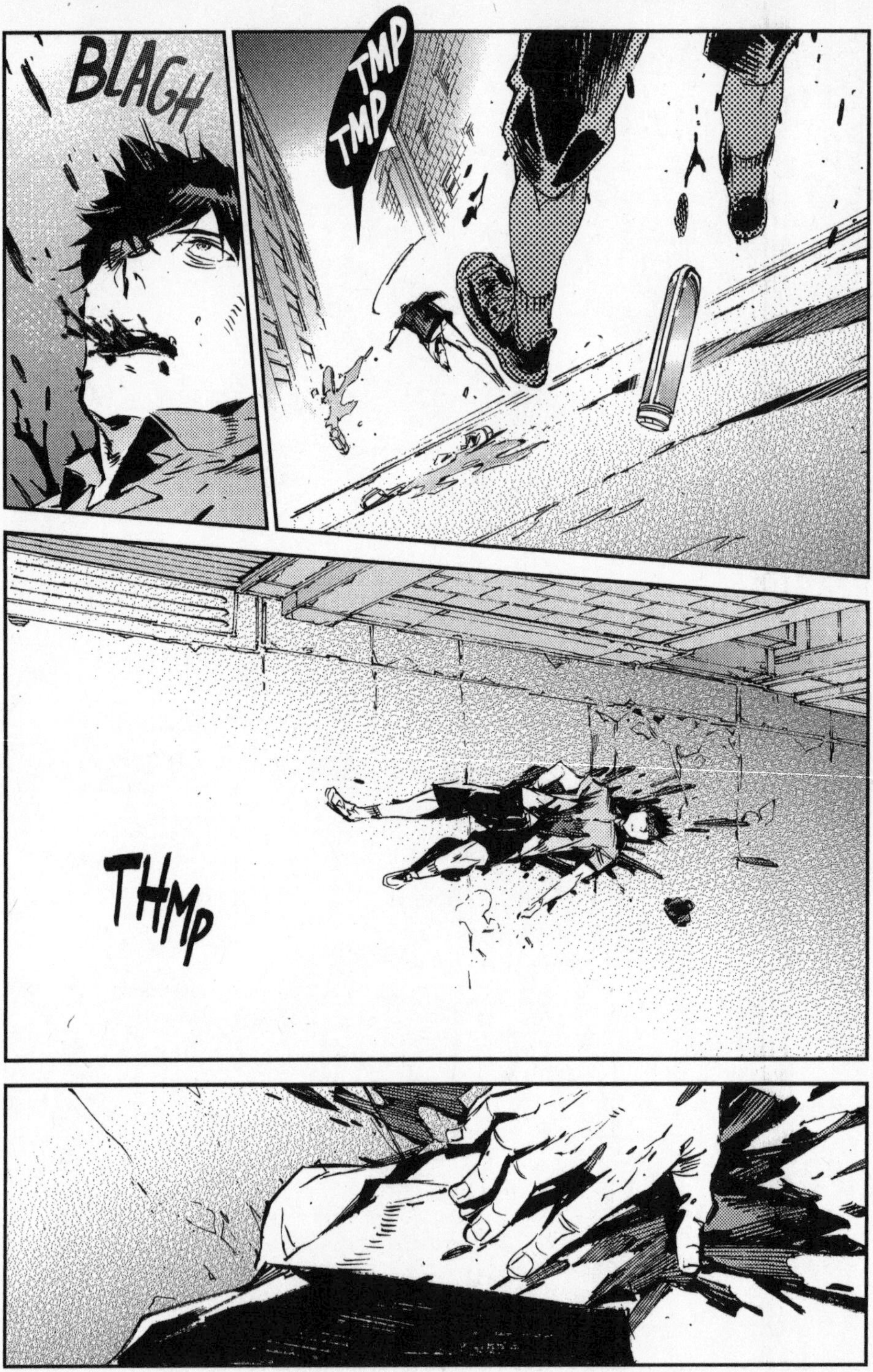
TMP
TMP
BLAGH
THMP

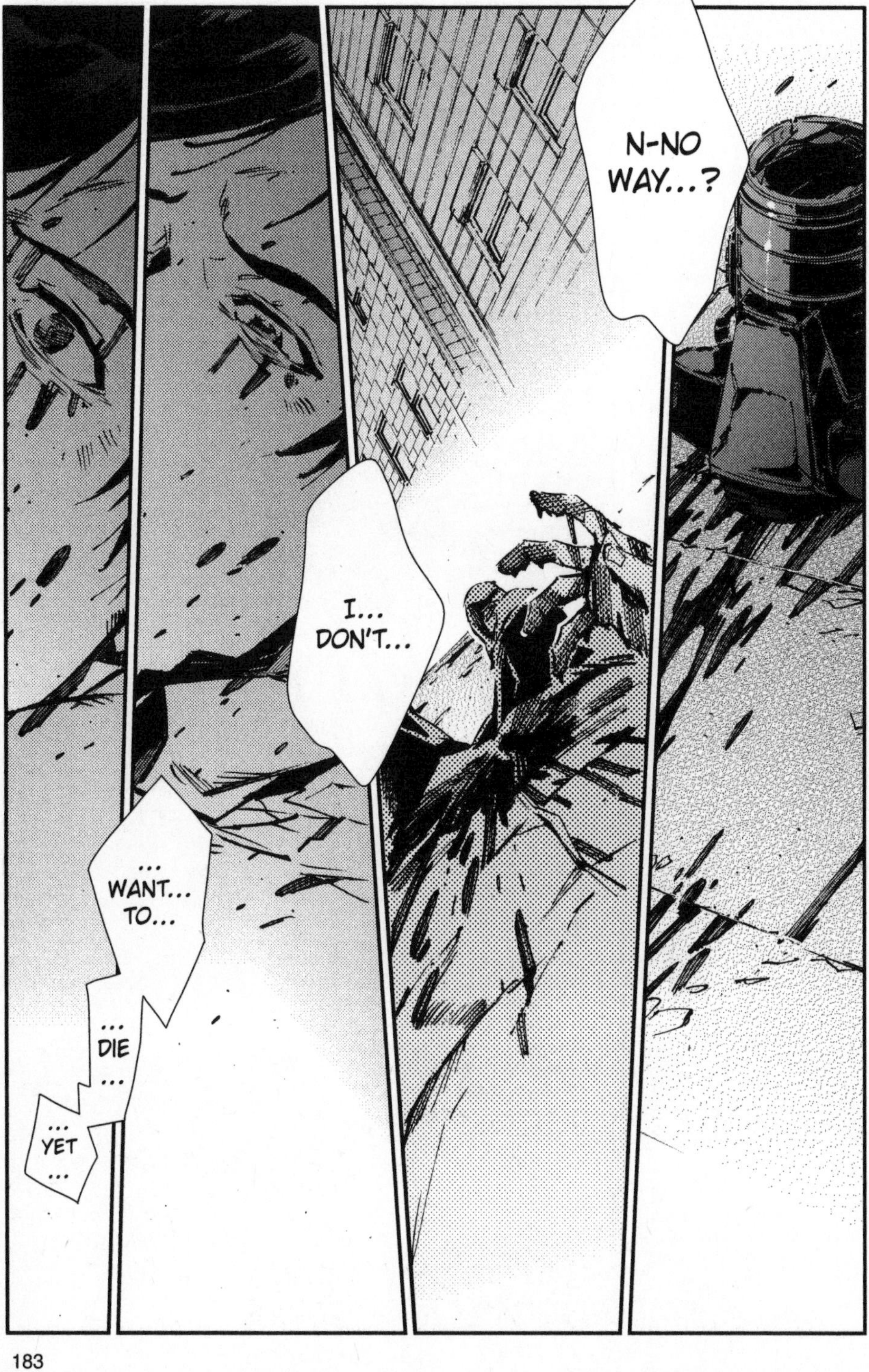
N-NO WAY...?
I... DON'T...
...WANT... TO...
...DIE...
...YET...

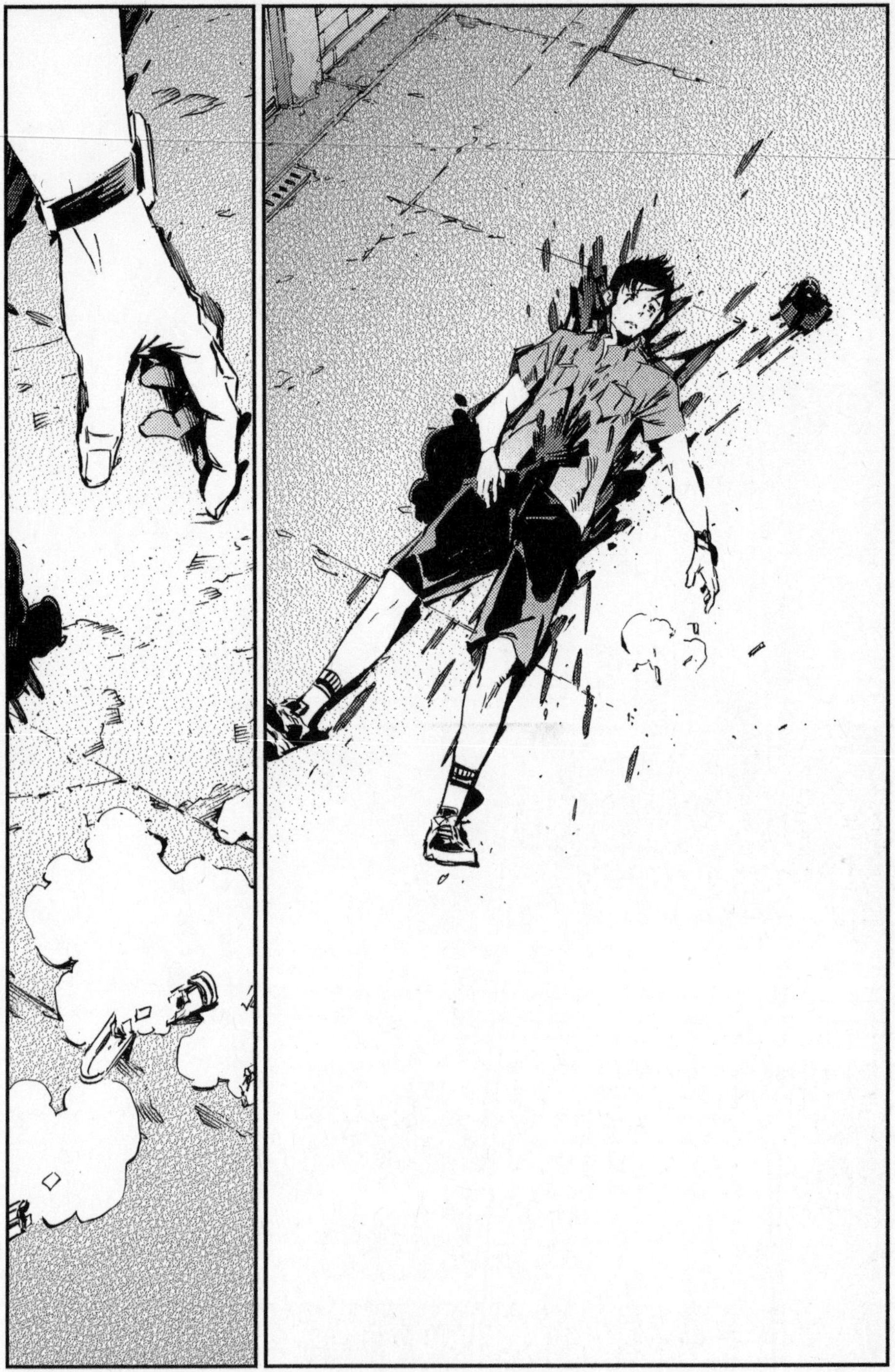

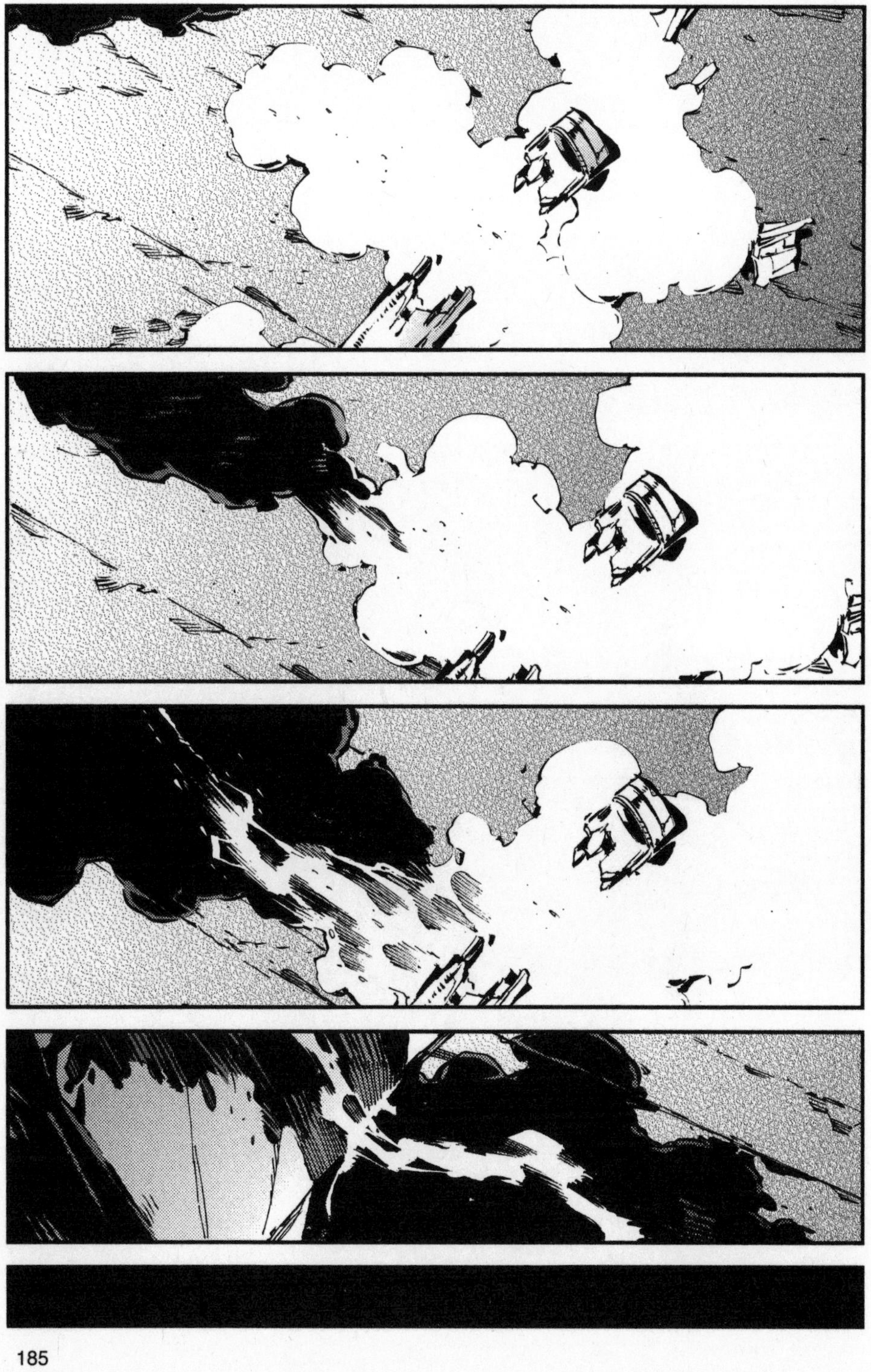

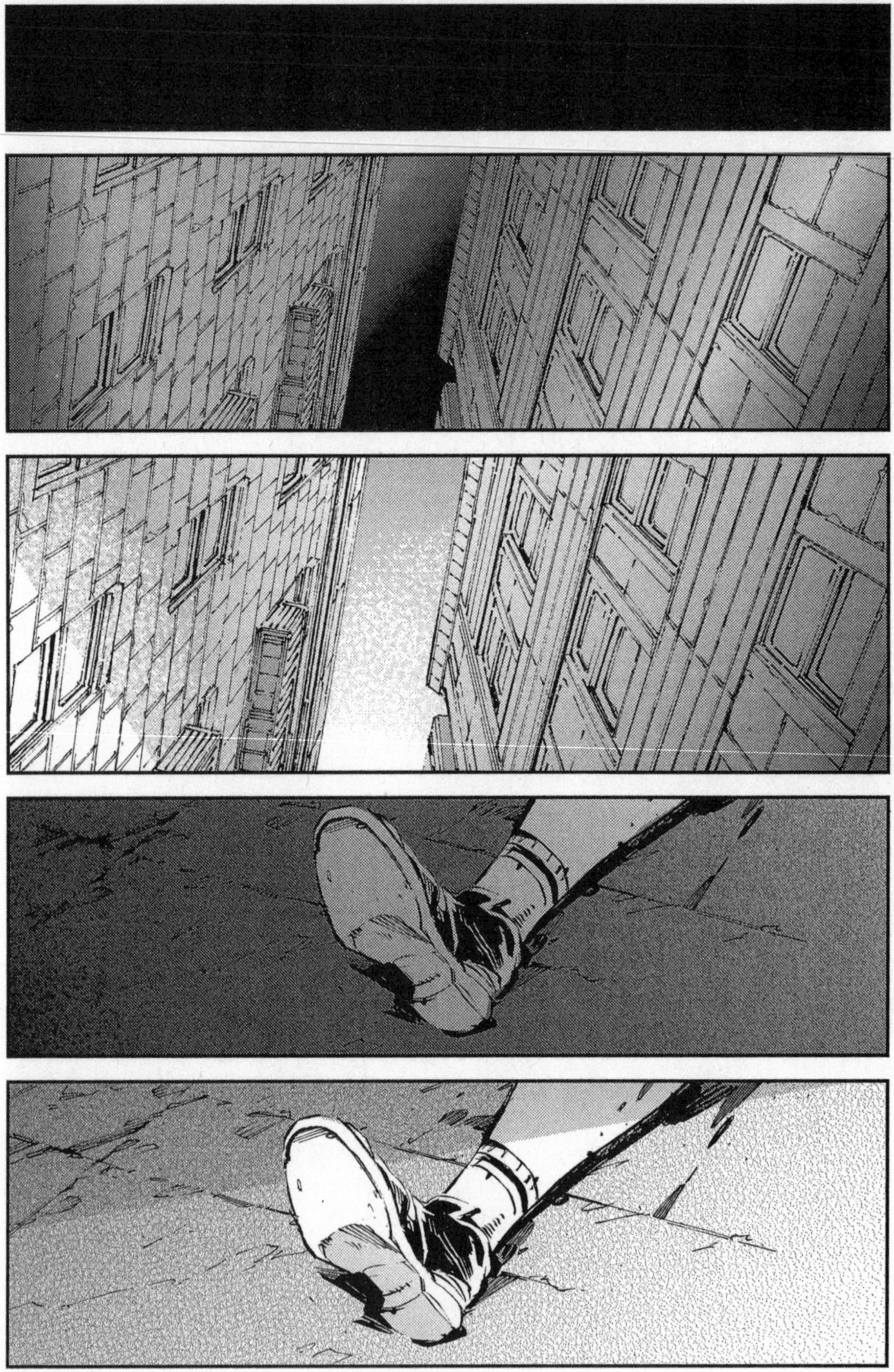

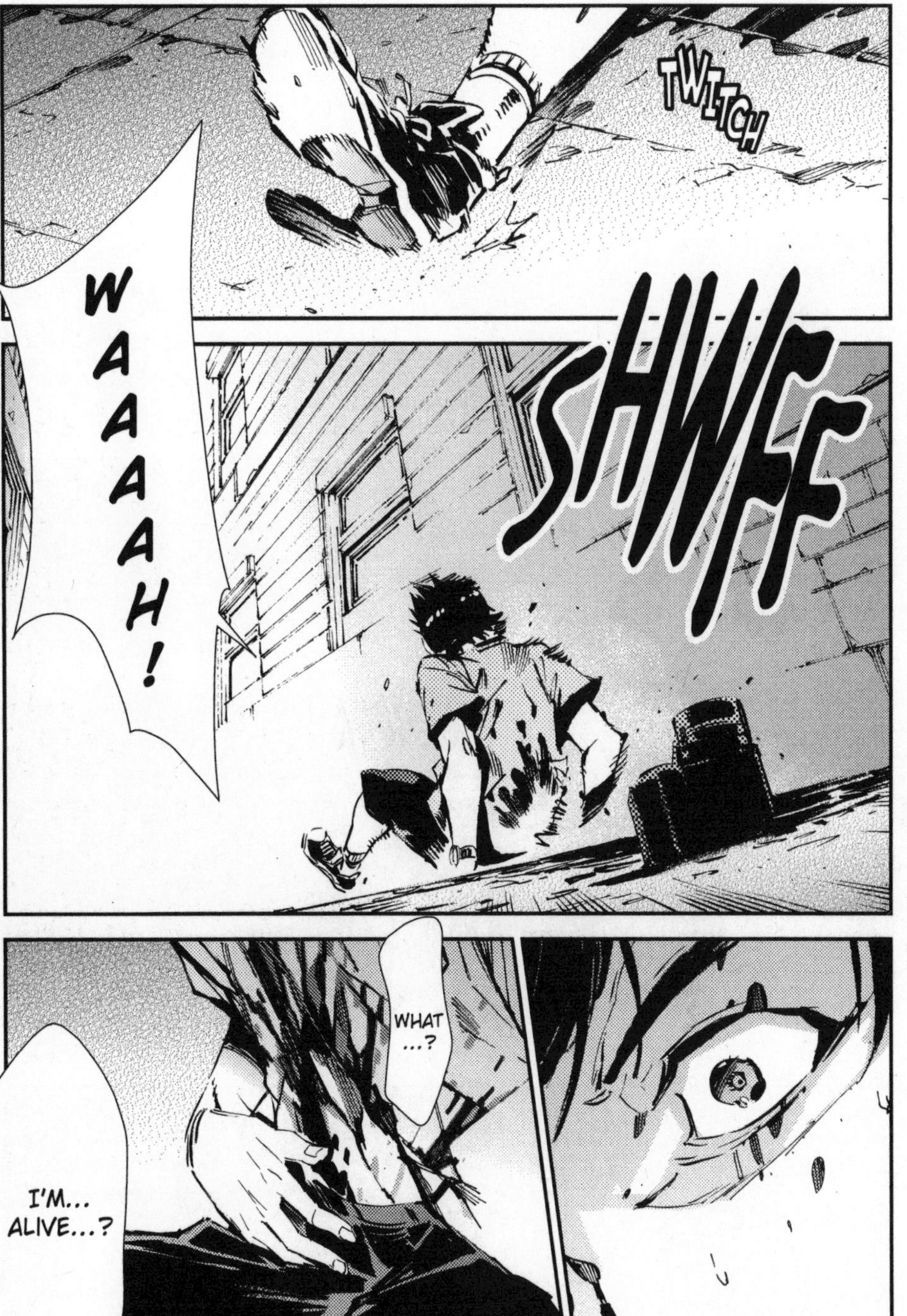
TWITCH
WAAAAAH!
SHWFF
WHAT ...?
I'M... ALIVE...?

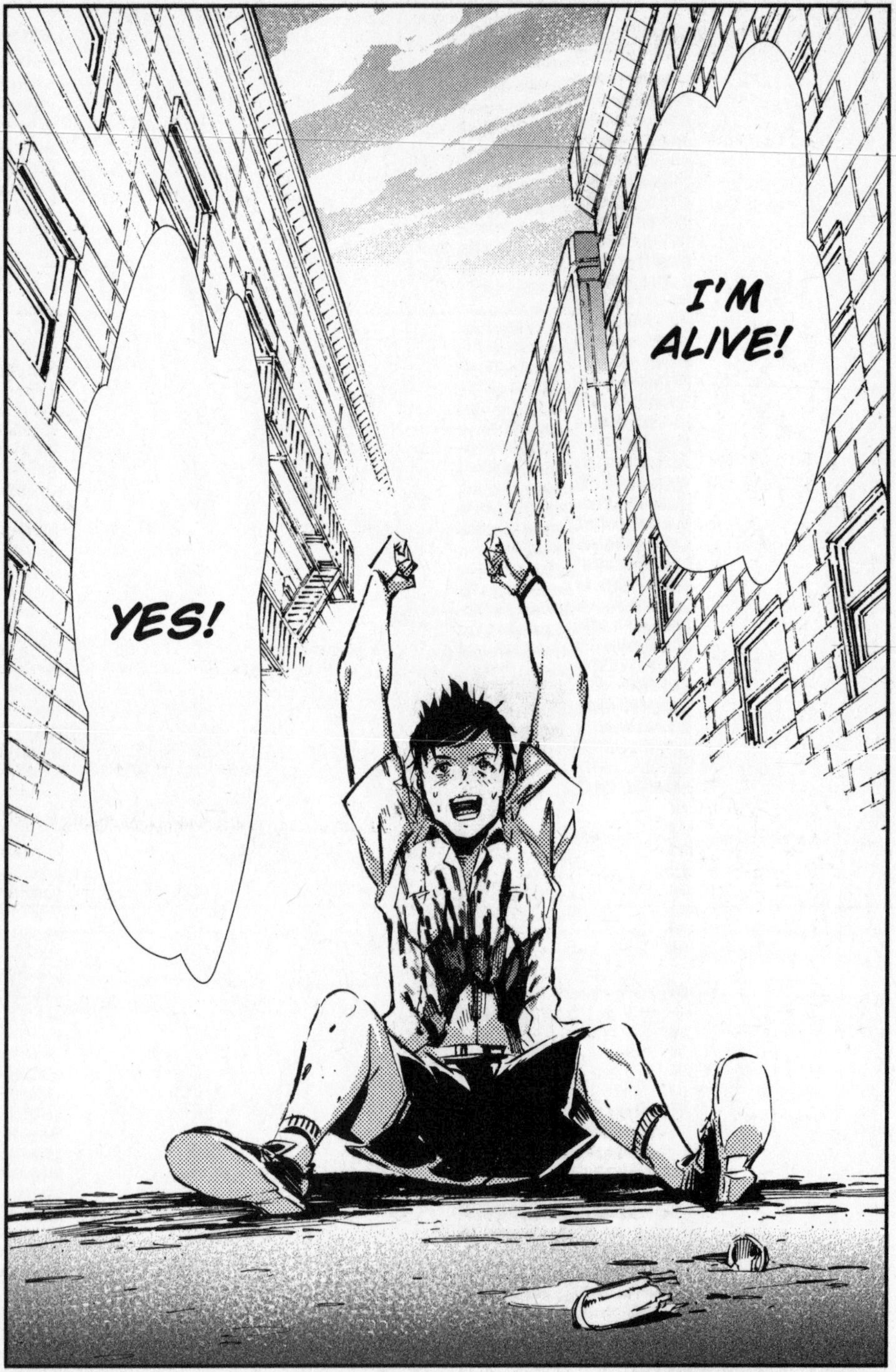
I'M ALIVE!
YES!

ULTRAMAN 8 - END

THIS IS THE BEGINNING OF A NEW AGE

■ **This is the prototype of the Ultraman suit Hayata wears. It's called the Convenience Prototype. It's a modified prototype suit that's ready to be used in actual combat. When Hayata wore it against Ace Killer, additional modifications and a prototype mask were added. As with Shinjiro's suit, its power source—the Spacium Core—has been replaced with a newer version.**

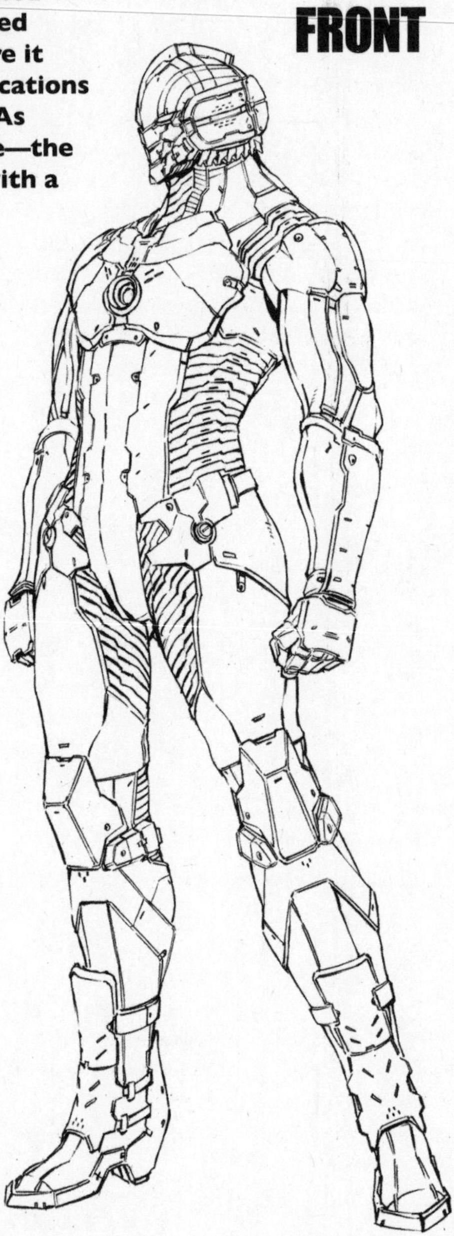
FRONT

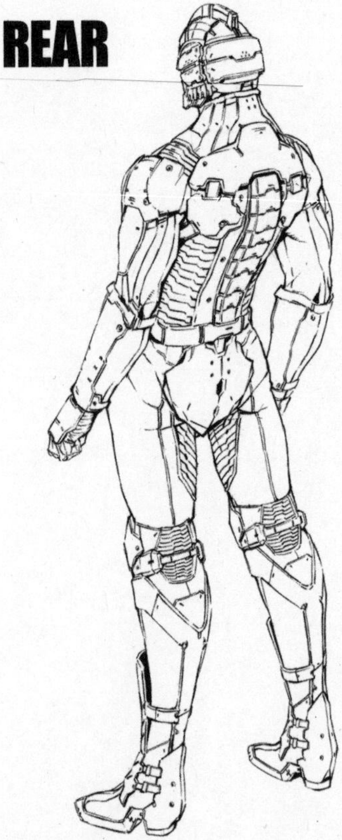
REAR

■ The leader of the mercenary team that does dirty work for the Star Cluster Council. As a side job, he also supplies corpses to aliens that have a taste for feeding on humans. Primarily known as Ace Killer, his real name and background are unknown. One theory says that he's an organic weapon created by an unknown scientist, but the truth is not known. What he looks like underneath the mask also remains unknown since he was blown up by Hokuto.

HATCHET

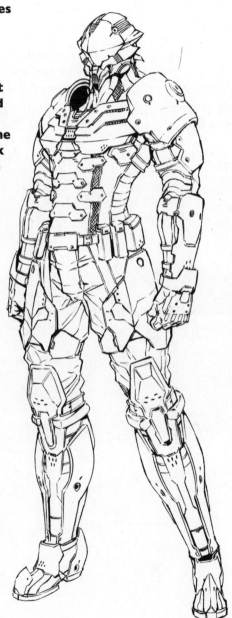

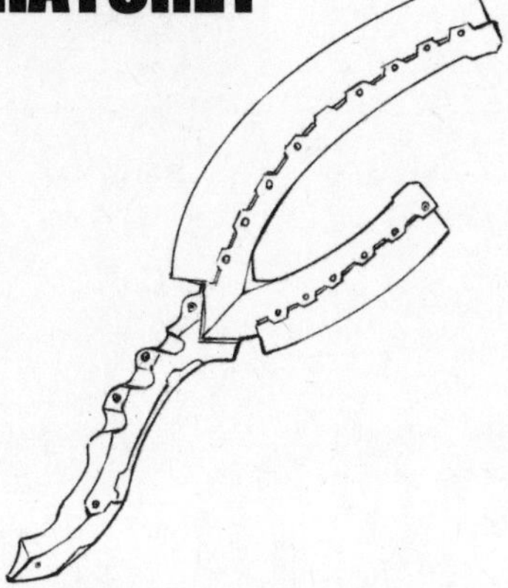

■ A hatchet-shaped weapon Ace Killer is fond of using. Can be used like a *sasumata* (spear fork) due to its shape.

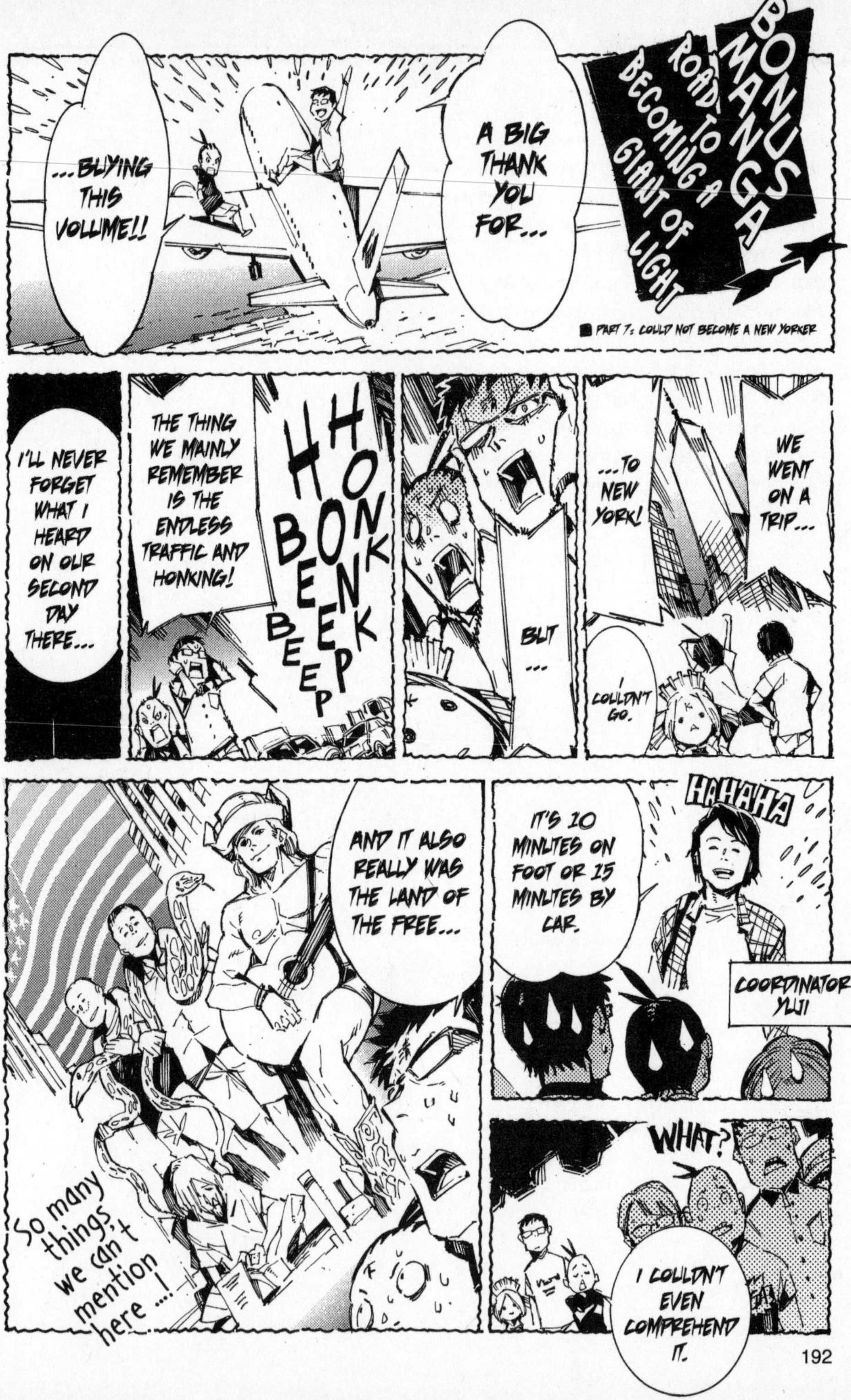
BONUS MANGA
ROAD TO BECOMING A GIANT OF LIGHT
A BIG THANK YOU FOR...
...BUYING THIS VOLUME!!
PART 7: COULD NOT BECOME A NEW YORKER
WE WENT ON A TRIP...
...TO NEW YORK!
I COULDN'T GO.
BUT ...
THE THING WE MAINLY REMEMBER IS THE ENDLESS TRAFFIC AND HONKING!
HONK
BONK
BEEP
BEEP
I'LL NEVER FORGET WHAT I HEARD ON OUR SECOND DAY THERE...
HAHAHA
IT'S 10 MINUTES ON FOOT OR 15 MINUTES BY CAR.
COORDINATOR YUJI
WHAT?
I COULDN'T EVEN COMPREHEND IT.
AND IT ALSO REALLY WAS THE LAND OF THE FREE...
So many things we can't mention here...!

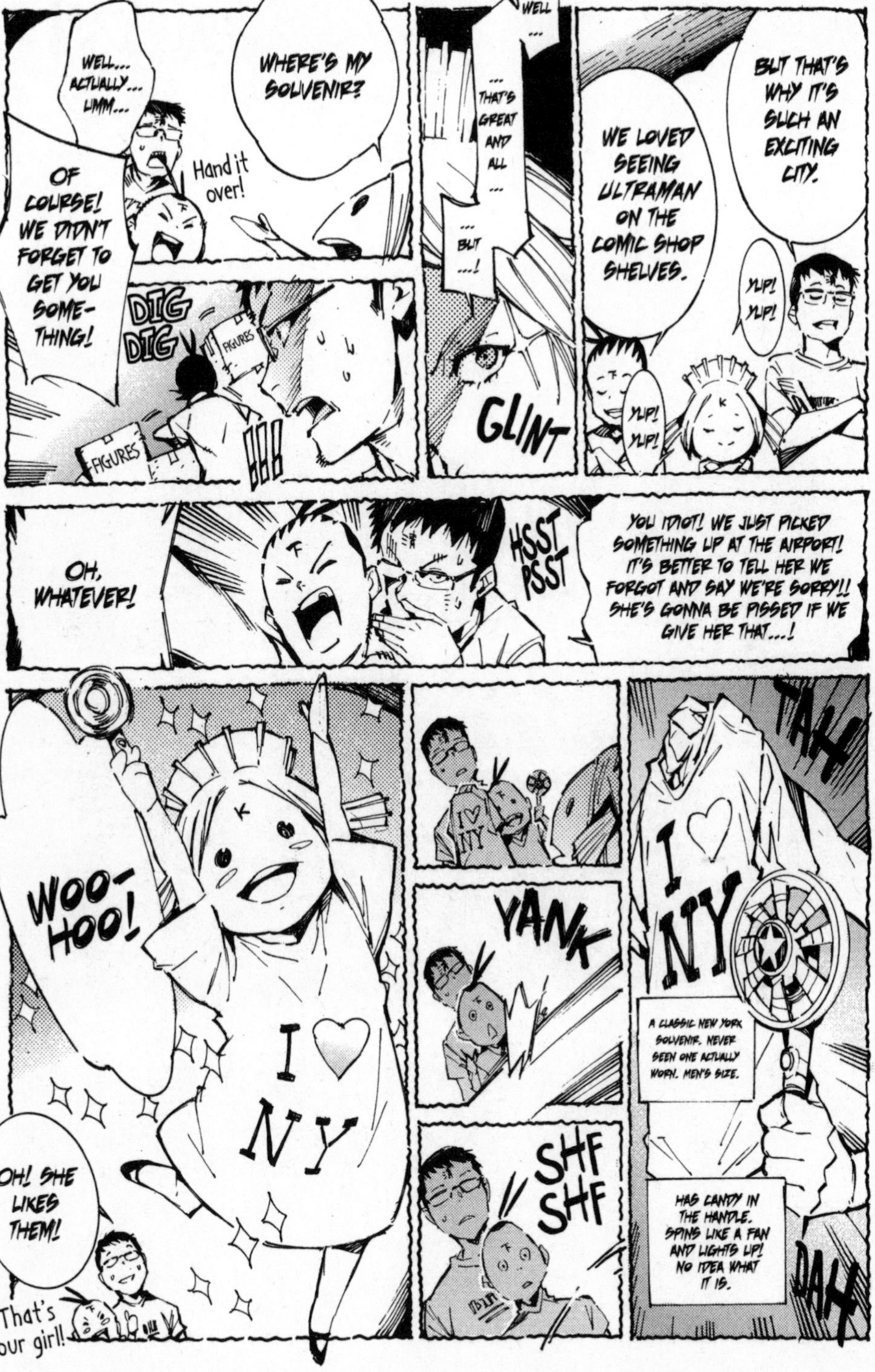
BUT THAT'S WHY IT'S SUCH AN EXCITING CITY.
YUP! YUP!
WE LOVED SEEING ULTRAMAN ON THE COMIC SHOP SHELVES.
YUP! YUP!
WELL ...
... THAT'S GREAT AND ALL ...
... BUT ...!
GLINT
WHERE'S MY SOUVENIR?
Hand it over!
WELL... ACTUALLY... UMM...
OF COURSE! WE DIDN'T FORGET TO GET YOU SOME-THING!
DIG DIG
FIGURES
FIGURES
YOU IDIOT! WE JUST PICKED SOMETHING UP AT THE AIRPORT! IT'S BETTER TO TELL HER WE FORGOT AND SAY WE'RE SORRY!! SHE'S GONNA BE PISSED IF WE GIVE HER THAT...!
HSST PSST
OH, WHATEVER!
TAH
I ♥ NY
A CLASSIC NEW YORK SOUVENIR. NEVER SEEN ONE ACTUALLY WORN. MEN'S SIZE.
HAS CANDY IN THE HANDLE. SPINS LIKE A FAN AND LIGHTS UP! NO IDEA WHAT IT IS.
DAH
I ♥ NY
YANK
SHF SHF
WOO-HOO!
I ♥ NY
OH! SHE LIKES THEM!
That's our girl!

EIICHI SHIMIZU ✕ TOMOHIRO SHIMOGUCHI

The year we are writing this in, 2016, is the
fiftieth anniversary of the *Ultraman* TV series.
Congratulations!!

Fifty years is truly amazing. Neither of us was
even born when it started!!

So to celebrate this historic year, we decided a
long time ago to have Hayata as Ultraman on the
cover of this volume. Of course, he doesn't actually
wear a cape.

But you know, it's an anniversary...

ULTRAMAN
VOLUME 8
VIZ SIGNATURE EDITION

STORY/ART BY **EIICHI SHIMIZU** AND **TOMOHIRO SHIMOGUCHI**

©2016 Eiichi Shimizu and Tomohiro Shimoguchi / TSUBURAYA PROD.
Originally published by HERO'S INC.

TRANSLATION **JOE YAMAZAKI**
ENGLISH ADAPTATION **STAN!**
TOUCH-UP ART & LETTERING **EVAN WALDINGER**
DESIGN **KAM LI**
EDITOR **MIKE MONTESA**

Printed in the U.S.A.

Published by VIZ Media, LLC
P.O. Box 77010
San Francisco, CA 94107

10 9 8 7 6 5 4 3 2 1
First printing, May 2017

www.viz.com

HEY! YOU'RE READING IN THE WRONG DIRECTION!

This is the END of the graphic novel

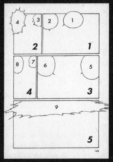

Follow the action this way.

To properly enjoy this VIZ graphic novel, please turn it around and begin reading from RIGHT TO LEFT. Unlike English, Japanese is read right to left, so Japanese comics are read in reverse order from the way English comics are typically read.

This book has been printed in the original Japanese format in order to preserve the orientation of the original artwork.

HAVE FUN WITH IT!